# MusicMedicine

RALPH SPINTGE, M.D.
ROLAND DROH, M.D.
EDITORS

INTERNATIONAL SOCIETY FOR MUSIC IN MEDICINE
IV. INTERNATIONAL MUSICMEDICINE SYMPOSIUM

ANNENBERG CENTER FOR HEALTH SCIENCES AT EISENHOWER
RANCHO MIRAGE, CALIFORNIA
OCTOBER 25 - 29, 1989

MMB MUSIC, INC.

# MusicMedicine

Ralph Spintge, M.D., Roland Droh, M.D., Editors

ISBN: 0-918812-72-0

Cover Concept: International Society for Music in Medicine
Cover Art: Linda Brown
Printer: Malloy Lithographing, Ann Arbor, Michigan
First Printing: July, 1992
PRINTED IN U.S.A.


For a complete catalog, write:

MMB Music, Inc.
10370 Page Industrial Boulevard
Saint Louis, Missouri 63132 (USA)

FAX: (314) 426-3590
Phone: (800) 543-3771

# TABLE OF CONTENTS

## I General Considerations

## II Aspects in Physiology and Physics

## III Applied Research

## IV Therapeutic Applications and Workshop Transcriptions

## V Aspects in Occupational Health Care

# VI Toward Standards of Research in MusicMedicine and Music Therapy

# THE AUTHORS

H.-H. Abel, Institute of Psychology, Free University, Berlin, Germany

Helmut Baitsch, Emeritus Professor, University of Ulm, Ulm, Germany

Karen L. Barton, MSS, The International Arts-Medicine Association, Philadelphia, PA, USA

Susanne Bauer, Psychologist and Music Therapist, Department of Psychotherapy, University of Ulm, Ulm, Germany

Yogi Bhajan, Master of Kundalini Yoga and Mahan Tantric, House of Guru Ram Das, Los Angeles, CA, USA

William Davis, RMT-BC, Associate Professor of Music, Colorado State University, Fort Collins, CO, USA

Bruno Deschênes, MMus, Composer, Montréal, Canada

Suzanne Dixon, MD, University of California at San Diego, La Jolla, CA, USA

Roland Droh, MD and PhD, Anesthesiologist and Head of the Department of Anesthesiology at the Sportkrankenhaus Hellersen, Lüdenscheid, Germany

Charles T. Eagle, PhD, Professor and Head of Department of Music Therapy: Medicine and Health, Southern Methodist University, Dallas, TX, USA

Nikolaus Ell, MD, Head Surgeon, Department of Hand Surgery, DRK-Clinic, Baden-Baden, Germany

Paul Fairweather, PhD, University of California at San Diego, La Jolla, CA, USA

Bella Abramowitz Fisher, PT, Jacobi Hospital; Einstein College of Medicine, New York, NY, USA

Reinhard Flatischler, Rhythm Projects, Vienna, Austria

Jonathan S. Goldman, Founder and Director of Sound Healers Association, Inc.; President of Spirit Music, Inc., Boulder, CO, USA

Fawzi P. Habboushe, MD, FACS, FCCP, FACEP, Clinical Assistant Professor of Surgery, University of Pennsylvania, Philadelphia, PA, USA

Suzanne B. Hanser, PhD, Research Health Scientist, Veterans Affairs Medical Center; Postdoctoral Fellow, Stanford University School of Medicine, Palo Alto, CA, USA

Arthur W. Harvey, DMA, Minister of Music, Waialae Baptist Church, Honolulu, HI, USA

Peter Haussmann, MD, Professor of Surgery and Chief Surgeon, Department of Hand Surgery, DRK-Clinic, Baden-Baden, Germany

Laura Hersh, Undergraduate Student of Psychology, University of California at San Diego, La Jolla, CA, USA

Horst Kächele, Professor and Chairman, Department of Psychotherapy, University of Ulm, Ulm, Germany

Avery Kenyon, Undergraduate Student of Psychology, University of California at San Diego, La Jolla, CA, USA

D. Klüssendorf, Institute of Psychology, Free University, Berlin, Germany

Hans Peter Koepchen, Institute of Psychology, Free University, Berlin, Germany

Vladimir J. Konecni, PhD, Professor of Psychology, University of California at San Diego, La Jolla, CA, USA

E. Koralewski, Institute of Psychology, Free University, Berlin, Germany

Ekkehard Kreft, PhD, Professor and Director, Institute of Music Pedagogy, University of Westphalia, Münster, Germany

Richard J. Lederman, MD, PhD, Department of Neurology and Director, Medical Center for Performing Artists, Cleveland Clinic Foundation, Cleveland, OH, USA

Richard A. Lippin, MD, President, The International Arts-Medicine Association, Philadelphia, PA, USA

Robyn Main, RN, MSN, Maternal Child Health Clinical Specialist, Mount Sinai Medical Center, Miami Beach, FL, USA

Cheryl Dileo Maranto, PhD, RMT-BC, Associate Professor of Music Therapy, Temple University, Philadelphia, PA, USA

Lisa Marchette, RN, PhD, Nursing Research Coordinator, Mount Sinai Medical Center; Associate Professor, University of Miami School of Nursing, Miami, FL, USA

Louise Montello, DA, CMT, Clinical Research Scientist, Department of Psychology, New York University, New York, NY, USA

John T. Myers, PT, Department of Physical Therapy, Cleveland Clinic Foundation, Cleveland, OH, USA

Philip Nader, MD, University of California at San Diego, La Jolla, CA, USA

Jonathan Newmark, MD, Departments of Neurology and of Anatomical Sciences and Neurobiology, School of Medicine, University of Louisville, Louisville, KY, USA

Paul Nolan, MCAT, RMT-BC, Director of Music Therapy Education, Hahnemann University, Philadelphia, PA, USA

Rosalie Rebollo Pratt, Professor of Music, Brigham Young University, Provo, UT, USA; Executive Director, The International Association of Music for the Handicapped

Ellen Redick, RN, MSN, CCRN, Critical Care Clinical Specialist, Mount Sinai Medical Center, Miami Beach, FL, USA

Paul Salmon, PhD, Associate Professor of Clinical Psychology, University of Louisville; Louisville Performing Arts Medicine Group, Louisville, KY, USA

Joseph P. Scartelli, PhD, RMT-BC, Dean, College of Visual and Performing Arts, Radford University, Radford, VA, USA

Judith E. Schaeffer, MSLS, The International Arts-Medicine Association, Philadelphia, PA, USA

John Schanberger, MD, University of California at San Diego, La Jolla, CA, USA

Sandra Schleiffers, PhD, Lecturer in Computer Science, Colorado State University, Fort Collins, CO, USA

Nicola Scheytt-Hölzer, Psychologist and Music Therapist, Department of Psychotherapy, University of Ulm, Ulm, Germany

Stefan Schmidt, Research Assistant, Department of Psychotherapy, University of Ulm, Ulm, Germany

Albrecht Schneider, University of Hamburg, Hamburg, Germany

David Shannahoff-Khalsa, President, The Khalsa Foundation for Medical Science, Del Mar, CA, USA

Arthur G. Shapiro, MD, Clinical Professor of Ob/Gyn, University of Miami, Miami, FL, USA

Thomas Sherman, MA, The International Arts-Medicine Association, Philadelphia, PA, USA

Olav Skille, VibroSoft a/s, Steinkjer, Norway

Ralph Spintge, MD, Neurovegetative Research Department, Sportkrankenhaus Hellersen, Lüdenscheid, Germany

Jayne M. Standley, PhD, RMT, Center for Music Research, The Florida State University, Tallahassee, FL, USA

Myra J. Staum, Professor and Director of Music Therapy, Willamette University, Salem, OR, USA

Michael Thaut, RMT-BC, Associate Professor of Music, Colorado State University, Fort Collins, CO, USA

Tonius Timmermann, Researcher, Department of Psychotherapy, University of Ulm, Ulm, Germany

Sara Scott Turner, Winnipeg, Canada

# I
## GENERAL CONSIDERATIONS

# INTRODUCTORY REMARKS

### Roland Droh

O nly seven years have passed since the foundation of the International Society for Music in Medicine. Even in our fast-paced age, this is only a short time span because the development and application of valid new methods take considerable time. Nevertheless the symposium program is itself evidence that we have made much progress in these seven years.

Music is physics, mathematics and art. It was already understood as such in ancient times. Music is divine, magical, mysterious and could not be notated until a few centuries ago. Pythagoras and his school of thought drew closer through the invention of the monochord which in the ensuing millennia became the measuring instrument for musical instruments and voices. The monochord became the basis for the measurement of organs and led to the invention for polychords, up to the clavichord. It also led to the notation of the octave scale. The Pythagoreans also discovered the phenomenon of intervals. The octave scale is a physical concept that was experimented with from the time of Pythagoras. However, it was not adopted into notated music until nearly two thousand years later when musicians and composers were searching for artistic parallels to the advances in physics and mathematics. Even nowadays the monochord remains the physical principle in MusicMedicine research. Like the philosophy of the ancients, it continues to lead the way. Music, like mathematics and language, has its own rationale, its own expressiveness, its own meaning, and even its own written medium. Music is a means of communication just like language, mathematics, painting and sculpture. Whoever has mastered musical communication is able to communicate with anybody else who has also mastered it, without speaking the other person's native language; just as mathematicians and physicists can in their respective fields. A German, American or a Japanese does not need a translator as long as the subject is music. They understand each other. One can listen to, understand, write, reproduce, and enjoy music worldwide. One can be moved by it and express thoughts and feelings. Music is able to stimulate, to soothe, to control our emotions, our vegetative nervous system. We are able to express fear, pain, happiness, grief, hope, despair, agitation and much more, through music. Music can be a pastime in the sense that it makes us forget time. Music can let thoughts flow. Music can occupy us and it can be abused. Nevertheless music will always remain an independent force.

Just what constitutes the power of music? Is it the dynamics or the rhythm? Is it the separate notes or the whole composition? Is it the melody? Is it physical vibrations or is it the mathematical concept of the physics of these vibrations in the context of the melody with its rhythm and dynamics? We must learn to live with it and we each need our own time span to develop an understanding of the composer's message in his and our time. Only in our time has it become possible to make these messages audible at any moment, in order to learn to understand them. In the past millennia of human kind this was not possible, it was reserved for only a handful of the privileged at special times or moments. Today each one of us can participate in the total spectrum of music and can make use of it at will—learning about its power, learning to estimate what kind of forces there are that move music and how great they are. Trying to discover how music can seduce, comfort, convince, delight and move us. Trying to discover what music can do with simple and complicated melodies, with sound patterns that use a greater or smaller range of dynamics and that possess a large repertoire of rhythms. Mankind has known for millennia that music can do this with conventional or unconventional compositions, with ingenious or simple constructions or vibrations in space and time and many have thought about this subject in centuries past. But we know little or nothing about how this is accomplished through music.

In medicine we have described, measured and weighed a multitude of physical, chemical and mathematical parameters. We have dissected and cataloged body and soul, and many regular measurements have been translated into mathematical and physical formulas. However, up to now we have barely started to explore a large area of our biological being: the neurovegetative system.

We know much about psychology and psychiatry and their somatic interactions, about heart-circulation, respiration, hormones, acid-base and water-electrolyte balances, the organs of the central nervous system and many other things, but up to the present day the neurovegetative system has remained virtually inaccessible in all its complexity. We have certainly invested a great deal of effort to advance in this area and much detailed knowledge has been amassed. Nevertheless, the uncharted areas on our map of medical knowledge in the area of the neurovegetative system are still gigantic. The secrets of the neurovegetative system, as well as the effects of music on it, are largely unresearched. Pythagoras and his school of thought had already developed the monochord with its diatonic octave scale and had placed music with astronomy, mathematics and languages in the center of his philosophical *weltanschauung* (world view). Plato continued this train of thought. He writes about the magical forces of music that affect the irrational part of the soul.

We have scarcely begun to research the effects of music on people and the workings of the neurovegetative system. If the following papers advance us only a little on our way in this adventure, we will still have achieved much. The investigation of the neurovegetative rhythms and the influence of music on them alone will open doors for the research of the neurovegetative system and will provide us with much new knowledge in the areas of respiration and heart-circulation research. We expect music to contribute decisively to evaluating the neurovegetative status of humans and its adaptive changes. We have started the research at our hospital along with the Physiological Institute of the Freie Universität Berlin, the Institute of Theoretical Physics and Synergetics of the Universität Stuttgart and the International Society for Music in Medicine.

# THE INTERNATIONAL SOCIETY FOR MUSIC IN MEDICINE [ISMM] AND THE DEFINITION OF MUSICMEDICINE AND MUSIC THERAPY

Ralph Spintge
Roland Droh

Since 1976 so-called anxiolytic music has been used in the Department of Anesthesiology at Sportkrankenhaus Hellersen in Lüdenscheid, Germany to alleviate perioperative anxiety and distress. In order to compare our own experiences with this kind of therapeutic use of music with data of other colleagues the International MusicMedicine Symposium on "Anxiety, Pain and Music in Anesthesia" was held in 1982 in Lüdenscheid. We were very surprised by the huge international interest and the number of well-researched contributions. In consequence the International Society for Music in Medicine (ISMM) was founded on the occasion of this first symposium, December 3, 1982.

The society was originally founded as a medical research society, two thirds of the members being medical doctors. According to the statutes of the ISMM up to third of the total membership may be made up of scientists and representatives of other academic specialities who have a special knowledge or skill in MusicMedicine. Also subsidiary members like institutions or companies can be accepted.

The scope of the ISMM is to initiate and coordinate interdisciplinary research into the physiological and psychological basis and the applications of music in medicine/music therapy. The scientific exchange is organized through international symposia on Music in Medicine and through the *International Journal of Arts-Medicine, (IJAM)*.

ISMM was incorporated as a nonprofit international scientific organization for the following purposes:

1. To foster and encourage research into the therapeutic mechanisms of music and to help improve the management of patients through musical means by bringing together scientists, physicians, musicians, psychologists and other professionals of various disciplines and backgrounds who are interested in MusicMedicine/Music Therapy and related research.

2. To promote education and training in the field of MusicMedicine/Music Therapy.

3.  To promote and facilitate the dissemination of new information in the field of MusicMedicine/Music Therapy including sponsorship of a journal.
4.  To promote and sponsor international congresses of the society and such other meetings which may be useful or desirable for the advancement of the purpose of the society.

5.  To encourage the adoption of a uniform classification, nomenclature, and definition regarding MusicMedicine/Music Therapy.

6.  To encourage the development of a national and international databank and to encourage the development of a uniform records system with respect to information relating to MusicMedicine, Music Therapy and related research.

7.  To inform the general public of the results and implications of current research in the area.

8.  To advise international, national and regional agencies and institutions of standards relating to the use of music and dance in therapy.

9.  To engage in such other activities as may be incidental to or in furtherance of the aforementioned purposes.

During the following years the international exchange of information and experiences in the field of music in medicine grew and so the Second MusicMedicine Symposium "Music and Medicine" took place in 1984 in Lüdenscheid again. This symposium brought together much clinical data on the therapeutic applications of music in different specialities in medicine. Thus the practical applicability of music as therapy for anxiety, pain, and stress was significantly demonstrated to the medical community.

Until then music as a complete artistic entity had been studied. Now interest focused upon the question of what part of music or what musical parameters were responsible for certain effects. We think that rhythm might be probably the most powerful and effective parameter in music. So the Third International MusicMedicine Symposium brought together many theoretical and practical presentations, demonstrations and workshops on rhythm in music and its impact upon the human soul and body. This third symposium again took place at Sportkrankenhaus Hellersen in Lüdenscheid in 1986.

For the future we intend to look further into different cultural spheres concerning music in medicine. So the Fourth International MusicMedicine Symposium took place in the United States. The fifth MusicMedicine symposium should probably take place in Asia in 1992 or 1993.

Looking at the proceedings of the first four MusicMedicine Symposia it is clear that this is only the beginning of a widespread and beneficial use of music as a therapeutic tool in most fields of medicine, especially where anxiety and pain are a problem. It can decrease emotional stress and pain for the patient, saving drugs and costs.

The ISMM deals with MusicMedicine in all its aspects, i.e., with therapeutic applications of music in medicine as a whole. Our understanding of MusicMedicine is that it deals with occupational health problems of musicians and dancers. This is a field of growing importance and interest in the work of our society. Music Therapy in this connection is understood as the psychotherapeutic applications of music being a part of MusicMedicine.

# THE NEW INTERFACE BETWEEN MUSIC AND MEDICINE

Rosalie Rebollo Pratt

In the last five years there has been a silent but dramatic revolution in which musicians and medical doctors have forged a relationship that has created: (a) a new partnership in the process of healing, and (b) the pursuit of interdisciplinary experimental studies in MusicMedicine. A serendipitous network has developed among these musicians and physicians, and much of the impetus for this liaison has been from the medical world. Three examples of MusicMedicine organizations primarily under the leadership of physicians are: The Biology of Music Making, Frank Wilson, M.D., Director; The International Arts-Medicine Association, Richard Lippin, M.D., President, and The International Society for Music in Medicine, Ralph Spintge, M.D., Director.

In addition to the above, there are other organizations in which leadership for MusicMedicine networking comes primarily from the music therapy, special music education, and music performance sectors. These groups include:

- The National Association for Music Therapy, Barbara Crowe, President;
- The American Association for Music Therapy, Concetta Tomaino, President;
- The Music for Health Services Foundation, Arthur W. Harvey, Director;
- The Institute for Music, Health, and Education, Don G. Campbell, Director;
- Instruments of Healing, Pamela Woll, Director;
- New England Sound Healers, Jonathan Goldman, Director;
- The International Society for Music Education Commission on Music in Special Education, Music Therapy, and Music Medicine, Rosalie Rebollo Pratt, Chair;
- The International Association of Music for the Handicapped, Rosalie Rebollo Pratt, Executive Director.

The International Society for Music Education Commission also acts as a network for music therapy and special music education programs and societies throughout the world.

Musicians and psychologists are also entering into the interdisciplinary venture as they expand their joint investigations of music therapy in psychotherapy. The recent conference co-sponsored by the International Association of Music for the Handicapped and the Netherlands Society for Creative Therapies, Holland, August 1989, featured research programs in this area. The Second International Symposium of Music in Medicine, held in October 1984, Lüdenscheid, West Germany, was an earlier forum for interdisciplinary research presentations as well as for studies of music specifically applied to medical practice. In addition, these organizations regularly present international symposia and publish conference proceedings, journals, and newsletters.

As the networking develops and breaks boundaries among the professions of music, medicine and psychotherapy, there are challenges that must be faced. First and foremost, we must eliminate jargon that serves only to disguise our research and clinical practice from other kinds of professionals who have a genuine interest in what we are doing. We must stop creating words and expressions that are outside the standard lexicon and effectively keep our discoveries from those who do not share our professional training. It is most frustrating to attend a session in which one genuinely wants to understand the research of another scholar and be inundated with jargon and acronyms that can have no meaning except to those who either created them or learned about them in a closed group. Certainly, we must understand the logic and basic science of each other's discipline and work. It is, however, another thing to feel alienated from that research by verbal camouflage that appears in no standard dictionary or glossary.

Secondly, we must make every effort to be aware of, and to disseminate information about, all interdisciplinary research being conducted internationally. Organizations such as the International Arts-Medicine Association, the International Association of Music for the Handicapped, the Biology of Music Making, the International Society for Music Education, and the International Society for Music in Medicine have been working to increase that database of common knowledge. The International Arts-Medicine Association (IAMA) has proposed a central international arts-medicine information clearinghouse called AMI (Arts-Medicine Information). "IAMA can serve as the 'central nervous system' or brain that can 'think globally' for arts-medicine by collecting, organizing, and appropriately disseminating information on arts-medicine around the world" (IAMA Newsletter 1989). Our pressing goal is to make a database available internationally and to include in it all up-to-date information about research and clinical practice that is of interest to music therapists, special music educators, physicians, psychologists, and others in allied health professions. The recent research articles in music therapy and music education journals and newsletters make it clear that the bonds between these two professions and the medical world are growing rapidly. Such an international and interdisciplinary database will help solve another serious problem, the urgent need for an international resource with analysis by topic. For example, a recent search for MusicMedicine publications made on Brigham Young University's library computer-assisted system revealed only those journal articles written in English. Fortunately, the searcher was aware of international resources available in international journals and other publications. The problem of identifying all research on a particular topic extends also to gathering information presented at symposia. Searches reveal articles from journals but often overlook studies that appear in texts and symposia proceedings. For example, articles about music and medicine written by Soren Nielzén (1985) and Jacqueline Verdeau-Paillès (1985, 1987) are included in two different volumes of proceedings of international symposia sponsored by the International Association of Music for the Handicapped. Yet these important contributions remain undisclosed to the scholar who does a routine computer search. An exhaustive international resource of current research and clinical studies is the obvious solution to the problem of searching all investigations of a topic.

Thirdly, the professions of music therapy, special music education, medicine, and psychology must free themselves of both distrust and condescension. If we are to have productive discussions among ourselves, they must be open and respectful of the contributions that can be made only when there is an atmosphere of true scholarship and desire to learn. From the early 1950s, when music therapy became defined as a profession, there was a genuine extension of friendship and collegial interest from those in medicine and psychology. Clearly, it is time to confess that no single discipline or profession has all answers to problems of healing. Together, information and perspectives may be shared and present all discussants with new clues to the healing process. Our methods of investigation must be scientifically solid, free of wishful thinking and unsubstantiated opinions. In our efforts to conduct interdisciplinary investigations, it may be necessary to work out research designs that accommodate studies of musical, psychological, and medical phenomena and data. This does not mean compromising accuracy and objective investigation; it may, however, mean that our new mode of investigation requires a new mode of thinking.

When music therapy became defined as a profession in the 1950s, the National Association for Music Therapy began a liaison with the medical profession, with a strong link between music therapy and psychiatry. A networking system is currently being sought among music therapy, music education, psychotherapy, and medical organizations. There is an underlying conviction that music is vital to the healing process, and these professional societies are now working to develop research and the kinds of hard evidence that prove the point. Such a move means, of course, that changes must be made in the way we investigate these data. The subjective and anecdotal report is simply not evidence that is supportable by the general scientific community. This does not mean, however, that intuition is to be discarded. Intuition has always served as the impetus for research questions, the dream that must be investigated with the greatest care. In addition, we must all look at our training programs and the library resources we currently offer our students. Interdisciplinary and international research means a substantial expansion of the readings we require of students. The training programs, themselves, must reach beyond the immediate speciality to embrace the basic logic and resources of those disciplines with which the program interfaces.

Another immediate challenge before us is to extend our concept of network to include our colleagues throughout the world. It is vital that there be a viable and efficient database of information that can be easily accessed by all international members of a network. In this way, the researcher in the southern United States who is exploring the effects of music on endorphin release can become aware of similar experiments in West Germany, and vice versa. We must also be aware of developments within the area of the healing arts among all cultures and societies throughout the world. The approach to music therapy is defined in many ways, and the careful scholar will be sensitive to the diversity of roots within this discipline. For example, European therapists often base much of their philosophy and technique on the work of people such as Juliette Alvin, Claus Bang, Edgar Willems, Jacqueline Verdeau-Paillès, Edith Lecourt, Paul Nordoff, Clive Robbins, and Christoph Schwabe. There is a rich heritage in the European tradition that should be a part of every music therapist's training. Yet, the current lack of effective networking and accessibility of information on an international basis tend to limit researchers to sources that are written in their native tongues, and are readily available to study. European research that involves music therapy and psychotherapy often deals with references centered around and sometimes strictly confined to sources such as those mentioned above. Yet, when one reads papers written by American researchers, there are references to a different group of therapists and psychotherapists (in this case, usually American).

The music therapist researcher and clinician must also be aware of the ongoing research and clinical work of international leaders such as Frances Wolf and Violeta Hemsy de Gainza in Argentina, Lia Rejane Barcellos in Brazil, Helmut Moog in West Germany, Graciela Sandbank and Chava Sekeles in Israel, Ruth Bright and Denise Erdonmez in Australia, as well as many others. The contributions of experts such as these are brought to the therapist's attention during symposia and seminars at the international level. Otherwise, it remains a matter of obtaining the same information in journals published in other languages and countries. A computer base that held brief abstracts of current research in English, French, and German would give the researcher enough information to determine whether a full translation of the article would be of benefit for his or her own study. It would, of course, be impossible, in a paper of this length, to name all the music therapists and special music educators who have made a lasting impact upon the profession, and the above list is only to offer a few important examples.

The time has come to erase these boundaries that only slow the progress of the profession and cause people to duplicate rather than replicate research. A network of research activity, properly classified, will lead to better understanding and joint research projects among international colleagues. Language, of course, is another barrier. Although publication of short abstracts in English, French, and German would do much to break down one of the major obstacles to international research, skill in several languages should be part of the training of the graduate therapist and the special music educator. Music therapists need to be able to read reports in English, French, and German in order to take advantage of the research currently available in the field. Efforts should also be made to translate the major works of leaders in the field into these three languages.

Another immediate challenge is that of strengthening already existing bonds and forging new links among musicians and physicians. For example, the area of psychoneuroimmunology is one currently being investigated by musicians, physicians, and psychologists. Donald E. Risenberg reports in the *Journal of the American Medical Association* (1986) that research in psychoneuroimmunology has indicated that this may be one of the areas of behavioral immunology that will prove most productive as it develops. Animal experiments being currently conducted by Steven Maier at the University of Colorado at Boulder "suggest a link between stress and immune function and indicate the importance of the subject's sense of control in a stressful situation" (Risenberg 1986, 313). The same report describes a study by Steven Locke et al. (1984) that has observed higher killer cell activity in subjects identified as "good copers" than was observed in those subjects identified as "poor copers." Medical researchers such as Locke, Charles Silberstein (1985), and Robert Ader (1981) are raising specific issues about the ability of the mind to influence the immune system. In the words of Ader, "given the fact that there are aberrations in the immune system, it is hypothetically possible that psychosocial factors exert an influence in the disease (p. xxiii). Siegel (1986) reports that imaging has helped shrink tumors and increased the number of circulating white blood cells and levels of thymosin-alpha-1, which can influence the patient's feelings of well-being (p. 152).

Spintge and Droh (1985), both medical doctors, edited a book that addressed much of basic research being conducted in the area of music in medicine. *Musik in der Medizin* includes presentations of research from a 1984 symposium held in Lüdenscheid, West Germany. The papers covered research in music perception, relationships between speech and music, anxiolytic music, music therapy for drug addicts, music processing by Type A and Type B personalities, amusia, music in psychotherapy, music in surgery, music and stress reduction, music during surgery, problems of musicians, the history of music in medicine, and a model for the interface between medicine and music.

Clynes (1985) refers us to a number of studies of the fruit fly that indicate that the courting songs of these insects are based on certain pulsation rates and that these differing rates affect mating choices. He postulates that studies such as these help us better understand the biologic basis for pulse in music. Clynes speaks of essentic forms, which he describes as "the biologically given expressive dynamic form for a specific emotion" (1985, 3). He further theorizes that "the neurobiologic process of recognition of pure emotion essentic forms may release specific substances in the brain which then act to transmit and activate those specific emotional experiences" (p. 8).

GIM, or Guided Imagery, has long been studied by Helen Lundquist Bonny, CMT, RMT. Bonny and her associates are currently pursuing this research at the Institute for Music Centered Therapies in Salina, Kansas. Her insights into GIM show how music can be at the core or center of a therapeutic process (Bonny 1983). Lisa Summer's *Guided Imagery and Music in the Institutional Setting* (1988) is another important resource. The iso principle technique reported by Altshuler (1948) is an important tool in matching the musical mood of the patient and helping him or her gain insight into internal thoughts and memories. There is but a short step toward establishing the relationship between this approach to therapy and implications of research in psychoneuroimmunology.

Siegel's book *Love, Miracles, and Medicine* 1986) is a best seller. He uses music in meditation therapy and also at the beginning of sessions for cancer patients.

> ...many kinds of music work quite well, such as many types of classical music, gentle ballads, and spiritual music from any era or culture...besides using music in meditation, we begin each ECaP (Exceptional Cancer Patients) session with some calming music. This makes it easier to enter the state of 'loving confrontation' we are trying to achieve. The music helps people relax and help each other face unpleasant truths, while remaining secure in the knowledge that we really care about each other (p. 154).

Borysenko (1987) gives us a focus for this new approach to healing with the title of her book *Minding the Body, Mending the Mind*. It is significant that at no less an institution than Harvard Medical School, the name of the area for which Professor Borysenko is the director is the Mind/Body Clinic. She advises her readers to use calming music, should they require a sound stimulus before going to sleep (p. 54).

Nagler and Lee (1987) have reported the use of microcomputers in the music therapy program for a musician suffering from postviral encephalitis. The patient was a spastic quadriplegic whose communication and physical problems were so severe that her former skill as a guitarist was no longer an option (p. 72). Mathew Lee, M.D., and Director of the Department of Rehabilitation Medicine at Goldwater Memorial Hospital in New York has encouraged a music therapy program there. Research projects that unite the efforts of the music therapist and the physician are also encouraged.

Frank Wilson, M.D., an associate clinical professor of neurology at the University of California/San Francisco who has recently conducted research in Düsseldorf, reports that the hospital affiliated with the institution had engaged a music therapist who, among other projects, is working with patients who have suffered severe loss of physical function.

Spintge and Droh (1987) are affiliated with the Sports Medicine facility in Lüdenscheid, West Germany, where anxiolytic music is used to reduce patients' trauma and anxiety before and during surgical procedures. Gatewood (1921) also reported use of music during surgery.

Petsche, Pockberger, and Rappelsberger (1985) report on EEG studies in music perception, audition, and performance. Electroencephalography is a method of measuring discrete hemispheric and interhemispheric brain responses. Factors analyzed in the studies were: absolute power, median frequency, and mean coherence. Topographic probability maps were also included in the analyses of data. Results of the studies indicate that rather large parts of the brain participate in processing musical stimuli, and both hemispheres participate in different ways. Trained musicians tend to analyze the stimuli through the left brain, whereas the naive listener is more prone to take the information in a holistic manner. Although both hemispheres participate in different ways to the processing of music information, there is no evidence of strict lateralization.

Roederer (1985) has also contributed to studies of the neuropsychological processes involved in music perception. The emphasis in this study is on the effects of somatic drives as they influence information acquisition, processing and storage, and the manifestations generally described as emotion. Roederer's investigation has focused on the cognitive process involved in listening to music, why we process and acquire auditory messages that are musical, and why we respond emotionally to music. He reminds us that only the human species is capable of having its motivational control system (mainly controlled in the limbic brain) overridden by the higher order cognitive system. It may also be true that our system of storing and retrieving information in the brain is holological rather than photographic. That is, a clear associative recall may be triggered by limited information in the stimulus, simply because this association can be recalled from an imprinting upon a larger, or holographic image. Simply put, our perceptions may be context-dependent. In musical tasks, the initial relationship of infant to the mother may involve the infant's desire to sort out its mother's musical and rhythmic sounds, react with its own sounds, and reap an emotional, limbic-based reward as a result of the process. Certain basic emotional states are elicited by music, regardless of cultural and ethnic orientations of the listeners. Roederer suggests that investigations of emotional states evoked by music in religious, sexual, militaristic, and proselytizing endeavors may lead us to a greater grasp of how music functions in medicine.

Carlin, Ward, Gershon, and Ingraham (1962) suggest that auditory analgesia may be effective in a clinical situation as a result of the joint use of suggestion and distraction. A choice of musical tracks or selections is now a common tool in many dentists' offices.

Music therapy is reported as useful with hospitalized infants and toddlers (Marley 1984) for the reduction of stress-related behaviors. This may be because, among other factors, children aged 1 to 3 feel significant stress in a hospital environment and lack the verbal skill to express this grief. Music can become a means of nonverbal communication that brings a sense of closeness and signifies goodwill to the child.

Pain reduction is reported by Rider (1985) in a procedure involving music-mediated imagery and muscle relaxation. The study indicated that imagery, particularly entrainment-mediated imagery that involves music, may be more effective than imagery or music alone. Wolfe (1978) had previously reported that music played during pain rehabilitation sessions appeared to improve patients' level of physical activity and verbal expression.

Rider (1985) also reported effectiveness of a taped music/Guided Image/Progressive Muscle Relaxation in significantly lowering amplitude of the corticosteroid rhythm and a significantly greater degree of body temperature and corticosteroid entrainment.

Kibler and Rider (1983) report that the combination of sedative music and PMR (Progressive Muscle Relaxation) appears to increase the relaxing effect (as measured by finger temperature response), although the effect was not significantly higher than that experienced with sedative music alone, or progressive muscle relaxation alone.

Hanser (1985) points out that research in relaxing music must be better defined if it is to be persuasive. For example, what are the criteria for selection of music to reduce stress? Are the physiological effects ascribed to this kind of music possibly the result of some attentional or arousal factor? Are measures for looking at the effects of music listening reliable and valid? How can electronically altered music control variables more carefully? What is the relationship between the music therapist's behavior and the technique used? All of these factors must be examined meticulously in order to judge the effect of music therapy on stress reduction.

An earlier study by Hanser and O'Connell (1983) indicated that mothers in labor emitted fewer pain responses in the presence of a specially designed music program as compared with those women in a background with no music. Music was experienced as a diversion from hospital sounds and discomfort. Spintge and Droh (1987) report positive effects of anxiolytic music during dental procedures on measures of: Mean Arterial Blood Pressure (MABP), pulse rate, Plasma Adrenocorticotrophic (ACTH) levels, Plasma Growth Hormone levels (GH), and Plasma Prolactin levels (PPL). Positive effects are also reported for music on Plasma levels of Noradrenaline, and Plasma levels of Cortisol in surgical patients with epidural anesthesia. A third type of experiment yielded significant differences at the .002 levels for effects of music on Plasma ACTH levels and Plasma B Endorphin levels during labor over a 24-hour period.

There are specific implications of the above research. First and foremost, the network among musicians of all specialties, physicians, and psychologists must be developed at the international level. Research and clinical data must become an easily accessible resource for all professionals within this global community. Language barriers must be conquered, and methods of dissemination must improve dramatically. Those who classify themselves primarily as practitioners must develop a responsibility toward this work by providing scientifically based and reported information that reaches the database. In addition, research and clinical practice must be reported in journals and newsletters with an international readership.

Secondly, musicians, psychologists, and medical researchers must approach their universities and institutional libraries to expand holdings to include the kinds of interdisciplinary information that is now essential to our research in the healing arts. For example, an in-depth study of the current holdings at Brigham Young University has resulted in a substantial commitment from the Collections Department of the library to provide resources that will meet the needs of today's graduate music student who is investigating areas of interface among the scientific and fine arts.

Thirdly, the music therapist, special music educator, psychologist, and physician who wish to engage in a meaningful dialogue and conduct joint research studies must learn enough about each other's arts in order to make their conversations and investigations fruitful. New models of conducting research will be developed from these conversations. However, each one of the participants must know the language of the others before work can begin. We need to emulate the relationship of an Orlando Lassus and Samuel Quickelberg, the latter, a physician who served with Lassus at the sixteenth century Bavarian court, and left a most useful set of commentaries on the problems of *musica reservata*, or that of Theodor Billroth and Johannes Brahms, whose rich friendship has left us many delightful and informative accounts of musical life in old Vienna.

Fourthly, let us develop new curiosity about these arts of music and healing. We suspect enough now about the power of music to influence healing to know that further rigorous studies must be done of all aspects of these phenomena. We have only begun to understand the ancient maxim, *mens regit corpus*. Music education and music therapy programs must develop new perspectives. For example, from fall 1990, Brigham Young University, Department of Music, has offered a master of arts degree in music education with an emphasis in music as it affects the human life process. All legitimate investigations of music as it influences human development and behavior from the fetus to the dying person will be relevant to this area of inquiry. Experimental research will go far beyond the conventional Kindergarten through twelfth grade investigations. It is hoped that this expanded perspective will uncover aspects of human learning and response to music that are yet unknown.

Let us continue the investigation of music in medicine in the spirit of collegiality and respect for each other's arts. The possibilities are incredible. What a glorious adventure is just before us!

## REFERENCE LIST

Ader, R. 1981. *Psychoneuroimmunology*. New York: Academic Press.

Altshuler, I.M. 1948. A psychiatrist's experience with music as a therapeutic agent. In *Music and Medicine*, edited by D. Schullian and M. Schoen, 266-281. New York: Henry Schuman.

Bonny, H.L. 1983. Music listening for intensive coronary care units: A pilot project. *Music Therapy* 3:4-16.

Borysenko, J. 1987. *Minding the Body, Mending the Mind*. Reading, MA: Addison-Wesley.

Carlin, S.; Ward, W.D.; Gershon, A.; and Ingraham, R. 1962. Sound stimulation and its effect on dental sensation threshold. *Science* 138:1258-1259.

Clynes, M. 1985. On music and healing. In *Musik in der Medizin* [Music in Medicine], edited by R. Spintge and R. Droh, 3-24. Basel: Editiones Roches.

Gatewood, E.L. 1921. The psychology of music in relation to anesthesia. *American Journal of Surgery, Quarterly Supplement of Anesthesia and Analgesia* 35:47-50.

Hanser, S.B. 1985. Music therapy and stress reduction research. *Journal of Music Therapy* 22(4):193-206.

Hanser, S.B., and O'Connell, A. 1983. The effect of music on relaxation of expectant mothers during labor. *Journal of Music Therapy* 29:50-58.

Kibler, V.E., and Rider, M.S. 1983. Effects of progressive muscle relaxation and music on stress as measured by finger temperature response. *Journal of Clinical Psychology* 39(2):213-215.

Lippin, R.A. 1989. President's message. *IAMA Newsletter* 1989, 4(1):7.

Locke, S.E.; Kraus, L.; Leserman, J.; Hurst, M.W.; Heisel, S.; and Williams, R.M. 1984. Life change stress, psychiatric symptoms, and natural killer cell activity. *Psychosomatic Medicine* 46(5):441-453.

Marley, L. 1984. The use of music with hospitalized infants and toddlers: A descriptive study. *Journal of Music Therapy* 21:126-132.

Nagler, J.C., and Lee, M.H.M. 1987. Use of microcomputers in the music therapy process of a postviral encephalitic musician. *Medical Problems of Performing Artists* 2(2):72-77.

Nielzén, S. 1985. Psychiatry, music and therapy. In *The Third International Symposium on Music, Medicine, Education, and Therapy for the Handicapped*, edited by R.R. Pratt, 187-198. Lanham, MD: University Press of America.

Petsche, H.; Pockberger, H.; and Rappelsberger, P. 1985. EEG studies in music perception of different music programs in man. In *Musik in der Medizin* [Music in Medicine], edited by R. Spintge and R. Droh, 187-198. Basel: Editiones Roches.

Rider, M.S. 1985. Entrainment mechanisms are involved in pain reduction, muscle relaxation, and music-mediated imagery. *Journal of Music Therapy* 22(4):183-192.

Risenberg, D.E. 1986. Can mind affect body defenses against disease? *JAMA* 256(3):313, 317.

Roederer, J.G. 1985. Neuropsychological processes relevant to the perception of music: An introduction. In *Musik in der Medizin* [Music in Medicine], edited by R. Spintge and R. Droh, 61-88. Basel: Editiones Roches.

Siegel, B.S. 1986. *Love, Medicine and Miracles.* New York: Harper and Row.

Silberstein, C. 1985. Major depressive illness in six AIDS patients. *Einstein Quarterly J. Biol. Med.* 3:136-143.

Spintge, R.; and Droh, R. 1985. *Musik in der Medizin* [Music in Medicine]. Basel: Editiones Roches.

_____. 1987. Effects of anxiolytic music on plasma levels of stress hormones in different medical specialties. In *The Fourth International Symposium on Music: Rehabilitation and Human Well-Being*, edited by R.R. Pratt, 88-101. Lanham, MD: University Press of America.

Verdeau-Paillès, J. 1985. Designing the music therapy treatment program. In *The Third International Symposium on Music in Medicine, Education, and Therapy for the Handicapped*, edited by R. R. Pratt, 227-236. Lanham, MD: University Press of America.

Wolfe, D.E. 1978. Pain rehabilitation and music therapy. *Journal of Music Therapy* 15(4):162-178.

## SELECTED BIBLIOGRAPHY

Bailey, L.M. 1983. The effects of live music versus tape-recorded music on hospitalized cancer patients. *Music Therapy* 3:17-28.

Boyle, M.E. 1987. Music in operant procedures for the comatose patient. In *The Fourth International Symposium on Music: Rehabilitation and Human Well-Being*, edited by R.R. Pratt, 49-60. Lanham, MD: University Press of America.

Chetta, H.D. 1981. The effect of music and desensitization on preoperative anxiety in children. *Journal of Music Therapy* 18:75-87.

Clark, M.; McCorkle, R.; and Williams, S. 1981. Music therapy-assisted labor and delivery. *Journal of Music Therapy* 18:88-100.

Eagle, C.T. 1985. A quantum interfacing system for music and medicine. In *Musik in der Medizin* [Music in Medicine], edited by R. Spintge and R. Droh, 319-342. Basel: Editiones Roches.

Field, T.M.; Dempsey, J.R.; Hatch, J.; Ting, G.; and Clifton, R.K. 1979. Cardiac and behavioral responses to repeated tactile and auditory stimulation by preterm and term neonates. *Developmental Psychology* 15(4):406-416.

Fischer, S., and Greenberg, R.P. 1972. Selective effects upon women of exciting and calm music. *Perceptual and Motor Skills* 34:987-990.

Froelich, M.A.R. 1974. A comparison of the effect of music therapy and medical play therapy on the verbalization behavior of pediatric patients. *Journal of Music Therapy* 21(1):2-15.

Fromm, M.L. 1982. The effects of music upon the values of compliant and noncompliant adolescents (Doctoral dissertation, University of Colorado at Boulder, 1981). *Dissertation Abstracts International* 42:1488A.

Gardner, W.J.; Licklider, J.C.R.; and Weisz, A.Z. 1960. Suppression of pain by sound. *Science* 132:32-33.

Gibbons, A.C., and McDougal, D.L. 1987. Music therapy in medical technology: Organ transplants. In *The Fourth International Symposium on Music: Rehabilitation and Human Well-Being*, edited by R.R. Pratt, 61-72.

Goldstein, A. 1985. Music/endorphin link. *Brain/Mind Bulletin* (Jan. 21/Feb. 11)2:1.

Gotlieb, H., and Konečni, V.J. 1985. Type A/Type B personality syndrome, attention, and music processing. In *Musik in der Medizin* [Music in Medicine], edited by R. Spintge and R. Droh;, 169-176. Basel: Edtiones Roches.

Harvey, A. 1985. Understanding your brain's response to music. *International Brain Dominance Review* 2:1, 32-39.

_____. 1987. Utilizing music as a tool for healing. In *The Fourth International Symposium on Music: Rehabilitation and Human Well-Being*, edited by R.R. Pratt, 73-87. Lanham, MD:University Press of America.

Hassan, T.H.A. 1985. The current crisis of medicine and science and the place of music. In *The Third International Symposium on Music in Medicine, Education and Therapy for the Handicapped*, edited by R.R. Pratt, 167-186. Lanham, MD: University Press of America.

Laudenslager, M.L.; Ryan, S.M.; Drugan, R.C.; Hyson, R.L.; and Maier, S.F. 1983. Coping and immunosuppression: Inescapable but not escapable shock suppresses lymphocyte proliferation. *Science* 221:568-570.

Lavine, R.; Buchsbaum, M.S.; and Poncy, M. 1976. Auditory analgesia: Somatosensory evoked response and subjective pain rating. *Psychophysiology* 13(2):140-147.

Livingston, J.C. 1979. Music for the childbearing family. *Journal of Obstetric and Gynecological Nursing* 17:363-367.

MacClelland, D.C. 1979. Music in the operating room. *AORN Journal* 29:252-260.

Masserman, J.H. 1986. Poetry as music. *The Arts in Psychotherapy* 13:6-67.

Nelson, J.D. 1949. Effects of music on the performance of the Rorschach test. Unpublished Master's thesis, University of Utah, Salt Lake City, UT.

Pratt, R.R. 1985a. The historical relationship between music and medicine. In *The Third International Symposium on Music in Medicine, Education, and Therapy for the Handicapped*, edited by R. R. Pratt, 237-269. Lanham, MD: University Press of America.

_____. 1985b. Music and medicine: A partnership in history. In *Musik in der Medizin* [Music in Medicine], edited by R. Spintge and R. Droh, 307-318. Basel: Editiones Roches.

Rider, M.S.; Floyd, J.; and Kirkpatrick, J. 1985. The effect of music, imagery and relaxation on adrenal corticosteroids and the reentrainment of circadian rhythms. *Journal of Music Therapy* 22:46-58.

Scartelli, J.P. 1982. The effect of sedative music on electromyographic biofeedback assisted relaxation training of spastic cerebral palsied adults. *Journal of Music Therapy* 19(4):210-218.

_____. 1984. The effect of EMG biofeedback and sedative music, EMG biofeedback only, and sedative music only on frontalis muscle relaxation ability. *Journal of Music Therapy* 21(2):67-78.

Schleifer, S.J.; Keller, S.E.; Siris, S.G.; Davis, K.L.; and Stein, K. 1985. Depression and immunity. *Arch. Gen. Psychiatry* 42:129-133.

Smith, G.R.; McKenzie, J.M.; Marmer, D.J.; and Steele, R.W. 1985. Psychologic modulation of the human immune response to varicella zoster. *Arch. Intern. Med.* 145:2110-2112.

Spintge, R. and Droh. R. 1987. *Musik in der Medizin* [Music in Medicine]. Heidelberg, New York: Springer.

Staum, M.J. 1983. Music and rhythmic stimuli in the rehabilitation of gait disorders. *Journal of Music Therapy* 10(2):69-87.

Summer, Lisa. 1988. *Guided Imagery and Music in the Institutional Setting*. Saint Louis, MO: MMB Music, Inc.

Tanioka, F.; Takazawa, T.; Kamata, S.; Kudo, M.; Matsuki, A.; and Oyama, T. 1986. Hormonal effect of anxiolytic music in patients during surgical operations under epidural anesthesia. In *Musik in der Medizin* [Music in Medicine], edited by R. Spintge and R. Droh, 285-292. Basel: Editiones Roches.

Tateno, K.; Fukuda, Y.; and Ishikawa, I. 1985. Breathing exercises for asthmatic children through singing songs: "Asthma music." In *The Third International Symposium on Music in Medicine, Education, and Therapy for the Handicapped*, edited by R.R. Pratt, 199-226. Lanham, MD: University Press of America.

Taylor, D. 1981., Music in general hospital treatment from 1900-1950. *Journal of Music Therapy* 18:62-73.

Thayer, J.F. Multiple indicators of affective response to music (Doctoral dissertation, New York University, 1986). *Dissertations Abstracts International*, 47:5068B.

Tyrrel, M.J. 1958. Affective reactions to musical variables. Unpublished Master's thesis, University of Utah, Salt Lake City, UT.

# A COMPREHENSIVE DEFINITION OF MUSIC THERAPY WITH AN INTEGRATIVE MODEL FOR MUSIC MEDICINE

Cheryl Dileo Maranto

*The author wishes to acknowledge Dr. Kenneth Bruscia, CMT-BC, for his assistance in the preparation of this article.*

The purpose of this paper, as the title implies, is to provide a working definition of music therapy in medical settings, to classify goals and types of interventions, and to project a model for interfacing the fields of music therapy and music performance medicine (specifically music medicine).

For purposes of this discussion, a clarification of terms is needed. The term "Music and Medicine" is used to refer to the interface of these two large, yet related fields. It provides a broad frame of reference and subsumes three categories: Music Performance Medicine or Music Medicine, Traditional Music Therapy, and Medical Music Therapy (C. Eagle, personal communication 1989; Ralph Spintge, personal communication 1989).

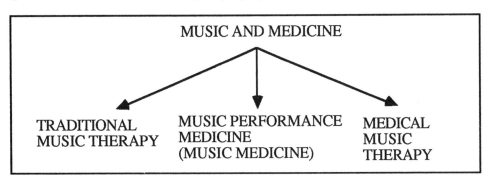

Music performance medicine or music medicine refers to the treatment of the medical and psychological problems of musicians.

Traditional music therapy refers to "a systematic process of intervention wherein the therapist helps the client to achieve health using musical experiences and the relationships that develop through them as dynamic forces of change." (Bruscia 1989, 47)

There are many applications of music therapy; the field is indeed a broad one, encompassing psychotherapeutic, educational, instructional, behavioral, pastoral, supervisory, healing, recreational, activity, and interrelated arts applications of music (Bruscia 1989).

Medical Music Therapy refers to the functional uses of music in medical specialties, e.g., surgery, cardiac care, etc. There are several requirements of medical music therapy based on Bruscia's definition: a client with some type of medical need, therapeutic goals based on initial diagnostic intake and ongoing assessment; a trained music therapist; musical experiences within the treatment session; and a therapeutic relationship which develops between the client and therapist (see Table 1).

---

# TABLE 1

## Necessary Components of Music Therapy

CLIENT WITH SOME KIND OF NEED

THERAPEUTIC GOALS

TRAINED MUSIC THERAPIST

MUSICAL EXPERIENCES

THERAPEUTIC RELATIONSHIP

---

In recent years, there has been an increased emphasis on and renaissance of medical music therapy, judging by the amount of published research, clinical interest, and media attention. This emphasis also corresponds to advances in behavioral medicine and psychoneuroimmunology during the past decade. The thrust in these areas has centered around the connections and interplay among the mind, body, and social environment of the patient, and how patients may take an active part in the treatment and prevention of illness. This is particularly evident as we begin to know the impact of stress and environmental factors on the immune system and subsequently on various types of illness.

Simultaneous with this thrust are advances in medicine, and in particular neuroscience, that facilitate methods of assessing the impact of psychological and social factors on disease and wellness.

And lastly, with the widespread occurrence of diseases such as AIDS, for which there are now no known cures, we are continuing to explore treatments to support medical interventions, with music therapy as one of these (Maranto 1988).

Medical music therapy can be classified both according to type of goal sought and level of intervention utilized. The biopsychosocial model of illness (Engel 1977) is an appropriate one for use in classifying goals of various applications of medical music therapy. Thus, medical music therapy goals may be biomedical, and/or psychosocial in nature. Examples of each of these are presented in Table 2.

# TABLE 2

## Goals of Various Applications of Medical Music Therapy

### Biomedical

EXAMPLES
- MUSIC TO INFLUENCE HR, BP, GSR, MUSCLE TENSION, ETC.
- MUSIC TO ENHANCE IMMUNE FUNCTION
- MUSIC TO FACILITATE RHYTHMIC AND DEEP BREATHING
- MUSIC TO SUPPRESS PAIN
- MUSIC TO DECREASE STRESS HORMONE LEVELS

### Psychosocial

EXAMPLES
- MUSIC TO REDUCE PREOPERATIVE ANXIETY
- MUSIC TO DISTRACT THE PATIENT DURING KIDNEY DIALYSIS
- MUSIC TO REDUCE DEPRESSION DUE TO SENSORY DEPRIVATION RESULTING FORM ISOLATION
- MUSIC TO REDUCE THE TRAUMA AND FEARS OF PATIENTS
- MUSIC TO ASSIST IN PATIENT DECISION-MAKING REGARDING TREATMENT
- MUSIC TO FACILITATE SUPPORT GROUPS AMONG PATIENTS
- MUSIC TO PROVIDE A SOCIAL OUTLET FOR PATIENTS IN LONG-TERM CARE
- MUSIC TO PROVIDE SUPPORT FOR FAMILIES OF TERMINALLY ILL PATIENTS

However, in keeping with the biopsychosocial model, the interrelationships among these areas are significant. That is, each of these areas influences and is influenced by the other. Thus, the music therapist who seeks to effect changes in either of these domains, (e.g., psychosocial) may also directly affect the other (e.g., biomedical).

Medical music therapy may be further classified as follows:

---

## TABLE 3

## Categories of Medical Music Therapy

MUSIC AS MEDICINE

MUSIC IN MEDICINE

MUSIC THERAPY AND MEDICINE

MUSIC THERAPY AS MEDICINE

MUSIC THERAPY IN MEDICINE

---

Criteria for the development of these categories include: the significance of the music in treatment; the significance of the therapeutic relationship in treatment; the role of the music and/or relationship in supporting medical treatment; and the role of the music and/or relationship as treatment.

When music is the primary agent for change, it is used directly to affect health. The therapeutic relationship is of lesser significance although a vital component of the process. When the therapeutic relationship is the primary agent for change, it is used directly to affect health. Music in this instance is of lesser significance, although a vital component of the therapeutic process.

In a similar manner, the role of medical music therapy in medical treatment may be either primary or supportive. When it is primary, it is used directly to affect health, as a medical treatment. When it is supportive, it is used to enhance or augment the effectiveness of the medical treatment.

## Music as Medicine

Music as Medicine refers to the use of music to affect health directly. Music, in this category, is subordinate to the therapeutic relationship in that it is primarily the music which effects the therapeutic change, on biomedical and/or psychosocial levels. An excellent example of music as medicine is the use of music as an audio-analgesia. Here listening to music may successfully diminish the patient's pain and be used in lieu of pain medication. The therapeutic relationship is necessary to provide support and encouragement to the patient in this process. Another example of music as medicine is the use of vibrational music techniques, such as the Somatron or sound bath to effect physiological changes, such as the lowering of blood pressure, heart rate, and muscle tension. Further examples include the use of music listening to increase immune function and peak air flow, and to decrease ACTH levels.

## Music in Medicine

Music in Medicine refers to the use of music as the primary agent in a role which supports or enhances medical treatment or procedures. In this category, music is of greater significance than the therapeutic relationship and is used most often in conjunction with medical procedures, but not as the sole treatment. Music can be used to effect biomedical and/or psychosocial factors which support the success of medical procedures.

Examples of music in medicine include: music to enhance the patient's mood during kidney dialysis; music to arouse patients following surgery; music to reduce length of labor; and music-electro-acupuncture.

## Music Therapy and Medicine

Music Therapy and Medicine is a category which includes those applications where there is equal importance of both the music and the therapeutic relationship. In addition, music therapy has an equal role in terms of significance with the medical treatment used. In this category also, the target goals of medical music therapy are the biomedical and/or psychosocial aspects of the patient. An example of medical music therapy is guided visualization and music to increase peak air flow of asthmatics.

In this case, the music is equally important with the relationship established between the client and therapist. Also, the music and medical procedures are equally significant in that both music and medical treatment are used to support each other.

### Music Therapy As Medicine

Music Therapy as Medicine refers to the use of the client-therapist relationship to treat medical problems directly. In this category, the therapeutic relationship is more important than the music used, and the procedures have direct impact on health, i.e., are not used to support medical procedures. Frequently, the patient's psychosocial well-being is addressed directly, with subsequent effects in the biomedical domain anticipated. An example of music therapy as medicine is the use of music therapy to facilitate changes in the patient's lifestyle which will help the client overcome the disease.

### Music Therapy In Medicine

Music Therapy in Medicine refers to the use of the therapeutic relationship, with music in a subservient role, to support medical procedures. The goals of music therapy in medicine are often psychosocial or psychotherapeutic in nature, with changes in the biomedical domain anticipated. An example of music therapy in medicine is the use of music therapy to reduce distress related to the specific illness, such as cancer or to facilitate decision-making regarding treatment.

## MUSICAL EXPERIENCES

Musical experiences in each of these five categories of medical applications of music or music therapy generally are classified as either passive or active. Either or both types are used in any of the categories.

Passive methods usually involve receptive music activities such as music listening, song discussion, music reminiscence, music-facilitated biofeedback, music and relaxation, and music-vibrational therapy. Mental imagery stimulated or facilitated by the music may also be an important component of passive methods, e.g., guided imagery and music.

In the category of active music, either music is performed, improvised or created, or activities are performed, improvised or created to music. Examples include music and exercise, therapeutic music instruction, individual or group vocal or instrumental performing, vocal or instrumental improvisation, and song-writing. Imagery may also be an important part of this method, in that it may stimulate the creative process (see Table 4).

The effectiveness of music therapy interventions for medical problems has been addressed on page 364 by Dr. Standley in this panel, and based on her data I conclude that the future of medical music therapy is a bright one and collaborations between music therapists and physicians in both research and clinical practice can only serve to further its development.

What are the implications of music therapy for music performance medicine or music medicine? The following model integrating music therapy and music medicine is proposed (see Table 5).

## Musical Treatment of Musicians

I would like to emphasize and provide a direction for the use of music therapy in music medicine, specifically its use in treating the psychological and physiological problems of performing musicians. In Part V of this collection of papers I provide a rationale for the use of music in treating the performance anxiety of musicians. I would now like to extend that concept to include the use of music in treating physiological problems of musicians in addition to other possible psychological problems. Doctors Staum (page 267) and Thaut (page 80) have provided important information on the use of music in physical rehabilitation and have made specific suggestions to that end elsewhere in this collection of papers. I would like to add that music therapists, as trained musicians, trained therapists and experts on the influence of music on health, are uniquely skilled in this area and have much knowledge and clinical expertise to contribute to this interdisciplinary field. Using music to achieve biomedical and psychosocial goals at various levels of intervention, music therapists may bring a new dimension and perspective to music medicine. Examples of uses in this area are presented in Table 6.

## Music Treatment of Physicians

It has been stated in the past that artists are among our most valuable resources. I will extend that to state that effective physicians are also among our most valuable resources; their psychological and physical health must be protected. These individuals may be particularly prone to stress-related medical and psychological problems. Music therapy may be instrumental in helping them cope with this stress.

# TABLE 4

## Classification of Music Experiences Used in Music Therapy

**Passive Experiences**

EXAMPLES

- ° MUSIC-FACILITATED BIOFEEDBACK
- ° MUSIC LISTENING FOR STRESS REDUCTION
- ° PROJECTIVE LISTENING
- ° MUSIC REMINISCENCE
- ° ANXIOLYTIC MUSIC
- ° VIBRATIONAL THERAPY

**Active Experiences**

EXAMPLES

- ° INSTRUMENT PLAYING
- ° SINGING
- ° MUSIC AND MOVEMENT (OR EXERCISE)
- ° CONTINGENT MUSIC
- ° MUSIC PERFORMANCE
- ° CONDUCTING
- ° INSTRUMENTAL IMPROVISATION
- ° VOCAL IMPROVISATION
- ° SONG-WRITING
- ° MOVEMENT IMPROVISATIONS
- ° SONG-DISCUSSION

## Music in Hospitals

Without a doubt music therapy plays a critical role in rehumanizing hospitals. I have already addressed the possibilities of music therapy in medical treatment. However, numerous ancillary uses of music therapy can be implemented in hospital settings for a variety of purposes: stress reduction; creativity; productivity; diversion; fatigue prevention; morale; mood elevation; and for emphasis on health rather than illness (these uses apply equally to staff and patients). Both active and passive types of music experiences have unique capabilities for use in these settings.

## Music Therapy in Medical Education

Music therapy should also be an important component of medical education. Needless to say, physicians in training need to be educated regarding medical music therapy so that they may be knowledgeable about techniques that may enhance the quality of the medical procedures they use, as well as noninvasive, nondrug alternatives to treatment. In addition, I will be so bold as to recommend that student physicians have the opportunity to experience music therapy at its various levels of intervention to assist them in self-knowledge, personal growth, stress management, and creativity.

---

# TABLE 5

# Integrative Model for Music Therapy and Music Medicine

° MUSICAL TREATMENT OF MUSICIANS

° MUSICAL TREATMENT OF PHYSICIANS

° MUSIC IN HOSPITALS

° MUSIC IN MEDICAL EDUCATION

In closing I would like to state that the connections between music and medicine are centuries old, yet have dissipated along the way. There are two fields that may facilitate this re-merger: medical music therapy and music medicine. The field of music therapy, with its centuries-old history of practice but only recent emergence as a science may provide an obvious link between these two areas. Music medicine, with its current renaissance of practice, can provide the other link.

Thus, medical music therapy and music medicine may serve as the bridges between the art and science of music and the art and science of medicine. However, in order for these two fields to be truly effective as links between music and medicine, they must first link and integrate with each other.

---

# TABLE 6
## Examples of Medical Music Therapy for Musicians

### Music as Medicine
° MUSIC LISTENING TO REGULATE BREATHING PRIOR TO PERFORMING
° MUSIC TO REDUCE CATECHOLAMINE LEVELS OF ANXIOUS PLAYERS PRIOR TO PERFORMING

### Music In Medicine
° MUSIC TO REDUCE DISCOMFORT DURING MEDICAL PROCEDURES INVOLVING OVERUSE INJURIES
° MUSIC TO STRUCTURE PHYSICAL EXERCISE IN THE REHABILITATION OF PLAYING-RELATED INJURIES

### Music Therapy And Medicine
° MUSIC SYSTEMATIC DESENSITIZATION FOR PERFORMANCE ANXIETY

### Music Therapy as Medicine
° MUSIC TO HELP MUSICIANS IMPLEMENT LIFESTYLE CHANGES RELATED TO THEIR INJURIES

### Music Therapy in Medicine
° MUSIC TO HELP MUSICIANS EXPRESS FEARS PRIOR TO SURGERY

## REFERENCE  LIST

Bruscia, K.E. 1989. *Defining Music Therapy.* Spring City, PA: Spring House Books.

Engel, G.L. 1977. The need for a new medical model: A challenge for biomedicine. *Science* 196:129.

Maranto, C.D. 1988. AIDS: Information and issues for music therapists. *Music Therapy Perspectives* 5:78-81.

This article first appeared in *Applications of Music in Medicine* published by National Association for Music Therapy, 8455 Colesville Road, Silver Spring, MD 20910 USA.

# MUSIC MEDICINE: THE CASE FOR A HOLISTIC MODEL

Richard A. Lippin

**T**he relationships between human health and music have been described from the ancients to the present. Many descriptive terms have been utilized to describe fields of study and practice based on those relationships, including music therapy, music medicine, neuromusicology, and others. This paper argues for the acceptance on one term, namely "music medicine," which encompasses all relationships between human health and music. In order to put forth this argument, certain scientific and social phenomena must be recognized which set the stage for this holistic model.

The first principle is a general recognition of the limitations of the excesses of a reductionistic approach in either music therapy or music medicine, the latter being defined as the treatment and prevention of music making induced injury and illness. A reductionistic paradigm, for instance, would usually seek to explore in detail what particular physical forces may have contributed to an injury of a musician, rather than understanding the musician as an entire human being in the context of the impact of music, music making, and his musical career on his life. Thus, music becomes both a potential etiology and a potential therapy for the professional and/or amateur musician.

Dr. Louise Montello (1989) of New York University found that group music therapy can be highly effective in reducing performance stress and increasing musicality in anxious musicians. Dr. Montello believes the key to the success of music therapy intervention is the use of music as a transformational tool as well as a self-reflecting tool.

Also, advances in neuroscience are allowing music therapy to enter rapidly into the realm of somatic medicine. Music not only affects mood and therefore has application in a traditional mental health setting, but also clearly affects human physiology through its impact on the brain and, through the brain, on the neuroendocrine and psycho-neuroimmunological systems. Music therapy can no longer be viewed as an ancillary therapy in a few limited medical specialties such as psychiatry and physical medicine and rehabilitation, but must rather be integrated into the mainstream of all medical specialties, recognizing music's potential impact on all body systems.

Frank Wilson (1988, 139-146), Associate Clinical Professor of Neurology, University of California, in his outstanding article "Music and Medicine: An Old Liaison, A New Agenda," states that:

> ... the connections between music and medicine are durable because the disciplines themselves are expressions of singular and deeply rooted human propensities.

Wilson goes on to state that music therapists are:

> ... in a position to assume a major responsibility in at least two extremely demanding areas of medical practice: the physical, cognitive, and emotional rehabilitation of patients with neurological disability; and the medical and surgical therapies of patients with malignancies, and those with immune degenerative disorders.

What do music therapists and "music medicine physicians" have in common? Both have an interest in music as a phenomenon, in music making activity, and in musicians. Both, I presume, have an interest in the creative process and inherently both value music and musicians. Both should presume that music can be used diagnostically as well as therapeutically. What disciplines should music therapist and music medicine physicians have in common? I would propose psychology, psychiatry, neurology, physiatry, ergonometry, sociology, musicology, music education, creativity, and work physiology as elements of a core curriculum.

Should the music therapist study the physiology of music making? How can one separate the physical act of playing from the impact of music on health? For example, in order properly to choose a given music instrument for therapeutic use in a nonprofessional musician, the music therapist must understand the physical forces involved in playing such an instrument.

Music is so universal that in a sense we are all "music medicine patients," whether we visit a clinic, have a music therapy session, play music, or listen to music. This universality was brought home to me when first reading Lewis Thomas' *Lives of a Cell* in 1974. Thomas (1974, 27-28) says that "the urge to make a kind of music is as much a characteristic of [human] biology as our fundamental aspects." He refers to music as a fundamental need for symmetry against entropy which he called a "grand canonical ensemble." This is the proper term for a quantitative model system in thermodynamics, borrowed from music by way of mathematics, borrowed by Lewis Thomas back again.

Dr. Frank Wilson, noted above, also quotes Dr. Lewis Thomas who replied when asked what music has to do with thinking:

> Instead of using what we can guess at about the nature of thought to explain the nature of music, start over again. Begin with music and see that it can tell us about the sensation of thinking. Music is the effort we make to explain to ourselves how our brains work... If you want, as an experiment to hear the whole mind working, all at once, put on the Saint

Matthew Passion and turn the volume up all the way. This is the sound of
the whole central nervous system of human beings, all at once.

Why, conversely, should a music medicine physician be interested in music therapy?
Performing arts medicine physicians often have windows on musical expression at the
highest levels. The cases of Gray Graffman and Leon Fleischer represented unique
opportunities to understand the impact of music making on dysfunction as well as the
impact of this dysfunction on music making. Music medicine physicians often request
that the patient bring his instrument to the medical session. This represents a unique
opportunity not only to observe the patient's technique, but also to listen to the music
for its diagnostic value where one could hear the pathology in a music work. As a
nonmusic patient articulates his disease through his words, perhaps the musician
articulates his diseased self through his music. Leonard Bernstein, lecturing on Mahler's
*Symphony No. 9*, states that one could hear in Mahler the valvular heart disease of this
great nineteenth century composer. Music therapists have using these diagnostic
techniques for decades.

Also, the use of specific, even prescriptive, music to rehabilitate psychological and
physiological dysfunction has several advantages for the music medicine physician. First,
music has a unique capacity to stimulate muscular movement, a key element in physical
rehabilitation. Music-paced exercise is a well-known phenomenon which contributes to
the rehabilitative process. Tapes for music-based exercise are available for such fitness
pursuits as stationary cycling, jogging and walking. These tapes feature instrumental
music designed to synchronize cardiovascular and muscular activity according to the
demands of the particular sport. Secondly, music interventions are noninvasive, hence,
less destructive therapies to a great extent. Thirdly, the very stimulus which may have
caused the dysfunction originally is now utilized at a lower dose with appropriate rest-
work cycles to permit some level of therapy and play to continue, thus reducing the
anxiety the patient may feel about not playing at all. Perhaps even listening to oneself
playing and the concomitant use of effective imaging techniques could enhance confidence
as it relates to returning to full capacity.

Through courses in music therapy, the music medicine physician can be exposed to the
advanced psychological training which is becoming increasingly important in the total
care of the musician. Serious illness or injury could be one of the most important events
in a musician's life, either ending his or her career or advancing it through the process of
personal transformation or maturation that a disease process often brings into one's life.
In his most recent book Dr. Bernie Seigel references a young lawyer who wanted very
much to be a violinist but whose parents convinced him to go to law school. When
informed that he had developed a brain tumor early in life, the young man decided that
with his remaining years on earth, he would follow his true love, to play the violin. A

year later this lawyer-musician reported to Dr. Seigel that he was still playing for a local orchestra without any evidence of the brain tumor.

Several leaders in music therapy have suggested holistic paradigms:

Dr. Cheryl Maranto of Temple University titled this joint presentation, "Music Therapy and Music Medicine: An Integrative Model," suggesting that a holistic approach should at least be explored.

Dr. Arthur Harvey (1986), then Professor of Music at Eastern Kentucky University, has stated that "although there are isolated instances of studies that suggest a positive relationship between music and its use in a remediative and preventive medicine, I would propose a comprehensive 'Brain-Model Approach.'" In the development of this holistic perspective, based on a brain analogy, Dr. Harvey's idea is conceptualized in the establishment of the Institutes for the Study of Music Mind and Medicine. His Institutes would have several divisions, including the behavioral and experimental studies division, the transpersonal and existential division and the synthesis and applied studies division which "would serve to provide a connecting link or bridge between differing psychological and philosophical viewpoints and would provide an integrated or holistic channel through which future studies of the application of music to the field of medicine would emerge."

Dr. Charles Eagle, Professor of Music Therapy and Head, Music Therapy, Medicine and Health, Meadow School of the Arts, Southern Methodist University, in correspondence to me describing his accomplishments in music medicine information systems (March 15, 1989), stated that the project for him has been fun and informative. His conceptual formulation of music medicine, combining words from music and from medicine into a coherent assembly for the understanding of both musician and physicians has been and continues to be his most interesting challenge. His basic goal in this project is to provide a database of information relevant to the function of music and medical specialties and the treatment of performing musicians—thus combining music therapy and music medicine.

From a sociological and historical perspective, Rosalie Pratt (1987) states:

> Let us emulate the inquisitiveness of the Greeks, the solid foundation of the early universities and the interdisciplinary mastery they required, and the intellectual adventure and excitement of the Renaissance. Let us bring back the dialogue of musicians and scientists who recognized the stimulation of interdisciplinary discussion and thought. Let us also remember the closeness of the nineteenth century physician and musician and rediscover the affection the two professions once shared.

And Madeleine Cosman (1978,1) from the Institute for Medieval and Renaissance Studies, City College, City University of New York, in an article entitled "Machaut's Medical Musical World," states:

> Music pervaded medieval medical practice and theory in an outstanding manner. Not only was music prescribed for good digestion and for bodily preparation before surgery, but also as a stimulus to wound healing, a mood changer and as critical accompaniment to bloodletting. Specifically composed medical music (the shivaree) graced the wedding chamber to assure erotic coupling at the astrologically auspicious moment.

In his eloquent paper, "Harmony and Beauty in Medical Research," Dr. Robert S. Root-Bernstein (1987, 1048), Department of Natural Sciences and Physiology, Michigan State University, explores the relationship between music and nature and health. He states:

> More exciting is the notion of music as a mode of thinking about, feeling and exploring the structures of nature. For music is not simply a set of sounds we hear and take pleasure in. Music differs from other forms of expression such as words or most forms of mathematics in being able to explore and convey numerous concurrent themes. Think about the difference between a series of equations or the monotonic, linear progression of a medical description, an argument or novel, and then consider the dozens of layers of information conveyed simultaneously by an orchestrated piece of music, or one written for piano or organ. The music, like the metabolic process or the physiology of the body is a result of the controlled synthesis or contrasts, rhythms, harmonies and forms. It requires practice thinking concurrently about complex patterns and sensing multiple levels of interaction—holistic thinking, if you will—rather than linear, reductionist analysis. Thus, as Sigmund Levarie, has suggested, music combines both 'quality and quantity precisely and spontaneously so that sense impression can be measured and proportion can be experienced.' One both knows and feels the system. Surely practice in this way of thinking cannot but benefit the physician or medical researcher who must daily deal with systems even more complex than any symphony: the systems we call human beings.

Thus music medicine leaders, as illustrated above (Maranto, Eagle, Pratt, Wilson, Harvey, and Root-Bernstein) either explicitly or implicitly embrace a holistic model of music medicine. Most important, however, is that today's world needs the reality and metaphors of music.

Clearly we are living in a world which needs more harmony and less dysrhythmia. Steven Diamond, an attorney from Los Angeles, wrote to me in 1985, stating that he was working hard all over the country to get men to come into harmony together through the benefits of barbershop quartets. He referenced both music theorists who explain that the harmonics are all consonant, and group psychologists who attest to the amplification of power brought about by group unity. He went on to state that these men find support of other men in the vibrating they do together because their goals all involve coming into closer and closer harmony with each other. In a subsequent letter, he quotes a wonderful barbershop song that is a commentary on the competitiveness and isolation of men and states that many men have been traumatized by early childhood experience into thinking that they cannot sing. He states that he is sure this self-limitation has resulted in closing off many men to their emotional selves in song as well as limiting their capacities to learn by forging ahead.

The capacity of music to heal has never been greater. I am certain that consciously or unconsciously this lies at the root of the growth of music medicine as a specialty and has always been a basic premise of the music therapy movement.

## REFERENCE LIST

Cosman, M.P. 1978. *Machaut's Medical Musical World*. New York: New York Academy of Sciences.

Harvey, A.W. 1986. *Utilizing music as a tool for healing*. NAMT Southern Division Conference, Clearwater, FL.

Montello, L. 1989. *Music Therapy Successful in Treating Music Performance Stress*. New York: New York University.

Pratt, R.R. and Jones, R.W. 1987. Music and medicine: a partnership in history. In *Music and Medicine* ed. R. Spintge and R. Droh. Berlin: Springer Verlag.

Root-Bernstein, R.S. 1987. Harmony and beauty in medical research. *Journal of Molecular and Cellular Cardiology* 19:1043-1051.

Thomas, L. 1974. *The Lives of a Cell*. New York: Bantam Books.

Wilson, F.R. 1988. Music and medicine: An old liaison, a new agenda. *Psycho-musicology* 7(2):139-146.

# II

## ASPECTS IN PHYSIOLOGY
## AND PHYSICS

*We thank Mrs. Mahoney-Heidelmeyer for assisting with the preparation of the manuscript and Mr. P. Holzner for preparing the figures.*

# PHYSIOLOGICAL RHYTHMICITY AND MUSIC IN MEDICINE

H.P. Koepchen
R. Droh
R. Spintge
H.-H. Abel
D. Klüssendorf
E. Koralewski

The relationships between music and medicine are manifold. Research in this rapidly developing field has many different aspects and requires an interdisciplinary approach. One of the basic theoretical sciences involved is physiology. This volume deals largely with the following three areas of music in medicine hereafter called "MusicMedicine."

1. Music as a therapeutic tool;
2. Effects of music on the organism;
3. Medical treatment of musicians.

What can physiology contribute to these fields? What justification is there in applying physiological points of view to musicology?

If we view music in its broadest terms, the justification becomes more obvious. Let us take Kepler's (1596) famous symbolic diction of the "harmony of the universe" as a classical model. This kind of music includes a very large spectrum of frequencies below those which are perceptible to our limited auditory senses. Kepler's concept encompasses periodically occurring sequences of cosmic rhythmic events. Here the harmony becomes apparent in the laws of physics which may be described in mathematical terms. It is noteworthy that in the classical epoch of Greek science and philosophy, where our kind of scientific thinking has its roots, music was derived from mathematics.

Taken in this very broad sense, nature as a whole is full of rhythms where frequencies cover an enormous range. These can be comprehended as interdependent as well as independent clocks, from the orbit of stars down to that of an electron in an atom from which we get our most precise measurement of time today.

## RHYTHMICITY OF THE ORGANISM

The world of living organisms originates from this rhythmic universe and represents one part of it. Therefore, the organism is part of the rhythmic order and life is a rhythmically organized process, again with frequencies extending over a huge range (Hildebrandt 1958).

More recently, in a rapidly progressing field, molecular biologists have realized that biomolecules, the most important elements of vital function, are not static but exert oscillatory movements in a slower order of time than the atomic clock. Inevitably human life, as part of the living world, is embedded into rhythmic orders. We are consciously aware of only a very limited part of all these rhythms. There is a broader spectrum which can be measured using objective methods.

Most of the macroscopically manifest rhythms are based on the mutual coordination of many single elements in a characteristic analysis of self-organization. Recently, a new mathematical analysis of self-organization has been developed (Haken 1983). It can be applied to very different living and nonliving systems which consist of a great number of microscopic or macroscopic constituent parts. Since most of the interacting biological rhythms are in turn the result of synchronization and self-organization among potentially or actually oscillating subunits, this new kind of mathematics may help us quantify and analyze the complex biological rhythmicity. Figure 1 schematically illustrates the scale of frequencies involved in the course of human life. We see that this scale extends over a range of about 17 decades.

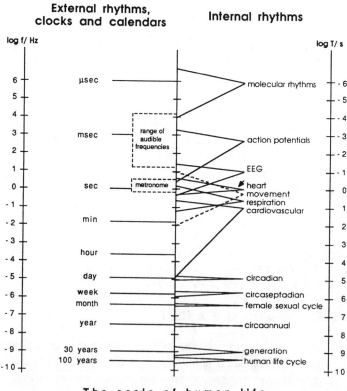

**The scale of human life**

*Figure 1.*

*Range of frequencies of human physiological rhythms drawn upon a logarithmic scale with frequencies on the left and periods on the right scale. External rhythms acting from the outer world on the organism are depicted on the left side, internal rhythms on the right side. The triangles on the right side symbolize the most characteristic frequency and the range of occurrence of the respective rhythm. Note the broad frequency with extensive overlapping of neurovegetative and motor rhythms as compared with the small variability of the slower rhythms evolved in adaptation to external cycles.*

The rhythms within the different ranges of this scale have different characteristic properties and interdependencies. At the upper end we find internal rhythms mainly determined by the physico-chemical properties of the elementary constituents at the molecular or membranous level, e.g., the action potentials. At the lower end we find the biorhythms which have evolved in adaptation to cosmic rhythms in the course of evolution, the most conspicuous and best studied of which is the circadian rhythm. The endogenous character of this rhythm was discovered using special methods of investigation (Aschoff and Pohl 1978; Wever 1979).

The rhythms, however, which are of particular importance to music are found in a medium range. At one end we find the EEG-rhythm overlapping with that of the action potentials; at the other end the cardiovascular rhythms extending to the diurnal range which manifests itself very distinctly in the cardiovascular parameters (Parati et al. 1988). The middle of this medium range between 10 Hz and $10^{-2}$ Hz is the proper domain of musical rhythms in the usual sense of the word. It is here that we find the inner rhythms of the heart-beat with all its variations, those of the respiratory system, and the frequencies of most of our normal movements.

It is remarkable and certainly more than pure coincidence that the range of frequencies installed in a metronome used in practical musical training corresponds exactly to the frequency range of heart beats occurring between quiet rest and intense physical activity. Regarding the biological internal rhythmicity this range has some characteristic features:

1. The rhythms show a fairly wide relative variability of frequency.
2. Their ranges overlap extensively.
3. They occur in systems with homeostatic feedback autoregulation of vital functions, e.g., the controls of arterial blood pressure and of blood gas concentrations.

These features lead us to the observation that:

a) There is permanent competition between the homeostatic function with the goal of constancy and the rhythmic change of the parameters whereby both these principles limit each other.

b)  There is intense mutual interaction between the different rhythms. These interactions comprise those between the vegetative and the somatomotor systems.

Moreover, these features show all modes of interaction between biological rhythms. One of these modes is the special kind of action on the frequency usually called "entrainment." Entrainment means that one rhythm synchronizes with another one. One well known example of entrainment is the synchronization of the inner circadian rhythm by the outer "Aschoff-Zeitgebers" of the 24 hour day-night cycle. The former is revealed when the influences of the latter are removed, as in the so-called "bunker experiments" with the subjects totally insulated from the environment.

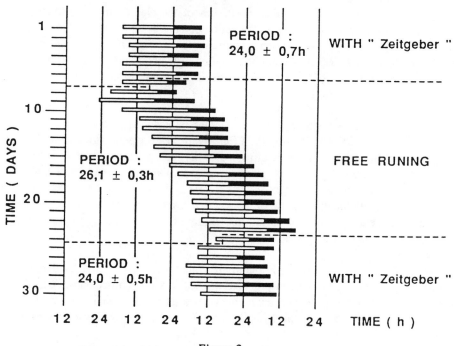

*Figure 2.*
*Duration of sleep (empty) and activity (dotted) cycles of a human subject plotted against the external diurnal time scale. Under normal life conditions (upper and lower part) the wake-sleep cycle is synchronized with the 24-hour period of earth rotation by the "zeitgebers" from the environment. In isolation from the outer world (middle part) the subject develops a slower "circadian" rhythm with a longer period of about 26 hours. [From experiments of Aschoff and Pohl (1978) and Wever (1979)]*

The qualitative phenomena of entrainment are well known, e.g., the synchronization between movements and respiration in rowers or runners. The precondition for such mutual influences and adaptations which are particularly noticeable in the medium range of biological rhythms is their variability, quite unlike physical clocks or the fixed beat of a metronome.

Quantitative analyses to detect the rules of interaction are much more difficult and require special approaches in the case of biological rhythms. Such a scientific analysis started with the pioneering work of Erich von Holst (1939). He carefully registered and analyzed the rhythmic fin movements with their mutual interrelations in fish without forebrains. Von Holst was able to reduce the complex physiological rhythmic phenomena to the concomitant action of two principles: the "Magneteffekt" (magnetic effect) and the "Überlagerung" (superposition).

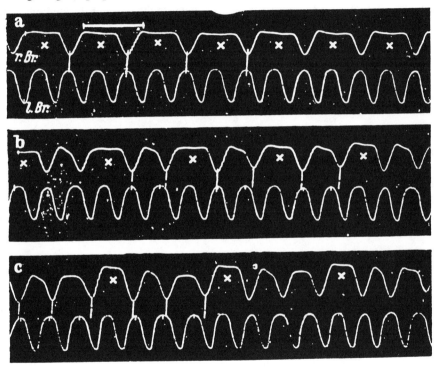

*Figure 3.*
*Simultaneous record of the movements of two contralateral fins from a fish without forebrain. Note the stable 2:1 frequency relation in a) and the spontaneous changes between 2:1 and 1:1 relation in b) and c). [From v. Holst (1939)]*

The magnetic effect is the basis of entrainment and can be demonstrated in the form of statistically preferred phase relations even when synchrony has not been achieved. All intermediate stages from complete independence to strong synchrony of different rhythms can be observed. Stages of multiple integer frequency relations are more stable than other irregular patterns especially those stages with low number relations like 1:2 or 1:3 in comparison to 3:5 or 6:7 for example (a well known experience for instrumentalists).

Usually one rhythm is the leading rhythm and the other is the dependent one. These roles can change if one of them becomes stronger or weaker due to external or internal influences. States of transition are characterized by alternating periods and/or amplitudes (Haken et al. 1985; Koepchen 1962).

Superposition simply means that the amplitude of one rhythm is added to the other or subtracted from it without influencing the phase. Mostly there is a mixture of magnetic effect and superposition. Both principles together lead to a resonance-like enhancement of the amplitude, when one rhythm's frequency approaches that of the other one. Von Holst has called these rules in their entirety "relative coordination." They are applicable not only to the interaction of different internal rhythms but also to the effect of the environment on internal rhythms. Later it was found that the rules of relative coordination represent a very general principle in nature. Corresponding phenomena have been demonstrated in the coordination of leg movements in running quadrupeds, in the coordination of suckling and respiration in babies, and in the coordination of human hand movements to cite only a few examples. Undoubtedly dancing will also be found to be governed by these basic physiological rules but as yet there has been no research in this area.

In the context of neurovegetative rhythmicity for the medium frequency range it is remarkable that a similar coordination was demonstrated in the relationship between the respiratory, cardiovascular, and motor systems and in the relationships between the individual components of these systems (Koepchen 1962, 1984; Koepchen et al. 1986; Koepchen, Abel, and Klüssendorf 1987, 1989). This also signifies the close functional connection between our inner world of neurovegetative rhythmicity and our motor activities which are used for interaction with the outer world and to express our feelings.

Now that the principles of biological rhythmicity have been introduced we come to our central theme and ask the following questions:

1.  What is the relationship between general biological rhythmicity and MusicMedicine?
2.  What kind of special phenomena can be found and evaluated in the realm of cardiorespiratory and motor rhythms?
3.  What is the relationship to homeostasis, stress, and relaxation?
4.  What are the possible applications to the concrete problems of MusicMedicine?

## GENERAL RELATIONSHIPS BETWEEN PHYSIOLOGICAL FUNCTIONS AND MUSIC

The manifold and mostly bidirectional relationships between these subjects can be depicted as in Figure 4.

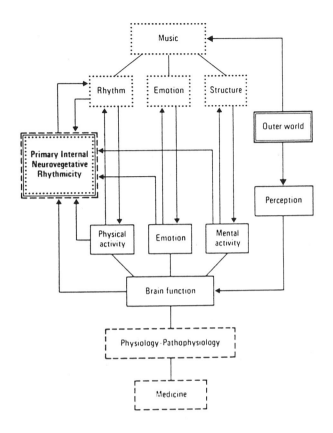

*Figure 4.*
*Scheme of bidirectional relations between the components of brain function and those of music, illustrating the role of neurovegetative rhythmicity in the frame of these relations. MusicMedicine is based on these interrelations. For further explanations see text.*

Music at an archaic level comes to man from surrounding nature. We can detect music in birdsong, the rustling of trees in the wind, the roar of the surging sea, or even, within a higher spiritual sense, in the harmony of the universe as Kepler did. All this becomes music only through the mediation of the human mind. Music in the narrower sense is a creation of man. The physiological roots of this creation can be found in his body as well as in his mind. In a certain sense man has projected the essential components of his brain and bodily functions into his creation called music.

Like music, brain function is an entity but we can differentiate a few main components in both which correspond to each other. In our brain we find the organization for the use of the motor system, for the function of abstraction and thinking and for the function of the involuntary neurovegetative control systems and closely linked emotions. The elements of music can be subdivided into rhythm, emotion, and structure which is expressed in the architecture of a melody or of a polyphonic fugue for example. These subdivisions correspond to the components of brain function: abstract mental activity and neurovegetative rhythms induced by the brain correspond to musical rhythm, and finally man's emotional experience corresponds to the emotional content of music.

Harmony, the fourth component of music, is based on numerical relations of frequencies and has no direct neurophysiological correlate in the time domain because it is transferred in the auditory system from a temporal to a spatial pattern. The subjective conscious perception of the latter as harmony or disharmony is still entirely enigmatic. There is no doubt, however, that this component also provides a powerful contribution to the emotional content of music. Thus, it may be expected that harmony can influence neurovegetative rhythms as do various emotions. This is one of the many open questions requiring investigation. In reality, of course, a complete separation of these basic elements never exists: rhythm is a constituent part of the structure of music, and both structure and more especially rhythm contribute to the emotional content of the music.

The relationships between brain activity and music are bidirectional. Man produces music and by hearing it and even more by performing it, this musical expression of human mental activity in turn stimulates the brain. This is particularly true where rhythm is concerned. In the terminology of von Holst's distinction between leading and dependent rhythms, man closely determines the rhythm in music as he has learned in musical education.

Conversely, music influences man's inner and outer rhythms in a much more variable manner. One can presume that this bidirectional process will be governed by the general rules of interaction between biological rhythms on the basis of entrainment and superposition. These have already been found in an archaic manner in the fin movements of fish. In other words, it will be a self-organizing system.

This supposition is not just a theoretical idea. It provides a basis for practical research programs for MusicMedicine. The fact that an enormous variety and variability of rhythmic phenomena in the organism can be reduced to a few principles makes this field accessible to scientific analysis. Thus we can measure and describe rhythmicity in a quantitative manner. As in other disciplines, only with quantitative analyses can research on the interaction of music and the organism develop from the simple observation of phenomena into a true science.

In the medium range, which encompasses musical rhythms, we find the following sources of human rhythmicity:

1.  Imitation of the outer world's rhythms, including the artificial man-made world of music and common walking and dancing;

2.  Rhythmic movements of the human body, governed by the central nervous motor control system and the mechanical properties of the involved parts of the body;
3.  Internal rhythmicity, controlled by neurovegetative mechanisms.

Restricting our theme to neurovegetative rhythmicity, the immediate subject of our research program, we must bear in mind that this area of study should always be seen in the broader context outlined above.

## NEUROVEGETATIVE RHYTHMICITY

"Neurovegetative" means governed by the nervous system and acting on inner organs and organ systems. In current medical literature in English we more frequently find the term "autonomic," i.e., independent of voluntary influence. In contrast, the term "vegetative" includes the closely linked respiration, a function accessible but not obligatorily bound to voluntary control.

Looking at the frequencies usually present in music, we find the rhythm of the heart beat and the rhythm of respiration. (For those not familiar with physiology we will recall that the rhythm of the heart beat originates in the pacemaker of the heart and is modified by central nervous influences whereas the respiratory rhythm is generated within the central nervous system.)

From the functional point of view, both are transport rhythms satisfying the metabolic needs of the body by moving blood through the circulatory system and air in and out of the lungs. Homeostatic neurovegetative control adapts this transport to the actual metabolic requirements which change extensively according to the degree of physical activity. Even with this basically functional point of view, these fundamental transport mechanisms must be rhythmic since the organism has no continuous movements like wheels. *Thus, external rhythms are not acting on a passive or static organism but on a dynamic and primarily rhythmic one.*

## Cardiorespiratory Rhythmicity

This survey includes the results of experiments on anesthetized animals where the underlying mechanisms can be studied more thoroughly. With some restrictions these results can be extended to humans since these functions are phylogenetically ancient and are common to all mammals and partly even to lower organisms.

### *The Respiratory Rhythm*

The respiratory rhythm is the result of complicated interactions between several populations of respiratory neurons located in the lower brain stem (Euler 1986). Early-inspiratory, late-inspiratory, end-inspiratory, early-expiratory, and late-expiratory neurons have been found. These neurons produce bursts of action potentials, each burst being related to a special phase of the respiratory cycle. It would take too long to enter into the details of the central nervous generation of the respiratory rhythm. We will confine ourselves to those basic principles which can also be studied in man.

Neurophysiological analysis results in a concept of respiratory rhythmogenesis caused by the interaction of several components each governing a certain part of the respiratory cycle. There is a mechanism for starting inspiration, another one for controlling the velocity of inspiration, and yet another for ending inspiration. Expiration is controlled by two mechanisms (Richter 1982). The first mechanism is active during the first part of expiration, preventing too rapid expiration by declining activity of inspiratory muscles. The second, late expiratory mechanism governs the maintenance and duration of the expiratory pause before the next inspiration begins. The latter partial mechanism is activated during enhanced metabolic needs and voluntary activation of expiration.

In humans, of course, it is not possible to register the activity of the corresponding brain stem neurons. However, we can differentiate between the respective phases of respiratory movement. A recording of respiratory movements can easily be obtained using belts fixed around the thorax and/or the abdomen. By means of this technique we have shown that during respiratory changes induced by mental activity, the different components of the respiratory cycle which have been revealed in animal experiments vary independently of each other (Koepchen et al. 1987a). This means that these components also exist in man. This kind of respiratory analysis has not yet been employed in research on MusicMedicine. (It would be of great interest to the relative contribution of the different respiratory phases to the amount of air flow in wind instrument players.)

*Cardiovascular Rhythms*
(Abel, Klüssendorf, Krause et al. 1991; Kitney and Rompelman 1987; Koepchen et al. 1961, 1968; Koepchen 1962; Koepchen, Abel, and Klüssendorf 1989).

Strange to say in medical terminology every change related to respiration is referred to as "rhythm" whereas when related to the functional state of the cardiovascular system it is usual to speak of sympathetic or vagal "tone." In reality, cardiovascular innervation and therewith cardiovascular parameters act in a basically rhythmic manner.

Terminology can have much more than merely semantic meaning. The use of the term "tone" suggests that the result of regulation can be understood as a state. The next step is the idea that the goal of regulation is constancy. Proceeding on the assumption of this goal it is widely supposed that normalization or relaxing therapy should result in the lowest possible and equal state of activity.

Cardiovascular parameters are the most representative and easily accessible expression of the acute neurovegetative condition. By nature they are unstable. This demonstrates significantly that *regulation is not a state but a process*. Thus, rhythmicity in the cardiovascular system is a fundamental phenomenon found both in animals and in man. It has been analyzed extensively in animal experiments. Here are some typical examples.

Figure 5 shows the time course of peripheral resistance against flow in the muscular bed of blood vessels in an anesthetized dog. The oscillations are caused by the variation of activity in vasoconstrictor sympathetic nerves.

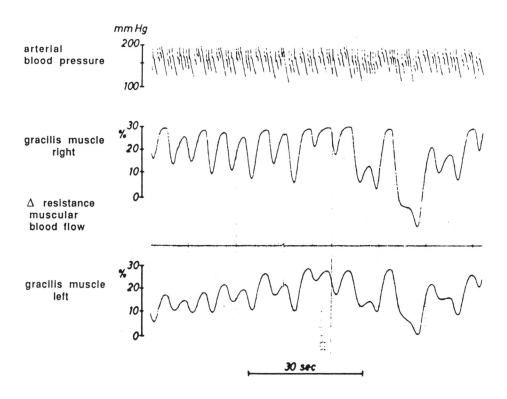

*Figure 5.*

*Rhythmic variations in the resistance to muscular blood flow, recorded simultaneously in the isolated perfusion of right and left gracilis muscle of an anesthetized dog. Note the synchronism between both sides, caused by bilateral synchronous action of sympathetic constrictor nerves. (From Koepchen et al. 1968)*

In Figure 6 we see the electrical record from a branch of the renal sympathetic nerve of a cat. This kind of spontaneous oscillation is characteristic for the time course of activity in nearly all of the hitherto recorded sympathetic nerves. It is evident that the term "tone" is not an adequate description for their mode of activity.

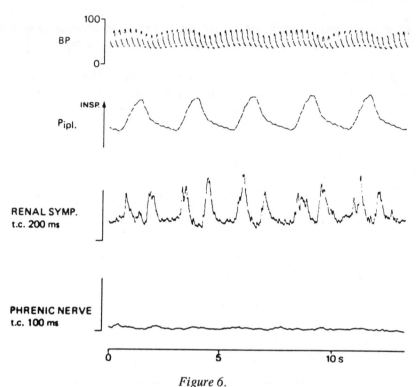

*Figure 6.*
*Rhythmic fluctuations in renal sympathetic nerve activity in an anesthetized*
*artificially hyperventilated cat. Absence of activity in the phrenic nerve indicates*
*silence of central respiratory rhythm caused by hyperventilatory hypocapnia.*
*Note the distinct sympathetic neural rhythm independent of central respiratory*
*rhythmicity as well as of the beat of artificial ventilation. BP: arterial blood*
*pressure. P_ipl: intrapleural pressure, indicating the rhythm of artificial*
*ventilation. t.c.: time constant of nerve recording. (From experiments of H.P*
*Koepchen, D. Sommer, and D. Klüssendorf.)*

All recordings of blood pressure, heart rate, peripheral blood flow, and recent direct
recordings of sympathetic nerve activity (Delius et al. 1972) taken from human subjects
have confirmed that the same rhythmicity is present in man (Abel, Klüssendorf, Krause,
et al. 1991; Akselrod et al. 1981; Eckberg et al. 1980; Golenhofen and Hildebrandt 1958;
Kitney and Rompelman 1987; Koepchen, Abel, and Klüssendorf 1987, 1989; Pagani et
al. 1986; Penaz et al. 1968).

The upper part of Figure 7 shows an example of a volume plethysmogram from a human
finger tip as an indicator of the spontaneous motion of blood vessel filling. We can see
the typical physiological temporal variations. In contrast, the lower part of the Figure 7
illustrates the same kind of recording from a patient suffering from renal failure where the
neurovegetative system is severely altered (Abel et al. 1990). We cannot enter into the
pathophysiological problems here. However, we can clearly see that the *pathological state*

*is characterized by a loss of rhythmicity* by comparing both recordings. This is only one example of this general principle.

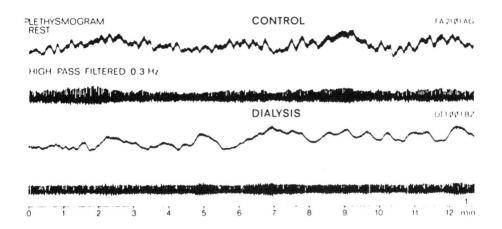

*Figure 7.*

*Fluctuations of the volume of a finger-tip as an indicator of rhythmic vasomotor changes in a healthy subject (upper part) as compared with a patient suffering from renal insufficiency, undergoing hemodialysis treatment (lower part). The second and fourth traces represent the high pass filtered registration showing the fluctuations in the amplitude of the superimposed pulse rhythmic fluctuations. Note the lower frequencies of the oscillations in the plethysmogram of the renal patient. (From investigations of H.-H. Abel, G. Schultze, D. Klüssendorf, W. Meyer-Sabellek, J. Sehested, and H.P. Koepchen.)*

Modern methods of data processing allow an automatic evaluation of the more or less hidden frequency contents of such periodical time courses (Akselrod et al. 1981; Kitney and Rompelman 1987; Pagani et al. 1986; Penaz et al. 1968). In the higher ultradian range there are two preferential frequencies in cardiovascular rhythmicity, one in the range around 0.1 Hz (MFB = mid frequency band) corresponding to a period of 10 sec (also called "10 sec rhythm") (Golenhofen and Hildebrandt 1958), the other frequency around 0.25 Hz (HFB - high frequency band). The latter range is that of the usual respiratory frequency at rest. For that reason cardiovascular oscillations in this range are often called "respiratory." This generalizing term, however, is problematic. One example of cardiovascular rhythm in this range is the well known "respiratory cardiac arrhythmia" or "respiratory sinus arrhythmia." Everybody can detect it simply be feeling his own pulse during quiet breathing.

Technically, these rhythms can be represented in the form of power spectra where the peaks indicate the frequency content of the process. Figure 8 shows the power spectrum with its preferential peaks of the heart rate from a quietly sitting subject. This kind of biological variation is rhythm as opposed to the fixed beat of a machine or a metronome. When we evaluate several power spectra in the same experimental session, e.g., in 2 minute successive sections, no spectrum exactly equals another but the main frequency contents can most often be found. Such a spectrum provides an informative survey of the neurovegetative state and its changes. Using the technique of power spectrum analysis it is interesting to go beyond the level of plain description and to know what physiological analysis in human and animal experimentation has revealed with regard to functional relations and the origins of rhythms.

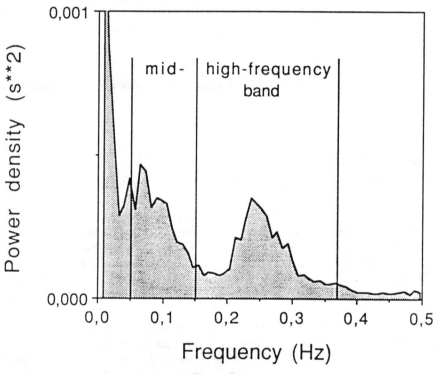

*Figure 8.*
*Typical power spectrum of spontaneous heart rate fluctuations in a normal young subject. Note the two peaks in the ranges around 0.1 Hz and 0.25 Hz. The latter corresponds to the frequency of respiration (so-called "respiratory sinus arrhythmia").*

The respiratory range in heart rate, variations of blood pressure, and movements of blood vessels are mostly considered as a combination of peripheral mechanical and central nervous "irradiation" from the respiratory to the cardiovascular system, i.e., a secondary side effect of respiration. Undoubtedly such side effects do exist but they are not the only cause (Koepchen 1962). A thorough analysis in animal experiments and casual observations in man have shown that the cardiovascular system has its own preferential high frequency range, even without respiration or when respiration takes place in another frequency range. The latter often occurs in states of relaxation where respiration tends to join the mid frequency range (Golenhofen and Hildebrandt 1958). In this case there is synchronization and superposition of both rhythms and especially large slow fluctuations of heart rate can be found. This physiological background is of value when judging the variations in heart rate since the contemporary respiratory frequency has an important role under otherwise equal conditions.

In both animal and human experiments the fact that cardiovascular-respiratory relations are not the result of pure "irradiation" reveals itself occasionally in multiple integer frequency relations (Koepchen 1962; Koepchen et al. 1989) like those found in the laws of motor coordination. Moreover, there are sliding transitory states between the more stable ones of synchronism, or multiple integer relation states (Koepchen 1962). In humans these transitory states are more frequent than in anesthetized animals. Unfortunately, the mathematical tools for a quantitative evaluation of nonstationary states are not yet available. Nevertheless, it can be expected that the aforementioned new developments in mathematics to describe complex systems will enhance future analyses of these phenomena.

Another factor correlated with the extent of heart rate variations is mean heart rate. (Koepchen and Thurau 1959). There is an almost logarithmic relationship between both heart rate variability and heart rate rhythmicity and the mean heart beat interval, i.e., the reciprocal value of heart rate (Abel et al. 1989b, Abel, Klüssendorf, Krause et al. 1991), for the medium range of heart rates. A further analogy between rhythms in music and those of the heart can be seen in music practice: the variability of frequency or tempo is usually greater in the low frequency range than in the high frequency range. We cannot go into the details of heart rate pattern analysis but as a general rule, heart rate rhythmicity is a very valuable and easily obtainable, sensitive indicator of the human neurovegetative state. Its evaluation, however, requires knowledge of basic physiological relations.

As far as the mid frequency band is concerned, this range is found not only in the heart rate but also in the time course of blood pressure and peripheral vasomotor changes as seen in the plethysmogram (cf. Figure 7). There are many simplistic explanations in physiological literature concerning the origin of these fluctuations. In reality, a more careful experimental analysis has shown that these fluctuations also have a multifactorial origin where several oscillatory systems interact with each other (Koepchen 1984). It has been demonstrated for example that the endogenous rhythmicity of the blood vessels interferes with the rhythms impinging on the vessels via rhythmic sympathetic nerve impulses (Seller et al. 1967). This interference again follows von Holst's (1939) rules of "relative coordination." Consequently, the variations seen in the peripheral plethysmogram are the result of such interference. Generally speaking, a state of quiet relaxation is correlated with regular rhythmicity also in this range.

Figure 9 summarizes the hitherto known potential oscillators acting and interacting in the genesis of blood pressure oscillations. Recent technical development allows continuous noninvasive registration of blood pressure in humans and as such an access to the rhythmicity of the important cardiovascular parameter. This major advance in technology has not yet been utilized in research projects for MusicMedicine.

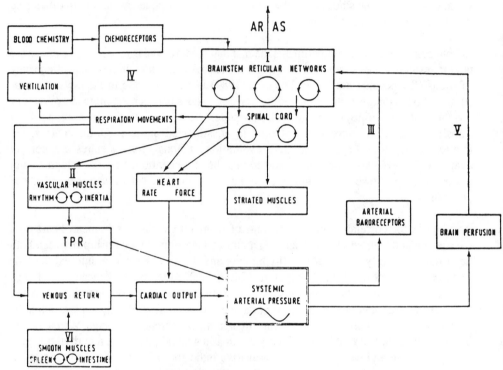

*Figure 9.*
*Functional scheme of the various rhythm generators and feedback circuits interacting in the generation of blood pressure waves. Circles symbolize central and peripheral rhythm generators. III: baroreceptor reflex feedback circuit. IV: chemoreceptor reflex feedback circuit. V: brain ischemic feedback circuit. (From Koepchen 1984.)*

## NEUROVEGETATIVE RHYTHMICITY, STRESS AND RELAXATION.

This topic is of practical importance for music as a therapy for stress and anxiety. In order to achieve a deeper understanding of the functional connections, it is necessary to be aware of some basic physiological facts. In the discussion of the frequency scale in Figure 1, the peculiarities of the medium frequency range were pointed out: cardiovascular, respiratory and motor frequencies overlap the temporal range of homeostatic cardiorespiratory regulation. Consequently, in this range the rhythms interact not only with each other but also with the autoregulatory feedback systems.

One prominent feedback control system for the circulation is the automatic control of blood pressure via the baroreceptor system. There are nerve endings in the large central arteries which register the pulsatile arterial pressure. Their excitation, present even at normal blood pressure, leads to a decrease in heart rate and dilatation of blood vessels. Peripheral resistance to flow and cardiac output is reduced. These effects counteract the increase in blood pressure. Reduction of blood pressure induces a reaction in the opposite direction. Besides the autoregulatory control of blood pressure, the baroreceptor system has a general dampening effect on central nervous activity (Dell 1952). Thus, this very effective mechanism tends to maintain constancy and seems to counteract variability and rhythmicity. Since the baroreceptor reflexes have a profound action on heart rate they must have an important role in the extent of heart rate rhythmicity.

At a first glance it seems surprising that enhanced baroreceptor activity does not diminish but elevates heart rate rhythmicity, at least in the high frequency band. Cardiac "respiratory" arrhythmia in fact is an indicator of intact baroreflexes. How can we explain this apparent contradiction? It was shown that sinus arrhythmia is a paradigm of the interplay between homeostatic feedback reflex control and centrogenic autorhythmicity. Baroreflex sensitivity varies during the respiratory cycle. It begins to decrease shortly before the beginning of the inspiratory movement, is minimal or absent in the late inspiratory phase, and on returning reaches its highest value during the first phase of expiration. (Figure 10) This phenomenon was first detected in anesthetized dogs (Koepchen et al. 1961) and later confirmed in humans (Eckberg et al. 1980).

Since heart rate is depressed continuously by the action of baroreceptor afferent nerve impulses, the inspiratory inhibition of the reflex causes a temporary departure from this depression resulting in the known inspiratory acceleration of the heart. The higher the continuous basic reflexogenic restraint of heart rate, the higher the variation in heart rate due to transient diminution of this restraint. The same inspiratory blockade of the reflex contributes to the inspiratory enhancement of sympathetic activity.

Closer analysis has shown that the phenomena and mechanisms of the "respiratory cardiac arrhythmia" are much more significant than being a side effect of respiration. The decrease of responsiveness to a dampening homeostatic reflex by every primary centrogenic activation is a general principle. There is a decrease in baroreflex sensitivity during exercise (Bristow et al. 1971) as well as during emotional excitation (Sleight et al. 1978). It always manifests itself in a decrease in heart rate variability and rhythmicity. Considered in this context every inspiration also induces a state of enhanced vigilance. This supports the finding that reaction time is shorter during inspiration than during expiration (Hildebrandt and Engel 1963). It would be extremely interesting to measure the respiratory related baroreflex sensitivity under the influence of various kinds of music with regard to their constituent parts. Similar combined changes in vigilance, baroreflex sensitivity and heart rate variability presumably occur in the lower frequency ranges—the

0.1 Hz band and below, i.e., frequencies below the proper range of musical rhythms. They have already been detected in the circadian activity cycle (Parati et al. 1988).

It is a fundamental question whether the rhythmic fluctuations of neurovegetative parameters represent an expression of physiological function or a disturbance or weakness of the homeostasis. There are several clinical studies with measurements of heart rate variability strongly favoring the first option (Pagani et al. 1986). Different pathophysiological states such as diabetes, renal failure (Abel et al. 1990), and cardiac disease are accompanied by a decrease in heart rate variability. We have seen the relative rigidity in vasal motility in renal failure (Figure 8). In contrast, high physical capacity as found in trained sportsmen manifests itself in a significant increase in rhythmicity in the resting state.

Normally loss of rhythmicity is the characteristic feature of states of high physical or mental strain (Abel, Klüssendorf, Droh, and Koepchen 1991; Abel, Klüssendorf, Krause, et al. 1991). With controlled increasing physical load, induced by exercise on a bicycle ergometer for example, heart rate rhythmicity decreases in both frequency ranges and practically disappears even at moderate work loads. As in other kinds of activity, the high frequency band is much more sensitive to even very light physical loads than the mid frequency band. (Figure 11) Thus, *low rhythmicity is a physiological accompaniment of high activity but a pathophysiological sign when occurring at a low degree of activity.*

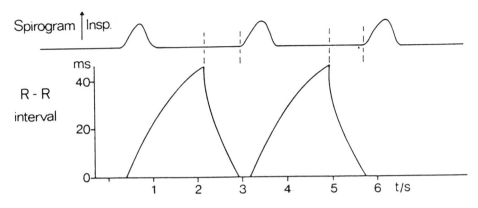

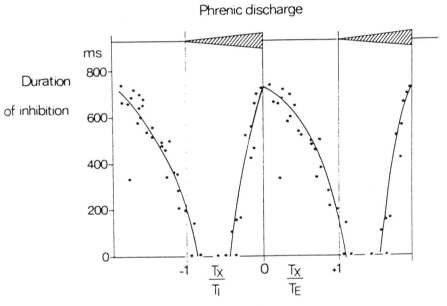

*Figure 10.*

*Respiratory variation of baroreceptor reflex efficiency in anesthetized dogs tested by bilateral rhythmic stimulation of afferent baroreceptor nerves. Upper part: Respiratory related changes of prolongation on heart beat interval induced by identical baroreceptor stimulation. First trace: respiration, second trace: reflex prolongation of heart beat interval. Lower part: respiratory related changes in the duration of baroreceptor induced inhibition of renal sympathetic nerve activity. $T_X/T_I$ and $T_X/T_E$: relative time of superimposed respiratory cycles. Results from numerous superimposed respiratory cycles. Both, the cardiac and the vasomotor reflex effects are smaller during the inspiratory phase. Note the beginning of decrease of reflex efficiency already before the beginning of inspiration. (Redrawn from Koepchen et al. 1961, upper part; and Seller et al. 1968, lower part.)*

Thus, it may be generally stated that the absence of fluctuations at a low heart rate, blood pressure, and sympathetic activity does not represent a physiological resting state and therefore cannot be the goal of any relaxation therapy.

It cannot be pure coincidence that the harmony of mind induced by many pieces of classical music is not based on constant low levels of tension as in drugstore background music but on the organic change of strain and relaxation around a medium level very similar to the natural time course of our neurovegetative parameters. This principle is expressed in its elementary form in the periodic change of homeostatic reflex sensitivity occurring with every breath.

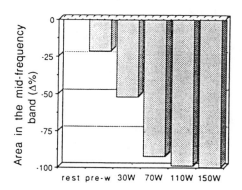 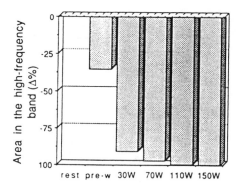

*Figure 11.*

*Relative changes in the rhythmicities superimposed on human heart rate in healthy young athletes during different degrees of physical exercise on an ergometer. Rhythmicities are evaluated by calculating the respective area under the power spectrum in the two ranges indicated in Figure 12. The zero level represents the control under resting conditions. It becomes evident that heart rate rhythmicity progressively disappears with increasing intensity of physical exercise, resulting in totally regular heart beat intervals when the work load approaches the value of about 100 Watt. In a medium range of work load the relative decrease in rhythmicity is stronger in the high frequency than in the mid frequency band. This applies also to the decrease in rhythmicity in the phase of expectancy of the starting signal (pre-w). (From Abel, Klüssendorf, Krause, et al. 1991)*

Figure 11 shows that heart rate rhythmicity decreases with the expectancy of work even before the exercise begins. Such "start reactions" or "feed forward adaptations" are a well known common feature in the animal kingdom as well as in man. The relative role of this neurovegetative pre-adaptation to motor action is outlined in Figure 12. Our motivations are governed by an interplay between internal signals like thirst or sexual drive and signals form the outer world perceived by the sensory organs. The outer world's signals do not induce stereotyped automatic reactions in man as they do in lower animals. They are compared with earlier experiences and analyzed with respect to their significance to the individual. Therefore, the reaction to these exogenic signals is different in different subjects. Music is a special kind of exogenic signal mediated by the auditory sense. Thus, it has to be expected that *the action of music will be quite different in different people.* Their constitution, education, and life history have a part to play. We can assume that this will likewise apply to the widely unknown action of music on neurovegetative rhythmicity

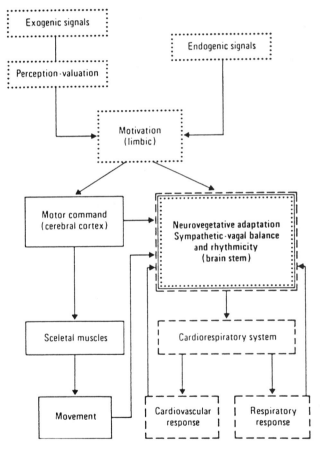

*Figure 12.*
*Scheme of the functional relations of central commands and feedback control circuits influencing the degree of neurovegetative activation and therewith that of heart rate rhythmicity under the influence of motivation. The latter can lead to motor acts or to neurovegetative pre-adaptation only, since the threshold for neurovegetative responses (right) is lower than that for the motor system (left). For further explanation see text.*

# NEUROVEGETATIVE RHYTHMICITY AND BEHAVIORAL ADAPTATION

In man, the inborn adaptive reaction pattern has an especially important role. Motivation and its overt expression in outward somatomotor activity is not as strongly coupled as in our animal ancestors. Subthreshold and widely unconscious pre-adaptation reactions take place in humans continuously, accompanying the permanent play of our thoughts. The fact that the threshold for the manifestation of this motivational activity is lower for vegetative efferents than for somatomotor ones conforms to the interpretation of neurovegetative variations as expressions of subthreshold adaptive processes. Since the degree of general central nervous activity is sensitively reflected in the degree of neurovegetative rhythmicity, the high variability of rhythmicity (cf. Figure 12) from moment to moment, even under resting condition, can be interpreted as an expression of this ever present activity in the mind of the human being.

The influence of mental activity can be studied systematically by replacing its spontaneous fluctuations with a standardized psychological test. We have investigated the effect of pure mental activation by means of the Raven test, a conventional psychological test procedure. It involved recognizing and coordinating various graphic patterns. There is a very distinct reduction of heart rate rhythmicity in the high frequency band during the test period (Koepchen, Abel, and Klüssendorf 1985) (Figure 13). It is remarkable that in this case the return of rhythmicity to the control value is distinctly delayed compared to the recovery of the mean heart beat interval. That means that here rhythmicity, in comparison with the usually measured parameter, namely mean heart rate, is a more sensitive indicator of enhanced mental activity which outlasts the test period.

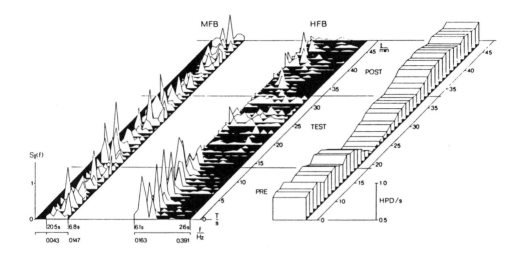

*Figure 13.*
*Series of power spectra of heart rate (left) and mean heart rate expressed as heart period duration (HPD) (right) from a healthy young subject, calculated for successive 2 min. periods before (PRE), during (TEST) and after (POST) the 15 min performance of a mental recognition test (Raven test). The two frequency ranges have been graphically separated for improved clarity. There is a strong decrease of rhythmicity in the high frequency range during the test, outlasting the test period for many minutes. Note the earlier return of mean heart rate to the control value as compared with that of high frequency range rhythmicity. (From experiments of H.P. Koepchen, H. -H. Abel and D. Klüssendorf.)*

It should be stressed that this experimental activation of the neurovegetative system does not at all represent an extraordinary load. Any mental exertion in everyday life produces similar unconscious neurovegetative reactions. This is shown in Figure 14 where the subject is simply reading a neutral text—about the geography of Northern Africa in this example. The distinct decrease in rhythmic variations in heart rate accompanying cardiac acceleration is particularly noteworthy among all the changes in the parameters registered.

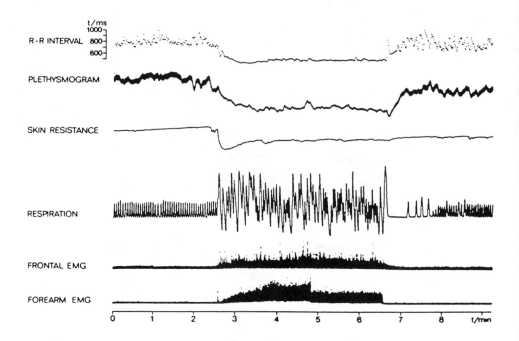

*Figure 14.*
*Record of neurovegetative parameters and electromyogram (EMG) during reading*
*of a normal text. Heart rate represented as beat to beat interval (R-R*
*INTERVAL). Plethysmogram and electrical skin resistance from finger. Surface*
*EMG recorded over a forearm muscle and forehead muscle. There is strong*
*reaction in all recorded somatomotor and neurovegetative parameters during the*
*period of reading. Decrease in the plethysmographic record indicates peripheral*
*vasoconstriction due to sympathetic activation. Decrease in skin resistance*
*unmasks the mental-emotional involvement of the subject. The general central*
*excitation also spreads to motor innervation, enhancing the resting muscular*
*tone. Note the disappearing of heart rate variability and rhythmicity during the*
*period of high heart rate and their distinct reappearance in the period of relaxation*
*immediately after the performance. The strong changes in respiratory pattern are*
*caused by the change of respiratory function, acting as an auxiliary mechanism*
*for speech. (From Abel et al. 1987.)*

It is difficult and indeed a psychological speciality to discriminate between the mental and
emotional content of various kinds of experimental mental tasks. In this context the third
component of mental activity and of music—emotion—must be taken into consideration
(cf. Figure 4). As we have seen, emotion has a considerable effect on neurovegetative
rhythmicity. Recently, successful attempts have been made to discriminate qualitatively
and to measure quantitatively the somatomotor, hormonal, and vegetative manifestation
and intensity of different emotions (Berger 1983; Bohus 1987; Clynes 1977, 1980;
Ekman 1982; Ekman et al. 1983; Ganten and Pfaff 1988; Giedke 1988; Harrer and Harrer

1980; Heath 1986; Henry 1985; Holsboer 1988; Laagmann 1987; Leibowitz 1985; Mandel and De Feudeis 1983; Mazzola et al. 1989; Meyerson and Höglund 1986; Panksepp 1982; Pert et al. 1985; Petsche et al. 1989; Spintge et al. 1988; Voigt et al. 1981; Voigt and Fehm 1983; Yaksh 1984). This makes the emotional content of music accessible to scientific analysis (Clynes 1987; David 1989; Spintge 1990; Spintge and Droh 1991). Since neurovegetative rhythmicity is coupled with emotions, the combination of these two approaches will lead to a new field of research in MusicMedicine. Through this approach we can investigate not only the effect of music on the organism but also the mechanisms involved when music is used as a therapy.

The interpretation of the neurovegetative variations during rest as subthreshold pre-adaptation is substantiated by the detection of subthreshold rhythmicity in the homeostatic baroreflex control. This was achieved by repetitive elicitation of baroreceptor reflexes (Koepchen et al. 1961). Similarly, the subthreshold activation of the somatomotor system can be demonstrated by repetitive elicitation of skeletomotor monosynaptic reflexes, for example by using the usual patellar tendon reflex in quietly sitting subjects (Schmidt-Vanderheyden et al. 1970; Schmidt-Vanderheyden, Heinrich and Koepchen 1970) (Figure 15).

The myographically measured amplitude of the reflex response unmasks the periodically occurring fluctuations of the motor innervation which are still subthreshold for inducing a leg movement. The autocorrelation function of the reflex amplitudes shows a very distinct respiratory rhythm with an increase in the reflex response during inspiration. Further studies revealed that other kinds of coordination also exist between this somatomotor manifestation and rhythms in cardio-respiratory parameters. They correspond to the mentioned rules of "relative coordination" seen in the coordination of motor rhythms. This means that there is a common rhythmicity comprising somatomotor as well as neurovegetative components (Koepchen, Abel, and Klüssendorf 1987).

The relationship to different branches of MusicMedicine is striking. Rhythmic movements guided by music are widely used forms of therapy. They can be supposed to induce not only rhythmic motor responses but also the variably coupled neurovegetative rhythmicity. Although this seems to follow from a wealth of physiological findings there is a lack of distinct experimental data in this field. Only recently have there been successful mathematical analyses of human motor coordination (Haken, Kelso and Bunz 1985). This approach could well be adapted and applied to research in MusicMedicine.

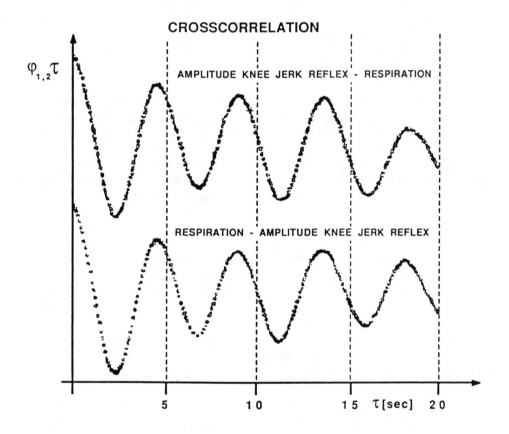

*Figure 15.*

*Crosscorrelation function between respiratory movements and the myographically recorded patellar tendon reflex elicited by constant periodic mechanical stimulation in a quietly sitting subject. The distinct identical rhythm in the crosscorrelation functions in both directions reveals the subthreshold manifestation of synchronous respiratory rhythmicity in the somatomotor nervous control. (From Schmidt-Vanderheyden and Koepchen 1970.)*

## GENERAL CONSEQUENCES FOR MUSICMEDICINE

In our considerations we have tried to unify the separate scientific approaches in the field of musicology, music therapy, psychophysiology of emotions, general control of vigilance, and the physiology of somato-vegetative rhythmicity and adaptation. This represents the framework for new areas of research. It would exceed by far the limits of this contribution to elaborate on the specific research programs. However, a common research program together with R. Flatlischer based on this concept has been devised (see also his contribution in this volume).

Flatlischer's investigations on the ethnology of fundamental components in rhythms created by man and the systematic therapeutic application of this rhythmicity would be made complete by studying the physiological background. What effect do externally created rhythms, which in turn are a projection of internal rhythms, have on the internal human rhythmicity? There are many factors interacting with each other. External rhythms can entrain and superimpose internal rhythms. Motor rhythms can synchronize, coordinate and enhance respiratory and neurovegetative rhythms. On the other hand, activation of the emotions as well as bodily activity decreases the degree of rhythmicity. Which of these actions will predominate? What effect does the intensity of the auditory stimulus have? How will the accompanying movements interfere with the passive effects of pure auditory perception?

Further questions are raised in relation to other neurovegetative research projects in MusicMedicine:

- Can we find physiological correlatives of the beneficial effects of music?
- Is there a correlation between the effects on anxiolysis or the immune system for example (see the contribution of C.D. Maranto in this volume) and the "neurovegetative personalities" as the basis for the different individual responses to the same therapy?
- Is the kind of "neurovegetative personality" influenced by professional musical education?
- On the basis of internal neurovegetative rhythmicity, can we predict the response to music therapy or the suitability of the individual to be a professional musician?

This is only a selection of many new questions arising from our concept. Thus, at the end of this contribution we must beg forgiveness for presenting more questions than answers. Hopefully this is compensated for by the proposal not only of concepts, but also of experimental methods of realizing them.

Modern technology lends itself to the realization of these concepts. Progress in medical engineering provides us with a method for continuous noninvasive registration of neurovegetative parameters in man. Computer assisted evaluation provides methods for automatically processing long time series comprising a huge amount of data (Abel et al. 1989a).

New developments in mathematics provide approaches less rigid than the classical mathematical ones and seem to be more suited to a quantitative analysis of living systems

(Haken 1983). These are far from the thermodynamic equilibrium and near the border between deterministic and chaotic behavior (cf. Schuster 1988). Thus mathematics, in which the earliest Western music music had its origins, is going to reappear in music and its relation to medicine.

Notwithstanding the optimism regarding these new opportunities for the future development of MusicMedicine, we are aware that it will be a long and painstaking path to realize the ideas presented above. It will require years if not decades. The special environment of the generous and farsighted Annenberg Center presents us with the artistic testimonies of classical medicine as well as with an orientation for future medical research. It is just the place for inspiring and encouraging us to open new scientific ways. With this in mind finally let us quote and modify a little the motto written over the entrance to the building where this conference was held:

"Devoted to the MusicMedicine of the 21st Century"

## REFERENCE LIST

Abel, H.-H.; Mottau, B.; Klüssendorf, D.; and Koepchen H.P. 1987. Patterns of different components of the respiratory cycle and autonomic parameters during speech. In *Respiratory Muscles and Their Neuromotor Control*, edited by G.C. Sieck, S.C. Gandevia, and W.E. Cameron, 109-113. New York: Alan R. Liss.

Abel, H.-H.; Klüssendorf, D.; and Koepchen, H.P. 1989a. A new approach to analyzing the neurovegetative state in man. In *Innovations in Physiological Anesthesia and Monitoring*, edited by R. Droh and R. Spintge, 21-34. Berlin, Heidelberg, New York: Springer.

_____. 1989b. Relation between tone and rhythmicity of cardiac chronotropic innervation. *Pflügers Arch.* 413:R11.

Abel, H.-H.; Schultze, G.; Klüssendorf, D.; Meyer-Sabellek, W.; Sehested, J.; and Koepchen, H.P. 1990. Spontaneity and reactivity of autonomic control systems in patients with end-stage renal disease: A new integrative approach. In *Blood Pressure Measurements*, edited by W. Meyer-Sabellek, M. Anlauf, R. Gotzen, and L. Steinfeld, 183-209. Darmstadt: Steinkopff.

Abel, H.-H., Klüssendorf, D.; Droh, R.; and Koepchen, H.P. 1991. Cardiorespiratory relations in human heart rate pattern. In *Cardiorespiratory and Motor Coordination*, edited by H.P. Koepchen, and T. Huopaniemi. Berlin, Heidelberg, New York: Springer (In press).

Abel, H.-H., Klüssendorf, D.; Krause, R.; Koralewski, E.; Droh, R.; and Koepchen, H.P. 1991. Spectral analysis of heart rate during different states of activity. In *Temporal Variations of the Cardiovascular System*, edited by J. Blümchen, T. Schmidt, and B.T. Engel. Basel: Karger (in press).

Akselrod, S.; Gordon, D.; Ubel, F.A.; Shannon, D.C.; Barger, A.C.; and Cohen, R.J. 1981. Power spectrum analysis of heart rate fluctuation: A quantitative probe of beat-to-beat cardiovascular control. *Science* 213:220-222.

Aschoff, J., and Pohl, H. 1978. Phase relations between a circadian rhythm and its zeitgeber within the range of entrainment. *Naturwissenschaften* 65:80-84.

Berger, M. 1983. Neuroendokrinologie der Angst (Neuroendocrinology of anxiety). In *Angst (Anxiety)*, edited by F. Strian, 71-85. Berlin, Heidelberg, New York: Springer.

Bohus, B. 1987. Endorphines and behavioral adaptation. In *Psychoneuroendocrinology and Abnormal Behavior*, edited by J. Mendlewicz and H.M. Van Praag, 7-19. Basel, New York: Karger.

Bristow, J.D.; Brown, E.B., Jr.; Cunningham, D.J.C.; Howson, M.G.; Strange Petersen, E.; Pickering, T.G.; and Sleight, P. 1971. Effect of bicycling on the baroreflex regulation of pulse interval. *Circ. Res.* 28:582-592.

Clynes, M. 1977. *Sentics—the Touch of Emotions*. New York: Doubleday.

_____. 1980. The communication of emotion. Theory of sentics. In *Emotion—Theory, Research and Experience. Vol. 1. Theory of Emotion*, edited by R. Plutchik and H. Kellerman, 271-300.

_____. 1987. On music and healing. In *Musik in der Medizin* (Music in Medicine), edited by R. Spintge and R. Droh, 13-32. Berlin, Heidelberg, New York: Springer.

David, E. 1989. Musikwahrnehmung und Hirnstrombild (Perception of music and brain waves). In *Musik—Gehirn—Spiel (Music—Brain—Play)*, edited by H. Petsche, 91-102. Basel, Boston, Berlin: Birkhäuser.

Delius, W.; Hagbarth, K.E.; Hongell, A.; and Wallin, B.G. 1972. General characteristics of sympathetic acitivity in human muscle nerves. *Acta Physiol. Scand.* 84:65-81.

Dell, P. 1952. Corrélations entre le système végétatif et le système de la vie de relation mesencéphale, diencéphale et cortex cérébral. *J. Physiol.* (Paris) 44:471-557.

Eckberg, D.L.; Kifle, Y.T.; and Roberts, V.L. 1980. Phase relationship between normal human respiration and baroreflex responsiveness. *J. Physiol.* 304:489-502.

Ekman, P. 1982. *Emotion in the Human Face*. 2nd Edition. Cambridge: Cambridge University Press.

Ekman, P.; Levenson, R.W.; and Friesen, W.V. 1983. Autonomic nervous system activity distinguishes among emotions. *Science* 221/4616:1208-1210.

Euler, C.v. 1986. Brain stem mechanisms for generation and control of breathing pattern. In *Handbook of Physiology, Section 3: The Respiratory System, Part 1 Volume 2: Control of Breathing*, edited by A.P. Fishman, N.S. Cherniak, J.G. Widdicombe, and S.R. Geiger, 1-67. Bethesda: American Physiological Society.

Ganten, D. and Pfaff, D. 1988. *Neuroendocrinology of Mood*. Berlin, Heidelberg, New York: Springer.

Giedke, H. 1988. Physiologische Korrelate affektiver Störungen (Physiological correlates of affective disorders). In *Affektive Störungen (Affective Disorders)*, edited by D. v. Zerssen and H.J. Moeller, 132-148. Berlin, Heidelberg, New York: Springer.

Golenhofen, K., and Hildebrandt, G. 1958. Die Beziehungen des Blutdruckrhythmus zu Atmung und peripherer Durchblutung (The interrelations between blood pressure rhythm, respiration and peripheral blood flow). *Pflügers Arch.* 267:27-45.

Haken, H. 1983. *Synergetics: An Introduction*. 3rd Edition. Berlin, Heidelberg, New York: Springer.

Haken, H.; Kelso, J.A.S.; and Bunz, H. 1985. A theoretical model of phase transitions in human hand movements. *Biol. Cybern.* 51:347-356.

Harrer, G., and Harrer H. 1980. Music, emotion and autonomic function. In *Music and the Brain—studies in the neurology of music,* edited by MacDonald Critchley and R. A. Henson, 202-216. London: Heinemann.

Heath, R. 1986. Neural substrate of emotion: Relationship of feelings, sensory perception, and memory. *Int. J. Neurol.* 19/20:144-155.

Henry, J.P. 1985. Neuroendocrine patterns of emotional response. In *Emotion—Theory, Research and Experience,* Volume 3, edited by R. Plutchik and H. Kellerman, 37-56. New York: Academic Press.

Hildebrandt, G. 1958. Grundlagen einer angewandten medizinischen Rhythmus-Forschung (Foundations of applied medical rhythm research). *Heilkunst* 71:117-136.

Hildebrandt, G., and Engel, P. 1963. Der Einfluss des Atemrhythmus auf die Reaktionszeit (The influence of the respiratory rhythm on the reaction time). *Pflügers Arch.* 278:113-129.

Holsboer, F. 1988. Neuroendokrine Regulation bei affektiven Störungen (Neuroendocrine regulation in affective disorders). In *Affektive Störungen,* edited by D. v. Zerssen and H.J. Moeller, 67-80

Holst, E.v. 1939. Die relative Koordination als Phänomen und als Methode zentralnervöser Funktionsanalyse (The relative coordination as a phenomenon and as a method for central nervous functional analysis). *Erg. Physiol.* 42:228-306.

Kepler, J. 1596. *Mysterium Cosmographicum.* Graz (Austria).
    Cf. Cramer, F. 1988. *Chaos und Ordnung.* Stuttgart: Deutsche Verlagsanstalt.

Kitney, R.I., and Rompelman, O. (Eds.) 1987. *The Beat-by-Beat Investigation of Cardiovascular Function: Measurement, Analysis and Application.* Oxford: Clarendon.

Koepchen, H.P. 1962. *Die Blutdruckrhythmik (The Rhythmicity of Blood Pressure).* Darmstadt: Steinkopff.

_____. 1984. History of studies and concepts of blood pressure waves. In *Mechanisms of Blood Pressure Waves,* edited by K. Miyakawa, H.P. Koepchen, and C. Polosa, 3-23. Berlin, Heidelberg, New York, Tokyo: Springer.

Koepchen, H.P., and Thurau, K. 1959. Über die Entstehungsbedingungen der atemsynchronen Schwankungen des Vagustonus (The origin of respiratory oscillations of vagal tone). *Pflügers Arch.* 269:10-30.

Koepchen, H.P.; Wagner, P.H.; and Lux, H.D. 1961. Über die Zusammenhänge zwischen zentraler Erregbarkeit, reflektorischem Tonus und Atemrhythmus bei der nervösen Steuerung der Herzfrequenz (Interrelations between central excitability, reflex tone and respiratory rhythm in the nervous control heart rate). *Pflügers Arch.* 273:443-465.

Koepchen, H.P.; Seller, H.; Polster, J.; and Langhorst, P. 1968. Über die Feinvasomotorik der Muskelstrombahn und ihre Beziehung zur Ateminnervation (Fine vasomotor changes in the sceletal muscle's vascular bed and their relations to respiratory rhythm). *Pflügers Arch.* 302:285-299.

Koepchen, H.P.; Abel, H.-H.; and Klüssendorf, D. 1985. Heart rate dynamics in healthy humans before, during and after a mental test. *Eur. J. Physiol.* 405:R50.

Koepchen, H.P.; Abel, H.-H.; Klüssendorf, D.; and Lazar, H., with technical assistance of Semmler, H. 1987a. Applicability of concepts of respiratory rhythmogenesis deduced from animal experiments to respiratory control in humans. In *Respiratory*

*Muscles and Their Neuromotor Control*, edited by G.C. Sieck, S.C. Gandevia, and W.E. Cameron, 103-107. New York: Alan R. Liss.

Koepchen, H.P.; Abel, H.-H.; Klüssendorf, D. 1987b. Integrative neurovegetative and motor control: Phenomena and theory. *Functional Neurol.* 2:389-406.

_____. 1989. Physiological concepts of cardiovascular and respiratory control: Theoretical basis and applicability in man. In *Innovations in Physiological Anesthesia and Monitoring*, edited by R. Droh and R. Spintge, 3-20. Berlin, Heidelberg, New York: Springer.

Laagmann, G. 1987. Neuroendocrinological findings in affective disorders after administration of anti-depressants. In *Psychoneuroendocrinology and Abnormal Behavior*, edited by J. Mendelwicz and H.M. Van Praag, 67-84. Basel, New York: Karger.

Leibowitz, M.R. 1985. *The Chemistry of Love*. Boston: Little Brown.

Mandel, P., and De Feudeis, F.V. 1983. *CNS Receptors—From Molecular Pharmocology to Behavior*. New York: Raven Press.

Mazzola, G.; Graber-Brunner, V.; and Wieser, H.G. 1989. Hirnelektrische Vorgänge im limbischen System bei konsonanten und dissonanten Klängen (Electrical phenomena in the limbic system in response to consonant and dissonant sounds). In *Musik—Gehirn—Spiel (Music—Brain—Play)*, edited by H. Petsche, 135-152. Basel, Boston: Birkhäuser.

Meyerson, B.J,. and Höglund, U. 1986. Neuropeptides, environmental and social approach behavior in the investigation of emotion. *Int. J. Neurol.* 19/20:156-162.

Miyakawa, K.; Koepchen, H.P.; and Polosa, C. 1984. *Mechanisms of Blood Pressure Waves*. Berlin, Heidelberg, New York, Tokyo: Springer.

Pagani, M.; Lombardi, F.; Guzzetti, S.; Rimoldo, O.; Furlan, R.; Pizinelli, P.; Sandrone, G.; Malfatto, G.; Dell-Orto, S.; Piccaluga, E.; Turiel, M.; Baselli, G.; Cerutti, S.; and Malliani, A. 1986. Power spectral analysis of heart rate and arterial presure variabilities as a marker of sympatho-vagal interaction in man and conscious dog. *Circ. Res.* 59:178-193.

Panksepp, J. 1982. Toward a general psychobiological theory of emotion. *Behavioral and Brain Sciences* 5:407-466.

Parati, G.; Rienzo, M. di; Bertinieri, G.; Pomidossi, G.; Casadi, R.; Gropelli, A.; Pedotti, A.; Zanchetti, A.; and Mancia, G. 1988. Evaluation of the baroreceptor-heart rate reflex by 24-hour intra-arterial blood pressure monitoring in humans. *Hypertension* 12(2):214-222.

Penaz, J.; Roukens, J.; and Waal H.J. van der. 1968. Spectral analysis of some spontaneous rhythms in the circulaiton. *Biokybernetik* 1:233-236.

Pert, C.B.; Rugg, M.R.; Weber, R.J. and Herkeham, M. 1985. Neuropeptides and their receptors: A psychosomatic network. *J. Immunol.* 135/2:820-826.

Petsche, H.; Lindner, K.; Rapelsberger, P.; and Gruber, G. 1989. Die Bedeutung des EEG für die Musikpsychologie (The importance of the EEG in musicpsychology). In *Musik—Gehirn—Spiel*, edited by H. Petsche, 111-134. Basel, Boston, Birkhäuser.

Richter, D.W. 1982. Generation and maintenance of the respiratory rhythm. *J. Exp. Biol.* 100:93-107.

Scherer, K.R., and Ekman, P. 1984. *Approaches to Emotion*. New York: Hillsdale.

Schmidt-Vanderheyden, W.; Heinich, L.; and Koepchen, H.P. 1970. Investigations into the fluctuations of the patellar tendon reflex and their relation to the vegetative rhythms during spontaneous respiration. *Pflügers Arch.* 317:56-71.

Schmidt-Vanderheyden, W., and Kopechen, H.P. 1970. Investigations into the fluctuations of proprioreceptive reflexes in man. II. Fluctuations of the patellar tendon reflex and their relation to the vegetative rhythms during controlled respiration. *Pflügers Arch.* 317:72-83.

Schuster, H.G. 1988. *Deterministic Chaos*. Weinheim: VCH.

Seller, H.; Langhorst, P.; Polster, J.; and Koepchen, H.P. 1967. Zeitliche Eigenschaften der Vasomotorik. II. Erscheinungsformen und Entstehung spontaner und nervös induzierter Gefässrhythmen (Temporal characteristics of the vasomotor system. Appearance and origin of spontaneous and nervally induced vascular rhythms). *Pflügers Arch.* 296:110:132.

Seller, H.; Langhorst, P.; Richter, D.W.; and Koepchen, H.P. 1967. Über die Abhängigkeit der pressoreceptorischen Hemmung des Sympathicus von der Atemphase and ihre Auswirkung in der Vasomotorik (The dependency of the pressoceptor inhibtion of the sympathetic nerve upon respiratory cycle and its effect on the vasomotor system). *Pflügers Arch.* 302:300-314.

Sleight, R.; Fox, P.; Lopez, R.; and Brooks, D.E. 1978. The effect of mental arithmetic on blood pressure variability and baroreflex sensitivity in man. *Clin. Sci. Mol. Med.* 55:381s-382s.

Spintge, R. 1991. The neurophysiology of emotion and its therapeutic applications in Music Therapy and Music Medicine. In "Music in Medical Science," special issue edited by C. Maranto. Washington: National Association for Music Therapy.

Spintge, R.; Droh, R.; Clynes, M.; Mulders, A.; and Hiby, A. 1988. Emotion und Sport—Sentic Cycle , auf dem Weg zur Schaffung eines leistungsfördernden emotionalen Status (Emotion and sports—Sentic cycle, on the way to the creation of performance enhancing emotional states). In *Schmerz und Sport (Pain and Sports)*, edited by R. Spintge, and R. Droh, 185-189. Berlin, Heidelberg, New York: Springer.

Spintge, R., and Droh, R. 1991. Towards a research standard in MusicMedicine/Music-Therapy—Proposal of a multimodal approach. in *MusicMedicine*, edited by R. Spintge. St. Louis, MO: MMB Music, Inc.

Voigt, K.H.; Weber, E., and Marten, R. 1981. Neuropeptides: Subcellular localization of ACTH and related peptides. In *Structure and Activity of Natural Peptides*, edited by W. Voelter and G. Weitzel, 297-303. Berlin, New York: De Gruyter.

Voigt, K.H., and Fehm, H.L. 1983. Hormone und Emotion (Hormones and emotions). In *Emotionspsychologie (Psychology of emotion)*, edited by H. Euler and H. Mandl, 124-131.

Wever, R. 1979. *The Circadian System of Man*. Berlin, Heidelberg, New York: Springer.

Yaksh, T.L. 1984. Multiple opioid receptor systems in brain and spinal cord. *Europ. J. Anaesthesiol.* 1:171-199.

# ON DEVELOPING A PROGRAM IN MUSICMEDICINE: A NEUROPHYSIOLOGICAL BASIS FOR MUSIC AS THERAPY

Arthur W. Harvey

*This presentation started with a musical excerpt from: "Jesu, Joy of Man's Desiring," by J.S. Bach.*

It seemed not only appropriate, but necessary that this presentation on the power of music to affect neurophysiological and neuropsychological responses begin with *music*, rather than *discussion about music*. My choice of the music by Johann Sebastian Bach was motivated by personal and professional experiences of the healthful benefits of his music, as well as a philosophical orientation in his composing that is consistent with the explorations of the role of music in medicine shared during this important and significant Symposium. Some words from Johann Sebastian Bach can aid in providing a structure for this paper.

> In the architecture of my music I want to demonstrate to the world the architecture of a new and beautiful social commonwealth. The secret of my harmony? Each instrument in counterpoint, and as many contrapuntal parts as there are instruments. It is the enlightened self-discipline of the various parts, each voluntarily imposing in itself the limits of its individual freedom for the well-being of the community. That is my message. Not the autocracy of a single stubborn melody on the one hand, nor the anarchy of unchecked noise on the other. No, a delicate balance between the two: an enlightened freedom. The *science of my art*, the *art of my science.*

It is this seeming duality, *the science of the art of music* and *the art of the science of music* as it relates to health, healing and medicine that has been the focus of all our presentations at the IV International MusicMedicine Symposium, and has permeated my ongoing exploration of how music affects our brains, and in turn our behaviors, thoughts, feelings, bodies, minds, and all that is *us*. Any serious teaching/learning endeavor needs to consider at least four aspects relative to that which is being examined, represented by four major questions: (1) WHY? (2) WHAT? (3) HOW? and (4) IF? Consistent with scientific methodology, most of our Symposium presentations thus far have dealt with *the science of the art of music in medicine* and have responded primarily to developing a more solid rationale for *Why MusicMedicine?*, or have presented methodological summaries of *What MusicMedicine* studies have shown. It is in dealing with the questions of *how* and *if* that the *art of the science of music in medicine*, that is, the creative and synergistic applications of sound and music to facilitate healthful changes in MusicMedicine practices, is emphasized.

While attending Gordon College, a liberal arts college in Massachusetts, in an Ethics course, our textbook title was *The Ifs and Oughts of Ethics* (De Boer 1936). As I share with you some of the *ifs* of MusicMedicine from my perspective, perhaps an appropriate subtitle for this paper would be "The If's and Ought's of MusicMedicine." It is my privilege to represent the University of Louisville School of Medicine Department of Psychiatry and Behavioral Sciences, Division of Behavioral Medicine and the unique Program for the Arts in Medicine established in 1988 under the codirection of Joel Elkes, M.D. and Leah Dickstein, M.D. The basis for such a program within a School of Medicine is to realize the following broad objectives:

1. To introduce the practice and appreciation of the arts as an accepted therapeutic modality into treatment settings;
2. To assess the effectiveness of such interventions by accepted methods of biomedical research;
3. To enhance the practice of art forms by health care personnel as an effective means of self exploration;
4. To identify and to attend to the special treatment needs of practicing artists which would enhance their personal well-being and creativity;
5. To develop educational programs (lectures, concerts, exhibits, workshops, conferences, etc.) to bring to the attention of the health community the place of the arts in the practice of medicine.

Each of us comes to this field of MusicMedicine from a variety of backgrounds and interests. Mine has involved many years of music education, with a specific emphasis upon music for special needs populations, teaching and research in psychology of music, the development, with Lance Brunner, Ph.D., of a Music for Health Services Foundation, and an ongoing study of the effect of music upon the human brain. It was with this background and expanding interest in the preventative as well as rehabilitative uses of music in health care that I received an appointment as Adjunct Professor in the School of Medicine and last year was appointed Visiting Professor to devote my time to exploring some of the *ifs of MusicMedicine*. Science focuses upon general principles, whereas the arts focus on individualizations. Many times throughout my 50 years I have experienced situations where music was the vehicle for facilitating a neurophysiological response. In regularly reviewing literature dealing with the effect of music, I find cited studies that support what I had already experienced, leading me to the point of this paper : *If music's impact as I observe it in an individual situation provides the type of response that would be beneficial for health care, and if I find other support from other researchers verifying the beneficial effects of music, **ought** we then to encourage, with confidence, the* *establishment of such a musical intervention as a standard component of health care, in the broadest sense of that term?*

Two weeks ago I was in a pre-op waiting room at the University of Kentucky Medical Center with a young lady awaiting neurosurgery. After she was prepped I entered the curtained area and found her tense, shaking, and breathing fast. I took a portable cassette player in and played "Musical Sea of Tranquillity"* for her. Within just a few minutes her breathing rate had slowed, she stopped shaking, color returned to her face, and she was calm. Within a few minutes of starting the tape, the attending nurse commented on how calming the music was, and one of the doctors passing by stopped, and made the comment "we ought to have more of that here."

There is extensive research on anxiolytic music in clinical practice showing evidence of music's ability to provide distraction, mood elevation, and relaxation at the same time, as well as maintaining contact through varied states of consciousness, altering perceptions of waiting time, and diminishing situation anxiety (Spintge 1988). "Sedative music ... proved effective in decreasing sympathetic nervous system activity and in reducing situational or state anxiety associated with surgery," Moss (1988) asserted in a study on the effect of music on anxiety with the surgical patient. In a preoperative study replicating and extending a study done by Bonny (1978) using the MUSIC Rx Hospital Music Program, Updike and Charles (1987) examine both physiological and emotional responses of patients to music, and found "the most significant emotional effect appeared to be an experienced shift in patients' awareness toward a more relaxed, calm state ... and music listening appeared to effect desirable pattern shifts in physiological and emotional states in the presurgical setting" ( p. 29).

If there is accumulating evidence from case studies as well as experimental studies which support what we know experientially about the power of music to activate a neurophysiological response that will reduce the anxiety and stress associated with surgical procedures, ought it not be included as a standard component of medical and nursing education, as well as a normal routine in perioperative care? To assist in realizing this goal, I taught a course, "Music and Medicine" at the School of Medicine at the University of Louisville in 1988 for medical students, presented lectures and seminars at medical schools and nursing colleges throughout the USA as well as several other countries, and continued our series of training seminars, "Music and Health," at Eastern Kentucky University for health professionals, as well as beginning a series of seminars at the University of Louisville.

---

* Musical Sea of Tranquillity (Audio Tape) 1987 by Chris Valentino. Jonella Record Co. P.O. Box 572, Englewood, NJ 07631.

Our Music for Health Services Foundation has sponsored two national conferences on "Music and Health," at which several of the presenters at this symposium have presented. Our third conference was May 10-11, 1990, and we changed our focus to deal specifically with "Music in Health Care."

Some time ago, I went to visit a lady who was dying of cancer of the pancreas and liver. She was carried from the second floor bedroom to the activity room where a piano was located. She was in continual pain, even with medication, and was unable to sleep through the night. As it was near the Christmas season, I began playing and singing familiar seasonal songs. As time passed she was obviously energized by the music, and participated in the singing. At the end of about an hour and a half, she was taken to her room. She died within a week, but at the funeral I was told that not only was the evening one of the most meaningful in the last weeks of her life for her and her family, but also that she had slept all night long and had been without pain.

While there are many theories concerning pain and pain management, recent uses of music as a nonpharmacologic method for treating pain have become a topic of interest among health professionals (Bailer 1986). Another study by Bailer (1983) compared the effects of live music to the effects of tape-recorded music of the same material, on hospitalized cancer patients, and found a measurable benefit of the live performance over the recorded one, including significant improvements in physical comfort, and as well as changes in mood, particularly relieving tension and promoting vigor. In another study done on patients with chronic cancer pain, Zimmerman et al. noted that the "results of this study indicate that listening to music with positive suggestion of pain reduction does have an effect on cancer patients' pain" (1989).

At the University of Louisville School of Medicine in 1989, one of my students completed a summer research project in the bone marrow unit, introducing "attitudinal music," a new name I have given "new age" music. This was part of a treatment regimen to determine its effect upon the attitudes of patients and staff during routine evaluations, as a component of Attitudinal Medicine. While I do not have the graphs to show you, when music was played prior to taking vital signs, there was a mean drop of 6 beats per minute in pulse rate and in a scale of 1 to 10, the nurses rated the addition of music favorable at 7.49 and overall indicated they would like to continue with the music as part of the treatment regimen.

We have also initiated a long term study at the Brown Cancer Center with breast cancer patients, to determine the comparative benefits of music and visualization to be utilized as a noninvasive means to enhance cancer treatment regimens. The study is designed to provide breast cancer patients with a positive therapeutic experience between blood workup and the treatment regimen itself. The effect of the music will be measured by the changes in blood pressure before and after the musical and or visual intervention, use of a

Pre- and Post-Intervention Survey, comparisons of trends in weight, temperature, white blood cell count, platelet count and hemoglobin count, and use of the Morrow Assessment of Nausea and Emesis Follow-Up Survey. A careful analysis on control responses and experimental responses will attempt to reveal any correlation between the relaxing effect of the music and toleration of cancer treatment.

In my work over the years with profoundly retarded individuals, I have become aware of the ability of music to effect neurophysiological responses of many types. While working weekly on an Extended Care Unit of a local hospital, providing music as a therapeutic experience, the staff asked me one week if I could do anything to help them with a 16-year-old profoundly retarded male who had been crying steadily for over a day and a half. Using the entrainment principle, or Altshuler's "Isoprinciple," I created a musical portrait of his anguish on the piano and mirrored through rhythmic, melodic, harmonic, and textural elements the changes in his emotive state. Once entrained, I was able to facilitate a neurophysiological change in him. Within forty minutes he was asleep.

I developed a study with anesthesiologist, Fred Schwartz, M.D. a participant at this Symposium, to examine the effects of taped music on the heart rate, mean arterial pressure, oxygen saturation and behavioral state of agitated, incubated premature infants in the neonatal intensive care unit. The music was a recording developed by Dr. Schwartz called "Transitions"* which is a combination of actual womb sounds, sound simulations and "attitudinal" music, composed by Burt and Joe Wolff. The study shows apparently beneficial increases in oxygen saturation and behavioral state changes in infants exposed to taped intrauterine sounds during periods of agitation (Collins et al. 1989). I have shared this tape and Don Campbell's "Birthing"** tape at several conferences of obstetric, gynecologic and neonatal nurses (NAACOG) and received much interest in its use.

My experiences with young children and low functioning retarded individuals have shown me the important roles that music can play in the neurophysiological and neuropsychological development. Starting in 1986 it has been my privilege to assist in the development of a therapeutic music program permeating all areas of the environment at Waimano Hospital and Training School, a residential facility in Pearl City, Hawaii for 200 severely and profoundly retarded, and multiply-handicapped adults. It has been exciting to have a total staff involvement in this program, using musical processes and experiences to facilitate motor development, perceptual development, language development, social development and cognitive development. The staff have all gone through in-service training in music with me. As an extensive use of the Omnichord was

---

* *Transitions: Soothing Music for Mother and Child.* Placenta Music, Inc. 2675 Acorn Ave. NE, Atlanta, GA 30305.
** *Birthing: Soothing Music for Prepared Childbirth.* Silverthread Marketing, Inc. P.O. Box 670573, Dallas, TX 75367.

found desirable, they purchased 14 of them and I completed two Omnichord songbooks for them. Music has been found to assist in most areas of their program, and an added benefit was noted last year in that there was significantly less staff turnover and a more positive attitude among staff due to the effect of music upon the staff.

Another study is currently underway at Frazier Rehabilitation Center, "The Effect of Music on the Attention Span of Traumatic Brain Injured Adults." Because music does affect subcortical areas of the brain directly, I created a tape utilizing a stimulus progression principle, increasing the dynamic, tempo, harmonic, textural, and timbral elements gradually to minimize habituation and increase attention in the patients. The nurse researcher, Karen Turner, is in the midst of data collection at this point, but preliminary results indicate that the increase of musical stimuli is having the anticipated effect upon the subjects.

At a nurses' training seminar called "Therapeutic Uses of Music" which I was leading in September 1989, a nurse told me of a recent incident that reaffirmed my conviction that an understanding of music in health care is as important for the nursing profession as it is for doctors. At a nearby hospital, a patient in ICU was in a coma. Each evening one of the nurses, while making rounds would sing as a spontaneous expression as well as to pass the time. After several days of balancing between life and death in a comatose state, the patient regained full consciousness, recovered and was released. Within a short time he returned to the ICU area and asked for the singing nurse. Upon inquiry, it was discovered which nurse was the one who sang, and the patient told her that he had come back to thank her for saving his life. While in a comatose state, he said he did not know whether he was alive or dead, or what was real until he heard the nurse singing, and her singing drew him back to life and was like a lighthouse guiding him.

Because I believe that music ought to permeate all areas of health care, I co-authored an article with Lois Rapp, a nurse from Eastern Kentucky University. We developed some principles for music in nursing, developed a model for a course, "Uses of Music in the Nursing Profession," and concluded that, "sufficient evidence supports the need for an inclusion of music in both nursing practice and nursing education" (Harvey and Rapp 1988).

To permeate all areas of medical practice with the arts is the ultimate goal of the Program for the Arts in Medicine. Music as a therapeutic medium with the elderly has been studied in considerable depth by Ruth Bright (1973, 1981). Jane Thibault, Ph.D. of the Division of Family Practice Medicine, and I designed a research project to study the effectiveness of providing instrumental music instruction to residents of two nursing homes, for the purpose of enhancing neurocognitive functioning, while at the same time providing a therapeutic and aesthetic music experience. The subjects were given instruction one hour weekly on soprano recorders, with supplementary instruction on an Omnichord and on chime bars. Only one subject had had previous music training, but not on the soprano recorder. The repertoire included exercises I wrote, short simple compositions, and as note reading and motor skills improved, folk songs, Christmas carols and simple hymn tunes were introduced.

Adaptive teaching strategies were utilized when appropriate. Music manuscript was enlarged, task analysis was used, and musical selections were modified to accommodate differing levels of motor development and musical knowledge. Throughout the eight weeks of the study, interest was constantly high and requests for continuation of the musical sessions beyond the project dates was expressed by those involved in the study. At one of the centers, musical development was sufficiently high to warrant an informal performance for other residents, and was performed well and received with enthusiasm. The musical goals of the study were limited to instructions in rhythmic and melodic elements, primarily. The nonmusical goals included motor development, perceptual development and social-emotional development.

Throughout the study, aesthetic perception increased noticably. Therapeutic benefits of expression, catharsis, social interaction, communication and outright pleasure were observed. Of significance to this study was the evidence that while both aesthetic and therapeutic goals were realized, the added value of music as a means of enhancing neurocognitive functioning was found to indicate sufficiently that music may be an important means of enhancing memory and other cognitive processes while serving important aesthetic and therapeutic purposes. The formal report of this study is completed and has been submitted for publication. The use of The Neurobehavioral Cognitive Status Examination [NCSE], as well as several other evaluation instruments, indicated a measurable increase in memory function as a result of our musical intervention. The development of a study to ascertain the effect of selected musical compositions on the "Sundowner Effect" in an institutionalized geriatric population is in process. A recent study by Millard and Smith (1989) has found that singing can be an effective activity to enhance the quality of care for Alzheimer disease patients.

A short documentary video of selected projects begun through the Program for the Arts in Medicine is in the final stages of editing. While not a formal study at this time, I have initiated a project in the Humana-University Emergency holding room, utilizing stimulus regression tapes to reduce out-of-control response patterns in the ER holding room, as well as a project with the Helicopter Emergency Transport nurses, utilizing music to facilitate reduction of anxiety in trauma transport.

The role of music in the development of the Program for the Arts in Medicine at the University of Louisville School of Medicine is similar to the mission I conceived for the second National Conference of Music and Health (Harvey 1974). This was to explore music, in all its simplicity and complexity—sound, rhythm, melody, harmony, form, and style in both active and passive uses—creating, playing, singing, moving, listening and naming—to facilitate optimal health—physical, mental, social, spiritual, and emotional—for ourselves and others for the specific situation, time, place, and space in which we find ourselves. Understanding health as both a continuum and an interaction, it will be our task to orchestrate and transcribe the music of our lives to create interpersonal and intrapersonal harmony.

As we seek individually and collectively to find more scientific answers to the *whys, whats, hows* and *ifs* of MusicMedicine, may we never forget that in the end it is the *art* of music and medicine that is instrumental in healing. May you, as Professor Fry (1971) so aptly described in *Some Effects of Music,* become aware "... that some music is aimed at your feet, some at your head, and some at your heart," and may this Symposium provide further direction in knowing the difference.

## REFERENCE LIST

Bailey, L.M. 1983. The effects of live music versus tape-recorded music on hospitalized cancer patients. *Music Therapy* 3(1):17-28.

Bailey, L.M. 1986. Music therapy in pain management. *Journal of Pain and Symptom Management* 1(1):25-28.

Bonny, H. 1978. Music listening for intensive coronary care units: A pilot project. In *Music Rx.* a Tape Set with Accompanying Booklet, Port Townsend, WA: Institute for Consciousness and Music.

Bright, R. 1973. *Music in Geriatric Care.* New York: St. Martin's Press. (Re-issue 1980 Musicgraphics, Lynbrook, NY)

Bright, R. 1981. *Practical Planning Music Therapy for the Aged.* Sherman Oaks, CA: Alfred Publishing Co., Inc.

Collins, S., and Kuch, K. 1989. Music therapy in the neonatal intensive care unit. Study conducted at Georgia Baptist Medical Center, Atlanta, Georgia. Submitted for publication, July 11, 1989.

De Boer, C. 1936. *The Ifs and Oughts of Ethics: A Preface to Moral Philosophy.* Grand Rapids, MI: Wm. B. Eerdmans Publishing Co.

Fry, D.B. 1971. *Some Effects of Music.* Kent, England: Institute for Cultural Research. Monograph Series, No. 9.

Harvey, A. 1988. *Conference Proceedings:* Second National Music and Health Conference, April 7-8, 1988. Richmond KY: Music for Health Services Foundation.

Harvey, A., and Rapp, L. 1988. Music soothes the troubled soul... *Ad Nurse* March/April:19-22.

Millard, K.A.O., and Smith, J. 1989. The influence of group singing on the behavior of Alzheimer Disease Patients. *Journal of Music Therapy,* 26(2):58-70.

Moss, V.A. 1988. Music and the surgical patient. *Association of Operating Room Nurses Journal* 48(1):64-69.

Spintge, R. 1988. Music as a physiotherapeutic and Emotional Means in Medicine. *Musik Tanz und Kunst Therapie* 1(2/3):75-81.

Updike, P., and Charles, D. 1987. Music Rx: Physiological and emotional responses to taped music programs of preoperative patients awaiting plastic surgery. *Annals of Plastic Surgery* 19(1):29-33.

Zimmerman, L.; Pozehl, L.; Duncan, K.; and Schmitz, R. 1989. Effects of music in patients who had chronic cancer pain. *Western Journals of Nursing Research* 11(3), 298-309.

# CHANGES IN EMG PATTERNS UNDER THE INFLUENCE OF AUDITORY RHYTHM

Michael Thaut
Sandra Schleiffers
William Davis

## 1. INTRODUCTION

**M**otor rhythmicity, i.e., the ability to organize complex motor acts into consistent and accurate temporal patterns, has been described in many research studies as an essential factor in skillful motor performance (Liehmon 1986). The question as to whether external auditory rhythm as superimposed time structure can be used to enhance the temporal organization of movement in motor performance has been of considerable interest in research and clinical literature regarding motor learning, motor control and motor rehabilitation.

The influence of external rhythmic stimuli on movement has been investigated in four areas that are pertinent to this study. First, studies have shown that auditory rhythm stimuli can serve as predictable timing cues to facilitate the anticipation, temporal accuracy and sequential organization of movement (Glencross 1970; Melvill Jones and Watt 1971). However, data from studies using rhythmic stimuli in rehabilitation settings point out that the translation of an audible rhythmic scheme into a motor rhythmic pattern needs to be carefully taught to the mover to create a coordinated perceptual-motor response (Staum 1983; Thaut 1985).

Secondly, when considering using an external rhythm to guide movement the personal tempo of an individual's motor response has to be considered. Rimoldi (1951), Melvill Jones and Watt (1971), Smoll and Schulz (1978), and Ruggieri and Milizia (1982) found that individuals chose their own preferred and repetitious tempos to perform the same activities. Deviations from one's preferred performance tempo may lead to decreases in performance quality.

Thirdly, from a neurophysiological point of view research has looked at the influence of sound signals on changes in electrical muscle activity. The results from these studies were of considerable importance to this study. Hass, Distenfeld, and Axen (1986) demonstrated the efficiency of auditory rhythm as a physiological entrainment signal or pacemaker to influence muscle activity in respiratory patterns. Paltsev and Elner (1967) found that sound signals of sufficient strength can shorten the latent period of motor reactions by changing the functional state of the motor nuclei on the spinal cord level, i.e., rise in the level of motor neural excitability, before supraspinal motor commands arrive at the segmental level.

In related findings Melvill Jones and Watt (1971) and Rossignol and Melvill Jones (1976) showed that, when pairing the elicitation of a muscle reflex with the presentation of a sound signal, the sound signals can increase the excitability of spinal motor neurons with a low habituation rate, thus leading to a shortening of the latent period in motor reactions. The central audio-spinal latency for the facilitation of the muscular response after the sound burst was 80 msecs, with a peak amplitude facilitation between 110 and 130 msecs, and a mean duration of facilitation of 200 msecs. When the time course of this audio-spinal facilitation was superimposed over the electromyographic (EMG) patterns of the gastrocnemius muscle during hopping to a simplified rhythmic musical beat the onset of EMG activity fell within the presumed facilitation period after the beat although the foot was still in its swing phase before contact with the ground and before any physiological stretch reflex could occur. Rossingol and Melvill Jones (1976) suggest therefore that during a movement pattern performed to an auditory rhythm the motor events should be timed to make best use of a potential audio-spinal facilitation effect.

Fourthly, whereas the previous studies demonstrated the effect of sound and auditory rhythm on muscle activity, a study by Safranek, Koshland, and Raymond (1982) compared changes in EMG activity with and without rhythm. They found an increase in duration and decrease in variation of EMG activity of the biceps muscle when the performance of a gross motor task was accompanied by an even auditory rhythmic beat. An uneven beat produced a significant increase in variation of muscle activity.

The aim of this study was to assess the influence of different audible rhythms on EMG activity in two antagonist muscles (biceps brachii and medial head of triceps brachii) when used as superimposed time structure (zeitgeber) during the performance of a gross motor task. Specifically, by assessing EMG patterns first when following a personal tempo without external rhythm and then adding auditory rhythmic stimuli that either matched or were slower than the internal rhythm, rhythm would be the only modified variable. Changes in EMG patterns under the rhythmic conditions could then be explained as unique neurological response rather than as merely the result of different performance tempos. If distinct muscular patterns emerge in the rhythmic conditions, rhythmic techniques then may be used to elicit these muscle patterns in motor rehabilitation in clinical settings.

## 2. METHODOLOGY

### 2.1 Subjects

Twenty-four randomly selected subjects from the undergraduate student population at Colorado State University agreed to participate in the study through informed consent procedure. All subjects were female and had declared music as major of their university studies. The subjects ranged in age from 19 to 32. None of the subjects had any known motoric and sensory impairment. A sample of music majors was selected for this study to provide comparison data for forthcoming research in order to test the notion that musicians do not perform better on motor rhythmic performance tasks than nonmusicians (Huff 1972).

### 2.2 Experimental Task and Procedure

Upon entering the laboratory subjects were seated on a chair in front of a table which had three target pads (8" *Remo* practice drum pads with 1" *Schaller* acoustic transducers attached to the pad surface near the upper [away from the subject] rim of the pad) mounted on its surface in a triangular configuration (Figure 1). Subjects were asked to sit upright with their backs in perpendicular contact with the back of the chair. Subjects were then taught the mechanics of the task.

Subjects were asked to hit each target pad twice with their nondominant arm in the following sequence which was repeated until being asked to stop: left pad, center pad, right pad, center pad. The hitting motion was carried out as follows: the hand was clenched in a fist without tensing the muscles, the ulnar side of the hand parallel to the table surface; the ulnar side of the hand made contact with the target pad when hitting; the arm was moved vertically up and down by flexing the elbow from a position of 130 to 145 degrees to an extension position upon target pad contact of 0 to 10 degrees. The wrist remained in a neutral position. Subjects were asked to hit the pads with as even a rhythm as possible in a tempo most comfortable to them. During Trial 2, subjects who followed an auditory rhythm were asked to synchronize their hits as closely as possible with the external beat.

After subjects had learned the task, preamp EMG electrodes were attached on the biceps brachii muscle belly and the medial head of the triceps brachii muscle belly of the nondominant arm. A practice performance of the experimental task was then recorded for 6 seconds. After that, the subject performed the task under experimental condition for 30 seconds. In the trials using an auditory rhythm, subjects had to demonstrate a synchronization of target hits with an auditory beat of 40 msecs or less before proceeding with the experimental task.

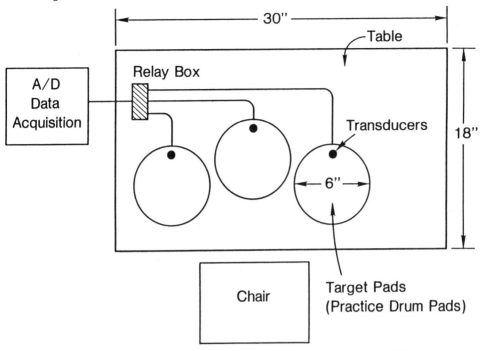

*Figure 1. Arrangement of Target Pads to Perform Experimental Task*

## 2.3. Experimental Design

During Trial 1, all subjects in the study performed the motor rhythmic task following their own internal tempo, without any external timing cues. For Trial 2, subjects were then randomly assigned to one of three experimental groups by drawing numbers from a table of random numbers. The three experimental groups were:

1.  Control group, performing the experimental task by following an internal tempo;
2.  Matched rhythm group, performing the task by following an auditory rhythm matched to the internal tempo used in Trial 1;
3.  Slower rhythm group, performing the task by following an auditory rhythm slower than the internal tempo used in Trial 1.

In Trial 1, internal performance tempos for all subjects ranged from 60 to 72 beats per minute as measured on the metronome function of an *Alesis HR 16* rhythm synthesizer when matching a single hit on the target pad with an auditory beat (clicking sound) from the synthesizer. For the matched rhythm group the auditory beat was played during Trial 2 at the internal tempo demonstrated during Trial 1. For the slower rhythm group the tempo of the auditory rhythm was set at 40 beats per minute. In absolute time units, 60 beats per minute equal a hit on the target pad one every second, 72 beats equal a hit every .83 seconds, and 40 beats equal a hit every 1.5 seconds.

## 2.4 Experimental Apparatus and Data Capture

A GCS 67 multichannel electromyographic system consisting of an MFB 12-67 power unit and EM 67 amplifier processor module with preamp electrodes was utilized to collect raw EMG signals from the biceps brachii and the medial head of the triceps brachii. This system returns a gain accuracy of +/- 10% and a gain linearity better than +/- .5%. Further, the input voltage range for full scale output is .1mV to 2.0 mV with an impedance of >25 Megohms at dc and >15 Megohms at 100 Hz. For this study the gain was set at an amplification level of 2000 with a frequency response setting of 40 Hz and a low-pass filtering time constant of 2.4 msec.

The EMG equipment was interfaced with a Hewlett Packard PC 6 computer via a Tecmar lab master A/D board. To control data acquisition the Asyst software package was programmed to collect inputs from 4 A/D channels consisting of 2 EMG signals, an auditory beat signal from a synthesizer, and the response signal composed of tapping one of three electronically rigged drum pads. The sampling rate across the four channels was set at 2 Khz/sec.

The auditory signal was generated by an Alesis HR 16 drum synthesizer, amplified and reproduced via a Kenwood Am-Fm KR-A47 stereo receiver and two Wharfdale 302 loudspeakers, at a loudness level of 70 decibels.

## 2.5 Measurements

The raw EMG data for each subject for the 30 second performance interval were printed and visually examined (see Figure 2). The duration of muscle activation was determined by measuring the distance from the first action potential spike deflecting the baseline to the last spike before the silent period, i.e., return of the action potential spikes to a nondeflected baseline indicating a resting muscle. The activation pattern of biceps (channel 1) and triceps (channel 2) were lined up with the electrical signal of its respective hand contact with the target pad (channel 3). The auditory signal was recorded on channel 4.

Two measurements were taken for each muscle: duration of muscle activation before and after target contact (Triceps before = Tb, Triceps after = Ta, Biceps before = Bb, Biceps after = Ba). Variation of muscle activity was determined by computing the standard deviations of the means of Tb, Ta, Bb, and Ba.

Coactivation or cocontraction of the two muscles was determined by measuring the duration of overlapping activation of the two muscles before and after target contact.

In a final step, the duration of each time interval between target contacts was measured. The separate time intervals were then averaged and the standard deviation from the mean was computed to yield a measure of rhythmic deviation for the performance of the motor task.

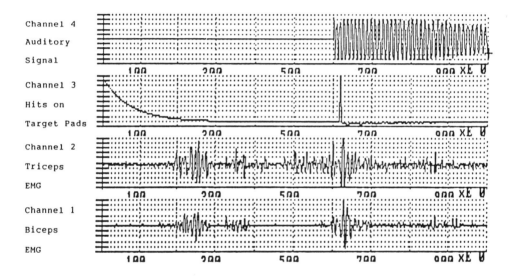

*Figure 2. Recordings of EMG-Traces, Hits on Target Pads, and Auditory Signal*

## 3. RESULTS

### 3.1 Visual Analysis

During Trial 1 a common type of EMG pattern emerged for most subjects (Figure 3). This pattern was evident again for subjects who performed the motor task under control group conditions during Trial 2. On the downswing of the forearm a short burst of biceps brachii occurred which was followed reciprocally by activity in the triceps brachii until target contact was made by the fist of the subject. Upon surface contact medial triceps activity ceased and within approximately 15 to 40 msecs after target contact the biceps became active moving the arm up and away from the target pad. Biceps then became silent before a short biceps brachii burst initiated the beginning of the new extension movement of the arm. The observed EMG patterns were identical with the three burst patterns in flexion-extension tasks described by Benecke, Rothwell, Day, Dick, and Marsden (1986).

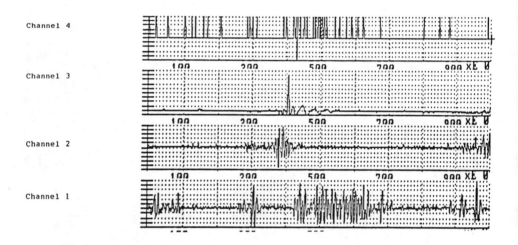

*Figure 3. Trial 1: 3 Burst EMG-Pattern of Triceps and Biceps during
Forearm Flexion-Extension Movement*

In some subjects, instead of reciprocal activation, brief periods of coactivation of biceps and medial triceps occurred before target contact. After target contact, about half of all subjects showed some continuous triceps activity along with the biceps activation.

When an auditory rhythm was imposed the most noticeable difference in visual analysis was the much earlier onset of biceps activity before target contact leading to a pattern of coactivation or coconcentration of biceps and triceps during the extension movement of the forearm (Figures 4 and 5).

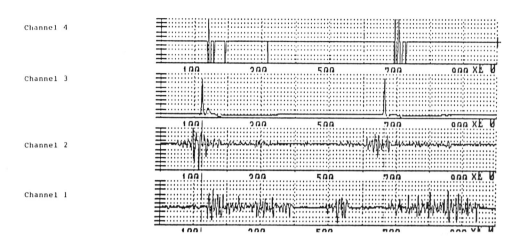

*Figure 4. Subject A: Reciprocal Activation of Triceps and Biceps
without Auditory Rhythmic Signal*

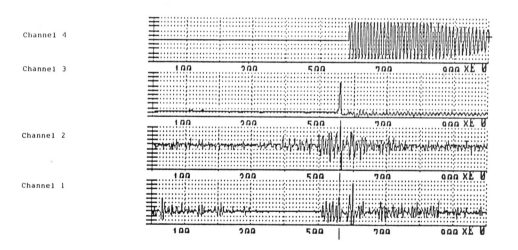

*Figure 5. Subject A: Coactivation of Triceps and Biceps during
Extension Phase of Forearm before Target Contact while following an
Auditory Rhythmic Signal*

In the rhythmic conditions, durations of muscle activation increased. That effect was most pronounced during the slower rhythm condition (Figures 6 and 7).

Channel 4

Channel 3

Channel 2

Channel 1

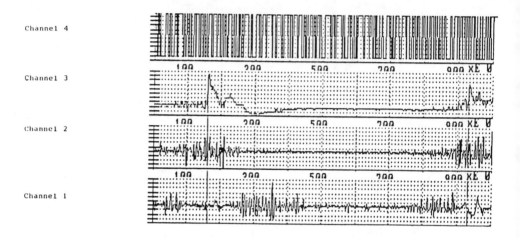

*Figure 6. Subject B: Duration of Biceps EMG-Activity after Target Contact without an Auditory Rhythmic Signal*

Channel 4

Channel 3

Channel 2

Channel 1

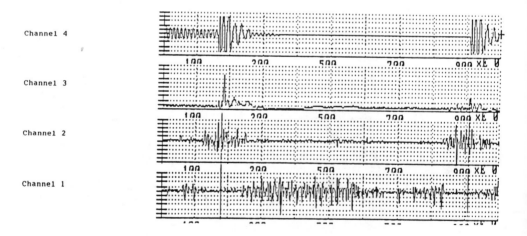

*Figure 7. Subject B: Increased Duration of Biceps EMG-Activity after Target Contact while Following an Auditory Rhythmic Signal*

Finally, in some muscle patterns (most noticeably triceps before target contact) variation of muscle activation decreased. This effect was enhanced mostly in the matched rhythm condition (Figures 8 and 9).

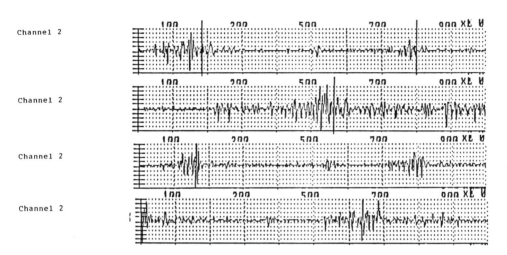

*Figure 8. Changes in Variation (Varied Duration) of Triceps EMG
Subject C: Trial 1 without Auditory Rhythmic Signal*

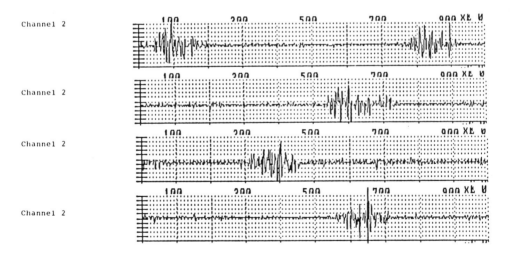

*Figure 9. Changes in Variation (Consistent duration) of Triceps EMG
Subject C: Trial 2 with Auditory Rhythmic Signal Present*

## 3.2 Statistical Analyses

As shown in Table 1, duration mean values for the experimental groups (matched and slow rhythm) increased in most instances from Trial 1 to Trial 2 as compared to the control group mean values. It should be noted that the slow rhythm group means depict the largest increase following the introduction of an external rhythm. As shown in Table 2, standard deviation mean values for Trial 2 tend to be below Trial 1 values in the control and matched groups vs. an increase in variation for the slow rhythm group in some instances. These descriptive statistics imply that the introduction of an external rhythm affects muscle activity responses. Table 3 shows the consistency of time intervals between hits for Trial 1 and the first and last 6 hits of Trial 2. Consistencies evident in Trial 1 tended to be skewed during the first six hits of Trial 2 but improved over time.

TABLE 1

Descriptive Statistics for duration of EMG activity among groups

| Muscle Activity (msec) | Group | | |
|---|---|---|---|
| | Control (n = 8) | Matched (n = 8) | Slow (n = 7) |
| *Triceps Before* | | | |
| Trial 1 | | | |
| M | 20.97 | 19.43 | 29.14 |
| SD | 8.07 | 6.15 | 18.05 |
| Trial 2 | | | |
| M | 17.49 | 35.26 | 45.83 |
| SD | 5.22 | 9.04 | 26.02 |
| *Triceps After* | | | |
| Trial 1 | | | |
| M | 22.67 | 28.78 | 20.30 |
| SD | 14.23 | 10.45 | 4.50 |
| Trial 2 | | | |
| M | 17.85 | 37.10 | 28.71 |
| SD | 19.72 | 11.95 | 12.13 |
| *Biceps Before* | | | |
| Trial 1 | | | |
| M | 9.84 | 12.53 | 12.83 |
| SD | 6.50 | 8.75 | 7.99 |
| Trial 2 | | | |
| M | 13.40 | 16.81 | 17.65 |
| SD | 9.20 | 5.13 | 5.01 |
| *Biceps After* | | | |
| Trial 1 | | | |
| M | 44.77 | 49.99 | 46.33 |
| SD | 11.00 | 9.59 | 8.68 |
| Trial 2 | | | |
| M | 45.58 | 44.16 | 71.40 |
| SD | 11.67 | 9.66 | 10.91 |
| *Cocontraction Before* | | | |
| Trial 1 | | | |
| M | 7.42 | 8.57 | 9.21 |
| SD | 4.66 | 8.32 | 4.22 |
| Trial 2 | | | |
| M | 5.60 | 13.91 | 16.09 |
| SD | 4.75 | 5.25 | 5.35 |
| *Cocontraction After* | | | |
| Trial 1 | | | |
| M | 20.83 | 29.22 | 23.44 |
| SD | 12.16 | 11.64 | 17.34 |
| Trial 2 | | | |
| M | 16.04 | 34.9 | 39.95 |
| SD | 19.33 | 10.90 | 22.22 |

TABLE 2
Descriptive Statistics for variation of EMG activity among groups

| Muscle Activity (msec) | Group | | |
|---|---|---|---|
| | Control (n = 8) | Matched (n = 8) | Slow (n = 7) |
| *Triceps Before* | | | |
| Trial 1 | | | |
| M | 5.50 | 7.25 | 5.87 |
| SD | 3.81 | 4.97 | 1.25 |
| Trial 2 | | | |
| M | 7.45 | 4.11 | 4.60 |
| SD | 4.02 | 2.06 | 1.46 |
| *Triceps After* | | | |
| Trial 1 | | | |
| M | 7.82 | 7.90 | 5.25 |
| SD | 7.09 | 4.90 | 2.71 |
| Trial 2 | | | |
| M | 5.33 | 5.40 | 6.18 |
| SD | 5.70 | 1.84 | 4.58 |
| *Biceps Before* | | | |
| Trial 1 | | | |
| M | 5.44 | 5.14 | 4.13 |
| SD | 3.93 | 1.81 | 1.35 |
| Trial 2 | | | |
| M | 5.97 | 4.09 | 5.45 |
| SD | 4.17 | 2.18 | 3.16 |
| *Biceps After* | | | |
| Trial 1 | | | |
| M | 8.50 | 5.13 | 5.73 |
| SD | 5.89 | 1.81 | 2.15 |
| Trial 2 | | | |
| M | 7.55 | 4.50 | 5.42 |
| SD | 5.92 | 1.88 | 3.12 |

TABLE 3
Standard deviations for consistency of time intervals between hits

| Subject | Trial 1 (msec) | Trial 2A (msec) | Trial 2B (msec) |
|---------|----------------|-----------------|-----------------|
| **Matched Rhythm** | | | |
| 1 | 5.16 | 4.58 | 2.29 |
| 2 | 4.29 | 4.34 | 2.29 |
| 3 | 2.98 | 6.18 | 3.96 |
| 4 | 3.53 | 8.97 | 3.50 |
| 5 | 6.23 | 7.27 | 5.58 |
| 6 | 3.68 | 5.05 | 2.86 |
| 7 | 3.31 | 10.24 | 4.52 |
| **Slow Rhythm** | | | |
| 1 | 1.33 | 4.16 | 1.32 |
| 2 | 1.50 | 3.11 | 1.29 |
| 3 | 0.81 | 2.35 | 1.92 |
| 4 | 2.67 | 2.83 | 2.16 |
| 5 | 4.48 | 5.75 | 1.41 |
| 6 | 3.33 | 3.23 | 2.29 |
| 7 | 3.23 | 1.06 | 2.94 |
| 8 | 1.59 | 2.51 | 1.11 |

One-way ANOVAs were computed to test the effect of an external rhythm on triceps and biceps activity and cocontraction properties before and after plate contact. Two dependent variables were examined. First, duration of muscle activity was assessed as the difference between mean values for Trial 1 and Trial 2 per subject concerning triceps, biceps, and cocontraction responses. Secondly, variation in muscle activity was assessed as the difference between standard deviation mean values for Trial 1 and Trial 2 per subject concerning triceps and biceps responses. Further, a two-way ANOVA was calculated to test for consistency of time intervals between hits across Trial 1 vs. the first six hits of Trial 2 (Trial 2A) and last six hits of Trial 2 (Trial 2B) for each of the experimental groups (matched and slow). Group and trial served as the main effects for the ANOVA with the average deviation of hits serving as the dependent variable. The Scheffe post hoc analysis was the statistical method of choice.

As shown in Table 4, a significant difference was demonstrated among groups for duration of triceps activity before plate contact. As depicted in Table 5, the post hoc analysis resulted in a significant difference ($p$<.05) between the control group and the matched and slow rhythm groups with the control group exhibiting the least amount of triceps activity before plate contact.

TABLE 4
Group by duration for triceps activity before contact: ANOVA

| Source of Variation | df | SS | MS | F | p |
|---|---|---|---|---|---|
| Equality of Means | 2 | 2029.50 | 1014.75 | 7.00 | .004* |
| Error | 20 | 2896.05 | 144.80 | | |

*$p$ < .05

TABLE 5
Scheffe post hoc analysis for triceps before

| Group | Group | | |
|---|---|---|---|
| | Control ($M$ = 3.47) | Matched ($M$ = -15.83) | Slow ($M$ = -16.68) |
| Control | | 19.30* | 20.15* |
| Matched | | | .85 |

SR - 16.27   *$p$ < .05

No significant differences were apparent for duration values concerning the triceps after or the biceps before responses (Tables 6 and 7)

TABLE 6
Group by duration for triceps activity after contact: ANOVA

| Source of Variation | df | SS | MS | F | p |
|---|---|---|---|---|---|
| Equality of Means | 2 | 906.51 | 453.25 | 2.45 | .11 |
| Error | 20 | 3686.05 | 184.30 | | |

*$p$ < .05

TABLE 7
Group by duration for biceps activity before contact: ANOVA

| Source of Variation | df | SS | MS | F | p |
|---|---|---|---|---|---|
| Equality of Means | 2 | 138.65 | 69.32 | 2.65 | .09 |
| Error | 20 | 521.82 | 26.09 | | |

*p < .05

However, a significant result was found for the biceps after plate contact (Table 8). A subsequent post hoc analysis (Table 9) revealed that after plate contact there was significantly less biceps activity in the control and matched groups vs. the slow group.

TABLE 8
Group by duration for biceps activity after contact: ANOVA

| Source of Variation | df | SS | MS | F | p |
|---|---|---|---|---|---|
| Equality of Means | 2 | 3881.30 | 1940.65 | 14.10 | .0002* |
| Error | 20 | 2752.02 | 137.60 | | |

*p < .05

TABLE 9
Scheffe post hoc analysis for biceps after

| Group | Group | | |
|---|---|---|---|
| | Control<br>($M$ = -.81) | Matched<br>($M$ = 5.83) | Slow<br>($M$ = -25.07) |
| Control | | 19.30* | 20.15* |
| Matched | | | .85 |

SR - 15.86   *p < .05

Finally, significant results emerged for cocontraction dimensions concerning before and after plate contact (Tables 10 and 11 respectively).

TABLE 10
Group by duration for cocontraction before contact: ANOVA

| Source of Variation | df | SS | MS | F | p |
|---|---|---|---|---|---|
| Equality of Means | 2 | 332.34 | 166.17 | 7.37 | .0004* |
| Error | 20 | 449.90 | 22.49 | | |

*p < .05

TABLE 11
Group by duration for cocontraction after contact: ANOVA

| Source of Variation | df | SS | MS | F | p |
|---|---|---|---|---|---|
| Equality of Means | 2 | 1692.47 | 846.23 | 5.19 | .015* |
| Error | 20 | 3256.96 | 162.84 | | |

*p < .05

Post hoc analyses (Tables 12 and 13 respectively) demonstrated that the control group responded with significantly less co-contraction before plate contact than the matched and slow rhythm groups, however, concerning co-contraction activity after plate contact, the control group again demonstrated significantly less activity than the slow rhythm group but not significantly less activity than the matched group.

TABLE 12
Scheffe post hoc analysis for cocontraction before

| Group | Group | | |
|---|---|---|---|
| | Control (M = -1.82) | Matched (M = - 5.34) | Slow (M = -6.88) |
| Control | | 7.16* | 8.70* |
| Matched | | | 1.54* |

SR = 6.41   *p < .05

TABLE 13
Scheffe post hoc analysis for cocontraction after

| Group | Group | | |
|---|---|---|---|
| | Control (M = 4.78) | Matched (M = -4.97) | Slow (M = -16.81) |
| Control | | 9.75 | 21.29* |
| Matched | | | 11.54* |

SR = 17.25   *p < .05

All variation ANOVAs resulted in nonsignificant findings except one. A significant finding was discovered for variation activity for the triceps muscle before plate contact (Table 14). As shown in Table 15, a significant difference emerged between the control group and the matched rhythm group.

TABLE 14
Group by variation for triceps activity before contact: ANOVA

| Source of Variation | df | SS | MS | F | p |
|---|---|---|---|---|---|
| Equality of Means | 2 | 106.13 | 53.06 | 4.23 | .03* |
| Error | 20 | 250.56 | 12.52 | | |

*p < .05

TABLE 15
Scheffe post hoc analysis for cocontraction after

| Group | Group | | |
|---|---|---|---|
| | Control (M = -1.95) | Matched (M = -3.14) | Slow (M = 1.27) |
| Control | | 5.09* | 3.22 |
| Matched | | | 1.87 |

SR = 4.78   *p < .05

As pictured in Tables 16 and 17, no other analyses demonstrated significant findings.

TABLE 16
Group by variation for triceps activity after contact: ANOVA

| Source of Variation | df | SS | MS | F | p |
|---|---|---|---|---|---|
| Equality of Means | 2 | 57.38 | 28.69 | .81 | .45 |
| Error | 20 | 708.04 | 35.40 | | |

*p < .05

TABLE 17
Group by variation for biceps activity after contact: ANOVA

| Source of Variation | df | SS | MS | F | p |
|---|---|---|---|---|---|
| Equality of Means | 2 | 1.54 | .77 | .06 | .93 |
| Error | 20 | 236.28 | 11.81 | | |

*p < .05

Results, concerning the consistency of time intervals between hits across trials, indicated a significant difference for both main effects (Table 18). The slow group ($M$ = 4.73) demonstrated the largest deviation between hits vs. the matched group ($M$ = -2.43) for the grouping main effect. A post hoc analysis (Table 19) showed that for the trial main effect Trial 1 was significantly different from Trial 2A but not from Trial 2B while Trial 2A was significantly different from Trial 2B. This result demonstrates that the average deviation between hits diminished as subjects practiced the task such that by Trial 2B the average deviation between hits was not significantly different from that displayed during Trial 1.

TABLE 18
Group by rhythmic deviations of time intervals between hits: ANOVA

| Source of Variation | df | SS | MS | F | p |
|---|---|---|---|---|---|
| Group | 1 | 59.16 | 59.16 | 29.66 | .0001* |
| Trial | 1 | 40.80 | 40.80 | 10.23 | .0003* |
| GT | 2 | 8.17 | 4.08 | 2.05 | .14 |
| Error | 39 | 77.78 | 1.99 | | |

*p < .05

TABLE 19
Scheffe post hoc analysis for trial main effect

| Group | Group | | |
|---|---|---|---|
| | Trial 1 ($\underline{M}$ = 3.21) | Trial 2A ($\underline{M}$ = 4.76) | Trial 2B ($\underline{M}$ = 2.55) |
| Trial 1 | | 1.55* | .66 |
| Trial 2A | | | 2.21 |

$\underline{SR}$ = 1.31    *$\underline{p}$ < .05

## 4. DISCUSSION

The main findings of this study are summarized as follows: In both rhythmic conditions the duration of triceps activity before target contact was significantly increased compared to the control condition. This finding suggests that we should consider the change in muscle activity as a distinct neurological response which is dependent on the presence of a rhythmic stimulus and which appears independent of changes in performance tempo. A similar finding was found for co-contraction patterns between triceps and biceps before target contact. Again, under both rhythmic conditions a significant increase in length of co-contraction was found which makes this a response unique to the addition of an auditory rhythm.

Duration of biceps activity increased significantly after target contact (during the arm-flexion phase) only in the slower rhythm condition. Since the matched rhythm condition produced results similar to the control condition the increase for the slower rhythm group may have been due to a change in performance tempo rather than the addition of a rhythmic stimulus. This can be verified only by adding an experimental condition where subjects are asked to perform slower than their preferred tempo without an auditory rhythm. The increase in cocontraction patterns after target contact for the slower rhythm group has to be interpreted then in the same light as the change in biceps activity.

The variation of triceps activity before target contact decreased significantly for the matched rhythm group. Since the addition of rhythm was the only modified variable here compared to the control condition this again appears to be a distinct neurological response and not an artifact due to different performance tempos.

An interesting result was found in the analysis of time interval consistency of target hits. The addition of an auditory rhythm initially caused a decrease in rhythmic accuracy. However, at the end of the trial period, rhythmic accuracy had improved to the point where it was slightly better than without a rhythmic stimulus present. This result confirms the findings by Hass et al. (1986) that the efficiency of an auditory rhythm as timing cue is not an automatic result but a function of training.

Several theoretical considerations may be put forward to explain the results of this study. The results imply that the auditory rhythm can serve as an efficient muscular entrainment signal to facilitate rhythmic performance accuracy (time interval consistency of target hits) as well as to influence EMG patterns in two antagonist muscle groups (biceps vs. triceps). The increase in cocontraction and duration of triceps activity before target contact under the rhythmic conditions may be explained as a distinct neurological response to facilitate the perceptual-motor match (synchronization between rhythm and muscular response) the subject is attempting. Prolonged triceps activity and earlier onset of biceps activity may facilitate the controlled extension of the forearm towards the target in timed synchronization with the auditory signal. Safranek et al. (1982) suggested that an increase in co-contraction indicates the shift of reflex-like muscle response to more volitional muscular activation. The decrease in variation, i.e., consistent onset and duration of triceps EMG before target contact, in the matched rhythm condition may be explained by Rossingol's and Melvill Jones' (1976) findings that when one follows an audible rhythm in movement the neurophysiological motor events become synchronized to the auditory stimuli. Furthermore, Paltsev and Elner (1967) and Rossignol and Melvill Jones (1976) have demonstrated that auditory signals via the audio-spinal pathways can shorten the latency of motor reactions by raising the level of motor neural excitability on the spinal cord level. We may speculate that the earlier onset of biceps activity before target contact, and the prolonged biceps activity after target contact all may have been effected by changes in the sensori-motor interactions between the audio-spinal pathways and the motor nuclei on the spinal cord level (Rossignol and Melvill Jones 1976).

In conclusion, several implications for clinical applications of these findings may be pointed out. A decrease in variation of muscular activity during motor performance indicates a more efficient recruitment of motor units as necessary in skilled movement. Using rhythmic techniques to teach movement in motor rehabilitation thus may aid in a quicker recovery of motor control and skill. Increased duration of muscular activity may translate into a greater exercise benefit to enhance strengthening of weak muscles. Finally, increased duration of muscle activity and cocontraction between antagonist muscle groups may add stability around the joints during therapeutic exercise or training of purposeful activities of daily living including walking and upper extremity movements.

## REFERENCE LIST

Benecke, R.; Rothwell, J.C.; Day, B.L.; Dick, J.P.; and Marsden, C.D. 1986. Motor strategies involved in the performance of sequential movements. *Exp. Brain Res.* 63:585-595.

Glencross, D. 1970. Serial organization and timing in a motor skill. *J. Mot. Behav.* 2:229-237.

Haas, F.; Distenfeld, S.; and Axen, K. 1986. Effects of perceived musical rhythm on respiratory pattern. *J. Appl. Physiol.* 61:1185-1191.

Huff, J. 1972. Auditory and visual perception of rhythm by performers skilled in selected motor activities. *Res. Q.* 43:197-207.

Liehmon, W. 1971. Rhythmicity and motor skill. *Percept. Mot. Skills.* 1986, 57:327-331.

Melvill Jones, G., and Watt, D.. Observations on the control of stepping and hopping movements in man. *J. Physiol.* 213:703-727.

Paltsev, Y.I., and Elner, A.M. 1967. Change in the functional state of the segmental apparatus of the spinal cord under the influence of sound stimuli and its role in voluntary movement. *Biophysics* 12:1219-1226.

Rimoldi, H. 1951. Personal tempo. *J. Abnorm. Social. Psych.* 42:283-303.

Rossignol, S., and Melvill Jones, G. 1976. Audio-spinal influence in man studied by the H-reflex and its possible role on rhythmic movements synchronized to sound. *Electroencephalogr. Clin. Neurophysiol.* 41:83-92.

Ruggieri, V., and Milizia, M. 1982. Rhythmic reproduction, arousal and chosen time. *Percept. Motor Skills* 54:527-537.

Safranek, M.; Koshland, G.; and Raymond, G. 1982. Effect of auditory rhythm on muscle activity. *Phys. Ther.* 62:161-168.

Smoll, F., and Schulz, R. 1978. Relationship among measures of preferred tempo and motor rhythm. *Percept. Motor Skills.* 46:883-894.

Staum, M. 1983. Music and rhythmic stimuli in the rehabilitation of gait disorders. *J. Music. Ther.* 20:69-87

Thaut, M. 1985. The use of auditory rhythm and rhythmic speech to aid temporal muscular control in children with gross motor dysfunction. *J. Music. Ther.* 22:129-145.

*I acknowledge assistance in the preparation of this paper by Arno Johann, Uwe Seifert and Andreas E. Beurmann.*

# ON CONCEPTS OF "TONAL SPACE" AND THE DIMENSIONS OF SOUND

Albrecht Schneider

## I.0 Introduction

A considerable number of studies in acoustics as well as psychophysics deal with the properties and perceptual determinants of sound (Benade 1976; Roederer 1975; Deutsch 1982; Zwicker 1982). Some papers discuss explicitly the notion of "tonal space" as a mainly psychic and cognitive concept as well as a phenomenon peculiar to music (Wellek [1934] 1963; Albersheim 1979; Kurth ([1931] 1947) while others have rejected that view as untenable (Révész 1937, 1946).

This paper aims at summing up some of the debate as well as submitting some findings and suggestions as to future research. I will try to evaluate basic concepts and empirical results in a concise way and also indicate some of the issues relevant to music therapy or music in medicine.

## I.1 Basic Psychophysical Concepts

Perhaps the best known approach to music perception is that of Helmholtz ([1863] 1870) where he tried to establish a clear-cut scheme of physical magnitudes and their sensory equivalents. According to Helmholtz, pitch is basically a function of the frequency of a pure tone (or the fundamental of a complex tone, resp.), loudness is a function of amplitude, and thus, intensity (sound pressure level), and timbre is by and large a function of the number and relative amplitude of partials of complex tones. This concept is based mainly on physiology and psychophysics though it cannot be reduced to physical dimensions. The idea however was to provide some scientific foundations of music theory and the psychology of music (Helmholtz [1863] 1870; Schneider 1988, 148ff). Carl Stumpf (1883, vol. 1; 1890, vol. 2) worked out a psychological concept of music perception and comprehension. His approach includes many aspects which are phenomenological and cognitive in that he gives a thorough description and evaluation of notions such as pitch, consonance, etc., timbre, noise, as well as of categories of sensory judgments such as sameness, similarity, likeness, dissimilarity, etc.[1] Stumpf's

---

1  Stumpf's *Tonpsychologie* to a certain extent is not merely a book on foundations of perception and comprehension, but also a treatise relevant to epistemics, as was Franz Brentano's (the teacher

elaboration of pitch proceeds from certain mathematical notions discussed in the 19th century by, among others, Gauss, Lobachevskij, G.F.B. Riemann, Helmholtz, and generally labelled "distance geometry."[1] The core of this most fascinating and also controversial discussion was the so-called "non-Euclidean geometries" and advanced concepts of space, and later also space-time relations (Minkowski [1909] 1911). It is sufficient here just to remember that Riemann (the mathematician and not the well-known musicologist Hugo Riemann!) in his famous lecture (1986, 134) did state that "...a geometrical space is but a special case of a threefold extended magnitude" and that there may be other objects conceived of in that way. In general, Riemann's idea was that any single item may be defined by a manifoldness of $n$ dimensions. Thus, ordinary space is a manifoldness of three dimensions, the plane is a two-dimensional manifoldness, and the straight line is a manifoldness of points on a single dimension.

Consequently, Helmholtz, contributing to the mathematical debate concerning axioms of geometry asserted that while time is a manifoldness of a single dimension, the sphere of tones (that is *pure* tones) could be described as two-dimensional by means of frequency and amplitude, or pitch and loudness respectively if we ignore timbre or tone color and duration (Helmholtz [1868] 1971, 200f). Helmholtz rightly claimed that though we are able to compare the distance of two pairs of points a ⟷ b = c ⟷ d, we are unable to compare two tones of the same pitch and different loudness with two tones having the same loudness but different pitch. The conclusion thus would be that comparisons of pairs of stimuli could be obtained only on dimensions which are treated separately and as independent scales.

Regarding pitch, then, we would have just one manifoldness, that of tones, arranged to result in one dimension. If we conceive of tones as defined by frequencies of vibrations (with constant amplitude), very slight differences in frequency would result in the above mentioned manifoldness. It is exactly this view which was adopted and reinforced by Carl Stumpf in his *Tonpsychologie* (1883:1, 57ff, 122ff, 247ff; 1890:2, 319f, 403ff) with respect to the theory of pitch and pitch perception. Consequently the difference of two stimuli, for example, pure tones, could be expressed as their *distance* on a certain dimension; the two tones thus are defined as points and their distance (difference of frequencies) $d$ can be expressed as:

(1)  $M = d\,(a,b) > 0$

---

and long-time friend of Stumpf) *Psychologie vom empirischen Standpunkt*, Vol. 1-3, Leipzig, see Schneider 1990.

[1]  See contributions by Alexitis and Freudenthal in Naas and Schröder (Eds.) 1957 and the book by Jammer [1969] 1980.

In this way with increasing dissimilarity (M) of two tones in pitch, spacing resp. distance will increase also, and on the other hand, with maximum *similarity*, the value for M should become zero. Simple as such considerations may appear, they still play a major role in psychological methodology, and especially in Multidimensional Scaling [MDS] (Borg 1981). Of course, here we find the notions of *distance* and *proximity* with regard to stimuli rated as subjects in terms of *similarity* or *dissimilarity*. Probably the simplest distance function used in MDS then could be given as:

$$(2) \quad d_{ij} = \sum_{a=1}^{n} | x_{ia} - x_{ja} |$$

Where for $p = 1$ the distance of $i$ and $j$ is just the sum of absolute differences on the systems of coordinates $a = 1, 2, ..., n$. Thus $d_{ij}$ is said to give the sum of differences judged to exist between a number of stimuli.[1]

The notions of *proximity, similarity, dissimilarity*, and *distance* as they were introduced by Stumpf (and approved soon after by W. James) function in *Tonpsychologie* to define categories of tone perception. The concept of pitch as outlined by Stumpf is in accordance with geometrical axioms usually stated as:[2]

(3)   $d(x, y) = 0 \quad X = y$         (axiom of minimum: if $x = y$, the value for $d$ is zero)

(4)   $d(x, y) = d(y, x)$         (axiom of symmetry)

(5)   $d(x, y) \le d(x, y) + d(z, y)$   (axiom of triangular inequality)

Here $x, y, z$ are three arbitrarily chosen points, and elements of a set $M$. The set $M$ (of points $a, ......, z$) together with the distance function $d$ is termed a "metrical space." In Euclidean geometry all distances will be straight lines while in non-Euclidean geometries making use of curved planes, distances could be drawn as geodesic lines.

Pure tones in particular can be conceived of as "points" on a dimension of pitch. Thereby each tone will have a distinct place defined by its frequency. Stumpf's concept (1883,122ff) basically follows mathematical notions of the single dimension that is an ordered manifoldness of points (see footnote 2 on page 2); as, by definition, a point in the strict sense has no extension, the theoretical number of points on a dimension is infinite.

---

[1]   See Borg 1981 who discusses various concepts: it is not possible here to enter into foundations of "scaling" or that of psychophysics in general. Most of the relevant problems are thoroughly treated in Falmagne (1985).

[2]   Basically the same approach is found in more recent models (Hake 1966, 502ff, 515f).

This view was expressed by Stumpf with respect to the dimension of pitch which he said will also have the properties of *continuity* and *homogeneity* insofar as we may create an infinite number of pitches by varying the frequency in very small steps (f/df). A series of such tones which will all be very similar yet not identical in pitch will result in a long glide so that in perceptual terms the dimension of pitch will correspond to a shift from *low* to *high* frequencies in *linear* fashion:

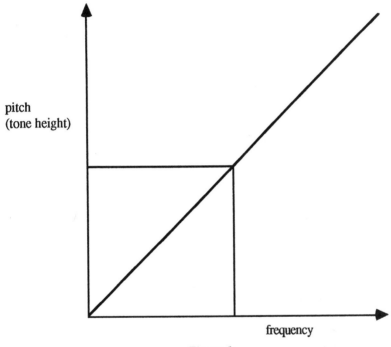

*Figure 1.*

It should be noted that Stumpf, at least in his *Tonpsychologie* of 1883, declared pitch to be *one*-dimensional, linear, continuous, and homogenous. Pitch is thus simply a function of the frequency of vibrations, and stretches from low to high.

To be sure, Stumpf's view was shared by a number of scholars and also adopted in principal by Carl Seashore who said ([1938] 1967, 53ff):

> ...that [pitch] denotes highness or lowness in the tonal continuum along which we locate the music scale.

Stevens and Davis (1938, 94f) consequently argued that on the continuum we may be able to distinguish between about 1,400 pitches in the range from 20 Hz to 12 kHz. Given the one-dimensional concept of pitch as outlined here, it is clear that the notion of *distance* will be of helpful in judging the location of tones on that continuum as well as in expressing the amount of similarity or dissimilarity in a pair of stimuli (cf. Abraham and Hornbostel 1926). The continuum could be conceived of as a kind of sliding rule where the notion of tonal distance is derived from indicating a section on the dimension which is equivalent to the ratios of the two frequencies ($f_1$, $f_2$) that are just points (see above) on the dimension of pitch.

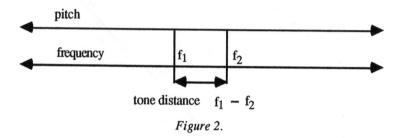

*Figure 2.*

Judging pitch differences thereby would be a kind of distance measurement where we estimate how far the tones may be apart from each other on the one linear dimension of pitch.

## I.2  Two-Componential and Multi-Dimensional Pitch

Approaches like those mentioned above have been labelled "single-componential" theories of pitch (Révész 1946, 63ff) as the sensation of pitch is traced back to the raising or lowering of tones which in turn are caused by shifts in frequency. However, pitch perception is a rather complicated process[1] with pitch itself related to more than one dimension. Already by the 19th century, Drobisch and Brentano had found out that besides tone-height, different pitches may have certain qualities. The distinction between tone height and tone quality was reinforced and experimentally demonstrated by Révész (1913) who established what has since become known as the "two-dimensional-theory" of pitch with the latter comprising a linear (tone height) as well as a cyclic element, tone quality, also labelled "tone chroma" (Bachem 1950). The tone qualities are recurrent because many subjects believe octaves to have almost identical quality though not having identical tone height and/or brightness (Wellek 1963; Heyde 1987). However it is reasonable to incorporate further relationships and elements into a theory of pitch as, besides the so-

---

[1]  Most of the relevant material is discussed in Keidel and Neff (1974-76:Vols 1-3) and Deutsch (1982).

called "octave generalization" found to be valid for many if not all cultures, "western" music in particular makes use of tonal relationships based on the fifth. Simple as these facts are, a combination of the "dimensions"[1] of tone height, the chroma circle and the circle of fifths will already result in a graphical representation of five dimensions while the combination of the two circles would require four and the combination of tone height with the circle of fifths three dimensions (Shepard 1982, 359ff).

Advantages of such models perhaps become more obvious when compared to purely psychophysical scalings such as the "mel-scale" developed by Stevens and Volkmann (1940). This one-dimensional theory does not concern itself greatly with fundamental musical experience, as experiments even attempted to eliminate basic structures such as the octave, and thus tone qualities which constitute melodic contour for example (Attneave and Olson 1971; Schneider and Beurmann 1989/1991).

As has been demonstrated by Shepard in a number of experiments, it is possible to separate tone height from the chroma and vary both independently. Moreover, there are additional variables, such as the circle of fifths, which have to be taken into account so that there are several components or dimensions which together make up the sensation of pitch (see "Attributes of Tone" diagram below). There is enough evidence to allow for the hypothesis that pitch is truly a multi-dimensional structure (Shepard 1982, 1983, Schneider 1991).

### I.3 Attributes of Tone and Phenomenological Approaches to Sound

Even before the "bi-componential theory of pitch" had been established, a number of studies were directed to tonal properties (Stumpf 1883, vol. 1; 1890, vol. 2). Brentano had hypothesized that the linear element of pitch would be brightness almost as there is such an element in different shades of grey.[2] Brightness thus would be an intermodal quality; the dimensions of low—high and dark—bright in this way are parallel, and indeed tone height has been suggested to be closely related to, if not identical with, brightness (Hornbostel 1926a; Schneider and Beurmann 1989/1990).

Research directed to tonal attributes resulted in findings that "*volume* is a phenomenal dimension of pure tones and that this dimension is a complex function of both frequency and the amplitude of the stimulus" (Stevens, 1934a, 406f). By varying only the intensity and frequency of pure tones (often ridiculed as "poor tones"), Stevens was able to generate different sensations of *pitch*, *loudness*, *volume*, and *density* (Stevens 1934b). Thus

---

[1]  It goes without saying that the notion of "dimension" does not have an identical definition in mathematics, physics, and psychology though "dimensions" in psychological models are very often figured as straight lines or vectors (Sixtl 1967, Falmagne 1985).

[2]  Brentano's theory which is both complicated and also speculative as far as any analogy to vision is concerned, is outlined in Résész (1913).

loudness is dependent on frequency and intensity, pitch rises of course with frequency, but is also dependent on the sound pressure level or intensity. The phenomenal dimension of volume increases with intensity and is greater with low and loud tones than with high and soft ones. Another phenomenal dimension, density, increases with both frequency and intensity. From this it becomes obvious that a small number of physical variables will produce fairly complex sensations with the psychic dimensions almost always exceeding the number of variables of the stimulus. However, there is evidence that some of the dimensions are correlated and are more "integral" than "separable" in perception, as has been demonstrated with respect to *pitch* and *loudness* recently (Grau and Nelson 1988).

A phenomenological description of attributes of sound has already been achieved by Hornbostel who pointed to characteristics such as brightness, volume, density (1926, 706ff). According to Hornbostel, besides the dimensions of bright ←→ dark and high ←→ low there is a third one so that tones appear as small and large, respectively. Sound thus contains three dimensions and is imagined in terms of a cube rather than in terms of a plane. Therefore, sounds may be assigned a certain "extension" and a "weight" by the listener, and because of different degrees of volume and density, the "big" sounds may appear to be more diffuse and mellow while the "small" ones are more dense, compact and acute (Hornbostel 1926). Even pure tones (sinusoidal stimuli) may account for such images, and several of them grouped together but varying a little in their respective frequencies will produce the sensation of a "tonal mass" (Ekdahl and Boring 1934) or, musically speaking, a *cluster*. This, then, again could be conceived of in three dimensions though (as is the case with a filtered noise band) the physical variables remain frequency and amplitude of sound. For complex tones, i.e., fundamental plus partials, it was claimed that such stimuli besides pitch and loudness do have "at least three attributes. These are brightness, roughness, and one tentatively labelled fullness" (Lichte 1941).

Perhaps the most detailed analysis of tonal attributes and dimensions of sound was supplied by Albersheim (1939) who distinguished basic tonal properties from those restricted to complex tones or sounds.[1]

---

[1]  This illustration is presented with the original German terms which are rather difficult to translate. "Complex tones" of course are signals which contain both fundamental and partials or, generally speaking, a number of components (a, b, ...., n) of different frequency and amplitude. It will be shown later, that the notion of *sound* in a strict sense points to another "dimension," that of time.

*Attributes of Tone (single pure tone)*

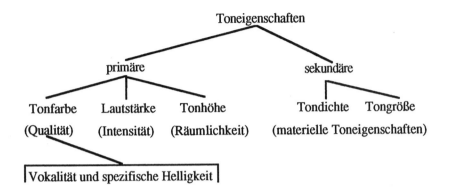

*Attributes of Complex Tones*

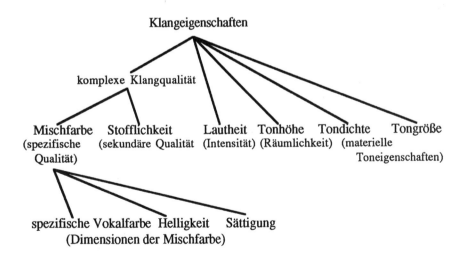

*Figure 3.*

It becomes evident that "Vokalität," that is, relatedness or closeness of sounds to the series of vowels (A-E-I-O-U) all of which are defined by spectral envelopes and maximum spectral energy due to resonance (Neppert and Pétursson 1984), is another characteristic of complex and even pure tones.[1]

According to Albersheim (1939), both pure and complex tones (sounds) are defined as such by "a specific *quality* of a distinct *intensity* and *spatial* determination (plus a number of secondary characteristics)." Complex tones all bear a certain "color" (Albersheim 1939, 266), by analogy to optics resp. vision one thus may speak of "Klangfarbe" (tone color or instrumental color), and *musical timbres* are distinguished in this way mainly by their spectrum envelope. Timbres in this way may be reduced to qualities where variation over a period of time has been omitted. It has been argued by Slawson (1981, 132) that *sound color* (Klangfarbe) "by definition... has no temporal aspect. Sounds may vary in color over time, but the variation in a sound is not itself a color."

This statement seems logical if one leaves aside temporal characteristics of sound, as, for example, transients and modulation processes (as does Slawson). However, there can be no doubt that sound in a very basic [e.g., $y = F(t)$] as well as in a psycho-acoustic perspective (Schügerl 1970; Keidel and Neff 1974-76) is very much a function of time, while the amplitude spectrum of course abstracts from the time domain and thus reduces the complex signal considerably.[2] To illustrate the fact that "sound color" is not just a function of the spectral envelope, but may be defined by temporal aspects, we may generate a specific sound on a synthesizer with an almost continuous shift of harmonics over time including variation of phase relationships. Figure 4 shows part of the sound as it develops in time (signal display as a function of time/oscillogram) with a slight modulation of the amplitude (see envelope). If we take a spectrum of that sound at a certain point in time, we will recognize a considerable degree of spectral density (Figure 5 plots only frequencies from 0 - 1 kHz) with a "fundamental" plus its partials as well as a number of other components which do not correspond to that harmonic series (frequency ratios 1:2:3:4:5:6:7:8... :n; see dotted lines of graph on Figure 5). Rather, there are at least two "complex tones" in this signal, one of which remains fixed while the other "travels" in that there is a sweep of its components and thus, a shift of the spectrum envelope as a function of time (Figure 6).

---

[1]  Relevant investigations had been carried out by Köhler (1909-1915), Stumpf (1926), Hornbostel (1926a), and others; the reader is referred to the discussion in Albersheim (1939).

[2]  Determination of the time function of a periodic vibration would require amplitude spectrum and phase (angle) spectrum. I will not discuss here relations of time to frequency and reciprocity of time function and spectrum as well as techniques like Fast Fourier Transforms etc. It should suffice to note that FFT-derived spectra normally have to be averaged and thereby the amplitude spectrum is that of a larger number of periods of vibration. (See Randall 1987)

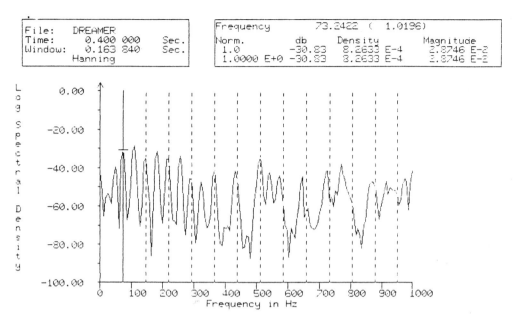

Figure 4. Signal Display

## SPECTRAL   DISPLAY                                **Sampled  Data**

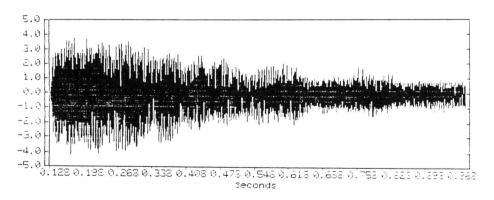

Figure 5. Spectral Display (Compressed)

**SPECTRAL  DISPLAY**                              **Sampled  Data**

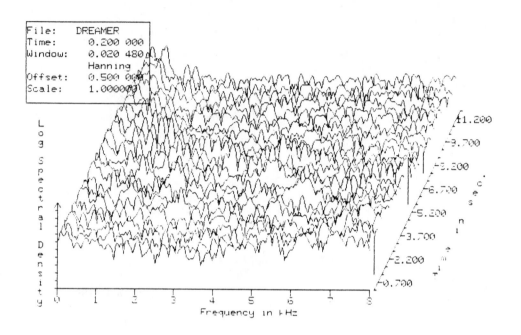

*Figure 6. Spectral Display 3-D Plot (Spectral Density/Frequency/Time)*

The sound, as it was actually programmed, allows each "state" of the spectrum envelope
to remain for a fraction of a second—just long enough to recognize that another step in
the shift has been reached. However, it is not too difficult to obtain a strictly continuous
variation that will appear as kind of a "spectral glide."[1] The "sound color," if understood
as the quality that allows identification on the one hand, and differentiation on the other,
is here quite obviously dependent on temporal *change* and not on the spectrum envelope at

---

[1]  Shepard (1983, 645) reports shifts "around the chroma circle" in the form of a continuous
glissando that reinforces the paradoxical effect of what is experienced as "Shepard-pitch," i.e.,
tones with "tone height" and "chroma" moving in  opposite directions. Schouten (1968, 142)
mentions change of spectral envelope (formant-glide) as a feature to shape timbre.

any given time. For if the sound were varied continuously, we would generate different spectrum envelopes and accordingly, different sound colors. Even if we allow for an integration of neighboring states over time (as the spectra obtained at points of time dt$_i$ ... dt$_j$ may be quite similar), the overall change that occurs within ten seconds, as is the case with this sound, is far too great for the average listener to recognize the initial and the final spectrum envelope as the same sounds. Moreover, it is exactly the shift of components that is considered characteristic to this sound. Strictly speaking, it is spectral *variation* that constitutes identity of this specific sound. Subjects who were asked to classify and describe this stimulus, unequivocally labelled it to be "voluminous," "spacious," and, certainly, "shifting."[1]

## II.0 CONCEPTS OF "TONAL SPACE"

As soon as research had established certain dimensions of sound, scholars endeavored to postulate that there was something like "tonal space" (German: *Tonraum*). According to conventional theories from antiquity to Newton and Kant (Čapek 1976), "space" is a three-dimensional structure, a view tackled of course by modern physics and mathematics for which "space" is at least a four-dimensional (including time), or rather a *n*-dimensional structure (Minkowski [1909] 1911; Jammer [1969] 1980; Naas and Schröder 1957).

Considerations as to tonal space seem to have proceeded from different angles. On the one hand research into localization of sound, visual and space perception provided evidence for diotic resp. binaural hearing and constitution of what was termed "hearing space" (German *Hörraum*) (Hornbostel 1926b); on the other hand, concepts of a psychology of music as developed by E. Kurth ([1930] 1947) and H. Mersmann (1922-1923, 1931) claimed that *music* causes images of motion in the listener as music is a dynamic complex of sounds. Thereby music evolves in time by means of what could be understood as kind of kinetic energy inherent in the music organism. According to Kurth, the motion is registered by the listener and projected into an imaginary *space* which cannot be viewed and which is not palpable (1947, 116ff). Even though this impression is inevitable—one cannot deny such projection of complex sound into imaginary space—little can be said with regard to the dimensionality of the spatial structures in question. While it is not difficult to visualize the dimensions low ⟷ high and dark ⟷ bright as the vertical of a three-dimensional space (or, generally speaking, the dimensions of tone height), the horizontal immediately introduces a nonspatial quality, namely time.[2] At least this was and still is

---

1 The sound in question was generated by means of Oberheim Matrix 6 and Oberheim Matrix 1000 synthesizers. The sound was recorded on tape via a standard mixing console in stereo and was played back both on loudspeakers and headsets to some 20 musicology students at the University of Hamburg.

2 This distinction holds true with respect to conventional theories of space and time that also govern most concepts of tonal space. As soon as one turns to modern physics (Minkowski [1909] 1911;

the most common approach to tonal space (Albersheim [1974] 1979, 1980), a view also supported by western notation that plots pitch/time-relationships in only two dimensions. However, while pitch motion is possible in two directions, up and down, time proceeds along the x-axis and is irreversible even though listeners will produce images of musical motion by means of retention or anticipation.[1]. Kurth rightly remarked that *reading* music of course proceeds from left to right while actually *listening* to it might arouse quite different images of what is the horizontal of the imaginary space. Yet the real problem would be a third dimension, that of depth. In music, sounds may appear to be removed, in the far distance, while others are near, present, almost palpable. This effect has been known for a long time and has been used in music compositions from Sweelinck's *Echo-Fantasy* to Ligeti's *Lontano*. Thus, depth of tonal space could be conceived of in terms of dynamics and loudness. As was stated earlier, tones are assigned a certain volume which in itself is a three-dimensional attribute. Wellek (1934) who discussed the problem of tonal space and its dimensions at some length, said that sounds may appear to be far or near not just because of their respective intensity, but also because of their timbre. By analogy to the two-componential theory of pitch (see above) he postulated an element (or dimension) of brightness to be part of the complex sound and relevant to perception of pitch as well as to the presence of sounds. As a rule, Wellek argued, a note produced by, for instance, a bassoon in the high range will appear to be much nearer and present than the same note produced by an oboe in its respective low range. So his third main dimension[2] was established as "nearness"/presence ⟷ "remoteness"/depth.

---

Jammer [1969] 1980; Naas and Schröder 1957) there is the problem of spatio-temporal continuity which is *not* completely out of sight as far as music is concerned; see also remarks on this subject by Wiener ([1964] 1976).

[1]  At this point, the reader is referred to categories of time consciousness elaborated by Edmund Husserl (1928), Brélet (1949), Klugmann (1961) and especially Ingarden (1962).

[2]  Wellek, who clearly recognized the problem of dimensionality of tonal  space, uses some irony when talking about the great number of "Dimensionen und Dimensiönchen" (German diminuitive of the noun "dimension") (Wellek 1934,422) that finally make up what he defined as the nonperceptive structure of "music space."

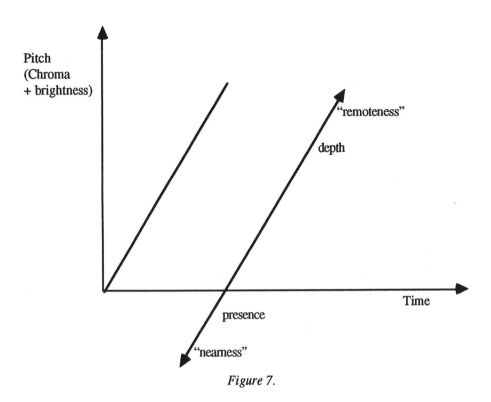

*Figure 7.*

A few years before Wellek's treatise, the problem of musical space was tackled in a brief article by Siegfried Nadel (1930/31) who correctly distinguished between the three-dimensional physical space relevant to geometry (a system of ordering that is of a *a priori* and objective nature), and the "space" of daily experience that is of a subjective and phenomenal nature. According to Nadel sounds will be perceived within the phenomenal and subjective "space" like other objects so that they may appear to be near or far, above or below the subject that listens to music (p. 330). In this way, Nadel's view comes close to Hornbostel's *Hörraum* (1926b). However, musical space as was outlined by Nadel is primarily a scheme of organization and ordering, much analogous to geometrical space. Besides the dimension of high ⟷ low, Nadel postulated several more like those of intensity and timbre, and he also mentions harmony with respect to the various relationships based on the circle of fifths (see above and Shepard 1982, 1983). What seems to be of particular interest in Nadel's concepts is that he points to what he calls the "nonhomogenous structure" of some of the dimensions (for instance, that of tone qualities or "chroma") as well as to the space-time-relations that are both basic and central to music. Nadel concluded that musical space is a complex and multidimensional as well as nonhomogenous structure that may come close to concepts developed in the field of non-Euclidean geometries and relativity theory as in music there is a complete interdependence of space and time. As an example that illustrates a kind of analogy to the theory of relativity, Nadel notes that the motion effected by low tones always appears to be much "slower" in time than the same motion produced by means of high notes, and thus, there is a dependence of musical time on musical space (Nadel 1930/31, 331). To those who think such reasoning is far-fetched and purely hypothetical, it may be of interest to know that the mathematician Norbert Wiener also saw parallels between modern physics and music both of which face the problem of spatio-temporal continuity (Wiener [1964] 1976).

## II.1 Sound, Music and "Spaciousness"

While the nature and exact number of dimensions that make up musical space are still a matter of debate (see below), there is much evidence at hand with respect to the factor of spaciousness of sounds in perception. Research in the fields of acoustics and psychoacoustics has revealed basic mechanisms and components that account for what has been called "spatial hearing" (Blauert 1974). Among the characteristics of stereophonic perception of sound, spaciousness is primarily determined by the relative magnitude of early lateral energy rather than specific temporal patterns (Blauert et al. 1986, 293). However, though spaciousness relates to physical magnitudes, this concept is also of cognitive and phenomenological importance as listeners usually are well able to classify sounds almost immediately with respect to three-dimensional properties and prefer conditions of listening that will materialize in the perception of the aforementioned quality of spaciousness (Blauert 1985, 75). Thereby, phenomenal properties of sound such as volume, density, and weight, are far from being sheer fancy or at best, illusion; as has already been argued by Dräger (1952), the properties in question were recognized by composers long ago and figure strongly in various works of music.

The same holds true with respect to the concept of space that seems to govern both music notation (Wellek 1931) and the process of composition since the Middle Ages (Kunze 1974). There has also been a constant interplay of acoustics and architecture again with the ultimate goal of providing spaciousness of sounds with respect to the conditions of listening to music. This approach in more recent times has led to quite sophisticated constructions of so-called "sound-cubes" and even spherical auditoria (Leitner 1978; Forsyth 1985), structures which were planned with the idea that sound should be able to "rotate" in space as well as to create "images" of spaces of changing dimensions (Leitner 1978). Thus, space here is not conceived of as the known three-dimensional structure that governs and orders perception but as a set of dimensions that may vary in size and arrangement with time as as a function of musical events (Barthelmes 1986).

## II.2  Localization and Cognitive Structuring

As has been determined from experiments over many years, subjects are mostly able to localize sounds (Boring 1926; Hornbostel 1926b; Blauert 1974) as well as to describe stimuli in terms related to space and spaciousness (Blauert 1985, 75). There is also evidence that the relative amount of spaciousness perceived is not dependent on "whether we have intracranial—as with headphones—or extracranial localization—as in free-field listening situations" (Blauert et al. 1986, 293). This finding perhaps suggests that spaciousness indeed is not only related to physical magnitudes but also a matter of cognitive structuring. To test this hypothesis, one may listen to stereophonic recordings which make use of sound sources that are more or less continually moved on the stereo basis from left to right and back. As soon as there are several such sources which are moved in opposite directions at the same time, subjects who listen to such music by headphones and are asked to describe their impression as to localization of sources (single instruments), quite unanimously have said that the moving sound signals appear to "go round inside the head," that is, horizontally on an intracranial plane.[1] Thereby, the distribution of lateral energy that would account in the first place only for left-right localization, is transformed into a spatial structure that represents the conceived (or just imagined) motion of the sound source.

To create such images,[2] a tape has been produced to be used in experiments with a piece of music (called *Sax Room*) based on synthesizer, drum computer and alto saxophone. The beat and the chord progressions, etc., have been designed to give a steady yet unobtrusive flow of sound as a background to the melodic lines of the saxophone that are featured and attract most of the listener's attention.[3] This piece has been recorded on multi-track and was mixed in such a way that the pan pot setting of the saxophone track as well as the fader position (level of loudness) have been manipulated to co-vary continuously as a function of time. Thereby the signal is shifted not only on the stereo basis from left to right, but also changes regularly in intensity with respect to loudness so that when in the middle position the level will be one time at maximum and one time at minimum loudness; as the whole cycle of stereo/intensity-manipulation is performed in exactly 60 seconds, one may conclude that 15 seconds of the signal will correspond to a shift of the sound source of 90° if we allow for the hypothesis that with presentation of the piece by means of a headset subjects will localize the moving source intracranially and

---

[1]  Intracranial localization of sounds is a basic experience in experiments where sound is fed into the ear by means of headphones. A piece of music to illustrate the effect and quite easily available is *Nimbus* by Beggar's Opera (Vertigo 6360 054)

[2]  The notions of image and imagery which are widely used in psychology again (see, for example, Segal 1971; Kosslyn 1980) of course point to the phenomenological approach as was outlined by, among others, Brentano, Husserl (1928), and also J.P. Sartre (1940).

[3]  I was joined in the preparation of the tape by Arno Johann (alto sax) whom I would like to thank here for his support.

build up mental images of the motion. The manipulation of the signal (saxophone track) could be illustrated according to the next scheme.

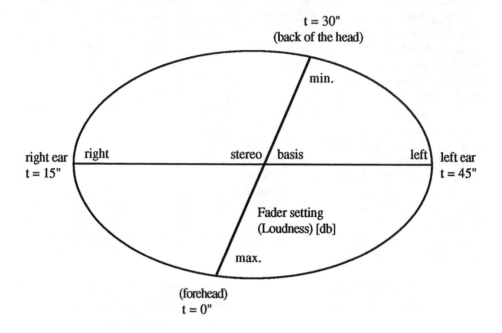

*Figure 8.*

This piece has been presented to a total number of more than 20 subjects (most of them students of musicology) who were asked to listen to the music, keep their eyes closed, and report on whatever might attract their attention. The response with the exception of one or two listeners always has been that subjects described the saxophone line as moving either "inside the head" or closely "around the head," that is, from the forehead to the right ear, from there to the back of the head, to the left ear, and back to the forehead. Most of the subjects reported intracranial localization of the moving sound source which was correctly identified to perform a (quasi-) circular motion. This motion of course captured much of the attention and led to conceptualization of the structure of the piece of music which might be interpreted according to schemes outlined by Sowa (1984, esp. Ch. 2.7). EEG-readings have been obtained from a few of the subjects while listening to the music although reservations have been expressed as to such measurement in diotic resp.

stereophonic conditions.[1] However it may not be inappropriate to point to the fact that diotic listening is the normal condition relevant also to the measurement of neural activity. The musical piece used in our experiment perhaps has the advantage that the characteristics of the main stimulus (the saxophone track used to create certain imagery, namely that of a intracranial rotation of a sound source) are defined with respect to the time basis, and thus are reproducible. It remains to be investigated in future research whether (and if, to what extent) there is a correlation of the changing time/localization patterns of the music used as a stimulus and patterns of cortical activity. (Roederer 1979; Roesler 1982).

## II.3 Hearing Space, Tonal Space, Music Space

Even though many of the characteristics of spatial hearing have been determined in psychoacoustical experiments, one has to admit that there is a certain subjective component already present in what has been conceptualized as hearing space (Hornbostel 1926b, 602f), a structure that seems to be closely related also to phenomenal attributes (Blauert 1985) that are difficult to measure in a strictly scientific approach yet a fact of daily experience. The problem of objective investigations becomes even more obvious when we consider concepts of tonal space as have been outlined by, among others, Stumpf, Hornbostel, Max Schneider (1930), Nadel, Wellek, Albersheim, Zuckerkandl (1963), and O'Connell (1962).

While the vertical of that space has almost always been identified with the dimensions of pitch (the latter understood to comprise one or several components with respect to dimensions, see above), time in most concepts figures as the horizontal, leaving a third dimension to incorporate various tonal as well as perceptual attributes (like intensity, volume, spectral density, etc.). As this third dimension seems to lack precision, some have denied it completely and also postulated that the dimensions of time and pitch (conceived of as a set of chroma-classes) are incommensurate (Albersheim 1979, 86ff) because there is neither the same measuring unit employed on both dimensions nor can we claim the fairly high consistency that governs the pitch dimension for that of time.

As far as geometrical *models* are concerned, if they are to be representations of perceptual and/or cognitive structures there is of course the question as to the true nature of the dimension. According to Eugène Minkowski (1971, 30), subjects tend to conceive of time as a straight line $\longrightarrow$ so that the concept of tonal space as a two dimensional plane of pitch and time as sketched by, among others, Albersheim (1979, 88) seems to be reasonable. However, it has been objected that "the use of an arrow for time is misleading

---

[1]   See Paulus (1985, 2) and literature quoted there. I will not discuss the methodology or limitations of EEG-measurements here.

for it suggests a direction in space. The only *direction* or *space* of time is from earlier to later and this can be along *any* direction in space" (Meredith 1970, 65). Moreover, psychologists have claimed that only physical time can be conceived of as a regular pulse or a straight line while *experience* of time is dependent on a number of subjective factors[1] and may result in a rather uneven flow of time segments each of which bears a certain quality (as is the case when listening to music, [Fraisse 1957]). Thereby, the time dimension (and also that of pitch) strictly speaking seems to lack homogeneity if we regard subjective experience. The geometrical model thus at best may be considered as an abstraction.

The same holds true with respect to the rectangular construction of dimensions. As we know from factor analysis and other models, dimensions are defined to build up *orthogonal* structures. In his *Theory of Perception* Reenpää has postulated that "the manifold of senses... is a phenomenal linear-orthogonal system" (1961, 18). Experiments carried out at Helsinki did yield the conclusion "that the perceptual manifold of the sense of hearing possesses an *Euclidean-Pythagorean* linear structure, where quadratic metrics apply" (Bergström et al. 1961, 10). It should be mentioned, however, that on the contrary, some scientists again on grounds of empirical data have argued that space even in elementary perception is a non-Euclidean structure, rather than a simple three-dimensional one,[2] a view put forward by Nadel (1930/31) also with respect to tonal resp. musical space.

In any case there is little doubt that music perception and cognition is comprised of more than three 'dimensions' resp. 'components' ( it depends on the approach which of these terms fits better into explanative models). Even if we allow for a basic concept of tonal space that is based on pitch, time, and timbre, as a three-dimensional plot, one has to remember that pitch in itself contains several components, and that *timbre* is understood as a multidimensional attribute of sound (Grey 1977; Wessel 1979) that seems to be as closely related to the time-domain as is pitch.[3] So in reality the dimensions are not as neatly separable as they are in a geometrical sketch, and although one may complain about the fact that in musical timbre, spectral and dynamic aspects are confused this is the very nature of the phenomenon in question (Crowder 1989, p. 477, and Figure 5.)

---

[1]  See E. Minkowski (1971), Husserl (1928), Fraisse (1957), Klugmann (1961). For a logical investigation of time, see Löfgren (1984) who points to the self-referential and *cyclic* nature of time respectively.

[2]  See Piaget (1970, ch. III, 9). The problems in question have been thoroughly treated already by Becker (1923) who in a phenomenological approach discusses the notions of space, spaciousness, and continuity. Different concepts of space are also discussed by Maurin (1981); both Becker and Maurin point to musical aspects of space here and there.

[3]  See also Monahan and Carterette (1986) who in a multidimensional study stated "that at least five dimensions were needed to a good accounting of the perceptual space" of melodies played in different rhythmic patterns with the major dimensions being time-related.

The temporal aspects of the problem become very obvious when we finally turn to the complex structure labelled "musical space" as was outlined by Kurth and Wellek. According to the latter, we may distinguish between *hearing space* (mainly a psychoacoustic structure), *tonal space* (a referential scheme related to perception that helps mental ordering of stimuli and thus functions as an aid to conceptualization), and *musical space* which again is based on perceptual facts but itself is imaginary and of unknown dimensionality though it reflects musical dynamics (Kurth [1931] 1947, 116ff) and is indispensable for aesthetic experience (Wellek 1934, 434ff; 1963, 295ff).

How these three spaces (if we accept the distinction as valid or at least as useful) might relate to each other, is an intricate and as yet unsolved question. Of course there are models of how reality is linked to inner experience (Ciompi 1988), and there are many theories of how perceptual data might be processed to produce mental images.[1] Marr's computational theory of vision is perhaps one of the best known achievements (Marr 1982) though not undisputed. One of the questions still debated (Kitcher 1988, 20) and also relevant to music cognition seems to be how structure is derived from motion. This is what basically happens when we listen to music as a more or less continuous auditory stream of music events that perhaps needs to be sliced as well as permanently scanned to yield meaningful units of cognition (McAdams and Bregman 1985; Deutsch 1982; Dowling and Harwood 1986). Thus one may consider building of conceptual structures as a steady process of abstraction that aims at establishing orderliness with respect to information (to put it in Wiener's terms). Though this process itself of course is time-related and the input may be of a temporal nature (as is the case in music), the result of the abstraction seems to be representations of structures at certain states.[2] There is evidence that the process of abstraction is dependent on the complexity of the input insofar as image formation in subjects tends to take more time if the signal resp. stimulus exhibits structural complexity (Hubbard and Stoeckig 1988). We know from listening to modern music that complexity may be considerable to the point where there is information "overflow," that is, too many events at a time to be processed in a way that yields adequate understanding. Generally, in order to conceptualize and comprehend musical structures, geometrical models as well as dimensional representations in a spatial arrangement may be of great help. Abstract phenomena as a rule seem to be better understandable if presented in a dimensional structure that is comprehensible as is even the four-dimensional cube (Tessaract) employed in biocybernetics (v. Foerster 1985, 72ff.) as a means to have subjects manipulate a quite complex body into different projections. Similarly, one may conceive of the spatial concepts discussed as tonal resp. musical space as supporting music cognition since tonal space seems to provide a kind of framework

---

[1]  Simply to name and list the relevant literature would require another article; it may suffice to point to Gibson (1966), Grossberg (1982), and Sowa (1984).

[2]  It is not possible here to discuss the neurobiological foundations of such a theory; see Grossberg (1982), Churchland (1986) and Kohonen (1988).

that guides structuring of perceptual stimuli. However, musical space which has been described phenomenologically to be imaginary yet unavoidable according to a hypothesis put forward recently by Bergström (1988), could be the result of a process of imagination induced by music in the brain that not only generates orderliness and information, but also a strain of nonpredictable ideas, new connections of various items stored in memory, and even a certain amount of entropy not to forget emotions (Roederer 1979) that play a major role in music perception and imagery as well as in the constitution of musical space (Wellek 1934).

The emotional and imaginative power of music has been derived from the interplay of more primitive parts of the brain (such as the brain stem and the limbic system) and the cerebral cortex in music listening and these features that seem to be specific to music also account for its therapeutical use as well as a nonverbal means of communication. It has been found, that sounds (sampled or synthesized) can be of special use in certain therapeutical applications (Schneider 1989), for example as an aid to address patients who suffer from depression and will not react otherwise. Such evidence, circumstantial as it may be, again suggests that music in general and certain soundscapes in particular may be suited to induce a process of imagination and to reestablish patterns of experience that are blocked or almost lost. It can only be hoped that future research into music cognition will reveal more of the structure and mechanisms that govern music imagery (Weber and Brown 1986) so that music therapy may benefit from a more systematic knowledge of how music is perceived and appreciated.

## REFERENCE LIST

Abraham, O., and von Hornbostel, E.M. 1926. Zur Psychologie der Tondistanz. *Zeitschrift für Psychologie* 98:233-249.

Albersheim, G. 1939. *Zur Psychologie der Ton-und Klangeigenschaften*. Strasbourg: Heitz.

_____. 1979. *Zur Musikpsychologie*. (2nd Ed). Wilhelmshaven: Heinrichshofen.

_____. 1980. *Die Tonsprache*. Tutzing: H. Schneider.

Attneave, F., and Olson, R.K. 1971. Pitch as a medium: a new approach to psychophysical scaling. *Am. J. Psychol.* 84:147-166.

Bachem, A. 1950. Tone height and tone chroma as two different pitch qualities. *Acta Psychol.* 7:80-88.

Barthelmes, B. 1986. Musik und Raum - ein Konzept der Avantgarde. In *Musik und Raum*, edited by T. Bräm, 75-89. Basel: GS-Verlag.

Becker, O. 1923. Beiträge zur phänomenologischen Begründung der Geometrie und ihrer physikalischen Anwendungen. In *Jahrbuch für Philosophie und Phänomenologische Forschung*, Bd. 6, 385-560. Halle: Niemayer.

Benade, A. 1976. *Fundamentals of Musical Acoustics*. London: Oxford University Press.

Bergström, M. 1988. Music and the living brain. In *Essays on the Philosophy of Music*, edited by V. Rantala, L. Rowell, E. Tarasti. *Acta Philosophica Fennica* 43 (1988):135-153.

Bergström R.M.; Häkkinen, V.; Jauhiainen, T.; and Kahri, A. 1961. Experimental demonstration of the Euclidean-Pythagorean structure and quadratic metrics in the perception manifold of the sense of hearing. *Annales Acad. Scient. Fennicae*, Series A:V Medica No. 84.

Blauert, J. 1974. *Räumliches Hören*. Stuttgart: Hirzel.

_____. 1985. Räumliches Hören. Nachschrift. *Neue Ergebnisse und Trends Seit 1972*. Stuttgart: S. Hirzel.

Blauert, J.; Möbius, U.; and Lindemann, W. 1986. Supplementary psychoacoustical results on auditory spaciousness. *Acustica* 59:292-293.

Borg. I. 1981. *Anwendungsorientierte Multidimensionale Skalierung*. Berlin, Heidelberg, New York: Springer.

Boring, E.G. 1926. Auditory theory with special reference to intensity, volume, and localization. *Am. J. Psychol.* 37:157-293.

Brélet, G. 1949. *Le Temps Musical*. T. 1/2 Paris: Pr. Univ. de France.

Čapek, M. (Ed.) 1976. *The Concepts of Space and Time. Their Structure and Their Development*. Dordecht/Boston: Reidel Publ. Co. *Boston Studies in the Philosophy of Science*, Vol. 22 = Sythese Library Vol. 74.

Churchland, P.M. 1986. Some reductive strategies in cognitive neurobiology. *Mind* 95:279-309.

Ciompi, L. 1988. *Außenwelt - Innenwelt. Die Entstehung von Zeit, Raum and psychischen Strukturen*. Göttingen: Vandenhoeck and Ruprecht.

Crowder, R.G. 1989. Imagery for musical timbre. *J. Exp. Psychol.: Human Perception and Performance* 15:472-478.

Deutsch, D. 1982. The processing of pitch combinations. In *The Psychology of Music*, edited by D. Deutsch, 271-316. New York: Academic Press.

Dowling, W.J., and Harwood D.L. 1986. *Music Cognition*. New York: Academic Press.

Dräger, H.H. 1952. Begriff des Tonkörpers. *Archiv. für Musikwissenschaft* 9:68-77.

Ekdahl, A.G., and Boring, E.G. The pitch of tonal masses. *Am. J. Psychol.* 46:452-455.

Falmagne, J.C. 1985. *Elements of Psychophysical Theory*. Oxford: Clarendon Press.

Foerster, H. von. 1985. Kybernetik einer Erkenntnistheorie. In *Sicht und Einsicht*, edited by H. von Foerster, 65-79. Braunschweig/Wiesbaden: Vieweg.

Forsyth, M. *Buildings for Music*. Cambridge, MA: M.I.T. Press.

Fraisse, P. *Psychologie du Temps*. Paris: Pr. Univ. de France.

Gibson, J.J. 1966. *The Senses Considered as Perceptual Systems*. New York:

Grau, J.W., and Nelson, D.K. 1988. The distinction between integral and separable dimensions: Evidence for the integrality of pitch and loudness. *J. Exp. Psychol.: General* 117:347-370.

Grey, J.M. 1977. Multidimensional perceptual scaling of musical timbres. *Journal of the Acoust. Soc. of Am.* 61:1270-1277.

Grossberg, St. 1982. *Studies of Mind and Brian: Neural Principles of Learning, Perception, Development, Cognition, and Motor Control*. Dordrecht: Reidel Publ. Co.

Hake, H.W. 1966. The study of perception in the light of multivariate methods. In *Handbook of Multivariate Experimental Psychology*, edited by R. Cattell, 502-534. Chicago: Rand/McNally.

Helmholtz, H. von. [1863] 1870. *Die Lehre von den Tonempfindungen als physiologische Grundlage für die Theorie der Musik*. Braunschweig: Vieweg (3rd Ed. 1870).

_____. [1868] 1971. Über den Ursprung und die Bedeutung der geometrischen Axiome (1868/69). In *Philosophische Vorträge und Aufsätze*, edited by J. Hörz and S. Wollgast. Berlin: Akademie-Verlag.

Heyde, E.M. 1987. *Was ist absolutes Hören? Eine musikpsychologische Untersuchung*. München: Profil.

Hornbostel, E.M. von. 1926a. Psychologie der Gehörserscheinungen. In *Handbuch der normalen und pathol. Physiol*. Vol. XI (1), 701-730. Berlin: Springer.

_____. 1926b. Das räumliche Hören. Ibid., 602-618.

Hubbard, T.L., and Stoeckig, K. 1988. Musical imagery: Generation of tones and chords. *J. Exp. Psycol.: Learning, Memory and Cognition* 14:656-677.

Husserl, E. 1928. Vorlesungen zur Phänomenologie des inneren Zeitbewußtseins (Ed. M. Heidegger). In *Jahrbuch für Philos. und phänomenol. Forsch*. 9:367-496.

Ingarden, R. 1962. *Untersuchungen zur Ontologie der Kunst*. Tübingen: Niemeyer.

Jammer, M. [1969] 1980. *Das Problem des Raumes (Concepts of Space*, 2nd ed. Cambridge, MA: Harvard University Press), 2nd enlarged German ed. Darmstadt: Wiss. Buchgesellschaft.

Keidel, W., and Neff, W.D. (Eds.) 1974-1976. Handbook of Sensory Physiology, Vol. V(1-3). Berlin, Heidelberg, New York: Springer.

Kitcher, P. 1988. Marr's computational theory of vision. *Philosophy of Science* 55:1-24.

Klugmann, F. 1961. Die Kategorie der Zeit in der Musik. Ph.D. dissertation, University of Bonn.

Kohonen, T. 1988. An introduction to neural computing. *Neural Networks* 1:3-16.

Kosslyn, S.M. 1980. *Image and Mind*. Cambridge MA: Harvard University Press.

Kunze, St. 1974. Raumvorstellungen in der Musik. Zur Geschichte des Kompositionsbegriffs. *Archiv für Musikwissenschaft* 31:1-21.

Kurth, E. [1931] 1947. *Musikpsychologie*. Bern: Krompholz. (1st ed. 1931, 2nd ed. 1947).

Leitner, B. 1978. *Ton : Raum/Sound : Space*. Köln: DuMont.

Lichte, W. 1941. Attributes of complex tones. *J. Exp. Psychol*. 28:455-480.

Löfgren, L. 1984. Autology of time. *Intern. J. General Systems* 10:5-14.

Marr, D. 1982. *Vision: A computational investigation into human representation and processing of visual information*. San Francisco: W.H. Freeman.

Maurin. K. 1981. Mathematik als Sprache and Kunst. In *Offene Systeme II*;, edited by K. Maurin, K. Michalski, and E. Rudolph, 118-244. Stuttgart: Klett-Cotta.

McAdams, St., and Bregman, A. Hearing musical streams. In *Foundations of Computer Music*, edited by C. Roads and J. Strawn, 658-698. Cambridge, MA: M.I.T. Press.

Meredith, P. 1970. Developmental models of cognition. In *Cognition: A Multiple View*, edited by P. Garvin, 49-84. New York: Spartan Books.

Mersmann, H. 1922/23. Versuch einer Phänomenologie der Musik. *Zeitschrift für Musikwissenschaft* 5:226-269.

_____. 1931. Zeit und Musik. In *Vierter Kongress für Ästhetik und Kunstwissenschaft Hamburg 1930*, edited by H. Noack, 216-231. Stuttgart: Enke.

Minkowski, E. 1971/72. *Die gelebte Zeit*, Vol. 1/2. Salzburg: O. Müller. German ed. of *Le Temps Vecu*, Paris, 1933.

Minkowski, H. [1909] 1911. Raum und Zeit. *Physikalische Zeitschr.* 10:104-111. (Reprinted in H. Minkowski, *Gesammelte Abhandlungen*, Bd. II, 431-444. Leipzig: Teubner 1911.

Monahan, C.B., and Carterette, E.C. 1985. Pitch and duration as determinants of musical space. *Music Perception* 3:1-32.

Naas, J., and Schröder, K. (Eds.) 1957. *Der Begriff des Raumes in der Geometrie*. Berlin: Akademie-Verlag.

Nadel, S. 1930/31. Zum Begriff des musikalischen "Raumes." *Zeitschrift für Musikwiss.* 13:329-331.

Neppert, J., and Pétursson, M. 1984. *Elemente einer akustischen Phonetik*. Hamburg: Institut für Phonetik, University of Hamburg.

O'Connel, W. 1962. Der Tonraum. *Die Reihe* 8:35-61.

Paulus, W. 1985. Der Einfluß musikalischer Reizqualitäten auf späte, akustisch evorzierte Potentiale. Medical Dissertation: University of Erlangen.

Piaget, J. 1970. *Tendances Principales de la Recherche dans les Sciences Sociales et Humaines*. P. I. Paris: Unesco/Mouton.

Randall, R.B. 1987. *Frequency Analysis*, 3rd ed. Naerum: Bruel & Kjaer.

Reenpää, Y. 1961. *Theorie des Sinneswahrnehmens*. Helsinki: Soumalainen Tiedeakatemia. *Annales Acad. Scient. Fennicae* Series A:5. Medica, No. 78.

Révész, G. 1913. *Zur grundlegung der Tonpsychologie*. Leipzig: Veith & Co.

_____. 1937. Gibt es einen Hörraum? *Acta Psychol.* 3:137-192.

_____. 1946. *Einfürung in die Musikpsychologie*. Bern: A. Francke.

Riemann, G.F.B. 1868. Über die Hypothesen, welche der Geometrie zugrunde liegen. *Abhandlungen der Königl. Gesellschaft der Wissenschaften zu Göttingen* 13:133-152.

Roederer, J. 1975. *Introduction to the Physics and Psychophysics of Music*. 2nd ed. New York: Springer.

_____. 1979. The perception of music by the human brain. *Humanities Association Review* 30:11-23.

Roesler, F. 1982. *Hirnelektrische Korrelate kognitiver Prozesse*. Berlin, Heidelberg, New York: Springer.

Sartre, J.P. 1940. *L'Imagination. Psychologie Phénoménologique de l'Imagination.* Paris: Gallimard.

Schneider, A. 1988. Musikwissenschaftliche Theorienbildung, außereuropäische Musik und (psycho-)akustische Forschung. In *Colloquium. Festschr. für Martin Vogel,* edited by H. Schröder, 145-174. Bonn/Bad Honnef: G. Schröder.

_____. 1989. Zur Anwendung von "Soundelekronik" in der Musiktherapie. *Musik-, Kunst- und Tanztherapie* 2:87-93.

_____. 1990. Pyschological theory and comparative musicology. In *Comparative Musicology and Anthropology of Music: Essays on the History of Ethnomusicology,* edited by B. Nettl and P. Bohlman. (pp. 293-317) Chicago: University of Chicago Press.

_____. 1991. On the acoustics and tuning of Gamelan instruments, in: *Indonesian Performing Arts.* ed. B. Arps. London: School of Oriental and African Studies.

Schneider, A., and Beurmann, E. 1989/90. Tonsysteme, Frequenzdistanz, Klangformen und die Bedeutung experimenteller Forschung für die Vergleichende Musikwissenschaft. In *Hamburger Jahrbuch für Musikwiss.* 11 (1989), Laeber 1991.

Schneider, M. 1931. Raumtiefenhören in der Musik. In *Vierter Kongress Ästhetik und Allg. Kunstwiss. Hamburg 1930,* edited by H. Noack, 207-215. Stuttgart: Enke.

Schouten, J.F. 1968. The perception of timbre, in: *Reports of the 6th Int. Cgr. on Acoustics, Tokyo,* SP-6-2,35-44.

Schügerl, K. 1970. Zeitfunktion und Spektrum in der subjektiven Akustik. In *Musik als Gestalt und Erlebnis, Festschr. W. Graf,* 215-226. Wein: Böhlau.

Seashore, C.E. [1938] 1967. *Psychology of Music.* New York: McGray-Hill 1938 (repr. Dover 1967).

Segal, S.J. (Ed.) 1971. *Imagery: Current Cognitive Approaches.* New York: Academic Press.

Shepard, R.N. 1982. Structural representations of musical pitch. In *The Psychology of Music,* edited by D. Deutsch, 343-390. New York: Academic Press.

_____. 1983. Demonstrations of circular components of pitch. *J. Audio Eng. Soc.* 31:641-649.

Sixtl, F. 1967. *Meßmethoden der Psychologie.* Weinheim: Beltz.

Slawson, W. 1981. The color of sound: A theoretical study in musical timbre. *Music Theory Spectrum* 3:132-141.

_____. 1985. *Sound Color.* Berkeley: University of California Press.

Sowa, J.F. 1984. *Conceptual Structures. Information Processing in Mind and Machine.* Reading, MA/Menlo Park CA: Addison-Wesley Publishing.

Stevens, S.S. 1934a. The volume and intensity of tones. *Am. J. Psychol.* 46:397-408.

_____. 1934b. The attributes of tone. *Proc. Nat. Acad. of Science* 20:457-459.

Stevens, S., and Davis, H. 1938. *Hearing: Its Psychology and Physiology.* New York: Wiley.

Stevens, S., and Volkmann, J. 1940. The relation of pitch to frequency: A revised scale. *Am. J. Psychol.* 53:329-353.

Stumpf, C. 1883. *Tonpsychologie* Vol. 1. Leipzig: Hirzel.

_____. 1890. Ibid. Vol. 2.

Weber, R.J., and Brown. S. 1986. Musical imagery. *Music Perception* 3:411-426.

Wessel, D. 1979. Timbre space as a musical control structure. *Computer Music Journal* 3: 45-52.

Wellek, A. 1931. Die Entwicklung unserer Notenschrift aus der Synopsie. *Farbe-Ton-Forschungen* ed. G. Anschütz, Vol.3 (Hamburg):143-153.

_____. 1934. Der Raum in der Musik. *Archiv für die Ges. Psychol.* 91:395-443. (reprinted in Wellek 1963: 295-343)

_____. 1963. *Musikpsychologie und Musikästhetik.* Frankfurt: Akadem Verlagsanstalt Athenaion.

Wiener, N. 1964. Spatio-temporal continuity, quantum theory and music. In *I Am a Mathematician*, edited by N. Wiener, 97-107. Cambridge MA: M.I.T. Press. (Repr. in Čapek 1976: 539-546.)

Zuckerhandl, V. 1963. *Die Wirklichkeit der Musik. Der musikalische Begriff der Aussenwelt.* Zürich: Rhein-Verlag.

Zwicker, E. 1982. *Psychoakustik.* Heidelberg, Berlin, New York: Springer.

# III
# APPLIED RESEARCH

# PAIN REDUCTION DURING NEONATAL CIRCUMCISION

Lisa Marchette
Robyn Main
Ellen Redick
Arthur Shapiro

## SUMMARY

The purpose of this study was to determine the effect of 2 interventions during unanesthetized circumcision on neonatal pain. Fifty-eight neonates were randomly assigned to 1 of the 3 intervention groups. Eighteen control infants received routine care, 25 infants had earphone music and 15 infants had a tape of intrauterine sounds played. During circumcision, monitors measured cardiac rhythm, blood pressure and transcutaneous oxygen. Pain was measured by analysis of videotaped facial expressions. The results showed that the mean heart rate tended to be slightly lower in the music group but no other differences could be substantiated in the other parameters monitored. The facial expressions analyzed showed that all 3 groups had pain much more than any other emotion during the procedure. Therefore, the intervention of music or intrauterine sounds could not offset the effects of circumcision pain. Music may not be an appropriate modality for pain relief in the neonatal period.

This study was funded by the American Heart Association, Florida Affiliate, National Association of Pediatric Nurse Associates and Practitioners (NAPNAP), and the National Association of Neonatal Nurses (NANN).

## BACKGROUND

Medical personnel have had concerns about the pain perceived by newborns during routine unanesthetized circumcision. More than one million newborns are circumcised each and year and most receive no medication to decrease pain (Wallerstein 1980). Unanesthetized circumcision has been found to cause significant abnormalities in physiological indicators of pain such as encephalographic (EEG) and rapid eye movement (REM) sleep patterns (Emde et al. 1971; Anders and Chalemian 1971), plasma cortisol (Talbert et al. 1976; Tennes and Carter 1982), respiratory rate (Rawlings et al. 1980), transcutaneous oxygen concentration (Rawlings et al. 1980), and heart rate (Holve et al. 1983; Rawlings et al. 1980; Williamson and Williamson 1983). In addition, profound crying causes modified Valsalva maneuver and blood flow changes that can delay and compromise cardiovascular adaptation post birth (Anderson et al. 1983; Lind et al. 1964).

One such treatment for pain reduction of neonatal circumcision is the dorsal penile nerve block but it is invasive and rarely used. Other literature recommends various nursing interventions to decrease neonates' pain (D'Apolito 1984; Sheredy 1984), but the benefits of these noninvasive methods had not been scientifically documented.

## PURPOSE

The purpose of this study was to determine the effect of 2 different noninvasive interventions during unanesthetized circumcision on neonatal pain, indicated by heart rate, arrhythms, blood pressure, rate-pressure product, transcutaneous oxygen level, alertness, and facial expressions.

## SAMPLE AND DESIGN

The sample included newborns scheduled for circumcision at a teaching hospital, with an APGAR score of at least 8 at 1 and 5 minutes of age, who had not undergone surgery, and whose parents gave informed consent. Data were collected on 103 infants who were randomly assigned to three groups. Missing data and/or usually prolonged circumcision deleted 45 newborns from the study. Of the remaining 58 newborns, 18 infants in the control group received the routine care; 25 infants in the "music group" heard by earphone a tape selected classical music during the procedure; 15 infants in the "intrauterine sound group" heard a commercially prepared tape of intrauterine sounds during the procedure. A time series design and repeated measures analysis of variance were used to compare the data collected at each of the 12 steps of the circumcision.

## INSTRUMENTS

Monitors measured cardiac rate, rhythm, blood pressure and transcutaneous oxygen. Rate-pressure product was computed by multiplying heart rate by systolic blood pressure.

Pain was measured by analysis of videotaped facial expressions with Maximally Discriminative Facial Movement Coding System (Izaard 1983). With this reliable and valid technique, assistants coded the facial movements of 3 facial regions and used the codes in formulas to determine emotions demonstrated during each step of the circumcision. Alertness was measured with the Brazelton's Neonatal Assessment Scale (Brazelton 1973).

## RESULTS

The mean heart rate of the control group was above normal limits during all the steps in which the infants were touched with surgical instruments (Table 1).

| TABLE 1. HEART RATE | | | |
|---|---|---|---|
| STEP | CONTROL | INTRA. SOUNDS | MUSIC |
| Strapping baby to circ board | 173 | 150 | 164 |
| Betadine prep/draping | 177 | 170 | 170 |
| Placement of 2 hemastats | 191* | 177 | 185* |
| Probing | 204* | 195* | 191* |
| Hemastat to mark cut | 203* | 193* | 196* |
| Cut; center of foreskin | 200* | 201* | 183* |
| Placement of Gomco bell (not clamped yet) | 214* | 198* | 186* |
| Clamping Gomco | 203* | 194* | 178 |
| Waiting | 183* | 178 | 170 |
| Cutting foreskin | 185* | 160 | 161 |
| Gomco removal | 180 | 162 | 162 |
| Normal = 110-180; abnormal values = * | | | |

The heart rate of the music and intrauterine sounds groups were within the normal range for more of the steps than the control group. The mean heart rate of the intrauterine sound groups and the music groups were above normal limits during 5 steps, while the heart rate of the control group was above normal in 8 steps. The heart rate of the music group tended to be lower with only 2 steps having rates above 190 and none above 200.

There were no differences noted in the systolic or diasatolic blood pressures except during the 2 minute waiting period after the Gomco clamp was tightened, when the obstetricians waited for hemostatis, when the systolic blood pressure was in fact lower in the control group than in the music group.

Mean rate-pressure product and TcP02 were normal at baseline but above normal limits the entire time the infants were lying on the circumcision board. An assistant analyzed the cardiac strips in a blinded fashion and found that cardiac rhythm was almost always sinus tachycardia with a few ectopic beats.

The facial expressions analyzed showed that all 3 groups expressed pain much more than any other emotion, during all the steps in which the infants were touched with surgical instruments. The Brazelton Neonatal Assessment Scale data showed that in all 3 groups, the infants cried during almost every step and were quiet and alert after return to their isolettes.


## DISCUSSION

Neonates must meet some of their greatest cardiovascular challenges in their first few days of life (Assali et al. 1968). Lung expansion and development of the adult circulatory pattern may take up to 5 days, during which time nursing care can foster successful adaptation by decreasing undue pain that causes crying and its cardiovascular effects (Gentile et al. 1981; Gill et al. 1984). Therefore, it would seem reasonable to evaluate various interventions for pain reduction in order to provide comfort and to offset the cardiovascular side effects of unanesthetized circumcision during the physically unstable first few days of neonatal life.

The heart rates of the music group tended to be lower than the other 2 groups. However, the systolic and diastolic blood pressures were similar in all 3 groups tested except for the higher systolic blood pressure in the music group during the 2 minute waiting period after the Gomco clamp was tightened. Therefore, the earphone music showed a limited beneficial effect only on the heart rate; this effect could not be documented by any of the other parameters tested including crying and facial expressions of pain.

It should be pointed out that music reduced pain sensation by its anxiolytic effect. Consequently, the pain reduction effect of music may hold true only when exposed to the more developed and conditioned interpretative brain centers of an adult as opposed to that of a child or, as in this case, a newborn baby. Further examination for pain relief of circumcision seems warranted and perhaps a combination of interventions may be demonstrated to be more effective than music alone.

## REFERENCE LIST

Anders, T.F., and Chalemian, R.J. 1974. The effects of circumcision on sleep-wake states in human neonates. *Psychosomatic Medicine* 36:174-179.

Anderson, G.C.; Burroughs, A.; and Measel, C.P. 1983. Nonnutritive sucking opportunities: A safe and effective treatment for preterm neonates. In *Infants Born at Risk: Physiological, Perceptual and Cognitive Processes*, edited by T.M. Field and A. Sosek, 129-146. New York: Grune and Stratton.

Assali, N.S.; Bekey, G.A.; and Morrison, L.W. 1968. Fetal and neonatal circulation. In *Biology of Creation*: Vol. 2., edited by N.S. Assali, 52-98. New York: Academic Press.

Brazelton, T.B. 1973. *Neonatal Behavioral Assessment Scale*. Philadelphia: J.B. Lippincott, Co.

D'Apoliton, D. 1984. The neonate's response to pain. *Maternal Child Nursing* 9:256-259.

Emde, E.N.; Harmon, R.J.; Metcalf, D.; et al. 1971. Stress and neonatal sleep. *Psychosomatic Medicine* 33:491-496.

Gentile, R.; Stevenson, G.; Dooley, T.; Franklin, D.; Kawabori, I.; and Pearlman, A. 1981. Pulse dopplar echocardiographic determination of time and ductal closure in normal newborn infants. *Journal of Pediatrics* 98:443-448.

Gill, N., White, M., and Anderson, G. 1984. Transitional newborn infants in a hospital nursery: From first oral cue to first sustained cry. *Nursing Research* 33(4):213-217.

Holve, R.; Bromberger, P.; Groveman, H.; Klauber, M.; Dixon, S.; and Snyder, J. 1983. Regional anesthesia during newborn circumcision. *Clinical Pediatrics* 22(12):813-181.

Izaard, C. 1983. *The Maximally Discriminant Facial Movement Coding System*. Newark, DA: University of Delaware.

Lind, J.; Stern, L.; and Wegelius, L. 1964. Human fetal and neonatal circulation. In *The Human Fetal and Neonatal Circulation*, Edited by S.Z. Walsh, W.W. Meyer, and J. Lind, 89-94. Springfield, IL: Charles C. Thomas.

Rawlings, D.J.; Miller, P.A.; and Engel R. R. 1980. The effect of circumcision on transcutaneous PO2 in term infants. *American Journal of Diseases of Children* 134:676-678.

Sheredy, C. 1984. Factors to consider when assessing responses to pain. *Maternal Child Nursing* 9:250-252.

Talbert, L.M.; Kiraybill, E.N.; and Potter, H.D.: 1976. Adrenocortical response to circumcision in the neonate. *Obstetrics and Gynecology* 48: 208-210.

Tennes, K., and Carter, D. 1973. Plasma cortisol levels and behavioral states in early infancy. *Psychosomatic Medicine* 35:121-128.

Wallerstein, E. 1980. Circumcision: An American health fallacy. New York: Springer Publishing Company, p. 216.

Williamson, P.S., and Williamson, R.N. 1983. Physiological stress reduction by a local anesthetic during newborn circumcision. *Pediatrics* 71:36-40.

# MUSIC THERAPY AND PSYCHONEUROIMMUNOLOGY

Joseph Scartelli

The health professions have reached, or grown to a point in which the patient, and specifically the brain, is recognized as a primary contributor to the resistance of disease (Ornstein and Sobel 1987). The Cartesian model of separation of mind and body, the premise on which medicine has functioned for many years, is now being replaced with a holistic model that recognizes a constant reciprocal action and communication between the mind and body. Irrefutable evidence of the influence that these domains have on one another is abundant. As a result, the specific disciplines of behavioral medicine psychology, physiological psychology, and psychoneuro-immunology have emerged (or evolved) to rethink how one resists, acquires and eliminates disease and to retrain professionals and patients as to methods and practices that will promote a more efficient communication between mind and body.

Ironically, the confirmation of the mind/body connection is, in large part, a result of the magnificent progress and technology of the very professions that shunned this connection. One example of this progress is the discovery of neurotransmitters—the chemical messengers of the brain. As the brain, particularly the hypothalamus, receives feedback from the entire body by way of the nervous system, it responds by commanding other portions of the brain to begin the process of chemical and hormonal secretion. These secretions, in turn, help the body to respond properly to the original stimulus in an effort to maintain internal homeostasis. As Ornstein and Sobel (1987) note, the brain is much more of a chemical factory or pharmacy than it is a computer, a common analogy. Each cell in the brain can release scores of chemicals which travel to other 'target' cells, tissues, and organs carrying messages that are primarily of excitation or inhibition of activity.

The triggers of these chemical discharges are many and varied. Reactions to environmental, emotional, physical, social and even spiritual changes produce subsequent and deliberate secretions of neurotransmitters which then effect autonomic nervous system, endocrine, and immune system functioning. These changes are perceived and transmitted by the nervous system with reactions to these changes being largely autonomic. It is not overtly necessary to command our lungs to inflate and deflate, to pump our hearts at an accelerated pace, to release certain chemicals or hormones in response to a changing condition. Since these functions are performed for us automatically and naturally by the body, it is not difficult to recognize why the patient has come to expect change solely from outside intervention when the process goes awry. The patient has been taught from childhood that there is simply no control over these functions. However, autonomic function is no longer an untouchable. Developments in self-management and regulation techniques such as meditation, biofeedback, hypnosis, imagery, etc. continually increase one's ability to *consciously* control previously autonomic functions, i.e., increase the patient's efficacy in dealing with his or her own illness.

As previously noted, the immune system response is included in one's reactions to changes in external and internal conditions. "The immune system is a defense system designed to protect the host on two fronts: it must protect from infective agents, without; from aberrance in self-structures, within" (Lloyd 1987, 19). Without the immune system, all cells, tissues, and organs would be unprotected from antigens that can injure and ultimately destroy the organism. Acting as a detective, this system can seek out antigens and, under normal and healthy conditions, acting as an enforcer, destroy them.

Today, it is widely known that events that lead to disruption of homeostasis through trauma, unwelcome changes, and prolonged stress have a deleterious effect on immune function. Stories of a surviving spouse who becomes ill or acquires a disease upon the loss of their mate are common. Even death is no longer considered an uncommon consequence of severe emotional trauma. To clarify, the trauma itself does not produce the onset of diseases or death in these examples, but more specifically, it is the surviving person's perception, interpretation, and designated meaning of that loss that creates the damaging state. Certainly, psychological and emotional factors have significant impact on immune function. For example, as stress persists, high level of corticosteroids (stress hormones) will be secreted to help the body defend itself during the period of stress. However, excesses of corticosteroid levels suppress normal immune function in the body (Suter 1986). As a result, viruses, cancer cells, and hosts of antigens are permitted to go on unchecked.

As trauma, or one's interpretation of loss or change can have varying degrees of negative effect on the health state of the individual, it must be emphasized that for every action there is an equal, but opposite reaction. As the immune system can be diminished by certain events, it can also be strengthened by opposite events. To illustrate, control, or a person's sense of control, appears to be an effective counter to stress and aversive conditions (Gatchel and Baum 1983).

Recognizing the contribution that emotions and patient belief systems have on health, new directions have emerged for pursuing maintenance of health and reduction of disease, including the discipline of psychoneuroimmunology. Psychoneuroimmunology is concerned with how "individual differences in adaption—differences shaped by personality, attitude, and behavior—predispose one to illness, wellness" (Weiner, cited in Lloyd 1987, xi). The psycho-neuroimmunologist, according to Lloyd (1987), focuses attention on "reactive patterns of emotion and behavior that may predispose an individual to autoimmunity" (p. 4).

Positive emotions, affect, control, and belief can result from many stimuli. One of the stimuli that maintains an eminent place in all corners of society is music. It is commonly recognized that music, in varying degree and intensity, depending on the setting, individual, type of music and specific selection, has known and sometimes predictable effects of psychological and physiological states of the listener. Certainly, one must first recognize that the degree and intensity of the impact of the music on the listener depends on the relationship of that particular individual with the specific music selection.

The effects of music take place in a number of environments and conditions including social, business and advertising, sports, television and movie soundtracks, religious ceremony, and in therapy to help address specific human conditions and disorders. The emotional domain of human function is the prime target of music. Filmmakers, advertisers, religious institutions, etc. rely on the fact that the right kind of music paired with their message will move the listener emotionally to the extent that this reaction will override rational decision making.

Music can also affect emotions to enhance one's energy level with obvious examples seen in long-distance running, aerobics, and competitive sports. In these activities, music is used to increase endurance and provide a diversion from pain. In the clinical setting, investigations report the positive contributions of music in pain management (Rider 1985; Clark et al. 1981; Christenberry 1979). While it is not precisely understood how this mechanism operates, it does show how music helps *patients* deal with pain through self-management strategies.

## MUSIC AND PSYCHONEUROIMMUNOLOGY

The physiological mechanisms that engage as a result of all external and internal stimulation channel through regions of the limbic system and hypothalamus which uses this information as it relates to emotion for ultimate effect on endocrine, immune, and autonomic nervous system function (Cox 1978). Among the prominent stimuli that affect these systems is music. The success of music in influencing healthy function of these systems may be in its inherent novelty as compared to most known brain processing and function. The novelty of music as a stimulus presented to the brain is noted by Roederer (1975) in which he states that it is one of the very few endeavors of the human species that has flourished, and continues to flourish throughout man's evolution, but contains no survival value to the species.

Music produces emotional reactions verbally and nonverbally. Its ability to communicate on many levels may promote the communication within the patient that is necessary for self-management strategies. As Scartelli (1987) contends, music signals are sent to the upper brain regions through the brain stem, reticular formation, and limbic system in a hypercharged manner by virtue of its rhythmic format. Because this information is rhythmically formatted, it is processed through all levels of the brain in a unique manner which is different from all other auditory stimuli. With regard to the reticular formation, Bloom et al. (cited in Rossi 1986) state that the reticular formation plays an important role in the information transduction within the mind/body connection. Rossi (1986) reveals that "it is the brain's ability to wake up, to become alert and attentive to novel patterns of sensory stimuli and information that enables it to focus its activity on new learning and creativity" (p. 28). Novel stimuli heighten the activity sent to higher cortical and limbic-hypothalamic areas of the brain (Rossi 1986).

Activities of the hypothalamus trigger activation of the pituitary gland, considered the "master gland," which will subsequently command chemical and hormonal secretion into the body, thereby activating the endocrine system. The limited scope of the present paper prohibits detailed descriptions of the abovementioned processes.

While researchers have demonstrated somewhat successful applications of music to affect neuro-endocrine activity (Rider et al. 1985), Goldstein (1980) presents a particularly strong case for using music to affect endocrine and immunological systems. Goldstein notes that the "right kind" of music will create a "thrill response" in the listener. Thrills are defined by sudden changes or shifts in mood or emotion and are accompanied by a number of visceral reactions such as palpitations, chills, and even weeping. Thrills commonly occur in response to music—primarily to those pieces that hold a special meaning to the listener and are generally associated with emotional arousal. Goldstein concludes by stating "that an emotional response involving the autonomic nervous system might be mediated by the recently discovered opiate peptides (endorphins) seemed an obvious conjecture, given the association of opiate receptors with the limbic system and the euphorigenic effects of the opiates" (p. 128).

It is important to note that music, arbitrarily heard, will not produce the effects suggested by this paper. Music specifically prescribed to the individual patient to assist in efficacy building and enhance self-management methods to increase a sense of strength and control appear to be the most prudent avenue. As Goldstein notes, use of the "right music." For the process to be effective in eliciting immunological and endocrine activity, the patient must practice the methods in order to create new learned habits and reconceptualize their thinking with regard to their own health maintenance and rehabilitation. For example, the patient might be taught to reconceptualize a perceived threat into a challenge. This change of definition of the threat redirects the patient's posture from one of defense to one of offense and as Lazarus (1966) notes, psychological and physiological stress have their roots in the perception of threat. As with biofeedback training, meditation, and imagery, the patient must learn the strategies that create desired results through continued and effective practice and drill, thereby indicating the importance of the therapist in the process. As Turk, et al (1983) note, of the ten leading causes of death, seven could be significantly reduced by changes in behavior patterns and "individuals require education in order to change (those) behavior patterns" (p. 28). To complement this behavioral education and training for greater autonomic control, one can learn to exploit the inherent appeal and innate effects of music.

## REFERENCE LIST

Christenberry, E. 1979. The use of music therapy with burn patients. *Journal of Music Therapy* 16:138-148.

Clark, M.; McCorkle, R.; and Williams, S. 1981. Music therapy-assisted labor and delivery. *Journal of Music Therapy* 18:88-109.

Cox, T. 1978. *Stress*. London: Macmillan.

Gatchel, R., and Baum, A. 1983. *An Introduction to Health Psychology*. Reading, MA: Addison-Wesley.

Goldstein, A. 1980. Thrills in response to music and other stimuli. *Physiological Psychology* 8:126-129.

Lazarus, R. 1966. *Psychological Stress and the Coping Process*. New York: McGraw-Hill.

Lloyd, R. 1987. *Explorations in Psychoneuroimmunology*. Orlando, FL: Grune and Stratton.

Ornstein, R., and Sobel, D. 1987. *The Healing Brain*. New York: Simon and Schuster.

Rider, M. 1985. Entrainment mechanisms are involved in pain reduction, muscle relaxation, and music-mediated imagery. *Journal of Music Therapy* 22:183-192.

Rider, M.; Floyd, J.; and Kirkpatrick, J. 1985. The effects of music, imagery and relaxation on adrenal corticosteroids and the re-entrainment of circadian rhythms. *Journal of Music Therapy* 22:46-58.

Roederer, J. 1975. *Introduction to the Physics and Psychophysics of Music* (2nd Ed). New York: Springer-Verlag.

Rossi, E. 1986. *The Psychobiology of Mind-Body Healing*. New York: Norton.

Scartelli, J. 1987 (November). Subcortical mechanisms in rhythmic processing. Paper presented at the meeting of the National Association for Music Therapy, San Francisco.

Suter, S. 1986. *Health Psychophysiology*. Hillsdale, NJ: Lawrence Erlbaum.

Turk, D.; Meichenbaum, D.; and Genest, M. 1983. *Pain and Behavioral Medicine*. New York: Guilford.

# MUSIC IN THE TREATMENT OF IMMUNE-RELATED DISORDERS

Cheryl Dileo Maranto
Joseph Scartelli

## INTRODUCTION TO PSYCHONEUROIMMUNOLOGY

The discipline of psychoneuroimmunology has its roots in many branches of medicine and psychology including immunology, psychiatry, neurophysiology, psychosomatic medicine, endocrinology, and behavior therapy. The connection between the functions of the mind and body has received increasing medical validation in the last two decades. Specifically, the knowledge that principal systems of the body's function—nervous, endocrine, and immune—do not, in fact, work in isolation form one another, but in an elegant cooperation and reciprocation. Additionally, these essentially autonomic systems have been shown to react to external and internal changes with a certain degree of consistency. Furthermore, it has been shown that these systems can develop the capacity to learn (Lloyd 1987). As these systems are integral to the psychoneuroimmunologic phenomenon, a short explanation of the makeup and function of each is in order.

The autonomic nervous system is an involuntary system that resides at various levels of the brain and body, and even in cellular composition. Moreover, it is responsible for the maintenance of the body's homeostasis. It is comprised of sympathetic and parasympathetic divisions which exist in somewhat antagonistic states to one another. The sympathetic nervous system responds to changes in the environment as well as internal fluctuations, thus preparing the body for emergency and stress situations by automatically and immediately increasing vital functions such as heart rate, respiration rate, arterial pressure, and pupil dilation/constriction. The result of sympathetic stimulation includes elevated energy, awareness, endurance, and overall visceral arousal. The parasympathetic nervous system will effect an opposing response to the sympathetic in decreased activity of the autonomic nervous system in an effort to conserve and restore energy for future use.

The endocrine system, a collection of organs located throughout the body, secretes hormones or chemical messengers into the blood stream with destinations to target organs and glands. This action creates metabolic changes in direct response to internal and/or external stimulation. The glands of the endocrine system include the pituitary, pinial, thyroid, adrenal as well as the testes and ovaries. As opposed to the autonomic nervous system which reacts with split-second immediacy to changes in environmental conditions, endocrine organs and tissues react relatively slowly. Additionally, the effects of the hormonal stimulation last much longer, as endocrine organs and tissues require more time to metabolize the chemical introduced in response to changing conditions. Common hormones active in the endocrine system include insulin, epinephrine, norepinephrine, cortisol, and ACTH (adrenocorticotropic hormone) ( Suter 1986).

The immune system is the body's defense mechanism against foreign invaders or antigens. This system is comprised or two operations, innate and acquired immunity. Innate immunity provides a general defense from a broad, nonspecific category of antigens. The most common of these is white blood cells or lymphocytes.

Acquired immunity, on the other hand, is a defense system developed by the body to fend off specific antigens, such as bacteria, viruses, and toxins (Rossi 1986). The principal structures of the immune system are the thymus gland, lymph nodes, the spleen, and bone marrow. As Rossi (1986) notes, neurotransmitters of the autonomic nervous system, the hormones of the endocrine system, and the immunotransmitters of the immune system all function as messengers to target organs, tissues, and glands of the body.

All of the above functions are mediated, to a great extent, by the pea-sized hypothalamus located in the mid-brain immediately below the thalamus. This densely compacted structure is responsible for the ultimate regulation of autonomic function, endocrine activity, hunger, thirst, fluid balance, body temperature, etc. Endocrine activity is innervated via pituitary stimulation by the hypothalamus, thus providing the beginnings of the anatomical link among the autonomic, endocrine, and immune systems (Lloyd 1987). The hypothalamus, in effect, receives messages from all portions of the nervous system, therefore providing a connection between behavior and the generally automatic functions of the autonomic, endocrine, and immune complex. In addition, the hypothalamus is an integral component in the emotional activity of the brain, further validating the anatomical connection of the emotional and physical state.

Ader and Cohen (1975) provided what is generally considered the breakthrough work that demonstrates the connection between immune functions and learning. In an attempt to train conditioned aversion to sweetened water, they added the drug cyclophosphamide to produce nausea in rats. Upon removal of the drug, which is also an immunosuppressant, the rats continued to experience nausea. However, a high mortality rate of the rats occurred in addition. The investigators concluded that not only was nausea conditioned to the sweetened water, but the immune system apparently learned to respond to the conditioned effects of the cyclophosphamide. The immune system, in effect, was suppressed or learned to suppress itself by the presentation of the sweetened water alone. This investigation paved the way for the bevy of research that followed connecting behavior, emotion, and immunocompetence.

The immune system is, in fact, extremely complex. It is made up of numerous types of cells that deal with antigens in unique fashions. The suppressed immune system, for example, limits the production of guardian cells including lymphocytes, T-cells, B-cells, and macrophages. As Hall (1989) reports, "some cells (monocytes) act as sentinels, others (antibodies and natural killer and cytotoxic T-cells) rouse or mute the general alarm, and other (macophages) come around to clean up the battle field and cart off the results of the carnage. Humans can generate up to one million different antibody molecules to attack foreign invaders" (p. 69).

Although the connections of autonomic, endocrine, and immune systems are only briefly described here, this tandem permits traumatic events, stress, loss, extreme change, and grief to encourage and cause illness by suppressing the immune system.

Selye's model for emergency and chronic stress reactions is useful for consideration in this discussion (cited in Achterberg 1985). Emergency stress reactions are sympathetic-dominated and cause reactions from the adrenal glands. Adrenaline and noradrenaline, the hormones which are secreted, diffusely immobilize the body, i.e., heart rate accelerates, sugar is released, pupils dilate, blood clots more quickly, and white blood cell activity increases. The body in essence has readied itself for a battle which may never occur. This heightened state must dissipate quickly or else become "the enemy within" (Achterberg 1985, 129). It is suspected that individuals who have cardiovascular condition cannot rid themselves of these reactions quickly enough and their prolonged emergency stress reactions may perhaps directly contribute to their diseases (Achterberg 1985).

In chronic stress, the glucocorticoids attempt to maintain the body in a state of readiness via sugar conversion and blood vessel sensitization to the adrenal hormones. However, to the body's great detriment, the main goal of ACTH and the glucocorticoids is to reduce inflammation, i.e., immune system function. So what is adaptive on a short-term basis may ultimately cause a host of diseases involving immune activity, such as cancer, infection, arthritis and multiple sclerosis. The effects of chronic stress may ultimately involve every gland targeted by the pituitary (Achterberg 1985).

Samuels (cited in Achterberg 1985) has proposed a stress/disease model which suggests that there are common causes for cancer, heart attacks, strokes, and other thrombotic diseases. These causes include: chronic stress, predisposing personality characteristics, and "chronic hyperactivation of neural, endocrine, immune, blood clotting (coagulation) and fibrinolytic systems" (Achterberg 1985, 130). He suggests that chronic stress both causes clotting mechanisms to become hyperactive and fibrinolytic mechanisms to fail. The subsequent blood clots are causally related to heart attacks and strokes. Furthermore, Samuels suggests the existence of "fibrin cocoons" which are created by excessive coagulation and act as sanctuaries for tumors. These cocoons shield the cancer cells from T-cells, as well as from radiation and chemotherapy interventions (Achterberg 1985, 30).

Also of interest in this discussion is the work of Pert and Ruff who have theorized about a neuropeptide and psychosomatic network wherein the mind and body continuously communicate using a language of biochemical. The result of this communication is the full gamut of human emotions. In their model, white blood cells are akin to little parts of the brain circulating around the body, manufacturing and discharging hormones. These receive communication directly from the brain and may perhaps also send messages back to the brain (Hall 1989).

While many of these theories, concerning the impact of stress and life factors on disease, point to the devastating effects of these factors, perhaps the picture is not as bleak as it may seem. It is noted that the mind-body dialogue can also be engaged to help strengthen and fine-tune the immunocompetence of the individual. While data are largely anecdotal at this point, mind-mediation to the ends of increasing the efficiency of the immune system has been reported (Simonton et al. 1978; Cousins 1979).

## SOME HYPOTHESES IN PSYCHONEUROIMMUNOLOGY

According to Melnechuk (1985, 22), "psychoneuroimmunology says that the immune system can be importantly influenced by psychological processes and that it can influence psychological processes in return."

Solomon (1985) has offered a number of hypotheses concerning the relationship between the immune and central nervous systems. One of these suggests that an individual's coping style as well as personality may influence his or her immunocompetence and subsequent susceptibility to disease. For example, persons having rheumatoid arthritis appear to have similar personality traits, such as masochism, moodiness, self-sacrifice, depression, and subservience. These traits are not apparent in nonarthritic patients who also show a physical predisposition to this disease (cited in Maranto 1988).

Similar personality profiles have also been noted in cancer patients. Nemiah and Sifneos (1970) have described the profile of alexithymia, or the inability to verbally express feelings, particularly negative ones. Alexithymic individuals appear to be predisposed to physical illness, are out of touch with their feelings, and are unable to express them. Solomon (1985) goes so far as to suggest that there is an "immunosuppression-prone personality" (cited in Maranto 1988).

Solomon (1985) also hypothesizes that there is a distinct relationship between emotional upset and distress and the incidence, severity of, and course of diseases that are immune-related. He states that "hardy" personality types are protected from the immunologic effects of upset and distress, and are typically characterized by having commitments to themselves, attitudes of vigorousness, control over their lives, and a sense of meaningfulness (cited in Maranto 1988).

Solomon and Temoshok (1987) have posed a variety of research questions in psychoneuroimmunology. With regard to the disease of AIDS, they question if emotional distress increases an individual's susceptibility to the AIDS virus. For example, homosexuals deal with the stressors of negative societal reactions and homophobic reactions, drug abusers demonstrate severe pathology with may be attributed to denial and the inability to deal with pain, and hemophiliacs have very stressful lives with limited existences and life-threatening incidences (cited in Maranto 1988).

## FACTORS WHICH AFFECT IMMUNE RESPONSE

Although the relationship is yet not fully understood, some researchers have suggested a relationship between psychosocial factors and immune responses (Broadhead et al. 1983; Coates et al. (1984); Fry and Weakland 1984; Jemmott and Locke 1984; McClelland et al. 1980; Palmblad 1981; Rider et al. 1985; Simonton et al. 1978; Wickramasekera 1987). Factors which may diminish immune function include: advancing age, over or under-nutrition, drugs and alcohol, stressful life changes, increased power-seeking, lack of sleep, loneliness, grief, bereavement, depression, dissatisfaction and helplessness.

Conversely, it has been suggested that the following may increase immune system functioning: hypnosis, meditation, imagery, relaxation, music, coping skills, and social support.

With regard to social support, Zich and Temoshok (1987) found the perceived availability of social support to AIDS patients was related to both the level of emotional distress and to the presence of symptoms and secondary disorders.

While continuing to utilize the psychoneuroimmunological model of the mind-body relationship, an examination is made of the current literature on the effects of music in medical interventions.

## REVIEW OF LITERATURE OF MEDICAL MUSIC THERAPY AS IT AFFECTS BIOMEDICAL AND PSYCHOSOCIAL DOMAINS

Standley (1986, 1989) conducted two meta-analyses of the literature of medical/dental applications of music. Based on the results of this analysis of 56 studies, the following dependent variables were positively affected by various applications of music (see Tables

1 and 2). The effect size of music on 130 dependent measures was analyzed, and it was found that music usage enhanced medical treatment in 126 of these.

Types of patients included in these research studies included surgical, burn, chronic pain, hypertensive, obstetric/gynecologic, spinal cord injured, stroke, brain-injured, neonatal, bronchoscopy, respiratory, dental, podiatric, respiratory impaired, terminal cancer, cerebral palsied, cardiac, and kidney dialysis.

## TABLE 1

### BIOMEDICAL APPLICATIONS OF MUSIC

| | |
|---|---|
| PAIN | GAIT IDENTIFICATION |
| USE OF OTHER ANALGESIA/ MEDICATIONS | LEVELS OF STRESS HORMONES (ACTH, CORTISOL, NORADRENALINE) |
| MOVEMENT | EMG LEVELS |
| WEIGHT GAIN | HEADACHE INTENSITY |
| CRYING | EFFECT OF ANESTHESIA |
| PERCEIVED LENGTH OF LABOR | CENTIMETERS OF DILATION |
| BLOOD PRESSURE | INFANT APGAR SCORES |
| PULSE RATE | GRASP STRENGTH |
| EXHALATION ABILITY | EMESIS INTENSITY AND LENGTH |
| MUSCLE TENSION | NAUSEA INTENSITY AND LENGTH |
| RESPIRATION RATE | INTRACRANIAL PRESSURE |
| WALKING SPEED | DAYS IN HOSPITAL |

**TABLE 2**

PSYCHOSOCIAL APPLICATIONS IN MEDICAL SETTINGS

PSYCHOSOCIAL APPLICATIONS OF MUSIC

| | |
|---|---|
| PERCEIVED PAIN | RELAXATION |
| ANXIETY | PERCEIVED BENEFITS TO PATIENTS/ VISITORS |
| PERCEIVED MOOD | SLEEP SATISFACTION |
| ATTITUDES | CHOICE OF ANESTHESIA |
| PERCEIVED CHILD BIRTH EXPERIENCE | HELPLESSNESS |
| PERCEIVED CONTENTMENT | NONSTRESS BEHAVIORS |
| RESPONSES ABOUT HOSPITALIZATION | PLEASURE |
| PERCEIVED DISTRACTION | |

## USES OF MUSIC IN MEDICAL MUSIC THERAPY

In Standley's analyses (1986, 1989) a variety of music techniques were utilized to affect positive biomedical or psychosocial changes in the medical subjects. These included taped music listening, group music sessions, music biofeedback, live music, instrumental playing, music relaxation, music an exercise, music and play therapy, music and Lamaze techniques, contingent music, music and imagery, and music and suggestion,

In addition to the music therapy techniques reported in the literature, there are a number of other techniques utilized in clinical practice which await initial and further investigation for possible efficacy in effecting medical changes and in enhancing immune function. These include music visualization (Simonton technique, Simonton et al. 1978), music systematic desensitization, music improvisation, music psychotherapy, guided imagery and music, music meditation, music acupuncture, music biofeedback, music vibrational therapy, and music entrainment techniques.

Some of these techniques, e.g., Simonton visualization, and psychotherapy have been utilized with some effectiveness in enhancing immune-related function. The research question is: Will music-based techniques (combining music with other techniques) and/or specific music therapy techniques serve to strengthen immune system functioning and thereby prevent or treat illness? As theoretical and research paradigms in behavioral medicine and psychoneuroimmunology develop, and continued evidence is discovered to support the role of psychosocial factors, i.e., emotions, stress, personality, social support and coping, in wellness and illness, it is believed that the role of music will be more clearly known and acknowledged. In addition, research on specific physiologic responses to music, e.g., in reducing stress hormones, in increasing beta-endorphin production, and in stimulating various neurotransmitter production, will further support the future role of music in preventing and treating immune-related dysfunctions.

Some preliminary work on the use of music in this regard has been positive and will be reported below.


## RESEARCH ON MUSIC AND IMMUNE FUNCTION

Several studies have examined the influence of music on immune function. Rider et al. (1985) proposed a specific model which demonstrates the mechanisms (neural and endocrine) by which music, imagery and progressive relaxation affect the adrenal corticosteroids (see Figure 3). Because large amounts of these hormones may be potentially detrimental to the immune system (Monjan 1981), this model has potential and indirect implications for the immune system. It is noted however, that this model does not provide for possible increases in immune response, but only decreases.

According to Rider et al. (1985, 47-49), the response to stress is initiated in the hypothalamus which has also been linked to immunological response.

> The music-imagery potential lies in the fact that the hypothalamus has strong connections to the limbic system. Achterberg and Lawlis (1980) have described a fronto-limbic system as the center of emotional processing, image formation, motor control and memory storage. The connection between Music/GI/PMR and health is very likely a mechanism involving a (neural) hypothalamic-frontolimbic loop and a (neuroendocrine) hypothalamic-immunologic loop.

In their study, these authors investigated the effects of taped music, progressive relaxation and guided imagery on the circadian amplitude, circadian reentrainment, and corticosteroid levels of shift workers. Results indicated a significant (p <0.007) decrease in circadian amplitude and a significant reentrainment of corticosteroids and finger temperature (p <.01). Corticosteroid levels decreased during the listening sessions, but not significantly so (p = .15).

Rider et al. (1988), in another study, investigated the influence of music and imagery on the production of secretory immunoglobin A (IgA) (from saliva samples). Results showed that both the music and the imagery groups produced higher levels of secretory IgA than the control group for all three trials. In addition, for the second and third trials, the imagery treatment was more effective than the music treatment in producing a secretory IgA increase.

Tsao et al. (1989) studied the influence of music, directed imagery, combined imagery and music, and no treatment on the immune responses of 99 college students. Secretory IgA (from saliva samples) and levels of emotional arousal were the dependent variables. Results showed significant increases in IgA levels for both the music (p <.006) an the imagery groups (p <.01). The combined music and imagery group showed an increase in IgA production, although this was nonsignificant (p <.10). Of interest is the fact that the control group had a significant decrease in immune response (p <.005).

With regard to levels of emotional arousal, it was found that compared to the control group, the combined music and imagery treatment produced significantly higher levels of relaxation and peacefulness (p <.05). Also, the subjects in the imagery treatment felt more relaxed than did those in the control group (p <.05). Further analyses revealed that subjects' stress levels related to finances and interpersonal relationships correlated significantly with their immune responses.

## CONCLUSIONS

The field of psychoneuroimmunology is a new one, still at a stage where various hypotheses are being developed and tested experimentally. These ideas regarding the connections between the mind and body and possible role of music therein are presented here not as conclusive facts, but rather as food for thought and future research. In this respect much caution should be exercised in interpreting the position offered, and no generalizations should be made at this juncture.

However, with these caveats aside, it must be stated that this field is a most exciting one for physicians and music therapists and offers a host of opportunities for future research.

We seem to have some good preliminary evidence at this point of the negative psychological factors which may affect immune functioning. Future research should investigate the role of music therapy in diminishing the effects of stress, in easing loss and bereavement, in providing social support, in modifying personality traits and coping types, and in facilitating expression of feelings (Maranto 1988).

The possible role of music therapy in increasing immune functioning and health also warrants further investigation, e.g., in increasing emotional hardiness, in increasing personal meaningfulness, and in supporting imagery and visualization.

Because music is able to affect both biomedical and psychosocial aspects of the person both individually and simultaneously, it may offer some, if not unique, benefits in the area of psychoneuroimmunology.

Music is without doubt an emotional communicator, and the right kind of music for the individual offers a positive emotional experience. Positive emotional experiences may enhance the immune system functioning. Therefore, it is logical to believe that the right type of music will function in a similar manner. It will require work on the part of music therapists to determine the right music for the individual, including selection, type, genre, etc., and this will require a very deliberate, controlled process.

Also, future research should consider the ability of music to create "thrill" responses in individuals (Goldstein 1980). These responses should be examined for their neurochemical bases and their relevance to immune system function.

Lastly, because the immune system is so complex, music's effects should be examined on a variety of immune measures, expanding upon the research already done with secretory IgA.

## REFERENCE LIST

Achterberg, J. 1985. *Imagery in Healing: Shamanism and Modern Medicine*. Boston, MA: New Science Library.

Ader, R., and Cohen, N. 1975. Behaviorally conditioned immunosuppression. *Psychosomatic Medicine* 37:333-240.

Broadhead, W.E. et al. 1983. The epidemiologic evidence for a relationship between social support and health. *American Journal of Epidemiology* 117:521-537.

Coates, T.J.; Temoshok, L.; and Mandel, J. 1984. Psychological research is essential to understanding and treating AIDS. *American Psychologist* 39:1309-1314.

Cousins, N. 1979. *Anatomy of an Illness as Perceived by the Patient*. New York: Norton.

Fry, W.F., and Weakland, J.H. 1984. Healing and hypnosis. *Advances* 1:60-63.

Goldstein, A. 1980. Thrills in response to music and other stimuli. *Physiological Psychology* 8:126-129.

Hall, S. 1989. A molecular code links emotions, mind and health. *Smithsonian* 20:59-74.

Jemmott J.B., and Locke S.E. 1984. Psychosocial, immunologic mediation and human susceptibility to infectious diseases: How much do we know? *Psychological Bulletin* 95:78-108.

Lloyd, R. 1987. *Explorations in Psychoneuroimmunology*. Orlando, FL: Grune and Stratton.

Maranto, C.D. 1988. AIDS: Information and issues for music therapists. *Music Therapy Perspectives* 5:78-81.

McClelland, D.C.; Floor, E.; Davidson, R.J.; and Saron, J. 1980. Stressed power motivation, sympathetic activation, immune function and illness. *Journal of Human Stress* 6:11-19.

Melnechuk, T. 1985. Why has psychoneuroimmunology been controversial? *Advances* 2:22-38.

Monjan, A.A. 1981. Stress and immunological competence: Studies in animals. In *Psychoneuroimmunology*, edited by R. Ader, 185-228. New York: Academic Press.

Nemiah, J.C., and Sifneos P.E. 1970. Affect and fantasy in patients with psychosomatic disorders. In *Modern Trends in Psychosomatic Medicine*, edited by O.W. Hill, 26-31. New York: Appleton-Century Crofts.

Palmblad, F. 1981. Stress and immunologic competence: Studies in men. In *Psychoneuroimmunology*, edited by R. Ader, 229-254. New York: Academic Press.

Rider, M.S. 1985. Treating chronic disease and pain with music-mediated imagery. *The Arts in Psychotherapy* 14:113-120.

Rider, M.S.; Floyd, J.W.; and Kirkpatrick, J. 1985. The effects of music, imagery and relaxation on adrenal corticosteroids and the reentrainment of circadian rhythms. *Journal of Music Therapy* 22:46-58.

Rider, M.S.; Achterberg J.; Lawlis, G.F.; Goven, A.; Toledo R.; and Butler, J.R. 1988. Effect of biological imagery on antibody production and health. Unpublished manuscript.

Rossi, E. 1986. The Psychobiology of Mind-Body Healing. New York: Norton.

Simonton, O.C.; Matthews-Simonton, S.; and Craighton, J. 1978. *Getting Well Again*. Los Angeles: J.P. Tarcher, Inc.

Solomon, G.F. 1985. The emerging field of psychoneuroimmunology with a special note on AIDS. *Advances* 2:6-19.

Solomon, G.F., and Temoshok, L. 1987. A psychoneuroimmunologic perspective of AIDS research: Questions, preliminary findings and suggestions. *Journal of Applied Social Psychology* 17:286-308.

Standley, J.M. 1986. Music research in medical/dental treatment: Meta-analysis and clinical applications. *Journal of Music Therapy* 23:56-122.

_____. 1989. Meta-analysis of research in music and medical treatment: Effect size as a basis for comparison across multiple dependent and independent variables. Paper presented at the VI International Music Medicine Symposium, Rancho Mirage, CA.

Tsao, C.C.; Gordon, T.F.; Maranto C.D.; Lerman, C.; and Morasko, D. 1991. The effects of music and directed biological imagery on immune response (S-IgA). In *Applications of Music in Medicine,* edited by C.D. Maranto. Washington DC: National Association for Music Therapy, Inc.

Suter, S. 1986. *Health Psychophysiology.* Hillsdale, NJ: Lawrence Erlbaum Associates.

Wickramasekera, I. 1987. Risk factors leading to chronic stress-related symptoms. *Advances* 4:9-36.

Zich, J., and Temoshok, L. 1987. Perceptions of social support in men with AIDS and ARC: Relationships with distress and hardiness. *Journal of Applied Social Psychology* 17:193-215.

RELAXATION                    MUSIC                    IMAGERY

FRONTO-LIMBIC SYSTEM

Neurotransmitters

HYPOTHALAMUS

PITUITARY

ADRENAL

Corticosteroids

IMMUNE SYSTEM

*Figure 3.*

# THE EFFECTS OF EARLY TRAINING IN MUSIC AND DANCE ON THE SOCIO-EMOTIONAL, SCHOLASTIC, AND AESTHETIC DEVELOPMENT OF PRE-TEENAGE AND TEENAGE GIRLS

Vladimir J. Konečni
Laura Hersh
Avery Kenyon

## 1. INTRODUCTION

Progressively younger age groups seem to be affected by the general societal emphasis on achievement and competition in our post-industrial world (e.g., Josselyn 1952). The dramatic entrance of women into the labor market on a large scale, and the changing perceptions of women's social, political, and economic roles since World War II, have combined to apply especially strong competitive and achievement pressures on young women (Gottlieb and Ramsey 1964). Perhaps more than ever, eager and ambitious parents may be insisting that their daughters succeed, and viewing as necessary to ensure such success the young women's ever-earlier and more time-consuming concerted effort, dedication, practice, and training.

The purpose of the present project is to focus on the pre-teenage and teenage girls who dedicate themselves, presumably with varying degrees of pressure from their parents, to *artistic* early training, specifically *music and dance,* respectively. The effects of such training on the girls' socio-emotional, psychological, sexual, scholastic, and aesthetic development will be examined. The underlying assumption is that intensive efforts in a particular area complement the influences of family members, teachers, and peers, as well as the maturation process, and will be reflected in the overall socialization and development process (Bandura and Walters 1963; Bronfenbrenner 1985; Gargiulo et al. 1987).

There is, of course, a large biographical and autobiographical literature on the development and experiences of particular, extremely gifted, dancers and musicians in childhood and adolescence. There are, furthermore, numerous "behind-the-scenes," "tell-all" accounts differing greatly in informational value. Finally, there are excellent sources dealing with the teaching of dance, voice, and instrumental music at different ages and other music education issues. What seems to be missing, however, in both the dance/music and psychological literatures, is reliable information about the effects of early training in dance and music (instrumental and voice) on average, "run-of-the-mill" students. None of these, by definition, is likely to rise to the exalted heights described in biographical accounts, yet music and dance nevertheless represent for them a considerable mental, emotional, and physical investment, at least for a period of time in the pre-teenage and teenage years.

In the present project, an attempt to gain a comprehensive perspective on this problem was made by administering a detailed, multifaceted questionnaire to music and ballet pre-teenage and early-teenage female students. Their responses were compared to those of girls who concentrated on: (a) science, computing, or mathematics (a nonartistic, nonathletic specialization, the latter feature being common with playing an instrument, but not with ballet), and (b) horseback riding (an athletic activity, like ballet, but a nonartistic one, unlike both ballet and playing an instrument). The science/mathematics and horseback riding groups can thus be thought of as special controls for the music and ballet students on the artistic/nonartistic and athletic/nonathletic dimensions. An additional control group with no particular area of concentration, but belonging to a similar socio-economic stratum, was also used.

In addition to an intrinsic interest in music and ballet, these particular areas of dedication were investigated because they require a considerable amount of time, focused energy, sacrifice, and commitment even of students who engage in these activities because of parental pressure and who are unlikely to decide on them as eventual career choices.

The science/computing/mathematics groups presented an interesting comparison because of the relatively greater encouragement (and pressure) that young women have presumably begun to receive in these areas as sexism—at least overt—has waned.

Finally, using horseback riding as an additional control presented an opportunity to obtain some information about this inherently interesting sports activity. Inexplicably, it has been almost entirely ignored in recent books on sport psychology (e.g., Alderman 1974; Carron 1980; Cratty 1981; Fisher 1976; Gill 1986; Lawther 1972; Ryan 1981). Yet because the sport, in addition to equitation per se, almost always involves caring intensely and being responsible for an animal on a daily basis, it is of interest from a developmental point of view.

## 2. METHOD

### 2.1 Experimental Participants

All 93 experimental participants resided in San Diego County, California. The girls attended classes in the various performing-arts academies, ballet schools, and horseback riding centers, respectively. Girls with a strong dedication to science, computing, or mathematics, as well as the controls, were contacted through various private and public ("magnet") schools. In the case of large classes, experimental participants were selected randomly (as opposed to teachers' recommendations being followed). In some cases, an entire group of girls that was, for example, studying with a particular teacher, was included in the study.

The composition of the five research groups was as follows:

*Music group* (M in further text: instrument and voice training): A total of 20 questionnaires was received form students attending classes at two different schools for performing arts and one private instructor (mean age = 11.6 years; range = 9-14 years);

*Ballet group* (B): A total of 18 questionnaires was received from students attending two ballet schools (mean age = 11.5 years; range = 10-14 years);

*Science group* (S): A total of 19 questionnaires was received from one private and one public ("magnet") school (mean age = 11 years; range = 9-14 years);

*Horseback riding group* (HR): A total of 14 questionnaires was obtained from students at two riding schools/centers (mean age = 10 years; range 9-13 years);

*Control group* (C): A total of 22 questionnaires was received from students at one private and one public school (mean age = 10.5 years; range 10-11 years).

The structure of the experimental-participant families did not differ across groups. There was a similar proportion of only (9 of 93 = 10% of the entire sample) first-born (38%), second-born (27%), middle (9%), and youngest (17%) children in the five groups.

## 2.2  Questionnaires

The entire questionnaire is included as Appendix 1. Questions on pages 208-209 of the Appendix were answered only by the ballet students (other groups answered questions specifically designed for them). The girls filled the questionnaires on their own, free of supervision or suggestions from parents, teachers, or the researchers (LH and AK, the second and third authors respectively; they were UCSD undergraduates at the time when the study was conducted) who contacted the schools/instructors/riding centers. The questionnaire was modified for each of the five groups (where necessary) in order to address the girls' different focal activities. In addition to the basic demographic information, the following areas of interest were dealt with:

*Daily routine:* This section was concerned with the distribution of the girls' time over the respective focal activities, schoolwork, and other activities on a typical day;

*Scholastic preferences and difficulties*: This section explored the relationship between the focal activity and schoolwork;

*Social activities:* This section examined the effect of the focal activity on friendship choices (female and male) and social interests, activities, and hobbies; an entire subsection dealt with television-watching preferences;

*Focal activity:* Details of the girls' involvement in the respective focal activities were obtained in this section, as well as how seriously these activities fitted in their future (including career) plans;

*Aesthetic preferences:* Some rudimentary information was obtained about the girls preferences in the areas of music and visual art.

## 3.  RESULTS

### 3.1.  Daily  Routine

Students in various groups spent roughly the same number of hours at school on the average (about seven), but differed in the amount of time they spent doing homework [$\chi^2$ (4) = 15.08, p<.01; B = 1.90 hours/day, HR = 1.43 h/d; M = 1.28 h/d, S = 1.07 h/d, and C = .88 h/d]. The B and M subjects also tended to go to bed later and get up earlier than did the girls in the other groups (p<.15).

None of the groups were particularly active in various school clubs, with the exception of drama, in which the M group seemed especially interested [$\chi^2$ (4) - 11.30, p<.05]. Presumably because of their involvement in the respective focal activities, the B, M, and HR groups spent significantly less time with their families than did the S and C students [$\chi^2$ (4) = 11.40, p<.05]. Furthermore, unlike the M subjects, the B and HR groups also tended to claim that there were no activities they regularly did with their families [$\chi^2$ (4) = 15.38, p<.01].

Within their families, the girls in all five groups tended to an overwhelming extent to spend time with their mothers, the time with their sisters being a distant second; a negligible amount of time was spent with fathers and brothers. The responses were analogous for the question about the family member who influenced the subjects the most.

## 3.2 Scholastic Preferences and Difficulties

There was a nonsignificant tendency [$\chi^2$ (8) = 12.72, p<.20] for C and HR students to like school the least. In terms of specific subjects, the five groups did not differ from each other, in that all liked art and physical education a great deal and equally; the one interesting exception was the M group, whose members did not much enrol in classes on, and did not like, (visual) art. C and HB students were similar to each other in that both groups disliked English, foreign language, history, mathematics, and science; in contrast, the B, M, and S students liked all of these subjects considerably and were similar to each other in this regard (all of the appropriate chi-squares were significant at least at the .05 level). The preferences of the B and M students in particular were strikingly similar.

In terms of the results for subject difficulty, art and English were rated as the easiest subjects by all groups, except for the M group finding art difficult. Science and mathematics courses were rated as easy by the S students, and difficult by the other four groups. In contrast, history was difficult for the S, HR, and C students, but rated as relatively easy by both the B and M groups. (All the relevant $\chi^2$'s were again significant at least at the .05 level).

Of the 93 students in the study, no less than 85 (91%) said they planned to go to college, but of the eight who checked "No" or "No response" to this question, five had ballet as the focal activity.

## 3.3 Social Activities

Students in all five groups stated that they had enough time to be with friends. In response to the question about where they tended to meet friends first, the B group subjects differed significantly from the other five groups [$\chi^2$ (4) = 51.78, p<.001) in that they overwhelmingly made friends through their "focal activity," ballet, whereas the others listed school, neighborhood, and so on. The B group also spent considerably less time with friends than did the other four groups ($\chi^2$ (4) = 18.14, p<.01]: whereas upward of 85% of the S, M, HR, and C groups stated that they spent 2-4 hours per day with friends on weekdays, only 41% of the B subjects spent that long, the remainder checking off the 0-1 hour option. A similar pattern of results also emerged for the time spent with friends on weekends, except that the M subjects' responses now resembled those of the B group.

In terms of the activity they engaged in when with friends, the B and HR subjects differed sharply from the other three groups in that they predominantly carried out their respective focal activities with friends [$\chi^2$ (4) = 48.84, p<.001]. The S and C subjects tended to watch more television, both alone and with friends, than the B, M, and HR subjects, but this effect was only marginally significant [$\chi^2$ (4) = 7.99, p<.10]. With regard to the type of program watched, the S and C subjects watched a great deal of MTV, the HR groups watched sports programs, the M group watched the PBS music programs, and the S and B groups liked the PBS educations programs more than did the other groups (all chi-squares were significant at the .05 level). The groups did not differ in how frequently they listened to music, played games, went to movies, or studied with friends. All the girls seemed to spend a great many nights at each other's houses. Time with friends was rated as very important by subjects in all groups and they did not differ in the number of close friends they listed as having.

A few of the C, M, and HR girls stated they had a boyfriend (not a single S or B girl said so), but considering the girls' age and their claim that the boyfriends did not take much of their free time, it seems likely that they interpreted the concept very loosely. Very few girls stated that they did not want, or have not looked for, a boyfriend: Instead the response of choice across all groups was that they had not been asked or that they had not found someone they liked. The general pattern of these results suggests that the girls were responding candidly to the questionnaire.

The girls reported having a wide variety of hobbies, with no clear pattern of inter-group differences emerging. The time spent on a hobby did not differ across groups, not did the girls' responses about hobbies they would pursue if they had more time.

## 3.4 Focal Activity

There are considerable and statistically significant differences (p<.01) in the extent to which the different focal activities were enjoyed by the subjects. On a 5-point scale, where "enjoy very little" was coded as 0 and "enjoy very much" as 4, the mean group results were: HR = 3.93, B = 3.89, M = 3.21, and S = 2.26. Thirty of the total 32 B and HR subjects marked the very top of the enjoyment scale. Subjects who engaged in their focal activity at school (S and 80% of M students), on the whole stated that they liked school much more because it gave them the opportunity to carry out the respective focal activity.

There were similar (also statistically significant) differences in the average response to the question "How important is it for you to be good at your focal activity?": HR = 3.57, B = 3.44, M = 2.65, and S = 1.27, where 4 = "very important" and 0 = "not important."

The groups differed greatly in how many times per week they took lessons in, or practiced, their focal activity. Fourteen of the 18 B subjects practiced ballet at least 4 times per week (7 of the B subjects 4 times per week, 3 of the B subjects 7 times per week). Ten of the 14 HR subjects rode at least 3 times per week. In the case of the M group, there was a bimodal distribution: of the 20 subjects, 7 practiced only once a week (presumably at school), whereas 10 did it at least 5 times per week (and 4 of these did it 7 times per week). The S subjects, in contrast, engaged in the focal activity much less intensely: Ten of 19 subjects had only one lesson per week, with another 6 equally split between 2 and 3 lessons per week. The average duration of a single class by research group was B = 1.73 hours, HR = 1.13, M = .79, and S = .78.

When information about the average frequency and duration of classes is combined on a weekly basis, it becomes evident that whereas the B subjects spent 8.04 hours a week engaged in ballet, and the HR and M subjects 3.31 and 3.00 hours per week, respectively, the S subjects average only 1.68 hours per week.

When the previously mentioned time spent by the various groups on doing homework (under Daily Routine) is added to the time spent on the respective focal activities, the following dramatically different average weekly totals are obtained for the various groups: B = 21.36 hours per week, HR = 13.32 hrs/wk, M = 11.96 hrs/wk, and S = 9.14 hrs.wk. By comparison, the C subjects, without a focal activity, do their homework 6.16 hrs/wk.

The parents of the M, HR, and B subjects were highly encouraging and supportive of their daughters with regard to the pursuit of the focal activity (upward of 3.0 on a 5-point scale where 4 was maximum for all three groups), and these girls, furthermore, tended also to be strongly encouraged by their friends (scores were in the 2.6 — 2.8 range on an analogous scale). In sharp contrast, the S subjects were encouraged by neither their parents nor friends (1.74 and 1.53 respectively).

The B, M, and HR groups were also highly similar to each other, and very different from the S group, in their claim that they would continue with their focal activity even if their parents did not want them to ($\chi^2$ (3) = 11.57, p<.001] and even if it meant losing their friends [$\chi^2$ (3) = 14.20, p<.001]. For example, whereas 15 of the 18 B subjects (83%) said they would continue even if their parents did not want them to, only 8 of 18 (44%) S subjects said so.

Analogous, and even more dramatic, differences were obtained for the choice between losing friends and continuing with the focal activity. In response to the question "How much time you presently spend with friends would you give up to become better at your focal activity?", on a 5-point scale, where 0 meant "Give up no time" and 4 meant "Give it all up," the average group results were as follows: B = 2.56, HR - 2.00, M = 1.65, and S = 1.11. In addition, whereas around 55% of the B and HR subjects said that they did not participate in school dances, plays, and clubs because the focal activity was more important, only 20% of the M subjects and none of the nineteen S subjects said so.

Finally, responses to the question "How serious are you about making your focal activity your career?" were instructive. Twelve of 18 B subjects (66%) indicated that ballet "would be" their career or that they were "fairly certain" of this. The percentages were 50, 30, and 17 for the HR, M, and S groups respectively.

### 3.5 Aesthetic Preferences

The subjects' aesthetic inclinations were crudely examined by asking them about the type of pictures or posters that adorn their bedrooms and their music-listening preferences.

In almost all cases, the subjects themselves chose what to put on the walls of their bedroom. While there was a considerable difference in the average number of pictures or posters (ranging form 6.02 for C to 4.73 for M and 3.81 for B), there were few unexpected differences in the type of pictures/posters preferred by the different groups (B subjects liked pictures of ballerinas, HR subjects liked those of horses, and so on). There was no evidence whatsoever that the B and M subjects had an artistically more advanced taste.

With regard to music-listening, C subjects claimed to listen to it the most (2.34 hours per day), followed by M and S subjects (2.15 and 2.09 hours per day respectively); B and HR subjects listened the least (1.49 and 1.41 hours, respectively). "Soft-rock," "hard rock," or "Top 40" were the most common top choices for all 5 groups. However, whereas 8 of the 18 B subjects and 11 of the 20 M subjects indicated classical music as one of their choices, none in the S group and virtually no other subjects mentioned it.

## DISCUSSION

One of the common and unflattering stereotypes about children and teenagers who are heavily involved in ballet and music is that they are working on one track only and often under an unpleasant degree of pressure from driving parents who are fulfilling their own ambitions, rather than doing what is good for the child. Such children are supposed to do poorly in regular school subjects, to have few friends and no time for them, and generally to be somehow stunted in their overall psycho-emotional and social development. Nothing could be further from the truth, given the results obtained the present study.

Most ballet and some of the music subjects, but also many of the horseback-riding ones, were indeed very serious about their respective focal activities: All three groups spent less time with their families than the S and C groups. They said they would continue practicing the focal activity regardless of the opinions of parents and friends, and that they would give up time with friends if it meant getting better at their focal activity (the patterns for the latter was B>HR>M). The total time spent on the focal activity and regular homework was three times as much as the control group spent (on homework) in the case of ballet subjects, and about twice as much for the HR and M groups. Both B and HR subjects also said that there were social activities they did not pursue at school because of their focal commitments. In fact, the B and M subjects had less time for sleep than other groups.

Such findings are more than balanced by the following facts. The B, HR, and most M students seemed to be thrilled by their participation in the focal activity, there being no indication whatsoever that parental pressure, the desire to please the parents, or pure snobbery were instrumental. Their parents were supportive, but so, importantly, were their friends. These friends could thus be presumed not to feel left out and, indeed, the subjects in these three groups valued their friendships as much as did the S and C groups. It is true that the ballet subjects' friends were typically other ballet students and that none of these subjects reported having a boyfriend (unlike the M and HR subjects, but like the S ones), but regarding such information negatively would seem to be an unjustifiable value judgement.

The ballet subjects in particular, but also the HR and M ones, in fact found more time to do homework than did the S and C groups. The B and M groups had similar preferences for different school subjects, preferences which differed from those of other groups, including HR; the B and M subjects also differed from other groups in their preference for the educational and classical music Public Broadcasting Service programming.

Overall, the impression one formed about the ballet subjects was highly positive. They took ballet very seriously, but still enjoyed it; they were very hard-working, but also seemed well-adjusted and content young people. The only reservation one might have is that too many of these subjects wished to make ballet their career. Considering the "market conditions" for ballet, this may not be realistic, but having grace and a well-proportioned physique may be an adequate compensation for such disappointment.

As is clear from the above review of findings, the music subjects were in many important respects similar to subjects with ballet as the focal activity, and the similarities are even more pronounced when the findings for the two "types" of music subjects are analyzed separately. It may be recalled that of the 20 subjects, 7 practiced only once a week, whereas 10 did it at least 5 times per week, and 4 of these did it daily. The former sub-group was playing an instrument as a school subject, "for fun," whereas the subjects in the latter sub group were clearly far more dedicated to their instrument or voice training, had private lessons, and practiced on their own.

Horseback riding turned out to be an aptly chosen control (physical) activity, in that these subjects displayed a remarkable dedication to their focal commitment. The similarities and differences between this group's responses and those of the B and M groups were informative. Much like ballet and music, horseback riding is for many practitioners a way of life, but here also there were no indications of poor psycho-social adjustment, failure in academic subjects, and so on.

To the extent that the main purpose of including the S group was its supposed considerable dedication to a mental (but nonartistic) activity, it is clear that these S subjects were not satisfactory controls. They simply did not work nearly as hard at either science/computing/mathematics or other school subjects as did the B, M, and HR groups. Even though they were more similar to the B, M, and HR groups than to the C group on a number of important dimensions, in a future study, S subjects would have to be more carefully chosen. The possibility remains, however, that it is difficult to find a large number of girls (or boys) *extraordinarily* dedicated to science or mathematics at this age even in the science classes of magnet schools.

Overall, the present research was able to answer successfully some preliminary questions about the impact of intensive involvement in ballet and music on girls' psycho-social development.

## REFERENCE LIST

Alderman, R.B. 1974. *Psychological Behavior in Sport*. Philadelphia: W.B. Saunders.

Bandura, A., and Walters, R.H. 1963. *Social Learning and Personality Development*. New York: Holt.

Bronfenbrenner, U. 1985. Interacting systems in human development. Research paradigms: Present and future. Paper presented at a meeting of the Society for Research in Child Development Study Group, Cornell University, Ithaca, NY.

Carron, A.V. 1980. *Social Psychology of Sport*. Ithaca, NY: Mouvement Publications.

Cratty, B.J. 1981. *Social Psychology in Athletics*. Englewood Cliffs, NJ: Prentice-Hall.

Fisher, A.C. 1976. *Psychology of Sport*. Palo Alto, CA: Mayfield.

Gargiulo, J.; Attie, I.; Brooks-Gunn, J.; and Warren, M.P. 1987. Girls' dating behavior as a function of social context and maturation. *Developmental Psychology* 23:730-737.

Gill, D.L. 1986. *Psychological Dynamics of Sport*. Champaign, IL: Human Kinetics Publishers.

Gottlieb, D., and Ramsey, C.E. 1964. *The American Adolescent*. Homewood, IL: Dorsey.

Josselyn, I.M. 1952. *The Adolescent and His World*. New York: Family Service Association of America.

Lawther, J.D. 1972. *Sport Psychology*. Englewood Cliffs, NJ: Prentice-Hall.

Ryan, F. (1981). *Sports and Psychology*. Englewood Cliffs, NJ: Prentice-Hall.

## APPENDIX 1

Date _____

Please complete this questionnaire to the best of your ability.

**All information will be kept strictly confidential**


Name _____ Age _____

Home Address _____
              Street                    City              Zip Code

Home Phone Number _____


### Education

School (Name of) _____ Grade _____

At what time do you arrive at school? _____ A.M. or P.M.

At what time do you leave school? _____ A.M. or P.M.

Do you receive any school credit for dancing? (ex. as an alternative to physical education)

Yes/No (please circle one)

Do you practice ballet under the guidance of an instructor while at school?   Yes/No

How much time to you usually spend doing homework each day? (Please check one)

_____ 0-30 mins      _____ 30 mins-1 hr.      _____ 1-2 hrs

_____ 2-3 hrs        _____ 3 hrs or more

Do you like school? (Please circle the number that best describes your attitude)

Greatly dislike school                                        Love school

        1              2              3              4              5

Please rank these subjects according to how much you enjoy them. (NE for never enrolled in that subject)

|  | Like very much | | | Dislike very much | | |
|---|---|---|---|---|---|---|
| English | 1 | 2 | 3 | 4 | 5 | NE |
| Math | 1 | 2 | 3 | 4 | 5 | NE |
| Foreign Language | 1 | 2 | 3 | 4 | 5 | NE |
| Science | 1 | 2 | 3 | 4 | 5 | NE |
| History | 1 | 2 | 3 | 4 | 5 | NE |
| Art | 1 | 2 | 3 | 4 | 5 | NE |
| Physical Ed. | 1 | 2 | 3 | 4 | 5 | NE |
| Other_____ | 1 | 2 | 3 | 4 | 5 | NE |
| (Please specify subject) | | | | | | |

Please rank these subjects according to how difficult they are for you.

|  | Very Easy | | Challenging | | Very Difficult | |
|---|---|---|---|---|---|---|
| English | 1 | 2 | 3 | 4 | 5 | NE |
| Math | 1 | 2 | 3 | 4 | 5 | NE |
| Foreign Language | 1 | 2 | 3 | 4 | 5 | NE |
| Science | 1 | 2 | 3 | 4 | 5 | NE |
| History | 1 | 2 | 3 | 4 | 5 | NE |
| Art | 1 | 2 | 3 | 4 | 5 | NE |
| Physical Ed. | 1 | 2 | 3 | 4 | 5 | NE |
| Other_____ | 1 | 2 | 3 | 4 | 5 | NE |
| (Please specify subject) | | | | | | |

Does ballet affect how much you enjoy school?

|  | No Effect |  |  |  | Greatly Affects |
|---|---|---|---|---|---|
|  | 1 | 2 | 3 | 4 | 5 |

Do you enjoy school more or less because of ballet?

|  | Much more |  | Neither |  | Much Less |
|---|---|---|---|---|---|
|  | 1 | 2 | 3 | 4 | 5 |

Do you participate in school related activities?

| Dances | Yes/No |
| Plays | Yes/No |
| Band | Yes/No |
| Clubs | Yes/No |
| Other | Yes/No | please specify _____ |

If you answered "No" to any of the above activities, is it because dancing takes up your time instead?          Yes/No

## Friendships

Do you have time to spend with friends?          Yes/No

If you have friends, how many to do you have?          _____

Where did you meet your friends? (Please check appropriate response)

School _____ Ballet _____ Neighborhood _____

Other (please specify where and/or how) _____

_____

How much time do you usually spend with your friend(s) each weekday? (Please check appropriate answer)

_____ 0-1 hr          _____ 2-4 hrs          _____ 5-8 hrs

_____ 8-12 hrs        _____ 12 or more hrs per day

How much time do you usually spend with your friend(s) on weekends?

_____ 0-1 hr          _____ 2-4 hrs          _____ 5-10 hrs

_____ 10-20 hrs       _____ 20 or more hrs

What do you do with your friends? (Check appropriate answers)

_____ practice ballet                    _____ study

_____ watch T.V.                         _____ go to movie

_____ spend the night at each            _____ go out to eat
               other's houses
_____ listen to music                    _____ spend school recess
                                                               together

_____ play games (please                 _____ other
               specify games                                 (please specify)

            _____

            _____

How important is the time you spend with your friends

            Very Important                          Not at all Important
                1        2        3        4        5
How much of the time that you presently spend with friends would you give up to
become a better dancer?

            Give It all Up                          Give No Time Up
                1        2        3        4        5

How many of your friends that you have thought about while answering these past questions were what you consider very close or best friends? (Please check appropriate number)

_____ 0     _____ 1     _____ 2     _____ 3     _____ 4     _____ 5

If more than 5, please specify how many _____

Do you have a boyfriend?          Yes/No

If yes, does your relationship take up a lot of your free time?          Yes/No

Would you give up your relationship for dancing?          Yes/No

If you do not have a boyfriend, is the reason because:

_____ you do not want one

_____ you do not have time for one

_____ you have not been asked to go out by anyone

_____ you have not found someone you like

_____ other (please specify) _____

## Other   Activities

Do you have any hobbies or interests that you spend time on each week          Yes/No

If yes, what _____

How many hours per week or day? _____

Do you wish you could spend more time doing it?     Yes/No

Are there any social activities or hobbies that you are not presently involved in, but would like to participate in?  Yes/No

If yes, what _____

Is dancing keeping you from getting involved?          Yes/No

Do you enjoy watching television?

|        Enjoy Very Much        |        | Don't Enjoy At All |        |
|:---:|:---:|:---:|:---:|:---:|
| 1 | 2 | 3 | 4 | 5 |

How many hours per day to you watch television?

_____ 0      _____ 1      _____ 2      _____ 3      _____ 4      _____ 5

_____ 5 or more hours

What kinds of programs do you watch?

_____ Sports

_____ Situation Comedies

_____ Soap Operas

_____ Wildlife Documentaries

_____ M.T.V.

_____ Science Fiction Shows

_____ High Action Drama

_____ Educational

_____ Consumer Reports

_____ News

_____ Suspense Drama Serials

_____ Religion Oriented Shows

_____ Disney Channel

_____ Movies

_____ Game Shows

_____ P.B.S.

_____ Special Performances
              (i.e. ballets)

_____ Musicals, Plays, Operas
              Symphonies

_____ Cartoons

_____ Televised Auction Channels

_____ Talk Shows

_____ Weather

_____ Congressional Channel

_____ Other
              (please specify)

              _____

**Family**

How much time to do you spend with your family each day?

_____ less than 1 hr        _____ 2-3 hrs        _____ 4-6 hrs        _____ 6-10 hrs

_____ more than 10 hrs

Do you have any sisters?        Yes/No        If yes, how many? _____

How old is/are your sister(s) _____

Do you have any brothers?        Yes/No        If yes, how many? _____

How old is/are your brother(s) _____

With which person in your family do spend the most time? (Check one)

_____ mother        _____ father

_____ sister        _____ brother

Which family member influences you the most?

_____ mother        _____ father

_____ sister        _____ brother

Do you have any activities that you do regularly with your family?        Yes/No

If yes, what? _____

With which family member(s)? _____

When or how often? _____

What time do you usually go to bed?

        Weekdays _____        Weekends _____

What time do you usually wake up?

        Weekdays _____        Weekends _____

## Ballet                  [This page and the next were for the Ballet group only.]

How much to you enjoy ballet?

|     Very Much |     |     |     |  Very Little |
| :---: | :---: | :---: | :---: | :---: |
| 1 | 2 | 3 | 4 | 5 |

How important is it to you to be a dancer?

|   Very Important |     |     |     |  Not Very Important |
| :---: | :---: | :---: | :---: | :---: |
| 1 | 2 | 3 | 4 | 5 |

How many times a week do you attend ballet class?

_____ 1      _____ 2      _____ 3      _____ 4      _____ 5

_____ 6      _____ 7

How long are your classes?

_____ less than 30 mins      _____ 30 mins - 1 hr      _____ 1 - 1.5 hrs

_____ 2 hrs      _____ greater than 2 hrs

How many times per week do you usually practice ballet or do something to improve your dancing?

_____ 1      _____ 2      _____ 3      _____ 4      _____ 5

_____ 6      _____ 7

How much time do these practices take?

_____ less than 30 mins      _____ 30 mins - 1 hr      _____ 1 - 2 hrs

_____ 2 - 4 hrs      _____ greater than 4 hrs

How serious are you about making dancing your career?

| It Will Be<br>My Career | | | | It Will Definitely<br>Not Be My Career |
| :---: | :---: | :---: | :---: | :---: |
| 1 | 2 | 3 | 4 | 5 |

Do you plan to go to college?        Yes/No

Do you get a lot of encouragement to be a dancer from your parents?

| A Lot of Encouraging | | | | They Discourage Me |
| :---: | :---: | :---: | :---: | :---: |
| 1 | 2 | 3 | 4 | 5 |

Do you get a lot of support from your friends to keep dancing?

| A Lot of Encouraging | | | | They Discourage Me |
| :---: | :---: | :---: | :---: | :---: |
| 1 | 2 | 3 | 4 | 5 |

Would you continue dancing if your parents didn't want you to?        Yes/No

Would you continue dancing if it meant losing your friends?        Yes/No

**Other**

How many pictures do you have on your bedroom walls?

_____ 0          _____ 1          _____ 2-3          _____ 4-5          _____ 6-7

_____ 7+

What kind of pictures are they?

_____ photographs of animals

_____ posters of animals

_____ drawings of animals

_____ photographs of landscapes

_____ paintings of landscapes

_____ drawings of landscapes

_____ poster of large sized cartoon
                characters

_____ photographs of people

_____ drawings of people

_____ other (please specify)

_____ drawings you made:
                of yourself

_____ of people

_____ of animals

_____ of landscapes

_____ abstract paintings

_____

_____

_____

_____

Did you choose to hang these pictures on your walls?          Yes/No

Do you enjoy listening to music?

|  | Like Music a Lot |  |  | Don't Like Music |
|---|---|---|---|---|
| 1 | 2 | 3 | 4 | 5 |

How many hours per day to you listen to or have music playing?

_____ less than 30 mins     _____ 30 mins - 1 hr     _____ 1 - 2 hrs

_____ 2 - 4 hrs     _____ 4 - 6 hrs     _____ greater than 6 hrs

What types of music to you choose to listen to?

_____ classical: baroque     _____ opera

_____ classical: Romantic 19th c.     _____ country

_____ classical: Romantic 20th c.     _____ reggae

_____ top 40/pop/conventional     _____ folk

_____ rock: soft/mellow     _____ rap

_____ rock: hard/new wave/punk     _____ jazz: fusion

_____ rock: heavy metal     _____ jazz: big band/dixieland

_____ new age     _____ jazz: modern/improvisational

_____ R&B/soul/motown     _____ jazz: blues

_____ other (please specify)

_____

_____

_____ _____

_____

# IV

# THERAPEUTIC APPLICATIONS AND WORKSHOP TRANSCRIPTIONS

*These techniques come from Kundalini Yoga as taught by Yogi Bhajan. We wish to thank Dr. Kenneth Klivington for his excellent editorial suggestions regarding this manuscript.*

## THE HEALING POWER OF SOUND: TECHNIQUES FROM YOGIC MEDICINE

David Shannahoff-Khalsa
Yogi Bhajan

## 1.0 INTRODUCTION

A map guides us in moving from place to place on the earth, and space travelers must have a fixed set of coordinates to navigate through the void. But what do we know of guidance systems for the realm of mental space? Space travel calls for absolute precision; why should things be different in the domain of the mind? Certainly many people have become hopelessly lost in the nether regions of mental space. While we are not always aware of it, the search for guidance has always been a primary pursuit of the human animal. The apparent inattention to the need for guidance stems from at least 4 reasons:

1. Some people think that the 5 senses coupled with the intellect and a conventional world view provide adequate guidance;
2. We have preset conventions for the way we think, or at least believe we think;
3. Conventions give us security, as the mind is partly dependent on habit and routine;
4. (Possibly dominant) most people are simply concerned with surviving on a day-to-day basis.

But today, among those who are thoughtful, increasing numbers are questioning our conventions, realizing that the current world view may be a harmful addiction. We must realize that the mind itself is a vehicle, a vehicle to carry us about within the world of consciousness. The question of how we guide this vehicle, however, is seldom central to our thinking. Thus we become restricted to the rutted roads of our mental routines. To leave these ruts and explore the rich landscapes of consciousness, we must establish a conscious relationship with our own minds.

In ancient times yogic medicine was developed as a science for healing and mental development. At its height it became a system for mastering the mind and developing its many facets. As molecular genetics is today the science of the gene, yogic medicine is the science of the mind for those who have acquired its knowledge. The metaphor of the gene is limited, however. The genetic program of the cell provides instructions that direct development; the same is not true for the mind. The science of the mind derives from ancient knowledge that is, in effect, a manual for mental operations.

Few may doubt that in time a science of mind will be developed, but to claim that it is here today may seem preposterous to the occidental observer. Nonetheless, yogic medicine is a science so advanced and refined and of such great power that few may accept its claims without extensive experimental evidence or direct personal experience.

Some recently published results of novel experiments based on concepts from yogic medicine have led to important insights into the relationship between mind and body (Werntz et al. 1983; Kennedy et al. 1986; Klein et al. 1986; Werntz et al. 1987; Shannahoff-Khalsa et al. 1991; for review see Shannahoff-Khalsa 1991). These studies corroborate the yogic claim that the cerebral hemispheres alternate in dominance with a 2 to 3 hour rhythm throughout the day. Yogis claimed that this mind-body rhythm is also manifested in the relative congestion and decongestion response of the 2 nostrils; called the nasal cycle. Right nasal dominance correlates with left cerebral dominance and vice versa. In addition, it was shown how forced nostril breathing through one nostril could "exercise" the opposite hemisphere regardless of the initial dominance.

Given the limited length of a lifetime, the opportunities for experimentation with mental technologies are severely limited. Consequently, most lives provide only a cramped and rather purposeless voyage within the realm of human consciousness. This voyage usually leads to a self-created unreality or twilight zone, to doldrums of depression, or to the endlessly repeating mazes of neuroses.

At best, we perceive an affective response to life's journey, but have little awareness of our own consciousness along the way. Life styles today are based primarily on feelings and emotions; there is scarce use of applied intelligence as a mode of operation. People too rarely do what they know is best for themselves, living instead by their rationalizations based on emotional convenience.

Potentially, birth can lead to a continuous process of awakening, an unfolding of the repertoire of mental talents. More commonly, however, the painful and callous reality of our environments suppress our mental development. Traumas forestall development and lead to the formation of a mental cocoon. Instead of enjoying the process of awakening, we find that life becomes an endless struggle to survive painful events. People grapple to understand life, and, simultaneously, do their best to avoid trauma. Life becomes an amazing tug-of-war between the hunger for exploration and understanding and the need to avoid harsh realities. On the one hand we have the drive to understand the unknown, but all too quickly we become conditioned to fear the known. Pain is layered upon pain, and the mystery of life remains unsolved.

There is an old proverb that says (Feild 1977):

> He who knows not, and knows not that he knows not, is a fool—shun him.
> He who knows not, and knows that he knows not, is a child—teach him.
> He who knows, and knows not that he knows, is asleep—wake him.
> But he who knows, and knows that he knows, is a wise man—follow him.

Without a guidance system, man tosses and turns in his dreamlike mental state, believing he is awake, but unaware of his destination and fate. This detached state is merely insulation against the throes of life, while the intellect merely uses unrealistic data to attempt to serve its sleeping master. Ultimately, death shatters the cocoon which has enclosed the mind. Death may be the first egoless experience of life, the first experience of a nondualistic state.

The word yoga translates to "yoked" or "union". It means a union of the subconscious, conscious and superconscious mind. This unified state of consciousness, also known as the state of God consciousness, is the pinnacle of human development.

The purpose of this paper is to introduce participants to the use of elementary techniques in yogic medicine. These techniques can awaken the dormant potential of the mind and help eliminate the subconscious blocks which impede development.

## 1.1  Theoretical Basis for the Healing Effects of Sound

In yogic medicine the guidance system for directing and correcting consciousness is sound. An earlier paper by Shannahoff-Khalsa and Bhajan (1988), discusses the mechanistic basis for this system. In the yogic system a pattern of 84 meridian points on the upper palate (see Figure 1) is known to act as a keyboard for the tongue, where different sounds impart state-specific effects. What is required to awaken the dormant mental potential is the correct code.

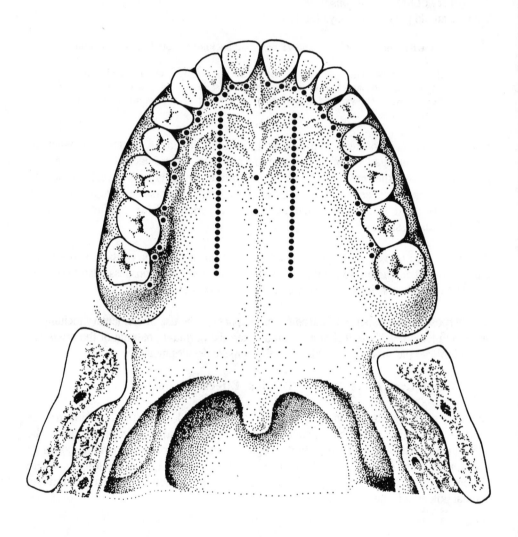

*Figure 1*

The upper palate is affected by the whole tongue, not just the tip. The 84 meridian points are related to the hypothalamus, and the effect of the tongue on these points is indirectly to stimulate specific regions of the hypothalamus. Signals are thus sent to various areas of the brain where they affect neural activity and brain chemistry. Shannahoff-Khalsa and Bhajan (1988, 183-192) state:

> ...this happens by creating a resonance on the upper palate that can differentially affect the regional metabolism of the hypothalamus. Different sounds affect different regions of the hypothalamus. As seen in Figure 1, the upper palate is drawn with the network of points arranged on the 2 sides almost as mirror images of each other. On the upper palate, along the row of sixteen possible teeth, are 2 points in front of each tooth on the gum. There are also 2 parallel rows of 25 pairs that are affected more by the tip of the tongue when it is erect in use during speech. Each side of the palate affects one half of the hypothalamus and the ipsilateral cerebral hemisphere and organ system. There are also 2 central points between the 2 parallel rows of points. The anterior point, or point closest to the front teeth, relates to the posterior fontanel. The posterior point corresponds to the anterior fontanel.

They discuss the yogic perspective on the indirect effects of sound on the autonomic nervous system on the 2 sides of the body, and the relationship of sounds to modes of quiescent and active states of metabolism. They also discuss the properties of different sounds that can affect the process of neural and mental development. Individual sounds and languages play an important role in the development of the human psyche. Examples given show how a word can be broken down and coded for meaning with effect. These principles were originally discovered in the systems called Nad Yoga and Mantra Yoga.

## 2.0 PREPARATORY ENERGIZING TECHNIQUES

The elementary techniques taught here can be practiced by any individual, and are useful for any stage of growth or development. Relevant cautions are given where needed. Advanced practitioners, as well as beginners, use them. They are very basic techniques that are effective for daily maintenance, healing and growth.

Prior to using the more subtle sound current techniques presented in Section 4, it is best to begin by using a technique that quickly raises energy and sets the metabolism for endurance. These techniques can help overcome the inertia due to emotional stress, fatigue, or neural chaos and dysfunction. The benefits of past practice become a source of motivation for a continued effort to cope, endure, excel and achieve. You learn that your success is dependent on your state of well-being and how the application of this technology can help quickly induce it. The following techniques in Section 2 are simple and effective ways to set yourself for any meditative strategy or effort to perform.

## 2.1 Spine Flexing for Vitality

The flexibility of the spine is a measure of youthfulness and vitality. This technique will help increase and maintain spinal flexibility. It will very quickly change ones metabolic state by raising energy up the chakras; energy centers along the spine and cranium that relate to different levels of consciousness and qualities of personality. The spinal fluid is also mixed in the canal and increased circulation in the cerebral ventricles occurs, allowing for enhanced nutrition of brain cells. Blood oxygen levels are increased and the electromagnetic field surrounding the spine is balanced and expanded in size. The circulation in the lymph system is also increased.

A psychological effect is that it can relieve depression if done for an adequate length of time (5-15 minutes). The mood becomes balanced, and one feels uplifted with a brighter sense of the internal and external environments. This technique can quickly elevate an individual who is feeling low or distressed. It should not be done by anyone under the influence of illegal mind-altering substances, although it is excellent for those under drug and alcohol rehabilitation. Individuals with spinal problems should use caution and take extra care in the use of this technique, as the vertebrae experience significant torsion.

*Description of Technique*

This technique can be practised either while sitting in a chair or on the floor in a cross-legged position. If in a chair, hold the knees with both hands for support and leverage. If on the ground, grasp the ankles in front with both hands. Begin by pulling the chest up and forward, inhaling deep at the same time. Then exhale as you relax the spine down into a slouching position. Keep the head up straight without allowing it to move much with the flexing action of the spine. This will help prevent a whip action of the cervical vertebrae. All breathing should only be through the nose for both the inhale and exhale. The eyes are closed as if you were looking at a central point on the horizon, where the eyebrows meet the origin of the nose (the third eye point). Eyes focused at the "third eye" equally activate both optic nerves and the consequent impact is to help balance the level of activity in both cerebral hemispheres. The pituitary gland also receives a balanced stimulation. Mental focus is kept on the sound of the breath while listening to the fluid movement of the inhale and exhale. Additionally, one can mentally create the sound "Sat" on the inhale and "Nam" on the exhale. These sounds relate to the pure state of consciousness of the newborn when the first recorded message is the sound and action of the breath. At this moment the nucleus of the psyche is formed. Begin the technique slowly while loosening up the spine. Eventually, a very rapid movement can be achieved with practice, reaching a rate of 2-3 times per second for the entire movement. A few minutes are sufficient in the beginning. Later, there is no time limit. Food should be avoided prior to this exercise. If a feeling of light-headedness develops, it is an indication of weak nerves. Be careful and flex the spine slowly in the beginning. Relax for 1-2 minutes when finished.

## 2.2 Shoulder Shrug for Increasing Metabolism

This technique stimulates the thyroid and parathyroid gland raising the level of glandular metabolism and basal metabolic rate. It also increases circulation of the blood and helps to reduce muscle tension in the neck and shoulders due to stress or poor posture. It can supplement for the use of caffeine and when done with a powerful breath can help cleanse the lungs.

*Description of Technique*

While keeping the spine straight, rest the hands on the knees if sitting in a cross-legged position or with them on the thighs if on a chair. Inhale and raise the shoulders up towards the ears, then exhale, letting them down. All breathing is only through the nose. Eyes should be kept closed and focused at the third eye. Mentally listen to the sound "Sat" on the inhale and "Nam" on the exhale. Continue this action rapidly, building to 3 times per second for a maximum time of 2 minutes. Going over this limit will overstimulate the thyroid and parathyroid glands. This technique should not be practiced by individuals who are hyperactive or diagnosed with attention-deficit disorder.

## 3.0 BREATHING TECHNIQUES

In yogic medicine, breath is understood to be the link between mind and body. And to conquer the mind, one must master the breath. With mastery each breath can be consciously regulated and calculated to drive the mind. In this sense, the individual breath gives us the perspective on the mind as a vehicle—"Mind is a unit energy given to you to serve you. Be its guide and not its slave" (Bhajan 1977). The breath is a tool for feeding fuel to the nervous system and bringing light, clarity, and expansion to the mind. Breath is the life force which supports life, both in a classical sense in respect to oxygen and in the esoteric sense for what yogis call prana (Shannahoff-Khalsa 1988). The yogi, a master of his nervous system, consciously selects the rate, rhythm, and nostril to channel the breath to achieve a state specific effect. Practice of the following technique will give an experience of how a specific pattern can produce specific effects.

### 3.1 Awakening Dormant Regions of the Brain—8 Part Breath with Sa Ta Na Ma

Life force or prana is guided by the action of the breath. The effect of an 8 part breath awakens dormant regions of the brain, and heals regions where damage has occurred. There is also a healing effect on the cranial nerves, and a balancing and stimulating effect on the pineal-pituitary- hypothalamic axis. This breath integrates mental activities and expands the mind. In yogic medicine there are 10 major regions of the brain, 5 on each side. They closely parallel the frontal, central, temporal, parietal, and occipital regions. Of these 10 regions, each is further divided into 4 additional regions. This technique begins to stimulate, heal, and equilibrate the 10 major regions of the brain.

In the use of this technique, the mantra called Panch Shabad (5 divine sounds), Sa Ta Na Ma, is given to help accentuate the effects of the breath and transform consciousness. The sound current of Sa Ta Na Ma brings the consciousness through the developmental cycle of infinity, life, death, and rebirth. The consciousness becomes molded, faceted, directed, and matured enabling an individual to experience the merging of his individual consciousness with universal consciousness. Eventually, one's actions become directed and committed to universal truth. The effect of the sound Sa gives the mind the ability to expand to infinity. Ta produces the effect to experience the totality of life. Na gives the mind the ability to conquer death. And Ma produces the quality of rebirth or resurrection. The fifth sound *ah* common to these 4, is the creative sound of the universe.

In ancient times certain sounds were found to have a state-specific effect on the mind that could guide and correct consciousness, and cleanse and restructure the subconscious mind. The mantra (mind-protector) used here has this ability. Sa Ta Na Ma gives the brain a working strength.

*Description of Technique*

Sit with a straight spine, with the lower vertebrae pressed slightly forward. Use a slight pressure to pull the chin toward the chest slightly, producing a neck lock which straightens the cervical vertebrae, however, the head remains erect as if looking straight ahead. If sitting in a chair, keep both feet flat on the floor. Eyes are focused at the third eye, as described in Section 2.1. Relax the hands in the lap. If you have the genetic ability, begin breathing through a curled tongue that is extended out of the mouth. The sides of the tongue are curled up so that it makes a "U" shape. Break the inhalation into 8 equal parts. Next, bring the tongue into the mouth, close it, and exhale through the nose in 8 equal parts. Do not pause after completing the full inhalation or full exhalation. Continue the cycle — 8 parts in through the curled tongue, and 8 parts out through the nose, taking about 10 seconds for each complete round. Use the sounds Sa, Ta, Na, Ma (repeat twice on the inhale and twice on the exhale) instead of counting 1,2,3,4,5,6,7,8 for each inhale or exhale of the breath. Mentally pair the sound of the breath with each of the different syllables in the proper sequence, or just mentally listen to the sound of the breath itself. If you cannot curl the sides of the tongue up in this fashion, inhale through the nose only in 8 parts, keeping the mouth closed and exhale through the nose in 8 parts. If you can curl the tongue in this way it will also help stimulate the thyroid and parathyroid glands. Start with 3-5 minutes, build the time up to 10-15 minutes, and then up to 31 minutes maximum. Upon completing this technique, take at least 3 long, slow, deep breaths through the nose, and relax.

## 4.0 SOUND CURRENT TECHNIQUES

In the paper by Shannahoff-Khalsa and Bhajan (1988) some of the scientific and religious aspects of sound are discussed. In science, the specificity of some sounds has been studied from the aspect of cerebral laterality (Tsunoda 1985) and (Zajonc et al. 1989) have recently reported on the emotional and physiological characteristics of the phonemes *u* and *e*. Pronunciation of the phoneme *u* resulted in elevated forehead temperature and negative subjective affect. Subjective reactions to *e* were found to be pleasurable and to produce a reduction in forehead temperature. In religion, some sounds combine to form the sacred "Word" with all its controversial interpretations and significance. Perhaps research efforts in medicine and healing can help create the needed overlap of these 2 otherwise separate fields. When you ask a yogi if yoga is a religion, the answer is, "It is and is not. In religion you have to believe something and in yoga you have to experience what you want to believe" (Bhajan 1977).

We have a respective relationship of the domains of science, medicine, healing, and religion. Each are subsets of a more comprehensive understanding achieved through the mastery of yoga. Yoga is a science that gives the healing experience of the spirit which otherwise comes under the domain of religion. These boundaries are largely artificial and exist mainly for socio-political conveniences. However, each domain professes to include a base of knowledge and reason which can provide a harmonious and objective perspective of the cosmos. One domain so strictly isolated from the other reflects the chaos, discord and disease of modern society and the fragmentation of mind. Today, each exists with little or no responsibility or relationship to the other. This dissociation is manifested when man becomes isolated within his consciousness from the pursuit of the experience of the soul, his innermost self, divine nature, or the realm beyond time and space. This present discontinuity between science and spiritual pursuits, as if they were so greatly different, symptomatically reflects the impaired communication between the left and right brains. As the left brain specializes in details, basic knowledge, and everyday skills, and the right brain in global perspectives, and sensitivity to the health and well-being of oneself and others, it could be argued that our modern western society may be overcome by the mentality of the left brain. From the yogic perspective, the left brain also supports the intelligence for aggression and defense. It argues against unity. The right brain specializes in the global view supporting union with less discretion for specifics and practicality. Yoga means union, union of the intelligence of both brains to provide a unified, effective, and realistic view of day-to-day life in the cosmos. It is a working knowledge to help facilitate the crossing of the great world ocean.

Words alone cannot describe the timelessness, the ecstasy and the state of mind of the healer, prophet or yogi. But the sound current can carry the practitioner's consciousness into this realm, where the reductionist mentality of the intellect fails. The sounds taught here, once kept secret because of their power, can help an individual begin his journey from the known realms of the mind, safely into the divine realms of higher consciousness. As the subconscious mind becomes cleansed and restructured, it is conditioned to support the individual's conscious union with universal consciousness.

A secret to chanting is to let the sound carry you in your consciousness without focusing on the intellectual content and interpretation of the words. Listen to the sounds you create. Experience the vibration created on the upper palate and within the cranium.

Caution is given that these sounds should never be chanted while driving a car or just prior to it, as their effects have the tendency to expand the mind beyond time and space.

## 4.1  Elementary Healing Sounds — Um, Ee, Oooh

Three simple but very effective and powerful sounds for healing are um, ee, and oooh (Shannahoff-Khalsa and Bhajan 1988). Although they can be chanted separately, they are most effective when combined and practiced in this order (the order is not to be altered). They each have an effect but no specific innate meaning as do some sounds (e.g. Sa Ta Na Ma). Combined in practice they have been known to heal diseases with no cure.

*Description of Technique*

Sit with a straight spine and focus the eyes at the third eye point. Hands can be relaxed in the lap, or in the posture called Gyan Mudra, where the tip of the index finger is touching the tip of the respective thumb. Hands are resting on the knees with palms up (whereby more healing energy is received through the hands) or down (whereby less healing energy is received through the hands). A good beginning time is 5-11 minutes for each sound. By chanting the continuous sound of ummmmmmmmm......, which produces an intense vibration on the lips, the energy patterns and flow of the left and right sides of the body and brain are balanced. Then chant eeeeeeeee..... continuously for an equal time, focusing on the vibration produced under the tongue. This raises the energy of the sushumna, or central meridian, increasing the life force. Finally, for the last period, chant oooh...... to complete the effect.

## 4.2 Stimulating and Balancing the 8 Centers of Consciousness—Ek Ong Kar Sat Nam Siri Whahay Guru

Besides simply considering the need for the balance of the left and right modes of intelligence, consciousness is also determined and affected by the amount of energy and activity in the 8 centers of consciousness, commonly called chakras. These centers are repositories for psychic energy. They are not related to the gross body alone, but are mainly situated in the subtle or etheric bodies. The intensity of activity in any one chakra imparts an effect that reflects a world perspective, understanding of cause and effect, and source of motivation and desire that is unique to each.

The consciousness of an individual who lives mainly in the first chakra is concerned primarily with survival. His action and values are based solely on the need to survive, regardless of other values. Fears and paranoia coincide with this center. The second chakra reflects mentality directed to reproduction and sexual activities. Overactivity here leads to sexual neuroses. The third chakra is the center of power, territory and ego, the "Me" mentality to the exclusion of others. The first 3 levels are the nature of the beast, or animal kingdom. They are not unique to the man. The biggest step in development is from the third to the fourth. The fourth chakra, the heart center, embraces the human element of compassion, the attitude to nurture and give without consideration of the cost to oneself. The fifth chakra is the center for creative communication and blunt truth. The sixth chakra, which is unique, allows for both sides of the coin to be seen and the dual nature of life to be understood in the terms of polarity. Supernatural abilities are also governed by this center. The seventh chakra, is the center for pure thoughts, where actions are based on concern for the highest good for all. It is the center of saintly intelligence. And the eight chakra is the aura, the realm beyond time and space, where past, present and futures merge. If an individual lives in the consciousness of this center too long, the world will pass him by.

Each chakra, or energy center, has a physiological correlate in the body. First chakra is the area of the rectum (sacro-coccygeal plexus), second chakra is the sex organs (sacral plexus), third chakra is the navel point region (solar plexus), fourth chakra is the heart center (cardiac plexus), fifth chakra is the thyroid and parathyroid or throat center (laryngeal plexus), sixth chakra is the pituitary gland or third eye, seventh chakra is the pineal and cerebral cortex, or crown center, and eighth chakra is the aura or the psychoelectromagnetic field surrounding the body.

The effects of chanting the mantra Ek Ong Kar Sat Nam Siri Whahay Guru is to awaken and balance all 8 centers, whereby the entire personality becomes balanced. In addition, it will equilibrate and balance the energy systems and metabolic correlates of the 12 major meridians described in the acupuncture system. This mantra will energize each center and raise the Kundalini, or evolutionary energy in man.

It is also said that if an individual chants it correctly and continuously for 2 hours and 31 minutes for 40 days before the rising of the sun, he will awaken his saintly nature. This mantra has the power to liberate the human from the cycles of life, death and rebirth.

The interpretation of the meaning of the mantra can be given in several ways. For example: Ek Ong Kar can mean "God is one", or "there is one God who created this creation", or "there is one universal creative consciousness", for Sat Nam; Sat is "the vibration of the infinite" and Nam is "its manifestation", or "truth is God's name or identity"; Siri Whahay Guru; "great is that universal wisdom that dwells through us", or "great is the true guru that manifests when the soul becomes awakened."

*Description of the Technique*

Sit with a perfectly straight spine using neck lock and pushing the lower vertebrae slightly forward. Eyes are closed and focused at the third eye. Hands are in Gyan Mudra (the circuit coupling divine knowledge and awareness with the ego), with elbows locked. Neck lock must be applied. Be sure to chant powerfully and vibrate Ong at the back of the neck. There are 3 phases to the chant. First, inhale deeply through the nose and chant Ek with a sharp cracking sound and pull felt at the navel region. It is very short. Continue to use the same breath to vibrate Ong (accentuating the nasalized *ng* as the sound stretches out) for equal time with Kar (accentuating the rolled *rrrr* as the sound stretches out). Then again, inhale deeply and fully through the nose only, and chant Sat but very short (like Ek), and feel the cracking sound and pull at the navel point. Then, using almost all of the same breath, chant a long Nammmmmmmmmm. But before completely running out of breath finish with Siri (pronounced Sree, but not Sri, Shri, or Seri). Then again inhale, but only a half breath through the mouth, and chant Wha and haaaaay (long *a*) then finish with Guru (pronounced Guruuu, rolling the *r* and accentuating the ruuuuuu over Gu) but not extending the ruuuu to far. A good beginning time is eleven minutes. Thirty seven and a half minutes, 62 minutes and 2 hours and 31 minutes are also different steps or plateaus for achievement. In addition, it is said that 72 continuous hours gives the equivalent effect of 40 days of 2 hours and 31 minutes before the sun. Take time to rest when completed, regardless of the length of practice.

## 4.3   Purity, Power and Prosperity—Har Har Har Har Gobinday, etc.

The nature and quality of potential in a fully developed consciousness is equivalent to comparing a thousand-faceted diamond to the beginning chunk of coal from which it came. Even God-conscious beings can have different levels of refinement, awareness, talent, and skill. It is impossible to define the limits of such a being. But their most divine quality is the ability to heal others and the destiny of the planet.

The mantra taught in this section establishes power and prosperity through the path of purity. Many seek power for the sake of power, they are doomed to failure. Only a rare few seek purity. In purity all powers come, powers that make the earthly powers of kings appear frail and of no consequence in comparison. In this state of consciousness, the value of ego is solely for the sake and convenience of an earthly or finite identity. A pure mind will always attract money and opportunities from the cosmos.

The complete mantra for purity, power and prosperity is:

> Har Har Har Har Gobinday
> Har Har Har Har Mukunday
> Har Har Har Har Udharay
> Har Har Har Har Aparay
> Har Har Har Har Hariung
> Har Har Har Har Kariung
> Har Har Har Har Nirnamay
> Har Har Har Har Akamay

The mantra contains the 8 facets of God that we all have to deal with. Gobinday, one who sustains us. Mukunday, one who liberates us. Udharay, one who uplifts us. Aparay, who is infinite. Hariung, who does everything. Kariung, for which grace everything is done. Nirnamay, the nameless one. Akamay, desireless is by itself. Har is the shakti yog (power) mantra. Har is the original God. The 4 repetitions of Har give power to all aspects, and provide the power to break down the barriers of the past. This mantra will bring stability to the cerebral hemispheres. It also works on the fourth center to help develop compassion, patience, divine tolerance, the ability to withstand irritation, pain and the onslaught of the time. It helps you to reach infinity.

*Description of Technique*

Sit straight with the same hand and eye posture as the previous technique. Inhale and chant the first section (Har Har Har Har Gobinday) pulling the navel point on each Har, then mentally focusing on Gobinday above and beyond the head. Then, inhale again, and do the second segment (Har Har Har Har Mukunday), the same way, except Mukunday is experienced at the seventh chakra or crown center (top of the head). The third segment is at the sixth chakra, and so on. Or the entire mantra can also be projected at the third eye. This method is easier when first learning the mantra until it becomes second nature and simply emerges without thinking which sound is next. The correct way to pronounce Har is with a quick light flick of the tongue on the upper palate behind the teeth with a slightly rigid tongue. Eleven minutes, 31, 62, or 2 hours and 31 minutes are excellent times for this mantra. Rest when completed.

## 4.4 Tranquilizing the Angry Mind—Jeeo

Anger is one of the most self-deprecating emotions. It is a killing poison of the mind. The challenge of life is to overcome lust, anger, greed, pride and attachment. Anger can virtually eat a person alive from within. In yogic medicine, this emotion is recognized as playing a primary role in the origin of many cancers. The effect of anger is to reduce all human mental qualities to zero, unless the energy is consciously channeled to overcome injustice.

There are numerous yogic techniques for dealing with anger, but this technique is the simplest, and certainly one of the most effective means to tranquilize the angry mind. Its tranquilizing effects can last for hours under the worst circumstances, and up to several days in mild cases.

*Description of Technique*

Sit with a straight spine and close the eyes. Simply chant Jeeo, Jeeo, Jeeo, Jeeo continuously and rapidly for 11 minutes without stopping (pronounced like the names for the letters G and O). During continuous chanting you do not stop to take long breaths, but continue with just enough short breaths to keep the sound going. Eleven minutes is all that is needed.

## REFERENCE LIST

Bhajan, Y. 1977. *The Teaching of Yogi Bhajan*. New York: Hawthorne Books, Inc.

Feild, R. 1977. *The Last Barrier: A Journey Through the World of Sufi Teaching*. New York: Harper and Row.

Kennedy, B.; Ziegler, M.G.; Shannahoff-Khalsa, D.S. 1986. Alternating lateralization of plasma catecholamines and nasal patency in humans. *Life Sci.* 38:1203-1214.

Klein, R.; Pilon, D.; Prosser, S.; Shannahoff-Khalsa, D.S. 1986 Nasal airflow asymmetries and human performance. *Biol. Psychol.* 23:127-137.

Shannahoff-Khalsa, D.S. 1988. A contemporary view of life force biology: The merging of Kundalini Yoga and the neurosciences. In *Energy Medicine Around the World.*, edited by T.M. Srinivasan, 89-110. Phoenix, AZ: Gabriel Press, pp. 89-110.

Shannahoff-Khalsa, D.S. 1991. Stress technology medicine: A new paradigm for stress and considerations for self-regulation. In *Stress: Neurobiology and Neuroendocrinology*, edited by M. Brown, G. Koob and C. Rivier, 647-686. New York: Marcel Dekker, Inc.

Shannahoff-Khalsa, D.S.; Boyle, M.R. and Buebel, M.E. 1991. The effects of unilateral forced nostril breathing on cognition. *Intern. J. Neurosci.*: in press.

Shannahoff-Khalsa, D.S., and Bhajan, Y. 1988. Sound current therapy and self-healing: The ancient science of nad and mantra yoga. *Intern. J. Music Dance Art Therapy* 1:183-192.

Tsunoda, T. 1985. *The Japanese Brain—Uniqueness and Universality*. Tokyo: Taishukan Publishing Co.

Werntz, D.A.; Bickford, R.G.; Bloom, F.E.; and Shannahoff-Khalsa, D.S. 1983. Alternating cerebral hemispheric activity and lateralization of autonomic nervous function. *Hum. Neurobiol.* 2:39-43.

Werntz, D.A.; Bickford, R.G.; and Shannahoff-Khalsa, D.S. 1987. Selective hemispheric stimulation by unilateral forced nostril breathing. *Hum. Neurobiol.* 6:165-171.

Zajonc, R.B.; Murphy, S.T.; and Inglehart, M. 1989. Feeling and facial efference: Implications of the vascular theory of emotion. *Psychol. Rev.* 96:395-416.

# SONIC ENTRAINMENT

Jonathan S. Goldman

I would like to share with you some important information about the the effects of sound upon the brain. Researchers in this field believe that is is possible to drive, or control the internal frequencies of the brain with external sound frequencies. This involves the use of extremely low pitched sounds to entrain the brain: to cause the brain to synchronize its wavelengths so they match this low pitched frequency. In this way, it is possible specifically to alter the brain waves of an individual by using sound waves and it appears also to be possible to affect their consciousness through this process.

The words "entrains," "drives," "controls," "alters" conjure up worrying images of mind control in such novels as *1984* or *Clockwork Orange*. It also sounds a little far fetched, like Buck Rogers or some other futuristic science fiction. Yet, from all the available written information and from the experiences of many people including myself, sonic entrainment of the brain is real. It works. And it is powerful.

The technology to create sonic entrainment is quite simple. The moral implications of its use merit much thought, however.

In fact, sonic entrainment has been used by medicine men and shamans from different cultures since the beginning of time. The ability to create altered states of consciousness through drumming, chanting and music is nothing new. It is probably as old as music itself. The ability to create specific changes in brain waves through exact intervals or beat frequencies is merely a refinement of the process.

These are exciting times with many exciting new discoveries being made. People now use frequencies and rhythms for relaxation, stress reduction and treatment of all sorts of illnesses and disease. Musicians and therapists are creating music and sounds to encompass all the newly discovered (or should I say rediscovered) theories, therapies and techniques.

I would like to present one aspect of the therapeutic use of sound and music. Yet the implications of this material are quite astounding and far-reaching. It is a great responsibility and one we should be aware of.

In the first part of this paper, I will be discussing the principle of entrainment. Then I will examine how it may be possible to entrain the brain with sound.

## THE PRINCIPLE OF ENTRAINMENT

Our understanding of entrainment begins with our understanding of the rhythms of life. The use of rhythm has always played an important role in the very fundamental concepts of music. And this is where we begin today, with the rhythm of life.

All life consists of rhythmic processes. From the simple pulsations of a single-cell organism to the rising and falling of our breath, life is filled with rhythm. This rhythm is also called "periodicity," meaning that the activity of something falls in cycles.

Much of life is directed by the external rhythms of nature. The earth spins on its axis and rotates around the sun. And the moon orbits the earth. We attune ourselves, for example, to the cycles of the sun and the moon, following different rhythms they create. With day and night, different behavior is created. We usually get up with daylight and go to sleep at night.

When our light-dark cycle is disturbed, if we take a long jet flight for instance, our ability to function in the new environment is affected for a day or two. We call this "jet-lag" of course. Different behavior due to rhythm is also true for different seasons of the year and the response of nature to this. Not only sleep patterns, but our eating patterns, digestional patterns, even our harvesting and mating patterns are affected by the rhythms of these cycles.

Sound can be understood as being rhythmic. Sound takes the form of waves, which are measured in cycles per second (or Hertz). This periodicity is rhythmic in nature. Each cycle of a wave may be recognized as a pulse of sound. Each individual frequency that we measure may be understood as being rhythmic, for the number of cycles per second that make up that frequency creates a rhythm. Low notes pulse much slower than high notes. The lowest note that you can hit on a piano will produce a frequency that vibrates at 27.5 Hz. The highest note on a piano will vibrate at 4,186 Hz.

The range of hearing for the human ear varies immensely. The upper range for normal hearing is somewhere between 16,000 and 20,000 Hz. The bottom limit of what we can hear is somewhere around 16 Hz. With very slow pulsed notes, below the threshold of hearing we cannot actually hear them as single tones, but we can perceive them as being rhythmical in nature. These extremely low frequencies (called "ELF"s) can sometimes even be counted. In particular, sounds pulsed in the range of 0.1 Hz to 8 Hz are perceived as being rhythmic in nature. Events slower than this are not perceived as part of an ongoing rhythm, while events faster than this become heard as a single tone.

Entrainment is an aspect of sound that is closely related to rhythms and the way these rhythms affect us. It is a phenomenon of sound, in which the powerful rhythmic vibrations of one object will cause the less powerful vibrations of another object to lock in step and oscillate at that rate. This phenomenon of nature has to do with the conservation of energy. It seems that nature finds it more economical in terms of energy to have periodic events that are close enough in frequency occur in phase or in step with each other.

## EXAMPLES OF ENTRAINMENT

An excellent example of entrainment is illustrated by Itshak Bentov (1988). If you have a room full of pendulum type grandfather clocks and start these pendulums in motion at different times, they will all swing differently. However, if you come back the next day, you will find that all the pendulums are swinging together at the same rate. This locking in step of rhythms is entrainment. This was discovered by the Dutch scientist, Christian Huygens in 1665.

Entrainment is actually as aspect of resonance. Resonance may be defined as the frequency at which an object most naturally wants to vibrate. One object may set another object into motion if it shares the same resonant frequency. For example, if you strike a 100 cycles per second tuning fork  and put it near another tuning fork of the same frequency, the second tuning fork will automatically be set into motion. Even though it has not been struck, it will begin to vibrate and sound merely by being in the same field as the vibrating tuning fork.

We have all seen a singer break a glass with the voice. This is another example of resonance. This same phenomenon exists between two guitar strings for example, one struck and one unstruck. Resonance is a cooperative phenomenon between two different objects sharing the same frequency. With resonance you stimulate the natural vibrations of an object with its own vibration frequency and thus set it into motion. I like to conceive of resonance as being passive in nature.

Entrainment, on the other hand, seems to be active. With entrainment you are changing the natural oscillatory patterns of one object and replacing them with the different oscillatory patterns of another object. You are actively changing the vibrations (the frequency or rhythm) of one object to another rate.

The oscillators of television sets, radio receivers and other similar equipment will lock on to each other and entrain. With television sets, when you turn the knobs, you are adjusting the frequency of the set's oscillators. When the two frequencies become close, they suddenly lock, as if they "want" to pulse together. Usually, it is the faster oscillator which will force the slower one to operate at its pace. Living things are like television sets in that living things also oscillate. They pulse, they vibrate, they have rhythm. These rhythms of life allow for entrainment.

As such, entrainment is also found throughout nature. Fireflies blinking on and off will entrain with each other. Female college roommates will often have a synchronous menstrual cycle. Muscle cells from the hearts when they move closer together, will suddenly shift in their rhythm and pulse together, perfectly synchronized.

This entrainment also takes place when two people have a good conversation. Their brain waves will oscillate synchronously. Such entrainment is seen in the relationship between students and their professors. Psychotherapists and clients entrain with each other. So do preachers and their congregation (Myers 1988).

Within our own bodies, we are constantly locking in rhythm with ourselves. Our heart rate, respiration and brain waves all entrain to each other. Slow down your breath, for example, and you will slow down your heart beat and your brain waves. Conversely, if you are able to slow down your brain waves, you can affect your heart rate and respiration.

It has been found that the frequencies of pulse, breathing and blood circulation, as well as their combined activities, all function harmonically. That is, their rhythms are strictly coordinated in whole number ratios—two to one, three to two (Berendt 1987).

## Brain Waves

Our brain waves, incidentally, pulsate and oscillate at particular frequencies that are measured, just like sound waves, in cycles per second. There are four basic delineations of different brain wave states, based upon the cycles per second of the brain.

1. Beta waves—these brain waves are from 13 to 23 Hz. They are found in our normal, waking state of consciousness. Beta waves are present when our focus of attention is on activities of the external world.
2. Alpha waves—these brain waves are from 7 to 13 Hz. They are found when we daydream and are often associated with a state of meditation. Alpha waves become stronger and more regular when our eyes are closed.
3. Theta waves—these brain waves are from 3 to 7 Hz. They are found in states of high creativity and have been equated to states of consciousness found in much shamanic work. Theta waves are also found in states of deep meditation.
4. Delta waves—these brain waves are from .5 to 3 Hz. They are found in a state of deep sleep or unconsciousness. Some of the newer brain wave work indicates that it is possible to be in a state of deep meditation and produce delta waves.

Two other delineations of brain wave activity have been noted by some researchers. They are:

1.  High beta—these brain waves are from 23 to 33 Hz. They are associated with hyperactivity and some types of anxiety.
2.  K Complex—these are brain waves over 33 Hz. They usually occur in short bursts and are often associated with the "aha" experience, where there is a sudden integration of ideas or experiences.

## Past Research in Sonic Entrainment

As the functions of the human body can entrain to each other, it is possible to use external rhythms to affect the internal mechanism of heart rate, respiration, and brain wave activity. I first became aware of this possibility several years ago while reading *Superlearning* (Ostrander and Schroeder 1982) which examines the Lozanov method of education from Bulgaria. Part of the program deals with using music to help induce states of consciousness effective in heightening the learning process. In particular, they focused upon music pulsed at about 60 beats per minute being helpful in inducing an alpha state of consciousness.

Something resonated within me when I read this. Intuitively, I had known that there was a relationship between external rhythms and internal rhythms. As a musician, I had been aware of this since I first began playing. If you wanted to have an audience up and dancing, you would play a fast song. If you wanted them to dance slowly or sit down and not move, a ballad was in order. Yet, I had never really contemplated the possibilities of affecting states of consciousness with rhythm until reading *Superlearning*.

At the time that I came across this concept, I was working with an associate who is a professor of music and psychology at Tufts University in Massachusetts. We used a computer to search the different scientific and medical journals to see what research had been done by others on this subject.

Studies suggested that resonance and entrainment of bodily processes can occur in response to external sound and musical rhythms. One paper by Kneutgen (1970), on the soothing effects of lullabies played for infants, noted that breathing rhythms became synchronized with the rhythm of the music. A paper by Landreth and Hobart (1974) found that heart rate changes were directly related to changes in tempo.

One series of extensive studies by Harrer and Harrer (1977) explored some of the effects that emotional musical experiences have on the autonomic nervous system, including blood pressures, pulse rate, respiration, galvanic skin response and muscle tension. They found that heart rate was sensitive to both music volume and rhythm. They also found that some subjects tended to show either a synchronization of their heart beat to the music, or a synchronization of their respiratory rhythm to the music.

There did not seem to be a one to one relationship between external rhythms such as drum beats, and internal rhythms. While an external rhythm of 60 beats per minute should reduce heart beat, it was not always directly proportional. Sixty musical beats per minute would not always produce 60 heart beats per minute. For example, some heart beats might go down to 64 beats per minute. Others might reduce to 68 beats per minute, from, say, 72. This difference makes it impossible to provide conclusive data for certain research studies, though it does not deny the ability of external rhythms to entrain internal rhythms.

It is also important to understand that different individuals being tested also had the ability to fight consciously against external rhythms and not be affected by the entrainment created by these rhythms. An additional factor is that the strength of the entraining rhythm may vary from person to person.

## Robert Monroe and Hemi-Sync

At the time I was exploring the research on external rhythms and heart beat, I was unaware that a great deal of private research was being conducted using specific frequencies to entrain the brain rather than specific rhythms to entrain the heart beat. This work was being pioneered by Robert Monroe, of the Monroe Institute.[1]

Robert Monroe was a business executive with a background in broadcasting. He was director of the Mutual Broadcasting System and owner of a group of radio stations and cable television corporations in the Southeast. When Monroe began having spontaneous out of body experiences in the 60s, he started private research into the effects of different frequencies to affect different states of consciousness. Part of Monroe's experience with these out of body travels involved hearing different frequencies which he felt triggered the experiences. He felt that sound could somehow play a role in helping others achieve states of consciousness similar to those he had experienced and with the help of a research team, he set out to discover if he could control or drive the brain with sound waves.

Through trial and error and probably much intuition, Monroe discovered that he could produce a driving or entrainment of brain waves through use of specific frequencies. Monroe found that much like a glass which could be resonated by a pure tone, the brain resonated when bombarded with pulsing sound waves. Monroe called this a "frequency following response," or FFR and patented this effect in 1975.

---

[1]   The Monroe Institute, Rt. 1, Box 175, Faber, VA 22938-9749.

The frequencies which Monroe used to entrain the brainwaves were in the same spectrum as the brain waves themselves—from .5 Hz to about 20 Hz. These were frequencies that the human ear is incapable of hearing. However, working with a psychoacoustic phenomenon called beat frequencies, Monroe found that is was possible to create very low frequencies from much higher sound. At the same time as Monroe was doing this work, Dr. Gerald Oster, a biophysicist at the Mount Sinai School of Medicine in New York, was independently investigating the effects of this beat phenomenon.

The phenomenon is this: if you use two independent sound sources, say for example, a tuning fork of 100 cycles per second, and another tuning fork of 108 cycles per second, they produce a sound that waxes and wanes in a pulsing wah-wah-wah sound or beat. The rapidity of the beat equals the difference between two frequencies. In the above illustration, between the two tuning forks of 100 and 108, you would create an 8 cycle per second beat frequency. If the sound sources come from external sources, such as a loudspeaker, these beats can be heard with both ears or only one ear. This is called "monaural" beat frequency. The phenomenon of beat frequencies is described in detail by Gerald Oster (1973).

If these independent frequencies are applied separately to each ear, a "binaural" beat frequency is created by both brain hemispheres working simultaneously. In his attempt to discover a technique to entrain the brain, Monroe had found a way to synchronize sonically the left and right hemispheres. In thousands of experiments using an EEG to monitor the brain waves of people hearing different signals in each ear, he verified that he could indeed entrain or drive brain waves using binaural beats. The entrainment or FFR took place not only in the area of the brain responsible for hearing, nor only in the left and right hemispheres, but the entire brain resonated, the waveforms of both hemispheres becoming identical in frequency, amplitude, phase, and coherence.

This paper is not on the potential uses of brain synchronization which may have remarkable implications for education, but rather on the ability of external sound stimuli to affect the internal rhythms of the brain. I mention this most interesting side affect—the ability to synchronize the hemispheres of the brain for those interested in further study of this.

In order for this patented process, which Monroe called "hemi-sync" to work, it appeared that it was necessary for those hearing the two sound sources to wear headphones. Later work with the FFR however, indicated that entrainment of the brain would still occur with external sound sources, such as stereo speakers, for example, if they were given enough separation in the room. While the effects were not quite as rapid or as powerful as with headphones, sonic entrainment still took place.

Monroe is not the only person who is utilizing different sonic phenomenon to entrain the brain. A number of other private institutions use similar processes. One person, a nonsectarian monk named Brother Charles, is head of Synchronicity Foundation,[1] which specializes in using sound to enhance and accelerate consciousness. Brother Charles was a disciple of the Eastern spiritual leader, Swami Paramahansa Muktandana. He found that through the new sonic entrainment technology, it was possible almost instantly to induce states of deep meditation, normally not available to people unless they had gone through years of meditational practice. Brother Charles uses a process called "Phasing" which employs a very similar mechanism to create states of altered consciousness. Indeed, it is the innate ability of the brain to detect waveforms phase difference which gives rise to binaural beats.

Another aspect of this sonic entrainment technology, brought to my attention by Sherry Edwards, a researcher at Ohio University (Letter to author, June 14, 1989), is that if the carrier waves creating the beat frequencies are harmonically related to these beat frequencies, a more powerful sonic entrainment would occur. Therefore, the most powerful form of entrainment to induce, for example, 7 Hz, would involve using two differentiated signals that were harmonic multiples frequencies of this—say 49 Hz and 56 Hz. Thus far there has been little research regarding this. It does make sense, however, and I mention it for those of you interested in working with this technology.

The tapes listed in the Addendum give several different examples of sonic entrainment and the brain.

### Earth Hertz

This technology of sonic entrainment does seem to work and these tapes expose one to frequencies designed to entrain the brain to alpha and theta states. These tapes are available to the general public; the first tape was created by scientist Robert Pollaksen. It is called "Earth Hertz"[2] in which two different tones create a beat frequency of 7.8 cycles per second.

It is of interest to note that the earth's ionosphere, the electromagnetic field around the earth, has been measured. This is called the Shumann Effect, and it appears that this frequency of the earth is somewhere around 7.83 cycles per second. This frequency is identical to the alpha wave spectrum of the human brain. It has been speculated that when we meditate, our brain waves lock in and entrain with the energies of the earth.

---

[1] Synchronicity Foundation, Rt. 1, Box 192-B, Faber, VA 22938.
[2] "Earth Hertz" by Robert Pollaksen, Psycho-Acoustic Research Consultants, Boulder, CO.

Itzhak Bentov (1988) theorized that when a person was vibrating at these frequencies during meditation, they would entrain with the geomagnetic energies of the earth and lock in resonance with it. There are also some researchers who, like Bentov, believe that this 7.8 Hz frequency is the resonant frequency of the human body.

It has been suggested by Dr. Robert Beck (1988) that perhaps this frequency is a "cosmic carrier of information" and could be the "drummer" to which these psychics, healers, dowsers, etc., were entrained? Give yourselves a moment to experience the beat frequencies from this tape and feel what, if anything, they are doing to you. They may produce the resonant frequency of the earth's aura. And, perhaps this particular set of tuning forks many be useful in helping you lock in resonance with the earth.

## The Way of Hemi-Sync

The next tape is from Robert Monroe's "Way of Hemi-Sync" tape.[1] Unlike the "Earth Hertz" which created beat frequencies of 7.8. Hz, that is, in the alpha frequency sound spectrum, most of these beat frequencies focus more on delta and theta waves mixed with beta frequencies. Additionally, unlike many of the other sounds on the tapes, Monroe does not deal with one specific frequency, but uses many.

With hemi-sync, the delta signal is usually 1.5 Hz. The theta signal is 4 Hz. The beta signal is 16 Hz. Alpha signals are not included on this or other hemi-sync tapes. Their research has shown that they are not of particular value in achieving the hemi-sync affect.

The carrier waves—that is the original frequencies used to create the different beat frequencies which produce the ELFs—vary, depending upon what they are trying to create. For delta, they generally use frequencies from 70-199 Hz. For theta, from 150 to 600 Hz. For beta, the carrier wave is below 350 Hz.

The following is a description by Bob Monroe (Hutchinson 1987) of the various frequencies used on hemi-sync tapes:

> The carrier frequencies that create the hemi-sync signals are introduced within the first minute of the music. The initial signal is a theta signal created from a carrier frequency of approximately 150 Hz. A delta signal with a carrier frequency under 100 Hz is faded in after approximately five minutes.
>
> The theta and delta patterns cycle together throughout the remainder of the music. Its amplitude is lower than that of the first theta signal. Its carrier frequency is generally a harmonic of the first carrier frequency.

---

[1]   "The Way of Hemi-Sync" by Robert Monroe, Monroe Institute, Faber, VA.

This provides a deeper or more enhanced experience for the listener. If the second theta signal is used, it is faded out in the final third of the piece. during the final five minutes the delta signal is gently faded out. This is followed by a gradual fading out of the theta signal and a gradual fading in of a low beta signal with a carrier frequency of approximately 350 Hz.

## Synchronicity

Next is one of Brother Charles' "Synchronicity" tapes which uses a technique called "phasing." Brother Charles defines phasing as "a vibrato sound, a tone that contains two tones, the top and bottom of the vibration. Phasing is the interval between the tones. The sound we call the interval is heard only in the brain. Your brain creates that sound from the two tones." This definition sounds surprisingly like the "binaural" beat frequency phenomenon employed by hemi-sync.

Brother Charles tapes also claim, like Robert Monroe's hemi-sync, to synchronize the left and right hemispheres of the brain. Brother Charles and Synchronicity Foundation have not published, or made available papers on their "holodynamic" technology. However, I have spoken with Synchronicity Foundation Research Coordinator Linda Burns personally about this (phone conversation 10/1/89). They have spent hundreds of hours with sophisticated EEG neuromapping on various subjects and found a consistent relationship between the phasing on the tape and the predominant brain wave activity of the subjects. The phasing technology is found processed into the ocean sound, as well as into the voice on this tape. Sometimes, it's easier to feel than hear. This tape is called "Genesis."[1] It is ocean sounds with a theta frequency of 4 Hz processed into the sound.

## Hermetic Harmonics

The next tape is "Hermetic Harmonics"[2] which I created to induce deep states of meditation. It is composed entirely of overtone chanting and Tibetan bells, multitracked and looped together. I created this recording for myself before I had any knowledge of the subject of sonic entrainment. As it turns out, this tape seems to be highly effective in inducing a theta state of brain wave activity, around 5 or 6 Hz. Intuitively, I had mixed the voices slightly out of phase. Tibetan bells or Ting Shas are also slightly out of tune and produce different tones which, depending on the bells, will create ELFs somewhere between 4 and 8 cycles per second. Many people have recorded and released meditation tapes which feature just the sounds of these bells.

---

[1]  "Genesis" by Borther Charles, Synchronicity, Faber, VA.
[2]  "Hermetic Harmonics" by Jonathan Goldman, Lyghte, Spirit Music, Boulder, CO.

I have wondered if Tibetan culture, which seems to have a sophisticated knowledge of the effect of sound on consciousness, did not create these bells because they knew of the ELFs created by them and their ability of alter consciousness.

"Hermetic Harmonics" is composed of these Tibetan bells and overtone chanting looped together. This tape is full of many different extremely low frequencies that seem to help entrain the brain to very deep states of consciousness. Recently, at Dr. Edgar Wilson's Center for BioBehavioral Health in Boulder, I was hooked up to a 24 channel Neuromap EEG while listening to this tape. The neuromap showed a predominance of theta activity in the 5 to 6 Hz range throughout my brain, accompanied by sporadic bursts of beta activity at various times.

Overtone, or harmonic chanting, incidentally, is the ability of the human voice to create two or more notes at the same time. At the last International Symposium, I presented a workshop, "Awakening the Lost Chord" on this subject (Goldman 1984). We've been receiving some very interesting information on the effects of overtone chanting which I hope to be able to share with you in the future.

## Peruvian Whistling Vessels

The next recording is of Peruvian whistling vessels—ancient pipe-like instruments.[1] On the tape they are actually replicas of the original whistling vessels, but they sound just the same. For some time, it was thought that they were just water jars buried with the mummies in Peru. Then some people began to experiment with them blowing on them as whistles. The psychoacoustic effects of actually blowing these vessels are quire amazing and powerful. The sounds are not particularly melodic and I have not found recordings of them to be nearly as effective as the actual experience of blowing them, where your entire cranium seems to act as a resonating chamber—an effect that does not reproduce on record. These vessels are usually blown in sets of seven, with a large number of beat frequencies being created.

Incidentally, the Science Section of the *New York Times* (March 29, 1988) was about these vessels (Broad 1988). The headline read, "Complex Whistles Found to Play Key Roles in Inca and Maya Life." The subtitle read "Much more than toys, the whistles were genuine musical instruments." Stephen Garrett and Daniel Statnekov (1988) were quoted in that article. They tested the tonal ranges of these vessels using spectrum analyzers and frequency meters.

[1] "Peruvian Whistling Vessels" by Daniel K. Statnekov and Steven Halpern, Sound Rx, San Anselmo, CA.

"The bottles are generally regarded by anthropologists as utilitarian liquid containers with the whistle providing an amusing method of venting," they wrote in the Journal of the Acoustical Society of America. "We are suggesting an alternative interpretation of the bottles as having been specifically produced as whistles." In an interview, Dr. Garret said their revision was driven by the fact that curious sounds were produced when two or three bottles of the same culture were blown simultaneously. Their higher notes would interact to produce deep, lower notes that could not be tape recorded but only heard in the ear, where the effect is generated, he said. "The idea is that these low frequency sounds were important in religious rituals for changing states of consciousness," he said.

We might contemplate that perhaps these ancient cultures which utilized beat frequencies in their instrumentation knew more than we have given them credit for.

The Peruvian whistling vessels and the Tibetan bells are two examples of shamanic tools that employed the concept of sonic entrainment and the brain. I am convinced that these and other ancient cultures knew of these principles for using ELFs to alter consciousness. Jeanne Achterberg (1985) notes that analysis of shamanic drumming encompasses a frequency range from .8 to 5.0 cycles per second, referred to as "theta driving capacity."

Though they may not have had a name for it, entrainment has been a tool for shamanic cultures since the beginning of time. The use of drumming and chants, as well as other instruments (perhaps such as the Peruvian whistling vessels) has always been implemented by shamans as they healed through the use of altered states of consciousness.

Today, as healers and therapists working with sound and music, we can follow in the paths of the ancient shamanic traditions, combining magic and mysticism with modern day science and technology. And I must be aware of new discoveries of using sound and music in this manner.

## Other Sonic Entrainment Researchers

As I was preparing this presentation, it was necessary for me to go through my collection of tapes which utilize some form of sonic entrainment. There are a number of very effective tapes which I outline below. Most of these tapes utilize the same technology as Monroe.

Tom Kenyon, head of Acoustic Brain Research in North Carolina,[1] produces various sonic entrainment cassettes called "Waveforms." Along with Differential Signalling, Tom's

---

[1]  Acoustic Brain Research, 100 Europa Drive, Suite 430, Chapel Hill, NC 27515.

term for the hemi-sync process, he also utilizes the pulsing of low tones at specific rhythmic patterns to entrain the brain into the desired state. He claims (1989) that an advantage of this form of entrainment is that a person with ear deafness can still get the "entrainment," whereas in Differential Signalling, there would be no entrainment since one of the signals is not being received. Tom has worked with researchers using a 24 channel Neuromap EEG recording of subjects after they had listened to his "Waveform" tape. This research showed a shift of dominant alpha brain activity and a powerful increase in theta (4-7 Hz).

Dr. Jeffrey Thompson, a chiropractor working with sound at Sound Sphere productions[1] has produced the "Isle of Skye" which incorporates music as well as sonic entrainment technology. This tape, according to Dr. Thompson, "contains specific frequency modulation designed to induce the production of alpha and theta waves in the human cerebral cortex... I use multiple variations of alpha and theta wave frequencies, phasing the wave forms through the 3.5 to 13 Hz range." Jeffrey uses a number of other sonic therapies besides these tapes and his work merits further investigation.

The use of music to accompany these sonic entrainment frequencies is becoming more and more common. Many of Monroe's tapes utilize music as well as the hemi-sync frequencies, with most of the hemi-sync frequencies at a subliminal listening level. They have found that these subliminal frequencies are as effective as the audible ones. The sounds from the tapes mentioned above were for the most part devoid of music in order to give a clear understanding of experiencing sonic entrainment through just beat frequencies. Particular music can, of course, help induce sonic entrainment as well.

It is important to understand that with these extremely low frequencies any music which may accompany the sounds must be pulsed slowly. As we discussed before, music pulsed at about 60 beats per minute is ideal for helping to induce alpha states. If you use music that was pulsed much faster, the entrainment of the heart to faster rhythms would clash with the slow brain wave pulses created by the beat frequency process. The effect would be minimal, if at all. Therefore, slow music must be utilized with this.

Ronald de Strulle, director of Holistic Programs in New York City,[2] has produced a series of tapes created for enhanced learning and meditation. In correspondence to me (letter to author, October 10, 1989), he writes:

> All programs contain natural (harmonic) alpha-theta bilateral entrainment; <u>not</u> as added (dissonant) signals such as hemi-sync, but by taking the bass frequency band such as created by cellos, string bass or

---

[1]  Sound Sphere Research, 312 So. Cedros, Solana Beach, CA 92075.
[2]  Holistic Programs, Inc., 1601 Beverly Road, Brooklyn, NY 11226.

lower octave voices, splitting and deturning one of the signals to the desired alpha or theta resonant pulse. Thus the entrainment is sympathetic or harmonic with the musical arrangement rather than dissonant and catalysing unwanted resonances.

Like Robert Pollaksen, de Strulle utilizes the 7.8 Hz frequency which he feels creates a geo-magnetic field. He also uses a frequency of about 1.45 Hz. to create entrainment between the hypothalamus, pituitary and pineal centers of the brain. This is a frequency with which Brother Charles is experimenting in a select group of test subjects. Brother Charles also believes it stimulates the pituitary.

## The Future of Sonic Entrainment

I have not discussed frequencies such as 1.45 Hz, but mostly those of either 7.8 Hz or 4 Hz. While I believe that such frequencies may indeed by effective for stimulating the pituitary for example, we must surely wonder what such an effect would produce on the brain and the total person. Especially worthy of contemplation is the long term effect of such resonance.

I believe that the technology of creating sonic entrainment may be an important aspect of the therapeutic use of sound and music. Private research from the Monroe Institute (Varney 1988) indicates some positive results for the enhancement of education. Recently, a paper from the Monroe Institute described some significant changes in the development of individuals with Downes Syndrome. The potential uses of such technology are limitless.

However I am by no means convinced that sonic entrainment is the cure-all or answer to the potential use of healing with sound. And I am somewhat concerned that with such a simple technology, it is becoming quite easy for anyone with recording equipment to produce tapes that create sonic entrainment. Without proper research and study, we may be unleashing a Pandora's box to an unsuspecting public. Along with research into how this technology can be utilized, I believe equal thought should be given to the moral implications of using this knowledge, i.e., when should it be utilized. A final question that we should contemplate regards brain wave activity itself. Does specific brain wave activity indicate specific states of consciousness? Simply registering alpha brain wave activity, for example, does not necessarily indicate a state of meditational bliss. Is there a specific relationship between particular brain waves and particular states of consciousness and if so, what is it and what does this mean?

## REFERENCE LIST

Achterberg, J. 1985. *Imagery in Healing*. Boston: New Science Library.

Allesch, C.G. 1981. A study of the influence of music on pulse and respiration frequency. *Zeitschrift für experimentelle und angewandte Psychologies* 1981, Vol. 29.

Atwater, F.H. 1987. The Monroe Institute's hemi-sync process. Unpublished research, Monroe Institute.

Beck, B. 1988. ELF waves and EEG entrainment. *Kiplinger Magazine* Jan/Feb.

Bentov, I. 1988. *Stalking the Wild Pendulum*. Vermont: Destiny Books.

Berendt, J-E. 1987. *Nada Braham: The World is Sound*. Vermont: Destiny Books.

Broad, W. 1988. Complex whistles found to play a key role in Inca and Maya life. *New York Times* Tuesday, March 29.

Clynes, M., and Walker, J. 1982. Neurobiologic functions of rhythm, time and pulse in music. In *Music, Mind and Brain*, edited by Manfred Clynes. New York: Plenum Press.

Fontana, A.E., and Loschi, J.A. 1979. Combined use of music with sound of heart beats and respiration rhythms in psychotherapy. *Acta Psiquiatrica y Psicologic de America Latina* March, 1979.

Harrer, A. and Harrer, L. 1977. Music, emotion and autonomic function. In *Music and the Brain*. M. Critchley, and R. Henson (Eds.). London: Heinemann.

Hutchinson, M. 1987. *Mega Brain*. New York: Ballantine Books.

Kenyon, T. 1989. *Acoustic Brain Research*. Faber, VA: Acoustic Brain Research, Inc.

Kneutgen, J. 1970. On the effects of lullabies. *Zeitschrift für experimentelle und angewandte Psychologie, Vol. I*.

Krier, B.A. 1987. Meditation on tape: Enlightenment made easy. *Los Angeles Times* January 30.

Landreth, J.E., and Hobart, F. 1974. Effects of music on physiological response. *Journal of Research in Music Education* Vol. 22.

Leonard, G. 1978. *The Silent Pulse*. New York: E.P. Dutton.

Morris, S.E. 1987. The structure of metamusic. *Breakthrough*. March. Monroe Institute of Applied Sciences.

Myers, J. 1988. Human rhythms and the psychobiology of entrainment. Unpublished, Bell Communication Research.

Oster, G. 1973. Auditory beats in the brain. *Scientific American*. Vol. 229, **4**, 94-102.

Ostrander, S., and Schroeder, L. 1982. *Superlearning*. New York: Dell.

Varney, K. 1988. Metamusic with hemi-sync as an adjunct to intervention with developmentally delayed young children. Virginia Commonwealth University.

# MUSIC THERAPY WITH BONE MARROW TRANSPLANT PATIENTS: REACHING BEYOND THE SYMPTOMS

Paul Nolan

The use of music in medical treatment can be traced to the earliest reports of medical practice. Currently, the practice of music therapy in medical settings is usually limited to the use of music as an auditory stimulus. Models of music therapy which use the musical expressions of the patient are not well documented. This chapter will attempt to illustrate a model of improvisational music therapy in a medical setting.

In this age of medical specialization each member of the treatment team is oriented toward the reduction of symptoms. Professional sub-specialization may inhibit a clinical understanding of the landslide affects of the dysphoria and demoralization which can occur from hospitalization, especially following periods of relapse (Weisman 1986). A common service available in many urban hospitals designed to treat these affects is the Liaison/Consultation Psychiatry service. However, for some patients this intervention signifies to the patient that they are not in control of their response to their illness. Also, to the general public, psychiatric consultations still carry a negative stigma relating to mental illness. For these and other reasons patients may resist, either directly or indirectly, psychiatric consultations when a dysphoric response to catastrophic illness occurs.

Throughout the course of one's hospitalization it is quite possible that virtually all interpersonal contact can become centered upon one's symptoms. In observing the patient's interactions with treatment staff, family, and friends it appears that the patient's illness dominates all conversation. Within this model, the music therapist maintains an awareness of the medical course of events but he or she is not directly invested in the symptoms of the disease. The music therapist can fill a void in the patient's life by identifying and attempting to reintegrate his/her preexisting health. The therapist attempts to make contact with the person who is living with the disease. In distancing oneself from the physical symptom-reducing process, the music therapist can provide an opportunity for patients to express their feelings directly about their illness or about their health care providers without the real, or fantasized, threat of compromising their personal care. In our hospital we have found that referred patients are rarely reluctant to participate in any of the offered art therapies. From the patients' reports, we have found that they feel that it makes sense to involve themselves in a therapeutic application of the arts to help combat the sensory deprivation and isolation which accompanies illness and hospitalization.

The basic orientation which underlies this model is found in the Supportive Therapy model (Werman 1984). The basic tenets of this approach include the strengthening of ego functions with the concomitant self-awareness of these strengths. In other words, the therapist attempts to connect the patient with preexisting resources which have become dormant due to the regressive response to illness and hospitalization. The therapeutic relation is not constructed along the lines of analytically oriented insight therapy. Therefore, the therapist limits the transference and the length of treatment. Treatment goals are facilitated through live music making whenever possible. This practice is based upon the premise that the initiation of musical sounds, either in response to an outside or self-initiated stimulus, represents the inherent health within that person. A basic assumption of this model is that music expression facilitates the activation and recognition of that health. Live music making in a music therapy context allows for the discharge of feelings as a symbolic expression within a supportive relationship. The therapist creates an environment in which patients may become aware of their control in the nonverbal and verbal expression of feelings in an otherwise dependent period of their life. The reduction of distress through the supportive relationship, along with the opportunities for nonverbal expressive discharge may offer the patient a means to keep emotions within bounds which does not warp judgement. The music therapist is also in a position to monitor the psychic health of the patient and to report back to the treatment team.

The materials used in this model include musical instruments which allow for melodic and rhythmic expression, yet do not require expertise or training in music. Xylophones with movable tone bars may be arranged by the music therapist so that a sequence of music pitches may be struck with a musical result. With certain pitch arrangements a random sequence can be played to produce sounds which makes sense as a musical statement. The creation of musical statements is not the goal of therapy, but this element allows for an expression of ideas and feelings with an accompanying sense of control. The therapist employs the musical expressions of the patient to construct a framework in which interaction can occur. Within the development of a music improvisation the therapist encourages exploration, reflects rhythms, dynamics, and melodic ideas, develops affective qualities within the patient's musical expression, and adds consequent responses to partially developed melodic ideas. Following the improvisation the therapist encourages verbal responses which may pertain to mood, extramusical associations, and other awareness experienced by the patient. The therapist may use this period to encourage the elaboration of thoughts and feelings which may have been stimulated by the music. Within this model the therapist offers feedback which is intended to support and strengthen mental structures which have become damaged from the response to life-threatening illness. The therapist nurtures, guides, suggests, and helps the patient distinguish fantasy from reality. The use of a tape recorder allows the music to be played back, thus offering a source for reality testing. This material becomes available as a bridge upon which the therapist may help the patient to identify and support the healthy resources which emerge through the musical interaction.

## CASE EXAMPLE

Mary, a thirty-three-year-old white mother of two children, was diagnosed with leukemia ten months prior to music therapy treatment. She underwent a bone-marrow transplant six months after the diagnosis. Due to frequent infections she was again hospitalized three months after the transplant. During this stay it was observed that her usually vibrant mood was deteriorating. Although she refused a psychiatric consultation, she was willing to try music therapy. She remained in the hospital for seven weeks. Six months after discharge she returned to the hospital and passed away suddenly. Mary's music therapy sessions provided a means of exploring feelings about her illness which fortified her sense of control. Within her early improvisations she seemed to use her gradually developing sense of control over the musical materials as a metaphor for the emerging inner control over her response to her illness. Her associations with her musical expressions gradually connected her to people and things outside the hospital which were important to her. She recomposed the lyrics of a popular folk song to portray her imagined physiological therapeutic response to the transplant. This humor-filled and spontaneous re-creation was performed to the musical accompaniment of the music therapist and her attending physician on guitar and banjo. This event was a turning point in Mary's emotional response. Her presence on the unit became a source of encouragement to the nurses; her physicians could offer increased support and allow for the mutual expression of positive feelings; her mother became less preoccupied with her illness. Mary's final music therapy sessions were characterized by further exploration and acceptance of her moods and response to her ordeal. She described her emerging musical expressions as "blue, but not totally depressing;" "intense, caring feelings of love;" and "fun, uplifting... it sparked something different in me." She begun to feel strongly about documenting her response to music therapy in the hope that others may benefit from her example. She agreed to participate in a nationally televised program on music and healing and became a local celebrity on the ward. Although appreciating the reality that at any time her symptoms could worsen, Mary was able to overcome the withdrawal and depressive responses to her trauma through the reactivation of her inner resources. It appears that this process was mobilized through her musical expressions and the cognitive processing which seemed to help her identify and eventually trust her emerging psychic health. She stated that she appreciated the opportunity to talk after each improvisation because it allowed her to talk about her feelings in a "way that makes it seem easier."

## SUMMARY

Mary's involvement in music therapy illustrates the role that musical expression can play within a therapeutic relationship. Her response to the prolonged illness began to produce signs and symptoms of depression which jeopardized her involvement in the treatment process. Music therapy seemed to assist in the restoration of her preexisting ego strengths and brought with it a new level of adaptation. Her health-oriented interactions with staff and family seemed to open up paths of relating which were less focused upon illness and more focused upon the person living with the disease.

## REFERENCE LIST

Weisman, A.D. 1986. Emotional problems in the management of cancer. In *Emotional Disorders in Physically Ill Patients*, edited by R. Roessler and N. Decker. New York: Human Sciences Press, Inc.

Werman, D.S. 1984. *The Practice of Supportive Psychotherapy*. New York: Brunner/Mazel, Inc.

# HOLISTIC NEUROMUSCULAR FACILITATION: THE USE OF MUSIC AND DANCE WITHIN A MULTIFACETED TREATMENT FOR THE DISABLED

Bella Abramowitz Fisher

Holistic Neuromuscular Facilitation (HNF), a unique synthesis of old and innovative ideas, is a complex physical therapy group treatment. Using many therapeutic approaches blended with physical therapy, the therapist tries to engage every aspect of the patient as a human being in a milieu both structured and spontaneous, joyful and solicitous. This facilitates the release of the body's natural healing forces toward wholeness.

In addition to the benefits of standard physical therapy, HNF provides an interplay between body, mind, and spirit; individual and environment; individual and group. It also provides a vehicle aimed at reaching the subcortical level of the patient. Such total involvement maximizes motivation and enhances improvement. Greater neuromuscular, cognitive, psychosocial, emotional, and spiritual responses are facilitated.

This rehabilitation treatment was pioneered in 1945 while I was treating traumatic injuries during the Battle of Okinawa during the Second World War. The present format, conceptualized in 1970, had evolved to include neuromuscular as well as the muscoloskeletal conditions.

Music is one major component of HNF, both as it sets the atmosphere prior to treatment, and as an integral driving force of the treatment itself, eliciting the return of movement through dance. Any and all forms of dance may be used, depending upon the functional level of the patient and the background of the therapist. These might include free-flowing or structured; sitting or standing; single or couple; line, circle, folk, square, ballet, modern, or ballroom dancing; and in any and all combinations.

Other new concepts included are: "Dynamic Relaxation;" sense-memory; separate room facilitating integration of all sensory input; Progressive Dance Training in lieu of progressive ambulation training; and the Party format.

An end in itself, as well as the means to an end, HNF provides the transition between hospital and home, and between home and the mainstream. This is accomplished by offering the opportunity to practice a returned or limited skill through song, dance, games, and socialization, under the professional guidance of a physical therapist. This is especially effective when using "Ballroom Dance Training" as a means for gait and ambulation training, and as an end for developing a social dance skill.

In the hospital, the session itself starts as the patient enters the special HNF room or area in which a party-like atmosphere has already been created with decorations and music. While establishing the state I call "Dynamic Relaxation," spontaneous reactions to music are stimulated. This is followed by simple structured movements to music, and builds with progressively more complex coordinated movements, ending with some popular dance and/or song forms. Real and/or imaginary props and games are used for change of pace. Refreshments are served as each individual receives progressive "Ballroom Dance Training." The session ends with the singing of a popular song which continues as the patients exit.

In order to allow internal processes to function uninhibitedly during this session, (such processes as the commanding powers of the mind, the healing capacity of the old, the generative capacity of the new, and any possible pre-patterned central programming of the brain), "Dynamic Relaxation" is used. This is a process to achieve relaxation for and during activity by encouraging the patient to feel so totally accepted within a safe, joyful ambiance, that she/he can function in the most accessible mental and emotional state, and free enough to actively participate physically as instinctively as possible. When this wholehearted active involvement is achieved the state of "Dynamic Relaxation" is realized.

The Progressive Dance Training mentioned is quite an effective technique for progressive ambulation training. Social dancing, after all, is ambulating to music in all directions, using various rhythms. Of course, the premorbid dance recall is also very strong.

The social dance position, modified to meet the deficit and assistive needs of each patient, fosters a more normal gait. The inhibiting and distorting effects of assistive devices, such as canes and walkers, are minimized and often eliminated. Length of steps becomes more equal and posture improves. The steady beat of the music also promotes equal length, as well as equal timing of steps.

Sessions in post-hospital support group Stroke Clubs in the community are similar but with additional emphasis on ambulatory and social skills in the form of line, circle, square, and disco dancing as well as a little more advanced ballroom dancing. All patients benefit greatly from these, but especially those with cognitive, perceptive, and aphasic problems.

Confusion and anxiety when mingling with crowds are decreased significantly when the patients get the repeated opportunity to do just that in the controlled chaos of the safe supervised line and circle dancing. Making decisions about when and how to circumvent a person blocking one's way during this dancing helps the patient develop some problem-solving skills. Left/right discrimination and body awareness in space relating to sense of direction get favorable practice time for improvements. Processing commands in this functional situation develops keener concentration efforts.

Being able to respond to ballroom dance stimulation on a subcortical level generates much pleasure and a sense of accomplishment. Developing mental flexibility is encouraged by helping the patient to change his former style of dancing and to accept a new one accommodating his/her new status, thus helping to assure continued dance enjoyment. Those who have never danced before are pleased to discover that it is truly never too late to learn, and they are surprised at the paradox that they had to get sick to learn to dance.

For almost 16 years I have used Holistic Neuromuscular Facilitation for a wide range of conditions, on three separate recovery levels. For acute services and rehabilitation this has been at three hospitals, and for post-hospital rehabilitation and maintenance, at six Stroke Clubs.

Results have been positive and sometimes dramatic as indicated by patients' questionnaires, referring doctors' re-evaluations, peer analyses, family and friends' commendations, and my evaluations, documented data, video, and informal clinical research.

The carry-over to improved patient management and motivation was often reported by the hospital team. In the post-hospital Stroke Clubs, improvements were noted at a rate faster than at any other time during the post-hospital period. The carry-over to other areas of the patient's life was also reported.

In addition to improved physical functioning, some general results noted on all levels were a decrease in pain, tension, blood pressure, depression, confusion, and fear; an increase in motivation, energy, self-image, and psychosocial functioning; and an improvement in speech, sense of direction, ability to dance, laugh, and enjoy.

In both the hospital and post-hospital settings, HNF tended to elicit earlier mobilization and incorporation of unused and weak muscles, and more control over ataxic movements, than did calisthenic exercises. One of the reasons for this, I believe, is the major impact of music and rhythm.

I observed that rhythmic music directed the patient into continuous coordinated movements. As part of this natural coordinated pattern, weaker components became more active, and in some cases were elicited for the first time. The insistent rhythm tended to have a compelling force that seemed to command, or almost pull forth, the weaker components. The closer the tempo of the music was to the tempo of the personality and the tempo of the physical capabilities, the more natural and coordinated were the responses, allowing the unused and weak muscles a better opportunity to join in.

The following are some general thoughts for music and rhythm selections. People respond more spontaneously to music they like, which makes "liking" a key factor. In fact, disliked music can facilitate inhibition. When liked and also familiar, music can help even more by its powers to stimulate physical responses associated with the sense-memory recall. All this applies to the therapist's likes as well, since his/her spontaneity will also help ignite the group.

Encouraging the singing of popular songs with lyrics adjusted to fit the situation and movements desired provides a framework for total involvement. This then elicits stronger emotional and physical responses.

In a group situation each individual should be encouraged to find her/her own most comfortable and successful beat. The choice is determined by ability and debility. For example, in 4/4 time, one person might move best on the first beat of each measure, another on the first and third, and still another on each beat or only the first of every other measure. However, being *on* the beat, and being *consistent* must be stressed. Upon improvement, variations and combinations of rhythm can be encouraged, but always *on* the beat—up or down.

Forcing a slower or quicker tempo upon a patient can be therapeutic only when dictated by the need to improve a particular neuromusculoskeletal deficit.

The beat can control, direct, and sustain movement, and therefore needs to be respected. Everyone is born with a sense of rhythm, but emotional pulls can affect it in some people. These individuals respond to their own inner drum played by anxieties and preoccupations, and heard through their misplaced emotions. These people, especially, need assistance to feel accepted and relaxed enough to respond to the outer drum played by others and heard through the ear.

Rhythm and music alone can facilitate neuromuscular responses. When inspired and directed by a physical therapist into dance reactions, this can be even more effective. When incorporated in a happy, accepting, social environment, and augmented by many other pleasant sensory stimuli, responses are even further enhanced. The evoked pleasant sense-memories could then intensify those good feelings, and thus hasten the creation of an optimal receptive state.

In fact, any one of these elements, when taken alone, could foster improvements. However, when taken as a whole, with overlapping sensory systems, the summation of this total integrated approach reaching maximal input has the most impact. Potential neuromuscular responses are more easily triggered, with more optimal results realized.

The disabled person with limited physical capacities has an enormous amount of work to do in his/her rehabilitation and ongoing life efforts. The one with additional cognitive, perceptual, aphasic, and/or emotional problems can be completely overwhelmed and needs all the help we can and should give. Holistic Neuromuscular Facilitation, with its use of music and dance, is a wonderfully joyous way to provide this help.

*This paper was not presented at the Symposium due to extenuating circumstances. The Editors, however, felt the material to be of such importance as to include it with the express permission of the author.*

# EXPRESSION THROUGH DANCE FOR THE WELL-ELDERLY

Sara Scott Turner

> Each art form expresses emotions which are particular to it. In exploring and learning new forms of expression, we are learning new forms of feeling, and thereby gaining and refining the capacity for experiencing new feelings. By presenting the possibility of expressing emotion in the medium of physical movement peculiar to dance, emotions are developed which could not be known in any other way. Thus, learning to dance can be a discovery of both formal and emotional qualities. Only through the physical movement which is the medium of dance can one acquire the possibility of expressing these emotions.

These thoughts expressed by David Best (1974, 159) illuminate our understanding of the procedures to be discussed in this paper.

Creative music making, movement (dance), drama and poetry have demonstrated a marked rejuvenating effect on the well-elderly person. Most middle-aged persons impose restrictions upon themselves, ruling out formation of new mental, physical and emotional patterns. Attitudes and postures are selected to fit an assumed dignity, so that certain actions such as sitting on the floor or jumping are rejected, which then soon become impossible to perform. Exploring means of creative expression through music, dance, drama, and poetry are long discarded dreams. Emotional nurturing is often limited to involvement with family and a few long-standing friends; relationships which may decrease in meaning and satisfaction.

In formulating processes toward more expressive, shared, self-actualized awareness, one is challenged to aid that core of self in which a sense of wholeness may surface through integration of inner and outer self.

The opportunity exists for a new start for those designing creative programs for the well-elderly. This is based on the participant having left behind the anxieties of work and the responsibilities of the family so that they are free to seize the opportunity more closely to resemble the inner self, rather than continue to conform to self-imposed and societal images of aging.

In a liberating group setting in which a childlike affection for others is based on a shared emotional experience, creative outpouring is infectious. It is possible to overcome the effects of isolation, withdrawal and depression on the elderly by providing an opportunity for verbal and nonverbal expression, using touching in social contact, stimulating rhythmic responses, building positive self-image and ego strengths through achievement, providing opportunities for relaxation, stimulating joyful, pleasurable participation in a group, and offering increased body awareness (Linder et al. 1979)

Being a part of a creative music and dance group stimulates growth and social awareness, creating an aura of fun and enthusiasm. Childlike simplicity strips away adult formed artifices and defenses, so that we may interact more honestly, recognizing a more authentic self. According to Al Siebert's indicators of self-motivated growth, qualities exhibiting a high level of maturity include "aimless playfulness for its own sake, like that of a happy child; a child's innocent curiosity; willingness to look foolish, make mistakes, and laugh at yourself, an active imagination, daydreams, mental play and conversations with yourself" (Siegel 1986, 164).

**TABLE 1** Workshop examples of exercises demonstrating therapeutic applications of music and dance.

## A. Mirroring

Pre-mirroring preparation
- Reach high to ceiling; stretch, inhale.
- Lower arms to feet; exhale. Repeat 3 or 4 times.
- Toes first, move about, receptive to the music.
- Try lilting, graceful, flowing large movements.
- Move throughout the room. Reach high, low, forward, to each side.

Mirroring
- Continue to move. Make intense eye contact with one person (first one you see). Place your palms toward the other, one or two inches from your partner's palms. Look at and accept the other's movements to develop awareness and recognition of your partner's response to changing moods indicated by music.

- Change, establishing eye contact with another person (first one you see) on suggestion of leader. Hold it intensely. Gain from the experience of mirroring the other, adapting your feelings to the other's movements. When carried out reciprocally, emotional bonding may ensue.

- Change partners on suggestion of leader. Direct pathways show openness and gladness; play cat and mouse, body cuts through space like a light beam; float, glide. Keeping eye contact, move far away from partner, then move closer.

- After changing partners several times, stop before interest and stamina wane.

Taped music included:
> Yamaha TSR 200 (electronic jazz)
> *This is Henry Mancini*
> *Solar Explorations* by Moe Kaufman's
> "Touch Her Soft Lips and Part" from *Henry V* by William Walton

## B. Moving Statues (relationships: meeting and parting)

- Form into groups of three. Think of being magnetically pulled toward each other.
- One person begins moving one body part.
- Others move with the same part. Each is drawn to fill up space, as though pulled magnetically, with movement expressive of provided music.
- Focus on sensitivity of others in triad.
- With palms outstretched as in mirroring, outline other's bodies with hands as more body parts are added gradually. Group becomes a moving mass, interlocking.
- Gradually untangle. One is adapting one's inner feelings toward other's experience.

Music:
> *Preludes for Piano* by Debussy
> *Symphony No. 2*, second movement,.by Rachmaninoff

## C.  Composition

- In the composition exercise, creativity is explored. Begin by notating motives for a composition on a blackboard in graphic representation, such as:

 etc.

serving as visual symbols of sound and movement.

- A participant who wishes to suggest a motive draws a graphic representation, suggesting vocal sounds and choreography to match. Four to six motives are needed.

- Participant divide into groups (4-6) with leaders being those who suggested motives. Each group works out a sound and movement expressing their motive, expanding and refining the original idea of their leader (approx. 5 minutes).

- Reassemble, keeping groups defined. One participant acts as conductor, indicating entry of each group, keeping their symbol in mind. Each group is given time to expand on their motive before indicating entry of another group. As groups interact, intertwining contrapuntally, both in sound effect and movement, the conductor, with hand and body indications, leads all to combine in an all-encompassing finale. Spontaneously, this usually takes the form of snake-like intertwining, or all moving towards the center in waves.

An informal opportunity for expressing reaction to the composition exercise immediately afterwards adds value to the experience. Sharing simple refreshments while sitting on the floor helps to solidify group identification, validating social and creative responses.


# REFERENCE LIST

Best, D. 1974. *Expression in Movement and the Arts: A Philosophical Enquiry.* London: Lepus.

Linder, E.C.; Harpaz, L.; and Lamberg, S. 1979. *Therapeutic Dance/Movement: Expressive Activities for Older Adults.* New York: Human Sciences.

Siegel, B.S. 1986. *Love, Medicine and Miracles.* New York, Harper and Row.

# MUSIC THERAPY WITH DEPRESSED OLDER ADULTS*

Suzanne Hanser

*This paper describes the effects of three music therapy techniques based on a cognitive-behavioral approach employed with the elderly. It presents music instruction, structured music experiences and a music stress reduction program designed to deal with the underlying anxiety associated with depression. Case studies of four older adults suffering from depression are provided.*

Thanks to medical advances, modern technology, and improved living conditions, the world's population is living longer than ever before. This trend is particularly significant in the United States, where elders are healthier and more active than they have ever been. While the group of people over the age of 65 is expected to increase dramatically in the next several decades, the number of people over 85 is projected to be seven times its present level by the middle of the twenty-first century.

With such longevity come new concerns about the quality of life of the older adult. Even when in good health, the elderly experience changes in their physical abilities and energy level as a function of normal physiological development. They must cope with major adjustments in life style, such as retirement, which is often accompanied by a change in financial status. New social roles and references contribute to difficulties in psychological adjustment. As the loss of loved ones becomes more prevalent, bereavement may also cause psychological problems. These factors and others can lead to depression, a condition which affects social and emotional functioning as well as physical health and well-being.

It has been estimated that three to six percent of the elderly population have a clinical diagnosis of major depressive disorder (Vernon and Roberts 1982). Treatment with pharmacotherapy is often effective with this syndrome, but side effects and contraindications with certain conditions are common (Strauss and Solomon 1983). Short-term psychotherapies, including cognitive therapy, behavioral therapy, and brief psychodynamic therapy have also been employed successfully with depressed elders (Thompson et al. 1987). These effective techniques are viable when the patient has access to treatment by a qualified psychologist. However, when the patient is homebound or unable to afford such psychological services, other treatment alternatives might be of value.

---

* This article is reprinted with permission from the *Journal of the International Association of Music for the Handicapped.*

It is the search for a psychoeducational strategy which is cost-effective and easily accessible that has produced the music therapy program described in this paper. The results of four case studies are described here as a pilot project for an experimentally controlled design incorporating home-based music therapy sessions, a comparison treatment condition, and a wait list control group.

## DEVELOPMENT OF A MUSIC THERAPY STRATEGY

In developing a strategy for coping with depression, one must be aware of the symptoms and behaviors associated with this diagnosis. These may include a sad affect; feelings of hopelessness; a sense of failure and dissatisfaction; low self-esteem; lack of interest, energy and appetite; poor decision making; somatic complaints; difficulty sleeping; and even suicidal ideation.

One basis for the use of music therapy with depressed patients is the notion that music listening is a palliative strategy for coping with the stress and anxiety underlying the depression. Music is also instrumental in facilitating a working through of problems when it relaxes and prepares the patient for clearer thinking. In numerous research studies, a successful music learning experience has been shown to improve self-esteem. Similarly, music has served as an effective means of stress reduction (Hanser 1987). Thus, music therapy holds great potential for the depressed patient.

A cognitive-behavioral theory served as the foundation for the specific music therapy techniques employed in this approach. Music therapy offered:

1. A stimulus for deep body relaxation;
2. A stimulus for positive imagery and mood;
3. A stimulus for clear thinking, incompatible with worrying; and
4. A pleasant, potentially reinforcing event.

Additionally, simple techniques which could be used by the patient with minimal therapist contact were most desirable. A short-term strategy was devised, involving one-hour weekly home visits by the music therapist over an eight-week period. Homework assignments necessitated daily use of a prescribed music therapy technique by the patient.

Three techniques were piloted as part of a broader research effort in the treatment of major depression. The first technique was instrumental music instruction for the purpose of developing new interests and improving feelings of self-worth. The second technique involved structuring active music participation for patients who worried extensively about specific problems. A music listening technique was also developed for stress reduction and sleep induction.

## Instrumental Music Instruction

When a patient expressed a desire to study an instrument, and scores on the self-esteem inventory were low, instrumental instruction was provided during weekly visits. A practice schedule was organized based on a reasonable expectation of available leisure time. Small increments of music learning objectives were set with a maximum likelihood of being met during the week. Simple performance pieces offered opportunities for successful music accomplishment over a short period of time. The lesson itself was used as a metaphor for observing and changing maladaptive behaviors which might interfere in other aspects of daily life.

## Structured Music Experiences

For the patients who had difficulty organizing time or tended not to engage in pleasant activities, a daily schedule was prepared. The patient was urged to participate in a variety of music activities, e.g., attending a concert, listening to favorite music, learning about music, or playing music (if the patient had musical skills) during some part of every day. In some cases, this special music part of the day temporally followed the accomplishment of less favorable tasks, in an attempt to reinforce such behavior. Sessions with the music therapist involved examining how changes in the amount of time spent in pleasant activities affected daily mood and the frequency of worrying and dysfunctional thoughts. New musical interests were also explored and when feasible, music stress reduction techniques were taught.

## Music Stress Reduction

Other patients participated in a music listening program designed to reduce stress. Musical selections were based on patient preferences and recommendations by the music therapist. When possible, the program included music from the patient's own collection to facilitate continued use of the techniques after the end of treatment.

The patient was then instructed in stress reduction exercises to be employed while listening to the music. The main objectives for these techniques were to achieve a relaxed body and a relaxed state of mind. To achieve body relaxation, three techniques were performed: light exercise to familiar, rhythmic music for identifying sources of muscle tension; gentle facial massage to familiar relaxing music to locate tension in facial muscles; and progressive muscle relaxation for the entire body accompanied by music specially composed for tension and release of individual body parts.

To achieve a relaxed mind, guided imagery to programmatic music encouraged the listener to become transported to a peaceful and wonderful place. After responding favorably to this technique, patients would meet an inner advisor in their mind's eye and maintain a dialogue with this being. This led to working out concerns and questions while in a relaxed state, using their own resources to solve problems.

The next step in this approach depended upon the appearance of particular symptoms. Individuals who displayed difficulty sleeping were taught to use these techniques before sleep. Those who found it challenging to get up in the morning or to get started on new projects were asked to listen to more active and rhythmic music in an exercise plan to promote stimulation and energy enhancement.

## ASSESSMENT

In the initial home visit, the music therapist assessed each patient's level of depression as well as musical interests and history. The following self-report scales were administered pre-treatment, mid-treatment after four weeks, and post-treatment after eight weeks: Yesavage Mood Assessment Scale [MAS] (Yesavage et al. 1983); Brief Symptom Inventory [BSI] (Derogatis and Spencer 1982); Rosenberg Self-Esteem Inventory [SEI] (Rosenberg 1979); and Beck Depression Inventory [BDI] (Beck et al. 1961). On each of these tests, the higher the score, the worse the condition; the lower the score, the better the condition. Scores range from 0 to 30 on the Yesavage MAS; 0 to 212 on the BSI; 10 to 40 on the Rosenberg SEI, and 0 to 39 on the BDI.

The patient's musical style preferences, musical interests and experience were recorded. Additionally, the patient was asked to relax while listening to musical selections as the therapist observed body tension.

This evaluation determined the most appropriate technique for a given patient.

## CASE EXAMPLES

### Case 1: E

| SCORES | PRETEST | MIDTEST | POSTTEST | PRE-POST CHANGE |
|--------|---------|---------|----------|------------------|
| MAS | 15 | 9 | 3 | +12 |
| BSI | 40 | 33 | 26 | +14 |
| SEI | 17 | 11 | 10 | +7 |
| BDI | 5 | 2 | 3 | +2 |

E is an 82-year-old female who had been treated for probable major depressive disorder two years before starting music therapy. E displayed a depressed affect and feelings of dissatisfaction, discouragement, irritation, and worthlessness. She avoided people and social situations, was distrustful of others, and frequently thought about death. After hip replacement surgery, E had difficulty getting out and exploring interests that kept her active when she was more physically able. In the initial home visit, E expressed an interest in learning to play the piano, something she had always wanted to do.

E progressed slowly on the instrument, pausing to perfect each simple exercise and piece. After teaching basic technique, the music therapist focused on improvisation at the keyboard to encourage a freer, more positive experience when playing. The piano lesson served as a metaphor when E displayed the compulsive and perfectionist tendencies which were common in the way she approached new tasks. After improvising, she was encouraged to consider how other compulsions could be changed by improvising around them. She enjoyed practicing and playing the piano for others. She started inviting friends over on a regular basis so that she could demonstrate her new skills.

E reported a significant change in her life as a function of learning the piano. At the final therapy session, she expressed this thought: "There is no need to be morose; there is something I can do now which makes me feel better." Interestingly, when the therapist followed up by recommending other piano teachers and suggesting ways to maintain piano technique and practice, E decided not to continue study. She stated that she could appreciate what she had accomplished and preferred to practice what she had already learned. She realized that this decision might reflect the lack of confidence and fear of trying new things that had plagued her in recent years, but this time, she felt that she was making a conscious choice to postpone further study until she was ready.

E's progress is evident on all of the standardized tests, where she demonstrated gains on all measurements. E obtained a posttest score of 10, the best possible, on the Self-Esteem Inventory, and extremely low scores of 3 on the Mood Assessment Scale and 3 on the Beck Depression Inventory. In addition, a sizeable gain of 14 points was accomplished over the eight-week treatment period on the Brief Symptom Inventory.

**Case 2: F**

| SCORES | PRETEST | MIDTEST | POSTTEST | PRE-POST CHANGE |
|--------|---------|---------|----------|-----------------|
| MAS    | 20      | 7       | 10       | +10             |
| BSI    | 41      | 16      | 27       | +14             |
| SEI    | 28      | 26      | 25       | +3              |
| BDI    | 12      | 10      | 7        | +5              |

F is a 76-year-old female who was diagnosed with Major Depressive Disorder. F's chief complaint was her inability to manage her life, to cope with disarray in her home, and find time for anything besides meal preparation and house cleaning. F reported frequent worries, compulsive thoughts, tears and upsets. She was easily annoyed and irritated, felt inferior to others, and believed that she was blocked in getting anything accomplished.

F was a trained violinist, but rarely found time to devote to practice. She enjoyed playing in quartets and chamber music groups, but due to the disarray of her home, refused to invite fellow players to rehearse with her.

It was clear to the music therapist that the first order of business was to establish some order in the home. Reasonable objectives were set for the first weeks of treatment, e.g., clearing space in the living room, removing clutter from the dining room table, sorting the mail. On a daily basis, F was expected to accomplish some household task and later in the day, to engage in violin practice and/or listening to music. It was important to engage in tasks that would bring a sense of accomplishment and also pleasant events, such as violin practice or music listening, every day. F was also encouraged to do something outdoors and something with other people daily, but most significantly, enjoy or succeed at whatever tasks were performed.

By the end of the eight-week treatment, F had invited chamber music players to her home for rehearsals several times. She had served lunch on many of these occasions, something she had set as a goal of treatment. She was asked to participate in amateur orchestra performances, and because of the regularity of her practice, was able to do so with a reasonable degree of confidence.

It is noteworthy that after four weeks of treatment, midtest scores are extremely low on the Mood Assessment Scale and the Brief Symptom Inventory. They climb somewhat at the posttest administration, but remain 10 and 14 points below pretest levels, respectively. F sprained an ankle and found herself on crutches during the last week of treatment, which could account for the increase from midtest scores. However, she coped with this decreased mobility with more positive affect than even she believed would be the case. Self-esteem scores showed slight improvement over the treatment period even though this was not the focus of music therapy, and degree of depression also improved from pre- to posttest.

**Case 3: S**

| SCORES | PRETEST | MIDTEST | POSTTEST | PRE-POST CHANGE |
|--------|---------|---------|----------|-----------------|
| MAS    | 15      | 8       | 3        | +12             |
| BSI    | 48      | 24      | 5        | +43             |
| SEI    | 17      | 12      | 10       | +7              |
| BDI    | 4       | 3       | 1        | +3              |

S is a 65-year-old female with major depressive disorder. She reported feeling lonely and blue, fearful and worried. She was often either agitated, tired or bored. S believed that she slept no more than two or three hours a night, finding it difficult to fall asleep and to stay asleep. She expressed the view that if only she could sleep better, she would be able to cope more effectively during the day and experience both less agitation and lethargy.

During the initial interview, S responded to slow flowing music by falling asleep on the spot. During the course of treatment, music stress reduction techniques proved to be quite effective. S preferred to use imagery to slow music to help her sleep. From the second week of treatment on, she was able to sleep for approximately six hours every night after listening to a few minutes of music at bedtime.

S improved dramatically on all measures. The Mood Assessment Scale showed a 12 point improvement for pre- to posttest. An incredible 43 point change revealed the disappearance of somatic complaint and other symptoms of anxiety or depression on the Brief Symptom Inventory. Self-esteem scores decreased to 1. Two-month follow-up demonstrates a maintenance of functional coping, positive attitude and good sleeping patterns.

**Case 4: H**

| SCORES | PRETEST | MIDTEST | POSTTEST | PRE-POST CHANGE |
|--------|---------|---------|----------|-----------------|
| MAS | 10 | 1 | 5 | +5 |
| BSI | 28 | 3 | 11 | +17 |
| SEI | 24 | 11 | 16 | +8 |
| BDI | 1 | 1 | 1 | 0 |

H is a 65-year-old male, treated two years ago for minor depressive disorder with group psychotherapy. After a recent recurrence of symptoms, H presented with sad affect, feeling blue, weak, restless, tense and worthless. He reported hot and cold spells, headaches, and gastric pain for which his physician could find no cause. He reported little interest in those things which he once enjoyed.

H was referred to music therapy to learn stress reduction techniques. At the first treatment session, H stated that he had a severe headache and considered cancelling the session. After practicing gentle exercise and facial massage with music, H announced that the headache was gone.

In subsequent sessions, H responded well to both body and mind relaxation techniques. He practiced these methods daily, and used them whenever he felt any unpleasant symptoms coming on. During one episode of extreme pain, music was influential in bringing on sleep. H was able to cope with his pain and his problems by using one of the stress reduction programs. He also experienced periods of extreme tension. Music was, likewise, functional in helping H through these times. H's physician had prescribed the use of a TENS unit to assist him with bouts of abdominal pain. At the close of the music therapy treatment, however, H no longer needed to apply the unit.

H improved significantly during the first four weeks of music therapy. He found the techniques very useful, particularly when he was able to use them as soon as the first signs of discomfort or anxiety presented themselves.

H's scores decreased on all measures except for the Beck Depression Inventory which maintained a low score of 1. This change was particularly evident during the first four weeks. The presence of a viral infection during the last two weeks of treatment could have affected posttest scores, as H complained of mood changes associated with the real aches and discomforts of that condition. Even so, scores on the Mood Assessment Scale and Brief Symptom Inventory decreased 5 and 17 points respectively, from pre- to posttest. Mastery of these techniques could have contributed to gains in self-esteem, a change of 8 points during treatment.

## CONCLUSIONS

A descriptive analysis of these four cases lends considerable support to the use of music therapy techniques based on a cognitive-behavioral model. This is a preliminary step in a plan to evaluate the effectiveness of music therapy with the depressed elderly. Only through the use of comparison and control groups will one discover the relative efficacy of music therapy. This pilot work will be followed by an experimental study to examine these effects. The successful clinical cases described here, however, demonstrate that music therapy holds potential as a home-based strategy for individuals who could not otherwise obtain psychotherapeutic services.

## REFERENCE LIST

Beck, A.T.; Ward, C.; Mendelson, M.; Mock, J.; and Erbaugh, J. 1961. An inventory for measuring depression. *Archives of General Psychiatry* 4:561-571.
Derogatis, L.R., and Spencer, P.M. 1982. *The Brief Symptom Inventory (BSI): Administration, Scoring and Procedures Manual.* Baltimore: Clinical Psychometric Research.
Hanser, S. B. 1987. *Music Therapist's Handbook.* St. Louis, MO: Warren Green.
Rosenberg, M. 1979. *Conceiving the Self.* New York: Basic Books.

Strauss, D., and Solomon, K. 1983. Psychopharmacologic intervention for depression in the elderly. *Clinical Gerontologist* 2:3-19.

Thompson, L.W.; Gallagher, D.; and Breckenridge, J.S. 1987. *Journal of Consulting and Clinical Psychology* 55:385-390.

Vernon, S.W., and Roberts, R.E. 1982. Use of the SADS-RDC in a tri-ethnic community survey. *Archives of General Psychiatry* 39:47-52.

Yesavage, J.A.; Brink, T.L.; Rose, T.L.; Lum, O.; Huang, V.; Adey, M.; and Leirer, V.O. 1983. Development and validation of a geriatric depression screening scale: A preliminary report. *Journal of Psychiatric Research* 17:37-49.

# THE DYNAMOGENIC IMPACT OF MUSIC

Bruno Deschênes

## INTRODUCTION

The expression "dynamogenic impact of music" refers to the impact and influence of music on the human body and emotions. Something is considered as having a dynamogenic effect on a system when it generates energy and strength. In physiology and biology, dynamogenesis is defined as an increase in motor functions under the influence of a stimulation (Henderson). Studies have shown that sound, and consequently music, has a direct impact on the human body's motor functions and vegetative system through processes of the ear and its connections to the cerebellum and the sympathetic system by the pneumo-gastric vagus nerve (Tomatis 1983). Music appears to influence directly the release of our emotions as imprinted in our muscles and viscera, (through our bodily expression) (Weiss 1981; Tomatis 1983). Furthermore, it also appears that these influences and impacts are molded and conditioned to a great extent by our minds. Namely the emotions and body sensations a listener will experience are contingent on the "instructions" (based on his/her values, beliefs, points of view, prejudices, etc.) sent by the mind to the body before or while listening to music (Francès 1972; Deschênes 1986, 1988, 1989).

In such a perspective, it is possible to create groups of exercises that will employ verbal inductive instructions aimed at freeing the states and attitudes imprinted in the listeners' minds and bodies. The purpose of these directives will then be to present the listener with explicit and purposeful directions that will orient his attention and concentration towards the initiation of psychological and/or psycho-motor states.

Research has shown that it is possible to induce different psychological states with the same musical content (Francès 1972). The function of the induction is then to focus the receptivity and the attention of the listener toward specific body, affective or aesthetic objectives, in order to unbind and release the emotions and memories imprinted and engrammed in the body and viscera. In this sense, the formulation of the verbal instructions will give a framework in which the delivery of these engrams could be taking place. It must be emphasized that it is not the semantic content per se of the instructions that "impel" the freeing of an emotion, but the affective context and state they create and into which they bring the listener. Moreover, other experiments have shown that when subjects were asked verbally to visualize music, the affective aspect of the images created by the instructions was emphasized, not their semantic content or significance (Weiss 1981).

From this brief overview of the subject we see that music appears to be a very good medium to help in externalizing repressed emotions by means of exercises or games using well-defined inductive instructions. In the following discussion I will first present a concise view of the role and impact of the ear on our body and motor functions, i.e., how music has the ability to initiate dynamogenesis for the release of engrammed emotions. In the second part, I will introduce a set of exercises taken from a series of music theater acting exercises (Weiss 1981) which will illustrate the proposals of my discussion.

## PART ONE: THE DYNAMOGENIC IMPACT OF MUSIC

### The Ear (Weiss 1981; Tomatis 1983)

The sound reaching the ear can be viewed as a cluster of frequencies which are rhythmically decoded first by the vestibule, and then frequentially analyzed by the cochlea. We must also keep in mind that a sound is not caught by the ear in the same way as by a recording apparatus, but is captured and deciphered in order to adapt the structure of the sound to the psycho-physiological preferences, capacities, and reactions of the ear itself. In this sense, the physical sound as recorded by any machine is transformed and modified through the different constituents of the different parts of the ear, favoring some types of frequency structures or qualities more than others to suit its capacities and characteristics.

Through the ear's connection with the cerebellum, the vestibule detects and coordinates the movements and body posture, including its orientation in space. The vestibule is also known to coordinate the sensory impulses sent to the muscles, thus revealing its influence on the sympathetic system. Furthermore, the vestibule influences not only the motor system, but also the vegetative system considered by many to be the seat of the emotions. We can conclude then that every auditory sensation has a corresponding muscular activity, and that the ear has an impact on the release of the imprinted emotions in our muscles, viscera, and nervous system.

On the other hand, the role of the cochlea is to manage the body posture and balance, and to analyze the frequency clusters received from the vestibule in order to send to the brain a fully decoded and defined sound. We can then propose (Weiss 1981) that the role of the vestibule is to regulate the movements of the body in space, while the cochlea manages the kinetics of these movements and the sensory stimulations received from the listener's environment.

### The Dynamogenic Impact of Music

Based on the preceding conclusions and different related studies and researches, Weiss (1981) endorses the conclusions that our emotions are engrammed and imprinted in our muscles and viscera. Thus, music is capable of provoking the release and relief of these imprinted emotions through the medium of the ear.

Evidently, this does not happen in a mechanical manner and cannot be interpreted from a cause and effect point of view. Responses to music differ from one listener to another because each one imprints his own personal emotions forged from his own life experiences, and will not imprint the same emotion in the same part of the body. Furthermore, experiments (Francès 1972) have shown, for example, that the listener's attitude or "instructions" sent by the mind during listening to music can influence the rhythms and amplitudes of the listener's breathing. The object of these experiments was to study the differences between a spontaneous response to music and an analytical one. The analytical answers showed more important variations on the E.E.G. than the spontaneous ones (Francès 1972), clearly supporting the role of the inductive instruction I sketched at the beginning. A verbal instruction could be used to trigger an analytical attitude that will activate and even regulate, among other things, particular biological rhythms in relation to the musical structures.

We must not ignore the fact that music perception per se and one's body image are contingent on cultural, social, psychological, philosophical, and personal determinants, directly influencing any psycho-physiological response to music. However, the sensory itinerary in itself is very similar for all listeners, being independent of the personal background. It is at this level that the dynamogenic effect of music can be used in music therapy and/or in any pedagogic method using music. As stated before, the purpose of the instructions will be to bring the participants into a sensory and emotional state that will help the release of an emotion. Even though the leader may conceive an instruction that could include a strong emotional intent, we cannot assume that the listener will release the specific emotion stated in this instruction, as explained above: no two people will imprint the same emotions in the same parts of the body.

The first musical ingredient to help establish the dynamogenic effect of music is rhythm. Any muscular activity is originated by the periodical electrical flux flowing along the nervous system paths (Weiss 1981). By definition it is a rhythmical activity. On the other hand, the body in movement is inclined to synchronize with the rhythms and fluctuations of the music. This synchronization influences and spreads into the whole body, regulating the body's motor functions. Thus rhythms with which the body can more easily synchronize will have a greater impact. For example, in rock and disco music, the heart beat is inclined to synchronize with the beat of the music.

The second ingredient that plays a prominent role in the dynamogenic impact of music is the link that is easily and spontaneously created between the symbolic ingredients of music and the movements of the body. As mentioned before, even though an instruction actuates an analytical attitude on the listener, it is the affective context created by the affective and symbolic images that captures the listener's conscious and unconscious attention during the exercise, not their semantic content. For example, it is the expanding and magnifying symbolic meaning of the crescendo in Ravel's *Bolero* that is significant to the listener, not just the fact that a crescendo as such has been identified or in musical terms it is called a "crescendo." Along this line of thought, since any gesture is intimately linked to a known and learned visual representation, the uses of visual images or symbols in an instruction will then greatly help to amplify the effect of music. For example, it is possible to ask the participants to represent visually or spatially a melodic contour, requiring the participants to visualize symbolically the instruction. Clearly one's symbolic representations are not innate but learned and influenced by one's cultural conditioning. Thus, the expression of an emotion is obviously subordinate to this cultural conditioning of our symbolic imagery.

Weiss (1981) indicates that music does not express a precise and explicit semantic content. Contrary to spoken language, music does not convey significant or meaningful objects but reaches directly the symbolic stratum of the unconscious (that, in a manner of speaking, precedes such meaning) bypassing many of the defense mechanisms of the participants. We might say that music offers a representation of the objects it refers to that will unbind the emotional content that is engrammed. By analogy, music creates a context in which the emotional content can be freed and released.

We must not forget that the released affective states are linked to the psycho-muscular imprinting of the participants manifested during their life experiences (i.e. linked to location where each emotion is imprinted). As a result, the emotional outcome of any exercise cannot by any means be forecasted or predicted. Each participant may express any emotion in a unique way, emotionally, affectively, culturally, and physically. Nonetheless, the movement used to express a particular emotion can be interpreted by the instructor based on his knowledge of the participant, or on his understanding of the participant's state. Thus, the purpose of any instruction will not be to induce a definite emotion, expressed in a specific way, but to induce symbolically the unconscious state of an emotion engrammed in the psycho-motor structure of the participant. No music and no inductive instruction can claim to activate directly a specific emotion from a listener. It can only create an affective context that will give a basis to exteriorize engrammed emotions that this music and/or instruction will be able awaken in the listener, relative to his cultural background, but also relative to his personal willingness to let these emotions out.

## SECOND PART: THE APPLICATION

### The Workshop

The workshop which I will outline is in fact an acting workshop. The training of an acting student includes learning to express emotions without barriers or blocks. Since repressed emotions produce fears, blocks, tensions, frustrations, etc., this type of training helps the actor to cope, overcome, or "exorcize" the grip which these emotions have over his or her self-expression.

In this endeavor, Weiss (1981) proposed three types of induction: guided (with a specific motive), semi-guided (looking for a emotional state, images, movements, nonspecific motive), and free (no motive). Since the purpose of the instruction is to encourage the bringing to the surface of affective and emotional states, its formulation will have to take into account the physical and emotional sensations the instructor wishes to trigger in the participant. The formulation of the instruction should first contain directives that will aim to produce body movements and gestures, which will in turn permit the triggering of a psychological state or an emotion. These instructions do not necessarily have to include an emotional aspect. They can easily take a building-up outline that could start with a simple body movement responding to the music, gradually adding directives with a more emotional connotation. An exercise can take many forms or structures. The triggering process can be slow (using a slow and gradual build up in the development of the exercise) or fast (getting directly into the releasing of a particular emotion). The possibilities of this type of instruction are wide and are limited only by the leader's creativity.

Moreover, in order to make these exercises interesting and entertaining, they can take the form of a game and can easily involve a sense of play. Piaget, for example, considers playing as a means for the child to learn and discover (Weiss 1981). It is through this type of action that the child develops its cognition and adapts himself to his environment. This idea can certainly be applied also to adult training. Playing refers to an outside situation with children, while in today's workshop, playing will pertain to an inner state that will be discovered introspectively and analytically. The role of music in this type of playing is to serve as an important stimulus for the objective of the exercise.

## The Exercises

EXERCISE 1
*Objective*:      Body awareness through rhythms.
*Instructions*:   Move different parts of the body on the leader's instructions, while following the music's rhythmical patterns.

The purpose of this guided exercise is to direct the listener's attention towards his body. Since the listener's attention will be focused towards these body parts, the tensions will be noticed and will even magnify. Then there should be some loosening up and releasing of some of the imprinted emotions. This exercise can be developed in the form of a build up structure. Gradually, specific body movements can be added; space recognition movement can be incorporated; dramatic or emotional instructions can be added; etc.

EXERCISE 2
*Objective*:      Emotional awareness of the emotions imprinted in the body.
*Instructions*:   Standing still, visualize the music penetrating the body, through the muscles and viscera. Gradually, pay attention to the emotions that music seems to trigger and note in which parts of the body each emotion seems to be felt. Do not censor them or focus on them. Just let them be.

This is a semi-guided exercise. The emotional state looked for is not defined. It asks the participants introspectively to pay attention to the body's sensations in relation to the emotions arising, independently of the emotions themselves.

EXERCISE 3
*Objective:*      Expressing spacially emotional states.
*Instructions:*   Use of two opposite directions in the movements: horizontal and vertical. The vertical movements will correspond to the tense or active sections of the music and the horizontal ones will correspond to the peaceful sections. During the vertical movements, the participants express a state of exaltation, and during the horizontal ones, they express a state of relaxation.

The objective of this guided exercise is to express spatially specific emotions.

EXERCISE 4
*Objective:*      Nonverbal communication.
*Instructions:*   In pairs, one participant will be passive and the other active. The active participant puts two fingers of his right hand (the left for the lefthander) on the passive one's forehead and two fingers of the left hand on the neck.

Guided by the music, the active participant leads the passive one who, in a trusting state of mind, follows. Afterward, they change roles.

The object of this guided exercise is first a communication of trust and secondly to achieve a sense of letting go. Usually, the state of the active partner is communicated to the other participant. For example, if the leader is tense, his partner will have to "submit" to the state of this communication. Another version of this exercise would be where participants change roles alternatively on the instruction of the class leader.

### EXERCISE 5
*Objective:*      Nonverbal communication of an attitude.
*Instructions:*   The group forms a circle. One participant is in the middle of the circle and starts a gesture representing an attitude. He moves towards one participant of the circle who will imitate the gesture; then he gets in the middle, transforms the gesture into something entirely different and "gives" to another participant. This game goes on until every participant has participated at least twice.

In this guided exercise, the participants try to imitate the gesture, the attitude and also the feeling that is expressed. The participants share emotions and attitudes without necessarily experiencing them themselves. They have to pick up these emotions and attitudes quickly and imitate them.

### EXERCISE 6
*Objective:*      Nonverbal communication of an emotion.
*Instructions:*   The class is divided in two groups, one on each side of the room. Both groups will be walking towards one another and, when they face one another at about three feet apart, the participants make a goodbye gesture, pass, and continue walking. At the end of the room they turn round and continue the exercise.

The situation is acting the final farewell of two close friends. With the help of music, the exercise can be very powerful, since there will be a sharing but also a build up of an emotion shared by the participants. This exercise is very good at provoking or generating an emotion in a group. This type of situation is not threatening for the individual participants since the emotion is shared by everybody. This exercise could easily be used to generate a great number of different emotions and states of mind.

### EXERCISE 7
*Objective:*      Psychological "clean-up."
*Instructions:*   The group forms a circle and the participants start "cleaning" themselves up—their body and around their body—they throw the dirt in the center of

the circle. On the instruction of the leader, they all move and start cleaning the others.

Cleaning in this free exercise refers to imagining the clean-up of our psychological debris with the help of music; then, letting others help with this personal clean-up.

EXERCISE 8

*Objective:*    Sculpting one's self-image.

*Instructions:*    Standing in the room, each participant with closed eyes visualizes and builds a statue of his/her own body. Afterward, upon an instruction of the leader, the participants "enter" the statue and freely do movements and gestures that the music encourages them to do.

The purpose of this free visualization exercise is to help the participant build and shape the self-image as he or she wishes to.

The reader will have noticed that I have not indicated any duration or any choice of music for these exercises. Neither of these factors can be pre-established. The emotional states the instructor wishes to awaken, the state of mind of the participants, and their answers to the exercises will indicate the length of each exercise and the choice of the music. For example, in Exercise 7, a slow movement of a Beethoven piano sonata or chamber music work might be suitable. But if the objective is to trigger the opposite emotions, a more rhythmical musical work would have to be used. An important point to remember is that the exercises should not be conceived for particular musical works, but in relation to the participants' situations and the objectives the instructor wants to set. Also, these musical works need not be in specific musical styles. I would recommend that any instructor should be open-minded by choosing as many classical works as popular or folk music; as much small ensemble as symphony orchestra; as much from our culture as from any other culture. One particular style of music might trigger positive emotions in some participants, and negative ones in others (Deschênes 1986). Choosing from a wide variety of styles, would give all participants the chance to get in touch with a wide variety of emotions. Because of the influence of one's cultural, individual, and aesthetic conditioning, this will also give them the opportunity to hear one piece of music that might trigger their emotions better than another. The choice of the pieces should not be forced on the participants, but should be made so that every participant will be able to find something to which he will be able to relate deeply.


## CONCLUSION

In the past few decades, the dynamogenic impact of music has been clearly proven. (No matter what the music used in a music therapy setup, no matter what the emotions imprinted and engrammed in one's body and nervous system, the impact of music can not at all be isolated and discriminated on the patients.) The social, cultural, psychological, philosophical, life experience, and even spiritual factors involved in one's personality will influence and shape the output of any exercise. Moreover, two participants will not engram exactly the same emotions in his body, still less in the same muscles or viscera. Thus, the emotions that can be triggered by an exercise cannot be predetermined or forecasted. Only the outcome can be interpreted. The purpose of the exercises used in this type of music therapy should be viewed as the creation of a context (initiated by music and the instructor's instructions) in which the emotions engrammed in the participant's body and mind can be expressed.

*My main reference for this workshop is by the Canadian acting director, William Weiss (1981). Weiss presents a very good synthesis of most of the work that has been done on the dynamogenic impact of music. The purpose of his book was to develop ways to use music in the training of the young actor to help him release physical and emotional tensions that could block the free flow of the expression of emotions needed in his work. His work on the dynamogenic effect of music may prove to be very valuable in music therapy in helping to understand the power of music on patients. Furthermore, the exercises he suggests can easily be used by music therapists.*

## REFERENCE LIST

Deschênes, B. 1986 (October). Music, health and consciousness. Lecture given at 3rd Symposium of ISFMIM, Lüdenscheid.

Deschênes, B. 1988 (April). Healing beyond music. Lecture given during a conference on Music and Health, Eastern Kentucky University.

Deschênes, B. 1989. Creativity in music: The role of our values. *The Creativity Research Journal*, Comments, September.

Francès, R. 1972. *La Perception de la Musique*. Paris: Librairie J. Vrin.

Henderson, I.F. 1989. *Henderson's Dictionary of Biological Terms*. Halsted Press.

Tomatis, A.A. 1983. *La Nuit Utérine*. Paris: Stock.

Weiss, W. 1981. *Introduction à la Pédagogie Musicale de l'Acteur*. Ottawa: Les Éditions de l'Université d'Ottawa.

# THE INFLUENCE OF MUSICAL RHYTHMICITY IN INTERNAL RHYTHMICAL EVENTS

Reinhard Flatischler

We know that rhythmic movements influence each other whenever they come into a field of common contact. Two pendulums swinging next to each other will start to synchronize their movements after some time. This is a law of nature. The same could be said about a crowd of people walking for a long time in the same room. They will also gradually synchronize their footsteps. But it could happen that some of the people will voluntary resist the process of synchronization and keep their own rhythm of walking. That picture gives us a first hint, that the quality of voluntary and involuntary movement plays an important role in the process of synchronization, especially if we talk about the interaction of music and human beings.

The human physiology is full of rhythm and I started a research project with Dr. H.P. Koepchen on the influence of elementary musical rhythm on the many levels of internal rhythms. It is reasonable to focus such a research project first on the two body rhythms that we feel most dominant in our daily lives: the rhythm of pulse and the rhythm of breathing. I do not want to present detailed scientific results in this paper. My goal is to give an overview and relate the rhythmicity that I am talking to practical experience. I also want to show a new vision of rhythm, that supplements existing knowledge with new approaches. That might help other researchers in this field to look at rhythmic phenomena from a different point of view.

Let us start first with a short examination of breathing rhythm:

Direct your attention to your nose. Feel how air streams through it into your body—and how it flows out again. Attentively follow this in and out flow. When the air flows through the nose into your body, give it space and allow it to fill you. When you sense that the movement is reversed and the air flows out, then feel how you let it go. Keep your attention on this process of releasing until you reach that point where the flowing ceases and a moment of stillness occurs before the air once again enters your body. You can experience that moment as one of "letting be." Remain attentive awhile to the flow of your breath, enjoying how the "releasing," the "letting be," and the "allowing to enter" always follow one another of their own accord: the "releasing" when exhaling, the "letting be" at the moment of transition and the "allowing to enter" while inhaling.

Taking in oxygen is only one function of breathing. Its vital force lies in the untiring rhythmic movement. You experienced the phases of breathing. The simplest case is merely an alteration of inhalation and exhalation. Your breathing flows on its own when you link the flowing of air into your body with the feeling of "letting in" and flowing out with a "letting go." In between, there are two points of transition which play an important part in the rhythm of breathing. They have the ability to expand. When we are in a state of rest, there is a brief moment when breathing comes to a standstill after letting go. This moment has the quality of "letting be." Breathing out has come to an end and breathing in has not yet begun. It is a moment of stillness. It is that very moment which begins to expand as though by itself when we detach ourselves from activity and enter deeper levels of our consciousness, as in sleep or meditation. As we allow ourselves to go deeper, this "letting be" extends itself to a period of time equal to each of the other two phases. Then we breathe in a triple cycle.

Inhalation phase  =  Exhalation phase  =  Stillness phase

However, when we are active, this space becomes ever shorter until it is finally just a point of transition. A dual cycle then arises in the alternation of inhalation and exhalation. After a fast run we clearly experience this dual cycle in breathing. You can best hear and see triple-time in someone in a deep sleep. In the rhythm of breathing, dual time is associated with an extroverted attitude while triple-time is a bodily expression of introversion. We will see that this fact has its counterpart in the rhythm of our pulse and is the way that musical rhythm changes our brainwaves. It also shows that duple-time and triple-time—two elementary phenomena in the music of every culture—are rooted in our physiology.

The point of transition *after* breathing in is potentially the fourth phase. There the moment when breathing stops does not happen "of its own accord." If we want to extend this point of transition, we must voluntarily retain the air that has streamed into us. This can happen effortlessly with practice. Nevertheless we must do something deliberately, or else the air simply continues to flow. Therefore I call the point of transition after inhalation the active pole and the point after exhalation the passive pole.

You may have discovered during our short examination of breathing rhythm, that this rhythm can happen in two different ways: we can breathe in and out with a voluntary movement and we can also let our breathing happen involuntarily. We can immediately increase or decrease the tempo of our breathing rhythm. We can also allow our breathing to happen of its own accord and find its own pace. Your pulse also beats of its own accord and you cannot change its rate immediately by voluntary action. However, both pulse and heartbeat will react to emotional changes or physical activities.

Whenever *musical rhythm* meets an internal rhythmicity that pulsates of its own accord, synchronization will occur in various ways. I will talk more about the possibilities of synchronization later on. But whenever a musical rhythm meets an internal rhythmicity that is connected with voluntary movement, the contact with this external rhythm can be manipulated: we can immediately enter into it or strictly avoid joining this rhythm.

But musical rhythm itself, played by a human being (in contrast to a rhythm from a rhythm machine) also has these two qualities: a voluntary and an involuntary quality. The first quality is connected with active action and creation and the second one is connected with a passive state of being carried by rhythm.

## THE HEARTBEAT—PRIMAL PULSE OF MUSIC

Long before we see the light of this world, we live in the pulsating sound world of the womb. Our mother's heartbeat and voice are the first rhythmic expressions which shape our consciousness. In this rhythmic sound world there arises the first communication between mother and child. At this time we experience an elemental pulsation. The mother's pulse, the pulsating rocking of her body and the sense of being carried create a totally integrated environment. The pulsating of music reminds us of this primal experience. The heartbeat is an elemental rhythmic measure within ourselves. Thus there exists a pulsation within ourselves which embodies a specific tempo which relates to all other pulsations and the rhythms we play. It may become faster, slower or synchronize itself with the pulsation of a musical rhythm, but sooner or later it always returns to its own tempo. When we feel our pulse we sense this primal rhythmic power. We ourselves are this power. We encounter ourselves in our pulse! As we get to know our pulse it becomes our companion in everyday life and we develop a relationship to our primal rhythmic ground.

The pulsing of the heart is produced by the alternating contraction and relaxation of the heart muscle. The contraction is known as the systole, and the relaxation as the diastole. Two parts of our nervous system, known as the sympathetic and the para-sympathetic are in constant control of the rhythm of the heartbeat. One stimulates, the other inhibits. The heartbeat is thus imbedded in the forces at work in our nervous system. But the final origin of this rhythmic power still remains a mystery. Put an ear to someone's chest and you will hear the heartbeat rhythm:

Bpp Bmm — Bpp Bmm — Bpp Bmm

This "melody" divides the intervals between beats into three subdividing pulses. When the body moves more actively, the "melody" changes, and we hear intervals divided into two:

Bpp Bmm Bpp Bmm Bpp Bmm

The heartbeat itself is a very complicated rhythmic event, but we can experience it as the simple, supportive pulsation anywhere within the body where the pulse can be felt. We hear music with our body and play music with our body. The body and its rhythms play a central role in music. This is why we find a knowledge of the inner pulse in the music of all cultures. There are drums which directly imitate the melody of the heartbeat. The drumming of Native American shamans involves a direct musical transposition of the heartbeat and so too does the main pulse of the Korean buk and the Japanese taiko. The heartbeat also forms the rhythmic foundation for complex Indian rhythms. The pulse tempo is the measure for the slowest basic speed in Indian music, known as the *vilambit laya*. Although this music uses many subtle tempo gradations, the Indian musician identifies three tempo ranges: *vilambit* (slow); *madhya* (moderate); and *drut* (fast). *Madhya* is twice as fast as the pulse and *drut* four times as fast. The music of Africa, Latin America and Asia is full of instances where a link with the pulse rate is clearly perceptible. However, this knowledge also lives in Western music. The *Tactus Intger Valor* was the basis of European music from the mid-15th century until the end of the 16th century. It is the underlying pulse in Bach's music, and, at around 60 beats a minute, corresponds to a slow heartbeat.

Drum rhythms act on the human heartbeat. This is an essential aspect in the healing rituals of all cultures. The body rhythms of all participants change in accordance with the impact of the music played. Every healing rhythm is, like our pulse, multi-dimensional and this quality enables pulse and drum to touch one another. By multi-dimensionality I mean a uniting of several rhythmic energies, just as the pulse has within itself possibilities of both duple-time and triple-time. Another important characteristic of a healing rhythm is its flexibility which allows subtle tempo variations—a phenomenon which strengthens the elasticity of our own pulse. The degree to which a natural pulsation fluctuates poses an interesting challenge for a musician: what does exactitude of playing involve? How exact is still alive? That leads us first to the question: What is a pulsation?

A pulsation is the primal rhythmic force in music and in physiology. A pulsation comes into being through the recurrence of the same event at a regular interval. That may sound very imprecise and we might be tempted to say: "Pulsation is the recurrence of identical events at identical intervals." But I know of no instance in nature that pulsates with exactly equal intervals. The subtle fluctuation of our inner rhythm can be felt in the pulse. Within certain parameters this inconsistency is not only a normal occurrence but an essential one as well in all naturally pulsating manifestations of life. But as soon as fluctuations within a pulsation exceed these parameters the pulse becomes disrupted and we experience it as arhythmical.

You certainly have felt your heartbeat—do you remember the *intervals* between those pulses? With every step you sensed your foot contacting the floor—do you remember the interval between the steps? The interval exists between one foot striking the ground and the next. If you live through this period of time by directing your attention to these intervals you will have a different experience of walking than you do when concentrating only on the feet striking the ground.

Pulse and interval are the two constantly alternating elements in pulsation. Even though we usually find it easier to direct our listening and feeling toward perception of the pulse, in fact it only marks the boundaries of intervals. We can think of the interval as the immaterial aspect, the soul, so to speak, of a pulsation, while the pulse on the other hand, corresponds to the material. From my observation, the interval is the part responsible for the for process of synchronization. Intervals are energy fields. They tend to melt together or synchronize into simple relationships such as 1:1, 1:2, 1:3, 1:4, 2:3, 3:4. These basic relationships can be found everywhere, where two or more pulsations vibrate of their own accord.

The pulse of a drum influences our heartbeat after some time. Whenever the pulsation of our heartbeat and the pulsation of a drum are connected with each other, the pulse will follow the increasing tempo of playing. I have found that this effect is even stronger when someone dances in synchronization with the drumbeat. But there is a limit: if the drummer plays ever faster, the pulse at a certain point "falls" back to a slow tempo and the same is true for the opposite. When the drummer plays too slow for a comfortable pulse rate, the pulse "jumps" back to its usual rate (between 60 and 80) finding sooner or later other forms of synchronization, such as half-time. From my twenty years' experience of teaching rhythm and from many experiments, I have found that it seems to be the easiest for most people to learn elementary rhythms in the tempo range of their heartbeat.

There are several ways to symbolize or depict pulsation that make clear its essential nature. The following is derived from a walking movement:

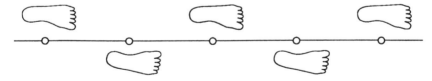

This representation of pulsation appears linear. But the essential nature of pulsation is cyclic as all rhythmic phenomena may be experienced and understood as cyclic. However, Western linear notation facilitates comprehension of very complex musical relationships—both the rhythmic and melodic structures. When the music is heard the cyclic effect begins. Everything we experience in the energy field of a cycle is perceived as a unity, therefore the appropriate visual image of a pulsation is a circle with an event at one point on its circumference. This event repeats itself time and again by way of an approximately regular movement on the circumference. The event in an audible pulsation is a sound. We may imagine that this event involves a bell which sounds every time that point is reached.

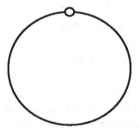

We can create pulsation on a drum. But at the same time pulsations are all around us. In a pulsation we encounter again an active and a passive quality. This is also true for the "event" of the pulsation: I call the two different aspects of the acoustic event "pulse" and "beat." The "beat" is established actively through our own creation, while the "pulse," on the other hand, occurs by itself just like our heartbeat. It is here that we meet again the two different spheres which are always interacting in music: the inaudible but perceptible rhythmic foundation as one sphere, and the audible rhythmic creations as the other.

## BEAT AND OFFBEAT

Once you have become acquainted with pulse and interval as constantly alternating elements within a pulsation, you will encounter a new pair of opposites: beat and offbeat. When you establish a beat you will also hear its counterpart, like an echo at the midpoint of each interval. This is generally known as the offbeat. This term is in fact imprecise since everything which occurs away from the beat, throughout the interval, is "offbeat." Offbeat here is used to indicate the exact mid-point in an interval.

With the following exercise you will feel the quality of the "offbeat."

Put your hand where you can feel your pulse and take time to contact your inner pulsation. As you feel your pulse, allow a sound to arise within yourself which imitates the sound of your pulse. First try to find this sound with your inner voice and when you have found it, link it up with the pulse. The pulsating of your heart will thus gradually be made audible. Take time to feel the pulse and voice unite and observe how your pulse reacts as it connects with your voice. Does it become stronger or weaker, faster or slower, or does it remain the same? Gradually separate your voice from the pulse and return to listening. Now direct your attention to the *interval* between the pulse beats. When you feel ready, give an inner voice to the syllable "GO" at the mid-point of one of these intervals. If you find it difficult at the beginning then pause before you continue whispering GO. The succession of pulse and voice thus become:

| Voice: | | GO | | GO | | GO |
|--------|-------|-----|-------|-----|-------|-----|
| Pulse: | Pulse | | Pulse | | Pulse | |

Do not worry if your pulse becomes more difficult to feel or even becomes irregular for some moments—this is a normal occurrence. Once again pay attention to how your pulse reacts. Does it become stronger or weaker, faster or slower? How loud can the GO become before you no longer sense the pulse. Allow your voice to become quieter again and return to whispering GO and finally to speaking with your inner voice. Perhaps the interval in your pulse can now be felt very clearly. When you have returned to quietness end the exercise at your leisure.

As I said, the interval is the "soul" of pulsation. Like any empty space the interval has the potential for dividing itself in certain ways. Whenever new pulses appear in the original empty space the quality of the pulsation is immediately changed. Remember, we can use a circle as an image for the recurrent interval. The circle itself symbolizes wholeness. When it is divided into three equal parts it is neither smaller nor larger than the original entity but it is *different*. It exhibits a new quality, one which relates directly to the laws governing vibrating strings, wood, metal, air columns and so on.

A string of a guitar, for example, reacts like an interval between two pulses. If we divide it by touching it gently at the midpoint (where the offbeat would be in an interval) we hear a new sound quality. When a string is set into motion it produces several tones simultaneously by itself but we are usually aware of only one of these. That one is the lowest and is called the fundamental. Once it begins to vibrate the string divides itself into shorter sections which give out higher tones known as overtones or harmonics. These harmonics can be heard clearly by gently touching the vibrating string at a point that divides the strings into halves, thirds, quarters, and so on. Every point produces a different tone and each point refers to another subdivision of an interval between two pulses. The rhythmic quality of an interval varies according to the number of its subdivisions. Thus an interval divided into three equal parts feels entirely different from one divided into two equal parts.

An increasing quantity of "subdividing" pulses thereby creates different rhythmic qualities. Of course, the tempo of the basic pulsation determines how many subdividing beats are musically meaningful in the interval. It is often the case that no additional beats are possible in rhythms based in a very fast pulsation. At slow tempi, on the other hand, a continuous change of color in an otherwise constant rhythm occurs when the subdivisions are varied.

My experience with various rhythmic traditions has revealed an interesting tendency regarding the impact of subdividing pulsations. Rhythms that have three subdividing pulses in each interval make the listener more introverted and bring him or her toward an inner stillness, whereas the intervals containing the movement of 2 or 4 subdividing pulses will direct the listener toward outer movement and greater extroversion. I assume that the change of subdivisions has a direct impact on our brainwave patterns. I found a correspondence of my discovery in the various rhythms of different cultures. Rhythms that are played to bring the listener or dancer to an introverted state of mind are mostly rhythms in triplets. Most of the carnival rhythms on the other hand are composed in 2 or 4 beat subdivisions—stimulating the participants to extroversion.

Finally I want to talk about one more fact that plays an important role in the interaction of musical rhythms and body rhythms: the relationship between rhythmic stability and falling out of rhythm. Most people tend to like rhythmic stability and try to avoid rhythmic instability. But physiology teaches us something different: it is not the final goal in any living system to reach a point of ultimate stability, but rather to fluctuate between more or less "chaotic states" and restabilization. It seems to renew a rhythmic system if this fluctuation occurs. From my experience of teaching rhythm it is the same. Rhythmic strength starts to grow if people are together in one rhythm and some allow themselves to fall out at times, while others continue with the rhythm. It seems to be the same with body rhythms. Whenever a heartbeat is challenged with tempo changes it will tend to resynchronize with the new rhythms and in this process develop a strong rhythmic power. If a heartbeat is constantly exposed to rigid rhythms that have an unshakable sameness the flexibility of its rhythm gets lost.

## DISCOGRAPHY

*Megadrums*—Schinore (1986)
*Megadrums*—Coreana (1988)
*Megadrums*—Worldlanguage Rhythm (1990)

*The Forgotten Power of Rhythm* — book (with CD and Cassette)

All products are available from:
Life Rhythm, P.O. Box 806, Mendocino, CA 95460, USA  Telephone: (707) 937-1825

# VIBROACOUSTIC RESEARCH 1980-1991

## Olav Skille

**V**ibroAcoustics can be defined as the use of sinusoidal, low-frequency (30 Hz - 120 Hz), rhythmical sound-pressure waves mixed with music for therapeutic purposes. Both principle and procedure were first described by Skille at the First International Society for MusicMedicine Symposium in 1982.

There are, at present, more than 20,000 hours of use on record. Most records are of anecdotal nature, and have basically been concentrated on testing Skille's descriptions and findings in practice. The effects may be categorized into three main areas:

1. Spasmolytic and muscle relaxing effect;
2. Increase of blood circulation in the body (brain included);
3. Marked, but variable, effects on the vegetative system.

VibroAcoustic [VA] therapy is a more physical method than most other therapies using music in medical contexts. Music and frequencies are transferred directly to the body. The patient is placed directly on a chair or bed filled with loudspeakers.

## RESEARCH AND EMPIRICAL FINDINGS

### Estonia

A research team, composed of Professor Saima Tamm, psychologist I. Ojaperv, and psychiatrist Erika Saluveer (1989) at the Medical Center of Tallinn Pedagogical Institute studied 40 neurotic patients and have concluded that 10 seems to be the most effective number of treatment sessions. Of the 40 patients, 25 had ten sessions, and a report was made. The data were processed by computer and were within the required statistical probability levels.

The patients were first examined by a therapist, a neurologist, and a cardiologist, and those with a diagnosis of hypertension were treated by the VA team. Another group of patients was selected by the psychiatrist from the Department of Neurosis in the Psychiatric Hospital of Tallinn.

*Methods Used*

1. The psychological condition of the patients was measured by the Taylor test. The Taylor test estimates neuropsychical, somatopsychical and somatogenic distress;
2. The asthenia was identified by a test compiled by Professor Tamm. The test consists of 59 questions and gives an evaluation in points. The average index is normally 68-70;
3. Blood pressure was measured before and after treatment during the ten sessions. The initial BP was measured after 5 minutes rest, lying on the VA bed;
4. ECG was done before and after the VA procedure;
5. EEG was done before and after the VA procedure.

*Patients Treated*

N = 25.    72% female, 28% male.
   Age:        21-30: 12%
               31-40: 32%
               41-50: 24%
               51-60: 28%

   Profession:   16% head of educational establishment
                 16% head of industrial enterprises
                 56% social workers
                 16% various professions

   Complaints, by main syndrome:
               36% depression
               32% asthenics
               16% hypochondria
               16% hypertension

   Characterization of main complaints (Tamm-scale)

   Normal index: 68 - 70.
               57.30 Neuropsychical distress
               46.68 Sociopsychical distress
               43.03 Somatic distress
               126.60 Asthenia

Subjective symptom reports:

| | | |
|---|---|---|
| 1) | Cry often | 50.0% |
| 2) | Headache | 58.3% |
| 3) | Tachycardia | 58.3% |
| 4) | Lack of concentration | 50.0% |
| 5) | Restless dreams | 75.0% |
| 6) | Constipation | 54.2% |
| 7) | Indigestion | 62.5% |
| 8) | Easily stirred up | 58.3% |
| 9) | Stomach troubles | 50.0% |
| 10) | Poor appetite | 42.2% |
| 11) | Sweating | 57.9% |
| 12) | Trembling of hands | 38.9% |
| 13) | Apathy | 66.7% |

A correlation analysis was carried out when evaluating the effect of treatment on individual symptoms. The results are described in the conclusion of the survey.

A histogram analysis of the changes in blood pressure shows the progress of BP changes during the 5 weeks of the described project:

| Weeks | Before Treatment | | After Treatment | |
|---|---|---|---|---|
| | RR syst. > 130 | RR diast. > 80 | RR syst. > 130 | RR diast. > 80 |
| 1. | 44.6% | 56.0% | 32.0% | 52.0% |
| 2. | 36.0% | 44.0% | 36.0% | 46.0% |
| 3. | 50.0% | 45.5% | 50.2% | 41.7% |
| 4. | 54.1% | 56.5% | 43.4% | 52.1% |
| 5. | 47.6% | 38.2% | 38.2% | 42.8% |

The Estonian research team summed up their findings by describing the results this way:

1. The treatment of elderly patients was more effective.
2. Women are more easily cured than men. (They became less tired, less prone to headaches, less distressed, less prone to trembling of hands).
3. During the course of treatment blood circulation was improved.
   a) Acro-cyanosis diminished. Temperature of limbs rose.
   b) Systolic and diastolic blood pressure decreased (was lowered).

    c) Headache and nausea vanished. Improvement of cerebral blood circulation.
4. ECG - no remarkable improvement after one procedure, studies continue in this field.
5. EEG - large individual differences but more research is needed.

The effect of treatment was as follows: raising of self confidence, less stomach troubles, less headaches, less depression and asthenia. The patients were more willing to work.

*Conclusion*

The Estonian team concluded that the VA methods can play a considerable part in the treatment of neurotic patients and patients with hypertension. Good results have already been achieved. However, there are many problems still to be solved and research at Tallinn Pedagogical Institute continues. In 1991 several new research projects will be initiated in hospitals and university clinics.

**England**

A.L. Wigram, BA, LGSM (MT), VATh, and L. Weekes, MCSP, SRP, conducted a single-blind study of the difference between the effects of VA therapy and the same procedure using music alone in reducing high muscle tone in multiply handicapped people and also the study of the effects of the same parameters on oedema in mentally handicapped people at Harperbury Hospital, Hertfordshire.

1. Three male and 7 female subjects in a large hospital for the mentally handicapped took part in trials to determine whether high muscle tone could be reduced by introducing low frequency sound at 44 Hz or 55 Hz into a treatment program involving music. The subjects' ages varied form 28 to 77 and their range of functioning ranged from very profoundly handicapped to moderately handicapped. All subjects had measurably high muscle tone which affected them in different ways. The average age of the male subjects was 51 and the average age of the female subjects was 44. The overall average age of the 10 subjects was 46.

2. Two male and 1 female subject were also involved in an experiment to evaluate whether the condition of chronic oedema could be alleviated and the size of limbs reduced by the use of VA therapy as opposed to music alone.

The subjects were all residents of a hospital for the mentally handicapped, and their average age was 52. The design of the study was identical for the two groups.

*Materials*

The equipment used was modelled on the descriptions Skille had made in the late 70s and early 80s with local modification.

Two 18" loudspeakers were used in the sprung bed designed for the study. On top of the springs were a single polythene sheet and a 1" pile sheepskin. One half of the end could be lifted up to an angle of approximately 30 degrees. The speakers were connected to an amplifier with 120 watts output per channel with the ability to increase and decrease the bass volume.

A cassette deck was used to play the therapy tapes used in the study. For the clients with high muscle tone a tape with a single tone of 44 Hz and another with a single tone of 55 Hz throughout were used. For the oedema group a tape with a single tone of 40 Hz was used.

*Design*

The experiment was set up as a repeated measures design across two experimental conditions. Each subject undertook a minimum of 12 trials, 6 in each condition. Condition A gave the subject 30 minutes on the VA unit with VA stimuli. In condition B the subject was given music alone. The the muscle tone trials, the dependent variables were the measurements taken on the subjects of their degree of extension before and after each session. The dependent variables were coded and are as follows:

1. Left shoulder to right shoulder;
2. Right shoulder to right arterial artery;
3. Left shoulder to left radial artery;
4. Right elbow to side;
5. Left elbow to side;
6. Nose to navel;
7. Right side greater trochanter to right side lateral malleolus;
8. Left side greater trochanter to right side external malleolus;
9. Base of right patella to base of left patella.

For each subject in each trial, an independent evaluator measured the maximum range between each of the two points in the dependent variables pertinent to each subject, and then was not present during the course of the trial. When the trial was finished, the independent evaluator repeated the same measurement procedure, without knowing which treatment condition (A or B) had been used. This formed the basis of a single-blind test, in which the subjects may have been aware of which condition they were in, but the evaluator was not. The course of the trials was randomly decided for each subject.

In the oedema group where 3 patients were monitored for oedema, the same design was used, and the same number of trials in the two conditions undertaken. The dependent variables were:

1. Base of right big toe;
2. Base of left big toe;
3. Instep of right foot;
4. Instep of left foot;
5. Right ankle round the heel;
6. Left ankle round the heel;
7. Circumference of right leg 3 cms. above lateral malleolus;
8. Circumference of left leg 3 cms. above lateral malleolus;
9. Circumference of right leg 10 cms. above lateral malleolus;
10. Circumference of left leg 10 cms. above lateral malleolus;
9. Circumference of right leg 20 cms. above lateral malleolus;
10. Circumference of left leg 20 cms. above lateral malleolus.

*Blood Pressure and Heart Rate*

Systolic and diastolic blood pressure as well as the pulse were measured before and after each trial in both conditions.

*Procedure*

Each subject was placed on a VA therapy unit with adequate head support. The body was given support by pillows containing polystyrene beads when this was necessary. Blood pressure and pulse were measured, and then the measurements were taken as specified for each subject. The evaluator then left, and the therapist in charge started the tape. The controls of the equipment were set uniformly in all trials and conditions. The treatment proceeded, and the therapist remained sitting quietly in the room with the client. At the end of the treatment all controls were turned to 0 and the independent evaluator came in and repeated the initial measurement procedure.

The patients were undressed as little as necessary to take the measurements, and always covered with a blanket.

The blood pressure and pulse were measured by digital blood pressure monitors. The following models were used:

1. Braun—Model DS-175 Auto Inflation BP Monitor.
2. Braun—Model DS-55p Digital BP Monitor

## Results

By measuring the difference in maximum range of movement achieved throughout the trial (found by comparing the "before" and "after" situations) and labelling increase of movement with a "+" and reduction of movement with "-" one is left with a mean improvement (or deterioration) due to introducing or not introducing low frequency sound.

The research team found that the best way to express changes in the observed parameters was to describe the changes in % increase or decrease in relation to the observed "before" levels before the trials started.

Table 1 gives the mean scores of increased or decreased range of movement within minimum and maximum ranges, shown as percentage scores for both conditions.

TABLE 1
Increase (+) and decrease (-) of movement range in %

| Measurement | 1 | 2 | 3 | 4 | 5 | 6 | 7 | 8 | 9 | % tot |
|---|---|---|---|---|---|---|---|---|---|---|
| LFS + music | +18 | +15 | +10 | +21 | +26 | +27 | +09 | +04 | +19 | +13 |
| Music alone | -04 | -02 | +01 | +03 | +10 | +16 | -01 | 0 | +01 | +01 |

LFS = Low Frequency Sound

Table 2 indicates the significance levels of percentages given in Table 1.

TABLE 2
Significance level of values in Table 1

| Total Measurements | + | — | P |
|---|---|---|---|
| n = 40 | 37 | 03 | < .004 |

Table 3 is a significance test on the mean scores of the measurement, where the number of subjects being measured at the given positions exceeded 5. The test was applied on the normalized data from Table 1.

TABLE 3

Significance levels of difference between Condition A and B where n at
each measurement# = < 5. * = not statistically significant.

| Measurement | + | — | P |
|:---:|:---:|:---:|:---:|
| 2 | 7 | 0 | .0079 |
| 3 | 7 | 2 | .0899* |
| 7 | 5 | 0 | .0313 |
| 8 | 5 | 1 | .1094* |
| 9 | 7 | 0 | .0079 |

Table 4 shows a significance test on the absolute data compared between the two
condition.

TABLE 4

Significance levels of difference between condition A and B - all
measurements. * = not significant.

| Measurement | + | — | P |
|:---:|:---:|:---:|:---:|
| 2 | 36 | 50 | < .0003 |
| 3 | 37 | 13 | .0005 |
| 5 | 05 | 00 | .0313 |
| 7 | 21 | 09 | .0214 |
| 8 | 22 | 10 | .0251 |
| 9 | 08 | 34 | < .0015 |

The data show a greater degree of extension when low frequency sound was used in the
trial.

Table 5 indicates the changes in BP and pulse levels. The table indicated that there is a
significant change in systolic blood pressure. However, the number of observations is
small, and there are indications that the significance might not be so clear if the test had
been taken on a more representative population.

TABLE 5
Significance levels of change in BP and pulse. * = no significance

|  | + | — | P |
|---|---|---|---|
| Systolic BP | 9 | 0 | .0020 |
| Diastolic BP | 4 | 4 | * |
| Pulse | 4 | 4 | * |

A very small group of three subjects were run for the oedema trial, and although 12 different measures were taken overall, only measures *a* and *b* were common in all three clients. The tests indicate that the low frequency sound condition gave a small, but significant, reduction in the measurement compared with the music alone condition.

*Discussion/Conclusion*

The outcome of the trial on clients with high muscle tone showed consistently that when low frequency sound (either 44 or 55 Hz) was used with the music, a greater reduction in muscle tone and an improved rate of motion was achieved than when music alone was used.

The results obtained from measuring blood pressure fluctuated quite considerably, and only the regular drop in systolic BP gave any level of significance.

The oedema difference scores, although very small, also gave significant indication of improvement due to low frequency sound.

The research in England continues, and more emphasis will be laid on obtaining data from subjects who are not hospital patients.

**Finland**

Petri Lehikoinen (1988) has completed a three month study of the effect of VA therapy on occupational stress in an insurance company. The 32 participants were divided in two groups.

Group 1 consisted on 15 people who were given traditional stress-reduction treatment. (Autogenous training, insight into interpersonal processes, communication training, etc.) Their treatment was given in 1 hour sessions once a week.

Group 2 consisted on 17 people who had two half-hour sessions of VA therapy every week.

The experiment was carried out from February to March 1987.

Parameters used:

1. Normal physical examination;
2. Psychiatric interview;
3. Spielberger scale;
4. Hamilton scale;
5. Stress-hormone analysis (adrenalin, noradrenalin, cortisol).

The hypotheses for the projects were as follows:

1. Education can help workers to cope with stress situations and to strengthen their professional identity.
2. Certain physical relaxation treatments can reduce situational stress.

The results confirm both hypotheses.

*Changes of Stress-Factors in the Tested Groups*

There is a remarkable difference between the groups when we look at the number who report unchanged or reduced stress level. In Group 1, 54% compared with 80% in Group 2.

*Changes in Anxiety Factors in the Tested Groups*

The anxiety level was decreased in both groups. Unchanged or decreased anxiety was reported by 77% in Group 1 and by 80% in Group 2.

*Hamilton Anxiety*

Unchanged or decreased anxiety was reported by 62% in Group 1 and 87 in Group 2.

*Changes in Depression Factors in the Tested Groups*

Unchanged or decreased depression was reported by 85% in Group 1 and 87% in Group 2.

*Discussion*

The research project was carried out on two groups, a total of 32 people. This number is too low to give the results statistical significance, but it is big enough to give us a strong indication that progress was made in both groups. Group 2 obtained better results in most of the factors measured.

If this trend is supported by other projects, it will be wise to develop the VA method further to suit the demands for stress-reduction in professional life.

## The Ronni-Project

A study of the effect of VA treatment on 9 severely retarded children by Ronni Keskuslaitos was conducted during September - December 1988. Each patient received 15 treatments. The nurses in the research team evaluated the following factors:

1.  **Changes in the general state of mind.** The results show that the immediate effect of VA-therapy was obvious. All patients became more aware of the treatment situation and showed positive emotional reactions. In three cases, this improvement was to some extent transferred to other, nontreatment, situations, but the most clear effects were limited to the treatment situation.

2.  **Changes in social interaction.** Social interaction was improved. Both eye and voice communication increased in the therapy situation. This improvement was not observed outside the therapy sessions.

3.  **Changes in motor behavior (mobility).** The motor activity improved in all cases. One patient reacted so well in the VA therapy, that the physiotherapist started to do all of his physiotherapy on the VA bed.

4.  **Changes in general behavior.** Changes observed in general behavior were not very obvious. However, in two cases remarkable improvement was observed: The severely aggressive behavior of one boy disappeared, and one severely autistic girl became more open and cooperative.

5.  **Changes in blood circulation.** One patient had severe problems with her blood circulation, and this problem was helped considerably by VA therapy.

The short term results in this group seem to be very positive. The long term changes are not so obvious. This is, however, understandable, because the patients suffer from very severe disability, and the described treatment period lasted only for a few months. The results were so satisfactory however, that the leading physician decided to continue the experiment, and to develop this project further.

## REPORTS FROM PRACTICAL USE IN VARIOUS CONTEXTS

**Norway**

*Variations in Blood Pressure and Pulse During VibroAcoustic Treatment. Pilot Study*
*Abstract*

In the TRILAX center, Steinkjer, routine measurement of blood pressure (BP) and pulse (P) are done to evaluate the effect of treatment on the clients. A sample of 82 measurements show a marked, but varying effect on the measured functions. The medium values were: Syst. BP –4.34. Diast. BP –5.35. Pulse 4.49. Rising values were found in about 25% of the cases. The measured values are checked initially (a), after 5 min rest (b), and at termination of treatment (c). The variation of values a-b, b-c, and a-c are described.

The necessity for further studies in order to increase the predictability for reduction of BP is emphasized.

*The Basis for the Study*

In TRILAX Center, Steinkjer, one has included measurement of blood pressure and pulse in the standard procedure of client reception. Systolic (SBP) and diastolic (DPB) are measured.

The study includes 82 randomly chosen measurement of patients coming for treatment during the fall of 1988. The overall distribution of patients show 30% men and 70% women.

Age distribution:

| | | |
|---|---|---|
| 20-29 years : 6% | 30-39 years : 17% | 40-49 years : 16% |
| 50-59 years : 18% | 60-69 years : 20% | 70-79 years : 14% |
| 80-89 years : 3% | | |

The equipment in use was a MultiVib chair VA 115 or a TRILAX Bed VB 555 and signal unit SU 225 from *VibroAcoustic a/s*[1]. The therapy programs are made by *VibroSoft a/s*[2] and are supplied on C-60 cassette tapes.

---

[1]   VibroAcoustics a/s, Granåsveien 9, 7040 Trondheim, Norway.
[2]   VibroSoft a/s, Høvdingveien 98, 7700 Steinkjer, Norway

The music which, for research purposes, is used to mask the low frequency signals is supplied by Spirit Music Inc., USA and the composers Otto Romanowski, Finland and Sven Grünberg, USSR Estonia, Soviet Union.

A Digital Electronic Blood Pressure Monitor from *Select a/s*[3] was used as measuring instrument.

A therapy session normally lasts between 20 and 29 minutes.

*Results* (SBP=Systolic Blood Pressure, DBP=Diastolic Blood Pressure, P=Pulse)

Basic Values:

| | | |
|---|---|---|
| SBP at arrival | m = 138.09 | sd = 14.37 |
| DBP at arrival | m = 86.72 | sd = 7.69 |
| P at arrival | m = 76.54 | sd = 16.01 |
| | | |
| SBP after 5 minutes rest | m = 127.54 | sd = 18.08 |
| DBP after 5 minutes rest | m = 79.84 | sd = 11.41 |
| P after 5 minutes rest | m = 72.44 | sd = 13.95 |
| | | |
| SBP after therapy session | m = 124.15 | sd = 16.90 |
| DBP after therapy session | m = 77.05 | sd = 11.41 |
| P after therapy session | m = 67.77 | sd = 11.60 |

---

[3]   available in the USA from Healthtech Corporation, 150 Sandbank Road, Cheshire, CT 06410

## TABLE OVER CHANGE IN VALUES

Group A = values measured after 5 min. rest at end of session
Group B = values measured at arrival and after 5 min. rest
Group C = values measured at arrival and end of session
SBP = Syst. BP,   DBP = Diast. BP   P = Pulse

| Group Rise | Unchanged N = | Rise N = | m = Rise | sd = Rise | Whole Group m = | | Fall sd = | m = N = | sd = Rise |
|---|---|---|---|---|---|---|---|---|---|
| ASBP | 1 | 24 | 8.92 | 9.94 | -4.34 | 9.44 | 57 | -9.98 | 7.6 |
| ADBP | 3 | 22 | 8.86 | 10.58 | -5.35 | 7.69 | 58 | -9.09 | 7.6 |
| AP | 8 | 18 | 4.78 | 4.16 | -4.49 | 7.20 | 56 | -8.43 | 5.0 |
| BSBP | 4 | 16 | 7.06 | 3.51 | -4.29 | 9.44 | 62 | -12.74 | 8.9 |
| BDBP | 5 | 22 | 7.41 | 7.73 | -4.23 | 10.67 | 55 | -8.51 | 9.9 |
| BP | 12 | 19 | 5.32 | 5.69 | -3.16 | 7.18 | 51 | -7.14 | 5.0 |
| CSBP | 3 | 12 | 8.33 | 6.09 | -12.20 | 12.94 | 67 | -16.75 | 9.3 |
| CDBP | 5 | 14 | 6.00 | 7.69 | -7.98 | 11.23 | 63 | -11.38 | 10.0 |
| CP | 2 | 13 | 5.40 | 5.84 | -7.40 | 8.25 | 67 | -9.86 | 5.5 |

*Discussion*

The statistics give an indication of what effects one can expect on SBP, DBP and P as a consequence of exposure to VA therapy.

The results cannot be directly compared with other studies dealing with the effect of 20 - 30 minutes *rest only* on SBP, DBP, and P as all persons were exposed to vibroacoustic stimuli in the corresponding period of time.

Clients who react to the therapy with a rise in the measured parameters have the same subjective feeling of stress-reduction, muscular relaxation and well-being after the end of the therapy session as clients in whom the same values are falling. The rise in values therefore has no correlation with physical discomfort.

## CHOICE OF MUSIC AND FREQUENCIES

The data collected on the use of tapes and frequencies for specific purposes are based on subjective feedback from clients.

However, the first study done by TRILAX Center, Steinkjer, based on 231 measurements of BP and pulse show us that we may expect a more uniform decrease in all three parameters when single-frequency tapes are used, than by use of multi-frequency tapes.

Research of this kind will be very important for the future development of VA therapy.

## CASE STUDIES

### Asthma Bronchiale

Three clients with Asthma Bronchiale, all women, 16, 56, and 83 years of age have used VA chairs for home use. all of them are invalided because of their asthma, and all have reported substantial relief of symptoms when the equipment is used regularly—i.e. several times a day. The effect seems to be good for the bronchospasms, and the general de-stressing and relaxing effect of the therapy seems to contribute to the rise in life quality of the clients. The study is continuing, and has now been going on for over 3 years. The results have not been altered. At especially severe times one of the patients uses the equipment up to 15 times a day. There are no adverse effects of her using it so often.

### Functional Dysmenhorrea

Five clients with functional dysmenhorrea have shown considerable improvement of both pain symptoms and mental stability in the premenstrual situation. Treatments have been given regularly, 21 times during a 3 month period. The project was terminated in February 1989, and at 4 months after terminating the test period, the subjects reported that the effects still lasted.

### Fibromyalgia/Fibromyositis

TRILAX Center, Steinkjer has treated 20 cases of fibromyalgia with positive results in about 50% of the cases. Best results have been obtained by giving concentrated treatments in a short period (11 treatment per week) and intervals of 3 to 5 months between the concentrated periods. The clients report that the pains gradually return during the intervals between treatments. The patients return for a new session when they feel the need of a "refill."

## Denmark

Using the MIMO 2 biofeedback equipment (from *Khepri Bioelectronical Development Company*[4]) which is doing numerical analyses of the spectral and amplitudinal conditions of brain waves, a study of the relative activity level in the two brain hemispheres has been made.

The results show a remarkable shift in the balance of activity between left and right hemisphere. The change in activity showed an increase in right hemispheric activity when the levels before and after VA therapy were compared.

The comparison was done between the reading before and after a 20 minute session in the VA chair.

## Sweden

Four top skiers from the Swedish national cross-country team have been using VA equipment to relax after extreme muscular strain during intensive training periods. The restitutional effect on muscles used under extreme conditions is considerable, and the physical discomfort is reduced to a remarkable extent.

## Finland

*Sport use*: At the Polar Rally 1989 considerable attention was given to the effect of VA therapy on sportsmen, when a driver with acute stiff neck was treated. The condition was so dramatically improved that the Finnish Olympic team is starting to explore how to use VA therapy in the psycho-physic relaxation of the team during intensive periods.

*Hard of hearing/deaf*: The Institute for the Hard of Hearing and Deaf (Kuulonhuoltoliitto) is treating their multiply handicapped patients from all over the country for periods of 3 to 6 weeks. The patients come for extensive examination and intensive therapy. Since December 1988 VA therapy has been included as an essential part of their daily rehabilitation program. The experiences are very positive and VA therapy is regularly used in auditive training, speech therapy and physiotherapy.

*VA therapy and stress in musicians*: VA therapy was started at the Sibelius Academy in Helsinki in Spring 1988 to treat stressed students. The Academy educates advanced level music students from all over the world. All students in this experiment reported improvement in muscle relaxation, better voice control, decrease of insomnia and reduced psychosomatic pains. In Spring 1989 the office staff of the Academy also started to use

---

[4]   Khepri, Bioelektronisk Udvikling, Chrostoffers Allé 1 th, 2800 Lyngby, Denmark

VA therapy for stress symptoms, especially headaches and muscle tensions. The results are also positive in these cases.

## CONCLUSION

VA therapy has now been used for 11 years, and The International Society for VibroAcoustics (ISVA) has reports from over 20,000 hours of use from approximately 60 different institutes, institutions and private persons.

There are clients who have been using VA therapy twice a day for 7 years, and private persons who have been using the chair up to 15 times daily for nearly 3 years. Over 90% of the clients react positively to the treatment. No negative effects have been reported from normal use. (Symptoms like muscular overuse syndrome can occur as over-exposure reactions when excessive volume is used.) In some cases of pain treatment, the pain increases initially and then gradually subsides.

It has been demonstrated that VA therapy has an effect beyond placebo reactions. However, the descriptions and research results collected do not satisfy the statistical requirements of medical research.

There are many projects of basic research lying ahead of us, if we are to develop the method and equipment to a satisfactory level.

We hope that there are many research institutions, institutes, hospitals or scientists with the interest, the capability, the creativity, and the capacity to join us in ISVA in our efforts to spread information and knowledge about this method which is in its infancy.

The VA method has been rejected my many Music Therapy institutes and groups in Europe but I am grateful to the ISMM for the moral support I have been given during the 7 years of more or less solitary work in opening new roads in MusicMedicine. We are now seeing the outline of an international team trying to develop the VA method, and this team will welcome new members who are willing to join us in this work.

## SUGGESTED READING

Carrington, M.E. 1980. Vibration as a training tool for the profoundly multiply handicapped child within the family. Lecture given at Castle Priory College.
Lehikoinen, P. 1988. The KANSA project. Report from a controlled study on the effect of VibroAcoustical Therapy on stress. Unpublished paper.

_____. 1988. Ääniaaltojen rentouttava vaikutus (The relaxing effect of sound waves). *Musikkiterapia* 1-2:21-25.

Saluveer E.; Tamm, S.; and Ojaperv, I. 1989. The use of VibroAcoustic Therapy on 40 psychiatric patients in the Dept. of Medicine, Tallinn Pedagogical Institute, USSR, Estonia. Paper read at 2nd International Seminar on the Use of VibroAcoustic Therapy, Steinkjer.

Skille O. 1985a. The music bath: Possible use as an anxiolytic. In *Music in Medicine,* edited by R. Spintge and R. Droh, pp. 253-256. Berlin, Heidelberg, New York: Springer.

_____. 1985b. Low frequency sound massage: The music bath—a follow-up report. In *Music in Medicine,* edited by R. Spintge and R. Droh, pp. 257-260. Berlin, Heidelberg, New York: Springer.

_____. 1987. Rapport fra symposium 13 - 15 Mars 1987 (Report from Symposium March 13-15, 1987). (available from VibroSoft a/s on computer disc only)

_____. 1988a. VibroAcoustics and sport: The beginning of a new approach to muscular stress? In *Schmerz und Sport,* edited by R. Spintge and R. Droh, 150-156. Berlin, Heidelberg, New York: Springer.

_____. 1988b. Fysmus: med en annen vri ("Physiomusic" — a new twist to music). *Musikkterapi* 3-4:48-63.

_____. 1989a. Behandling av funksjonell dysmenhorrea med VibroAkustisk behandling (Treatment of functional dysmenhorrea with VibroAcoustic Therapy). (VibroSoft, 1989).

_____. 1989b. Samlerapport fra 2. internasjonale brukerseminar omkring VibroAkustisk behandling. 14 - 15 April (Collected reports from The Second International Seminar for Practitioners of VibroAcoustic Therapy, April 14-15, 1989). (VibroSoft 1989 - Limited edition).

Swedish Defence Material Administration: INFRASOUND - a summary of interesting articles, p. 33. (FMV: ELEKTRO A12:142, May 1985).

Wigram, A.L. and Weekes, L. 1989. A project evaluating the difference in therapeutic treatment between the use of low frequency sound and music, and music alone, in reducing high muscle tone in multiply handicapped people, and oedema in mentally handicapped people. Paper read at the *Second ISVA Symposium* in Steinkjer, April 13-15, 1989.

# THE ROLE OF MUSIC THERAPY IN PHYSICAL REHABILITATION

Myra J. Staum

Human movement requires a certain "temporalness" in the performance of skilled motor patterns. In breathing, speaking, walking, or performing daily activities, accurate timing in coordination with the motor pattern is the factor most clearly differentiating normal from aberrant physical movement.

It has been suggested that a strong relationship exists between the auditory and motor systems (Gaston 1988; Licht 1946; Verdeau-Pailles 1985), therefore music used to accompany or stimulate movement has been a natural medium for the rehabilitation setting both in the regular medical hospital and in the private clinic. The rhythmic elements of music have been noted to override poorly established motor patterns particularly when reinforced by one's own production, as in singing or playing an instrument. While there is no definitive explanation for this phenomenon, it has been suggested that there is an internal drive to synchronize these two activities. It has been said that music tends to "activate the human rhythm" inherent in everyone (Altshuler 1960; Alvin 1966; Cotton 1965; Gilliland 1957).

While the rationale behind music's powerful influence when paired with movement may be obscure, research studies within the past fifteen years have consistently substantiated these results. Successful rehabilitation has been observed in the medical and rehabilitative settings (Staum 1988) within such different musical experiences as instrument playing, dancing, singing, listening and conducting.

In instrumental performance, activities and instruments have been adapted according to the physical limitations of the individual in conjunction with the needed rehabilitative objectives. These goals have been centered around developing coordination, strength, or endurance, and have been implemented in the context of small or large group ensembles, private lessons, and age appropriate musical combos. Mechanical adaptations of music instruments are widespread in the music therapy field and provide the necessary motivation for repeated exercise of the impaired body part (Brown-Wynkle 1956; Chadwick and Clark 1980; Clark and Chadwick 1979; Denenholz 1959; Dunn 1982; Erickson 1973; Elliot 1982; Miller 1979; Schoenberger and Braswell 1971).

Singing activities have been utilized primarily to strengthen the pulmonary system, and to alter the rate of respiration. The ability to inhale and exhale rhythmically and to sustain a vocalization with even consistency has been an important aspect particularly in language rehabilitation. Singing activities have been implemented primarily within private therapy sessions, private vocal lessons, and with choral groups.

Dance and related movement activities are the most parallel activities to physical movement. Dance choreographies have been developed specifically for the rehabilitative objectives, primarily to stimulate movement, increase coordination and muscular control, and to improve joint mobility and range of motion. These choreographed activities have been implemented in the context of large or small group dance experiences. The related activity of conducting had been used only infrequently for the purposes of developing upper body strength and coordination.

Listening activities have been implemented in physical rehabilitation as strong auditory cues to augment the rehabilitative process. Melodic variations have provided low-high cues to promote movement in the proper direction, stress patterns in music have helped with the emphasis needed to strengthen muscles, and the use of familiar or preferred melodic material has enabled the often repetitive nature of physical rehabilitation to be enjoyable. Attention to the rhythmic/temporal cues in music have aided all physical pursuits requiring timed, coordinated, or controlled motion.

While this body of research has not addressed the professional performing musician, the integration of this aspect of music medicine and music therapy is certainly an obvious one. With the most common overuse injuries of musicians occurring in the cervical and thoracic spine, the upper limbs, oral cavity, and respiratory system, the stress patterns of each instrument would need to be analyzed and exercises developed systematically approximating the physical demands of the actual instrument.

For instance, after sufficient rest, high pressure instruments like the oboe may require exercises which gradually restrengthen the embouchure and the intercostal and abdominal muscles, while simultaneously relaxing the throat. Performing musicians might choose to resume practice of the oboe after a designated period of rest at a reduced time schedule working up to the previous level or performance. For some individuals, however, particularly children and teens who are not under the pressure of a performance contract, it might be more motivating to work in the context of a structured music therapy session, redeveloping the necessary skills starting with instruments which require only a minimum of resistance such as a progression from whistle, to recorder, to kazoo, to a less demanding adapted instrument with a reed-like projection, and finally to the oboe. Within this context, enjoyable structured activities could be presented while physical improvement is monitored at each session. Specific exercise-compositions could be created by the youngsters themselves to assist in the process of rehabilitation, therefore continuing the creative, enjoyable process of music making.

The use of strong melodic and rhythmic cues would be useful for this purpose as well. For instance, to be aware of the proper proprioceptive sensation of a relaxed throat during a sustained instrumental passage, this same oboist might choose to compose a musical story in which both sanguine (staccato increasing to loud, accented passages) and morose (nonsupported sound or rest) fictional characters are present. Attention to the throat sensations would be guided by the therapist in the context of this creative activity. More sophisticated and professional musicians could develop their own progressive musical exercises with the aid of the physician who explicitly defines the physical areas requiring rest and /or rehabilitation. The fields of music medicine and music therapy blend naturally in the area of physical rehabilitation. Constant communication between the physician, music instructor, and musician can enable the rehabilitative process to be both functional and pleasant so that the process of learning or performing music continues to be a positive experience.

## REFERENCE LIST

Altshuler, I.M. 1960. The value of music in geriatrics. *Music Therapy 1959: Book of Proceedings of the National Association for Music Therapy*, 109-115.

Alvin, J. 1966. *Music Therapy*. New York: Humanities Press.

Brown-Wynkle, M.H. 1956. Devices as aids to rehabilitation through music therapy. *Music Therapy 1955: Book of Proceedings of the National Association for Music Therapy*, 79-85.

Chadwick, D.M., and Clark C.A. 1980. Adapting music instruments for the physically handicapped. *Music Educators Journal* 67:56-59.

Clark, C.A., and Chadwick, D.M. 1979. *Clinically Adapted Instruments for the Multiply Handicapped*. Westford, MA: Modulations.

Cotton, E. 1965. The institute for movement therapy and school for "conductors". Budapest, Hungary. *Developmental Medicine and Child Neurology* 7:437-446.

Denenholz, B. 1959. Music as a tool of physical medicine. *Music Therapy 1958: Book of proceedings of the National Association for Music Therapy*, 67-84.

Dunn, R.H. 1982. Selecting a musical wind instrument for a student with orofacial muscle problems. *International Journal of Orthodontics* 20:19-22.

Erickson, L.B. 1973. Keyboard fun for children with osteogenesis imperfecta and other physical limitations. *Inter-clinic Information Bulletin* 12:9-17.

Elliot, B. 1982. Guide to the Selection of Musical Instruments with Respect to Physical Ability and Disability. St. Louis, MO: MMB Music, Inc.

Gaston, E.T. (Editor). 1968. *Music in Therapy*. New York: Macmillan.

Gilliland, E.G. 1957. Music therapy. In *The Handicapped and Their Rehabilitation*, 628-649. Springfield, IL: Charles C. Thomas.

Licht, S.H. 1946. *Music in Medicine*. Boston: New England Conservatory of Music.

Miller, K.J. *Treatment with Music: A Manual for Allied Health Professionals.* Kalamazoo, MI: Western Michigan University Printing Dept.

Schoenberger, L., and Braswell, C. 1971. Music therapy in rehabilitation. *Journal of Rehabilitation* 37:30-31.

Staum, M.J. 1988. Music for physical rehabilitation: An analysis of literature from 1950-1986 and applications for rehabilitation settings. In *Effectiveness of Music Therapy Procedures: Documentation of Research and Clinical Practice*, edited by C.E. Furman, 65-104. Washington, DC: National Association for Music Therapy.

Verdeau-Pailles, J. 1985. Music and the body. *Musical Education for the Handicapped Bulletin* 1:8-21.

# V

# ASPECTS IN OCCUPATIONAL HEALTH CARE

# MUSIC THERAPY IN THE TREATMENT OF PERFORMANCE ANXIETY IN MUSICIANS

Cheryl Dileo Maranto

Health problems are a serious concern for musicians who are reported to have an average life expectancy of 22 % below the national average and who experience 5% more coronary disease than the general population (Tucker et al. 1971). In addition, musicians may be a high-risk group for psychological problems as well. Colligan et al. (1977) found that musicians were among the top five occupational groups (19.4 per 1,000) seeking treatment in a community mental health center in one state (cited in Wolfe 1989).

## MUSICIANS AND STRESS

Stress appears to be a significant problem in musicians. Middlestadt and Fishbein (1989) in a survey of 2,212 orchestral musicians found a significant correlation between perceived stress of musicians and the number of both musculoskeletal and nonmusculoskeletal problems.

These authors also found that perceived stress in musicians was most frequently associated with problems in their right hands, fingers and forearms. However, the greatest impact of stress was seen in players' back and neck problems. Players experiencing high stress also reported more frequent respiratory, cardiovascular, oral, jaw, dental, ear, and eye problems than players with low stress.

Musicians with high stress, according to the above authors, also experienced problems with anxiety, depression, and sleeping, and 41% of the high stress group also reported experiencing performance anxiety.

Middlestadt and Fishbein (1989) found that stress does not appear to be related to the gender of players, but is strongly and curvilinearly related to age. They found that the degree of perceived stress was strongly related to the player's function within the orchestra, with soloists experiencing the highest levels. Stress was also reported to be strongly related to the instrument played, i.e., stress levels were higher for oboe/English horn, French horn, trumpet, and tuba players, and for timpanists, percussionists, and harpists. Similarly, Schulz (1981) found that brass players were more likely to experience nervous stress than other types of instrumentalists.

## PERFORMANCE ANXIETY

Performance anxiety or stage fright is the most common nonmusculoskeletal problem of musicians according to a recent survey of over 2,200 International Conference of Symphony and Opera musicians representing forty-seven professional orchestras (Fishbein et al. 1988). Twenty-four percent of this group indicated that it was a problem, and 16% rated it as a severe problem. In a much smaller study of 100 European orchestra members, 63% of the respondents indicated that they experienced performance anxiety (James 1984). According to the ICSOM survey, stage fright appears to be related to a number of factors. Women more frequently experience stage fright as a severe problem than men. There appears also to be a curvilinear relationship between stage fright and age, with performers in the middle age group (35-45) experiencing this problem more severely than younger or older players. Brass musicians report more severe stage fright than players of other orchestral instruments, and members of smaller orchestras are more likely to have severe stage fright than members of larger orchestras. Raeburn (1987) found that performance-related anxiety was among the five top problems cited by rock musicians.

Performance anxiety may also be related to other health problems. Bayer (1982) reported that performance anxiety and problems with the player's stand partner were the best predictors of ill-health in his sample of orchestral players.

In an analysis of the research in this area, Maranto (1989) suggested that performance anxiety appears to be a function of a variety of factors, including the general state and trait anxiety of the performers, the demands of the situation, the influence of experience, and the composition of the audience. Also, it is suggested in the literature that there is a curvilinear relationship between the quality of performance and anxiety. Performance quality may be at its maximum at moderate levels of anxiety, whereas, performance is hindered when anxiety is either too low or too high (Sweeney and Horan 1981).


## TREATMENT OF PERFORMANCE ANXIETY

Musicians deal with performance anxiety in a number of ways. Forty percent of musicians who experienced stage fright reported that they had tried prescription medication with a 92% success rate. A sizeable percentage (27%) of musicians have used beta-blockers. Women, younger players (under 35), and brass players appear to be most likely to use these drugs. In the large majority of cases, beta-blockers are taken without a prescription and more frequently before auditions, solo recitals, and demanding or concerto performances (Fishbein et al. 1988)

Other methods sought to alleviate performance anxiety are most often psychological or psychiatric counseling, aerobic exercise, and hypnosis. Aerobic exercise was rated as the most effective of these nondrug methods of intervention (Fishbein et al. 1988).

A survey of the research on the effectiveness of various drug and nondrug treatments for performance anxiety revealed a number of different methods studied with varying degrees of treatment success: systematic desensitization, musical analysis training, cognitive restructuring, behavior rehearsal, psychotherapy, cue-controlled relaxation, coping skills training, thermal and EMG biofeedback, hypnosis, counseling, and music therapy (Maranto 1989). In general, the dependent measures in these studies have been behavioral observations, anxiety test scores, performance quality, pulse rate, and self-report measures. With the exception of coping skills training, all of these methods have demonstrated some significant effects on the dependent variable studied (Maranto, 1989).

A number of studies on the influence of beta-blockers as a treatment have also been reported in the literature. The drugs studied have been : propanalol, nadalol, pindolol, oxprenolol, alprenolol, and terbutaline (beta-stimulator). Generally, the dependent measures in these studies have been: heart rate, blood pressure, anxiety scores, performance quality, self-reports, and various other physiologic measures. The results of these studies for the most part suggest that beta-blockers do influence performers' heart rates. To some extent, these drugs also influence blood pressure, performance quality, and feelings of nervousness, although some of these results are contradictory and as yet inconclusive for beta-blockers in general. Moreover, these results vary with the specific drug tested (Maranto 1989).

## RESPONSES OF MUSICIANS TO MUSIC

The remainder to this paper will consider the unique and differential responses of musicians to music and will develop a rationale for the use of music therapy in the treatment of musicians' stress and performance anxiety.

### Mood Responses to Music

Persons with musical training appear to have different mood responses to music from nonmusicians as judged by the intensity and level of their responses (Brennis 1970), the number of their responses and specific responses to classical music (Sopchak 1955), and their tolerance for melodic tension in music (Trolio 1975).

However, no differences were found between musically trained and untrained subjects on response to harmonic tension (Winold 1963). It should be noted that researchers' definitions of "trained" versus "untrained" subjects vary and may account for some those conflicting findings.

Eagle (1971) studied music students' mood responses to a variety of musical stimuli. Results showed that the existing mood of these subjects affected their mood responses, the order of the music was not a significant influence on mood, and subjects' responses differed depending on whether the music was instrumental or vocal.

In addition, Lundin (1967) suggests that affective responses to music (for all types of listeners) are learned and are the result of a long-term interaction with the music.

## Music Preference and Taste

The results of several studies on the influence of music training on music preference and taste tend to suggest a relationship between these two factors (Long 1971; Duerksen 1968; Erneston 1961; Meadows 1970), although the specifics of this relationship are not yet known.

## Physiological Responses to Music

A number of researchers have investigated musician/nonmusician differences in physiological response to music. Results of these studies tend to support the idea that musical training is an important variable in assessing physiological responses to music. These data have been summarized by Hodges (1980, 395-396):

1. Fourteen studies have included data which indicate that musicians differ significantly from nonmusicians in their physiological responses to music (**HR**: DeJong et al 1973; Hyde 1927; Wascho 1948; **BP**: Hyde 1927. **Respiration**: DeJong et al. 1973. **GSR**: Dreher 1948; Henkin 1957; Peretti and Swenson 1974; Taylor 1973. **EMG**: Oleron and Silver 1963; Sears W. 1958, 1960. **EEG**: Inglis 1972; Wagner 1975a, 1975b. **Pilomotor**: Gray 1955. **Stomach**: Wilson 1957);
2. Only slightly more than half as many studies, eight, provided support for no significant differences between musicians and nonmusicians (**HR**: Ellis and Brighouse 1952; Sunderman 1946; Trenes 1937; Zimny and Weidenfeller 1963. **BP**: Miles and Tilly 1935; Misbach 1932; Sunderman 1946; Trenes 1937; Vincent and Thompson 1935; Wascho 1948).

It is interesting to note that all of the EEG, EMG, GSR, respiration and more unusual responses (pilomotor, stomach, etc.) studies fall into the category of significant differences, while all but one of the BP studies supported no significant differences; HR studies were nearly equally divided (pp. 395-396)

Several of these studies above are described herein. Shrift (1955) found that a piece of music could have differential sedative or stimulative effects on subjects, largely attributable to their previous musical training. Also, the subject's previous music experience (Taylor 1973) and the subject's preference for the music (DeJong et al. 1973) may be important in determining the potential stimulative or sedative effects of the music. Henkin (1957) found that previous musical experience was an important variable in GSR responses of subjects to various musical stimuli. Further, Peretti and Swenson (1974) in assessing the influence of music on anxiety, found greater decreases in anxiety for music majors as a result of the music treatment.

## MUSIC, STRESS AND ANXIETY

There have been some studies published involving the use of music to reduce stress and anxiety (Hanser 1985, 1988). Although results of these studies are in general supportive of the uses of music in treating stress and anxiety, it is difficult to generalize from these findings due to the various types of music utilized, the procedures used and the dependent measures employed. Also, in several of these studies, there is a discrepancy between the results of the various measures used, e.g., test scores may show decreases in anxiety, yet physiological measures may show no such differences.

According to Hanser, a number of reasons may account for these findings. "Relaxing" music has not yet been adequately defined for experimental purposes. Music categorized as either "sedative" or "stimulative" may have various elements which may prove ineffective for relaxation. Taylor (1973) warns against generalizing beyond a single piece of music.

It seems that because of the complex human responses to music in general, music for stress and anxiety reduction may have to be individually tailored (Hanser 1988, 213).

> Factors affecting the response to music, such as familiarity and preference, must be controlled. Structural elements of the music itself and subjective intervening variables, such as evoked images, should be considered. The definition of relaxing music is obviously unique to the listener.

Another reason which may account for these inconsistencies involves the attentional or arousal aspects of listening to music. While this phenomenon may indeed be a "positive" response to the music, it is not discriminated as such in physiological measurements. Thus, psychological and/or behavioral indices of stress reduction may provide more valid and reliable information (Hanser 1985).

In spite of these experimental and methodological difficulties in the research literature, clinical applications of music to treat stress and anxiety have yielded very positive results. Further, Ballard (1980), Crago (1981), and Franklin (1982) suggest that music is as effective as other stress reduction techniques and Yulis et al. (1975) recommend its use over other, traditional methods because of its apparent efficacy (cited in Hanser 1988).

## RATIONALE FOR THE USE OF MUSIC TO TREAT PERFORMANCE ANXIETY IN MUSICIANS

Although this review of the literature of psychological and physiological responses of musicians to music, and on the use of music in treating stress and anxiety is not an exhaustive one, and although some of this research is dated and has not been replicated, it does provide a basis of support for a rationale for the using music therapy techniques to treat the pervasive problems of stress and performance anxiety in musicians and for the identification of future research areas.

**Premise 1**: *Musicians, by virtue of their training, have differential responses to music both physiologically and psychologically.*

Although the research findings are inconclusive in this regard several important notions and areas for future research may be noted:

1. Musicians may be more sensitive to music than nonmusicians;
2. Musicians may have more intense responses to music than nonmusicians;
3. These response to music may heighten the effectiveness of music as a therapeutic modality.

Thus an important research question is: If musicians are more sensitive to music than nonmusicians, will music therapy be more or less effective as a treatment modality? Also, for which types of interventions will music therapy be most effective?

Interventions for performance anxiety reported into the literature may generally be classified according to four types: Psychotherapeutic, Cognitive/Behavioral, Stress Management, and Drug. Because of musicians' potentially heightened responses to music, will music psychotherapy therefore be more or less effective? Similarly, will musicians' behavioral or cognitive strategies be more or less effective? In addition, will musicians' responses to music enhance or contraindicate the use of music in stress management? Lastly, can music enhance or diminish the effectiveness of drug-treatment for performance anxiety?

The source of music performance anxiety has not been identified. Is music itself the source? If so, can the music be used to treat the problem or is it contraindicated?

If music is not the source, what then are the sources and can these be treated effectively with music?

Are musicians attracted to music because it is inherently gratifying to their psychological needs? what types of psychological needs does music gratify? If so, can this phenomenon be implemented to treat their problems?

**Premise 2**: *Music therapy shows great promise as a treatment for stress and anxiety.*

As mentioned above, preliminary research findings on the uses of music in treating stress and anxiety are very encouraging. Methodological issues in this complex area have been identified, and it is anticipated that future research will delineate more clearly and consistently the effects of music and the future role of music in treatment of these problems.

**Premise 3**: *Music therapy is a logical treatment for musicians whose own belief systems may support its efficacy.*

The importance of the individual's belief system regarding the treatment sought and undertaken appears to be a significant factor in its ultimate efficacy (Borysenko, personal communication 1988). Musicians, because of their choice of music as a career, may be very aware of its influence on them personally and of its importance in their lives. Through their performing experience they are also probably aware of its therapeutic effects on audiences. So, it is reasonable to suggest that musicians believe in the power of music both for themselves and for their audiences.

It is thus suggested that music as treatment for musicians may be particularly effective because of their inherent belief in its power to affect them deeply, access their feelings, and allow them insight into themselves. Also, music may be used to enhance the effectiveness of other types of interventions sought.

My preliminary work at Temple University with college music majors who experience performance anxiety is very encouraging. Music therapy techniques, as well as other techniques used with and without music (e.g. systematic desensitization) yielded positive results. Of interest is the preference of music students for music therapy and music-based techniques. In general, they could more readily relate to music therapy and music-based techniques. Further research into treatment preferences of musicians in indeed warranted.

The work of Louise Montello (1989) at New York University presented earlier in this conference is also of significance.

**Premise 4**: *Music is a safe, noninvasive, accessible, stigma-free treatment for stress and performance anxiety in musicians which may also complement their lifestyles.*

Music is every-present in a musician's life. As a mode of treatment, it is most available to them both through self-help and prescribed uses in treatment.

Music in the medium with which musicians may be most comfortable. It certainly provides for them a way of communicating nonverbally with others. In therapy, it may also be a vehicle for them to communicate nonverbally with a therapist or with themselves.

Music as treatment for performance anxiety offers little potential risk when compared with the possible side effects and risks of drug treatments. Music therapy, as with other nondrug interventions, affords the musician an opportunity to assume both an active role in treatment and some control over and self-reliance to combat the problems of stress and performance anxiety. These may be significant factors in the treatment of these, as well as other problems.

Finally, there may be a lesser stigma attached to the use of music as therapy for the musician when compared with the perceived stigmas of other types of psychological or psychiatric interventions. This factor may allow musicians to seek and continue treatment more freely.

## CONCLUSIONS

The stress and anxiety problems of musicians should not be taken lightly in view of the distress that it may cause them, as well as the other medical difficulties with which these have been associated.

While the cause of music performance anxiety is not clearly known, the use of music in its treatment deserves further consideration. Treatments, such as music therapy, which capitalize on the unique relationship the musician has with music and on the unique problems of the musician are recommended as topics for future research. It is also recommended that music therapists, who are both trained musicians and trained therapists involved in treating stress and anxiety, become involved in this emerging area of practice.

## REFERENCE LIST

Ballard, B.W. 1980. Effects of background music on anxiety during the initial counseling interview. *Dissertation Abstracts International* 41:3002-A.

Bayer, L.J. 1982. The stress process in professional musicians: An exploratory study. Dissertation, University of Cincinnati, OH.

Brennis, N.C. 1970. Mood differential responses to music as reported by secondary music and non-music students from different socioeconomic groups. Dissertation, Miami University, FL.

Colligan, M.J.; Smith, M.J.; and Hurrell, J.J. 1977. Occupational incidence rates of mental health disorders. *Journal of Human Stress* 3:34-49.

Crago, B.R. 1981. Reducing the stress of hospitalization for open heart surgery. *Dissertation Abstracts International* 41:2752-B.

DeJong, M.A.; van Mourik, K.R.; and Schellekens, H.M. 1973. A physiological approach to aesthetic preference-music. *Psychotherapy and Psychosomatics* 22:46-51.

Dreher, R.E. 1948. The relationship between verbal reports and galvanic skin response. Dissertation, Indiana University, IN.

Duerksen, G. 1968. A study of the relationship between the perception of musical processes and the enjoyment of music. *Council for Research in Music Education* 16:1-8.

Eagle, C.T., Jr. 1971. Effects of existing mood and order of presentation of vocal and instrumental music on rated mood responses to that music. Dissertation, University of Kansas, KS.

Ellis, D.S., and Brighouse, G. 1952. Effects of music on respiration and heart rate. *American Journal of Psychology* 65: 39-47.

Erneston, N. 1961. A study to determine the effect of musical experience and mental ability on the formulation of musical taste. Dissertation, Florida State University, FL.

Fishbein, M. et al. 1988. Medical problems among ICSOM Musicians: Overview of a national survey. *Medical Problems of Performing Artists* 3:1-8.

Franklin, C.E. 1982. The impact of music on the level of anxiety of high and low music listeners as measured by Spielberger's state trait inventory. *Dissertation Abstracts International* 42: 3419-B.

Gray, R.M. 1955. The pilometer reflex in response to music. Thesis, The University of Kansas, KS.

Hanser, S.B. 1985. Music therapy and stress reduction research. *Journal of Music Therapy* 22:193-206.

_____. 1988. Controversy in music listening/stress reduction research. *The Arts in Psychotherapy* 15:211-218.

Henkin, P. 1957. The prediction of behavior response patterns to music. *Journal of Psychology* 44:111-127.

Hodges, D.A. 1980. Physiological responses to music. In *Handbook of Music Psychology*, edited by D.A. Hodges, 393. Dubuque, IA: Kendall Hunt Publishing Co.

Hyde, A. 1927. Effects of music upon electro-cardiograms and blood pressure. In *The Effects of Music*, edited by M. Schoen. New York: Harcourt, Brace and Co.

Inglis, T.J. 1972. The effects of unfamiliar music on electroencephalograms of secondary school music students and nonmusic students. Dissertation, University of Minnesota, MN.

James, I.M. 1984. How players show stress symptoms. *Classical Music* Nov. 17:7.

Long, N.H. 1971. Establishment of standards for the Indiana-Oregon Music Discrimination Test based on a cross section of elementary and secondary students with an analysis of elements of environment, intelligence and musical experience and training in relation to musical discrimination. *Council for Research in Music Education* 25:26-32.

Lundin, R.W. 1967. *An Objective Psychology of Music* (2nd ed.). New York: Ronald Press.

Maranto, C.D. 1989. Performance anxiety: A meta-analysis of experimental research and clinical implications. Paper presented at the 7th annual symposium on medical problems of musicians and dancers. Snowmass, CO.

Meadows, W.S. 1970. The relationship of music preference to certain cultural determinants. Dissertation, Michigan State University, MI.

Middlestadt, S.E., and Fishbein, M. 1989. The prevalence of severe musculoskeletal problems among male and female symphony orchestra string players. *Medical Problems of Performing Artists* 4:41-48.

Miles, J.R., and Tilly, C.R. Some psychological reactions to music. *Guy's Hospital Gazette* 39:319-322.

Misbach, L.E. 1932. Effect of pitch and tone-stimuli upon body resistance and cardiovascular phenomena. *Journal of Experimental Psychology* 15:167-183.

Montello, L. 1989. Utilizing music therapy as a mode of treatment for the performance stress of professional musicians. Dissertation, New York University, NY.

Oleron, G., and Silver, S.E. 1977. Tension affective et effet dynamogéniques dus à la musique. *Anée Psychologique* 1963, 63:293-308. In Physical effects and motor responses to music (E. Dainow), *Journal of Research of Music Education* 25:211-221.

Peretti, P.O., and Swenson, K. 1974. Effects of music on anxiety as determined by physiological skin responses. *Journal of Research in Music Education* 22:278-283.

Raeburn, S. 1987. Occupational stress and coping in a sample of rock musicians. *Medical Problems of Performing Artists* 2:41-48.

Schulz, W. 1981. Analysis of a symphony orchestra and sociological and socio-psychological aspects. In *Stress and Music,* edited by Piparek. Vienna: Wilhelm Braumuller.

Sears, W.W. 1958. The effect of music on muscle tonus. In *Music Therapy,* 1957, edited by E.T. Gaston. Lawrence, KS: Allen Press.

Sears, W.W. 1960. A study of some effects of music upon muscle tension as evidenced by electromyographic recordings. Dissertation, The University of Kansas, KS.

Shrift, D.C. 1955. Galvanic skin response to two types of music. *Bulletin of National Association for Music Therapy* 10:5-6.

Sopchak, A.L. 1955. Individual differences in responses to music. *Psychology Monograph* 69:1-20.

Sunderman, L.F. 1946. A study of some physiological differences between musicians and nonmusicians: I. Blood Pressure. *Journal of Social Psychology* 23:205-215.

Sweeney, G.M., and Horan, J.J. 1982. Separate and combined effects of cue-controlled relaxation and cognitive restructuring in the treatment of music performance anxiety. *Journal of Counseling Psychology* 29:486-497.

Taylor, D.M. 1973. Subject response to precategorized stimulative and sedative music. *Journal of Music Therapy* 10: 86-94.

Trenes, N.E. 1937. Study of the effects of music on cancer patients. *Hospital Social Service* 16:131.

Trolio, M.F. 1975. Affective response to distorted melodies. Dissertation, Case Western Reserve University, Cleveland, OH.

Tucker, A.; Faulkner, M.E.; and Horvath, S.M. 1971. Electrocardiography and lung function in brass instrument players. *Archives of Environmental Health* 23:327-334.

Yulis, S.; Brahm, G.; Charnes, G.; Jacard, L.M.; Picota, E.; and Rutman, F. 1975. The extinction of phobic behavior as a function of attention shifts. *Behavior Research and Therapy* 13:173-176.

Vincent, S., and Thompson, J.H. 1935. The effects of music upon the human blood pressure. *The Lancet* 49:319-322.

Wagner, M.J. (1975a). Effects of music and biofeedback on alpha brainwaves, rhythm and attentiveness. *Journal of Research in Music Education* 23:3-13.

_____. (1975b). The effect of musical stimuli and biofeedback on the production of alpha brainwaves and verbal reports of musicians and nonmusicians. *Council for Research in Music Education* 41:1-10.

Wascho, A. 1948. The effects of music upon pulse rate, blood pressure and mental imagery. In *Therapeutic and Industrial Uses of Music*, edited by D. Soibelman. New York: Columbia University Press.

Wilson, V.M. 1957. Variations in gastric motility due to musical stimuli. Thesis, The University of Kansas, KS.

Winold, C.A. 1963 The effects of changes in harmonic tension upon listener response. Dissertation, Indiana University, IN.

Wolfe, M.L. 1989. Correlates of adaptive and maladaptive performance anxiety. *Medical Problems of Performing Artists* 4:49-56.

Zimny, G.H., and Weidenfeller, E.W. 1963. Effect of music upon GSR and heart rate. *American Journal of Psychology* 76:311-314.

# EXPLORING THE CAUSES AND TREATMENT OF MUSIC PERFORMANCE STRESS: A PROCESS-ORIENTED GROUP MUSIC THERAPY APPROACH

Louise Montello

## INTRODUCTION

Although musical performance stress has long proven to be physiologically, psychologically and artistically debilitating to professional musicians, only recently has this problem attracted the attention of researchers and clinicians in the behavioral and health sciences. Along with a number of epidemiological studies on the occurrence of performance stress in the musical community (Fishbein et al. 1988; Raeburn 1987; Piperek 1981), the psychological and medical literatures contain several outcome studies on the use of cognitive/behavioral techniques (Appel 1976; Sweeney and Horan 1982; Kendrick et al. 1982) and betablockers (Brantigan et al. 1979) in treating musical performance anxiety. None of these studies, however, contained qualitative data which described the underlying causes of subjects' performance anxiety, nor the process of therapeutic change as experienced by the therapy subjects.

In a recently published dissertation entitled "Utilizing Music Therapy as a Mode of Treatment for the Performance Stress of Professional Musicians," Montello (1989) found that group music therapy was effective in significantly reducing subjects' (anxious musicians) state and trait anxiety and increasing their confidence as performers. In a second study which partially replicated the results of the first study, it was also found that therapy subjects became significantly less self-involved, less stressed and more musical after groups music therapy intervention. Because the first study was exploratory in nature and the only empirical study of its kind (to date) which used a process-oriented "musical" approach to treating performance anxiety, the researchers added a qualitative component along with the quantitative measures which focused on the description and interpretation of subjects' "lived" experience of performance anxiety, as well as their "lived" experience of the group music therapy intervention. The purpose of this paper is to delineate the underlying components of music performance anxiety as experienced by subjects while actually performing in a group music therapy context (in Study I) and to describe how a multi-modal music therapy approach was used in dealing with these components.

## METHOD

### Subjects

Twenty musicians ranging from 18 - 48 years (M=28) were selected from 27 who responded to a flyer calling for volunteer participants in a study of the efficacy of music therapy as a treatment for musical performance stress. The criterion for selection of subjects was based on a minimum score of 12 (which represents a moderate level of anxiety) on the Personal Report of Confidence as a Performer Scale (Appel 1976). Subjects were randomly assigned to the "therapy" experimental group (n=10 initially but reduced to 7 by subsequent dropouts) and the "wait-listed" control group (n=10). The therapy group consisted of 4 females and 3 males (1 opera singer, six instrumentalists made up of 4 classical, 1 rock and 1 jazz), with 2-19 years of professional performance experience (M=8, SD=7.9) and 4-12 years of formal musical training (m=10, SD=2.3)

### Apparatus

The music therapy group was conducted in a large performance classroom at New York University. Subjects had access to a grand piano, an assortment of instruments for improvisation, as well as their primary instruments. The group met once a week for 90 minutes over a period of 12 consecutive weeks.

### Intervention

The group music therapy intervention focused on the here-and-now experience of the individual, using musical improvisation, performance, awareness techniques and verbal processing as catalysts for communication, change and personality integration. The therapy was influenced by Hesser's (1985) music therapy group training model for music therapy students.

The weekly sessions were structured into four components: a warm-up which included relaxation and breathing exercises; followed by an unstructured group improvisation; verbal processing of the group improvisation; leading to individual and/or group music therapy interventions. These interventions included techniques such as improvisational role playing, clinical improvisation, instrumental and vocal self-statements, "reality rehearsal" performances and guided imagery exercises.

### Therapists

The music group was led by two female certified music therapists with 12 and 4 years of clinical experience respectively.

**Measures**

Two instruments were developed by the researcher to obtain information from subjects regarding their "lived" experience of performance anxiety as well as their "lived" experience of group music therapy:

1.  Post-group questionnaire. This contained a number of open-ended questions regarding subjects' goal(s) for each session, their experience of group improvisation and individual interventions (if any) and what they learned about themselves during the group process.
2.  Weekly log. This contained a number of open-ended questions which related to subjects' performance experiences outside of the group. Nonmusical experiences which may have affected subjects' state anxiety were to be reported in the logs, as well as subjects' goals for each session. Also to be reported was the question of if and how insights gleaned from the music therapy group process were being integrated into their daily lives.

The bulk of the qualitative data came from the subjects' verbal dialogue, which was transcribed from weekly session videotapes. Giorgi's (1975, 74) phenomenological method was adapted for use in analyzing the raw data taken from the videotapes as well as from post-group questionnaires and weekly logs. In this method, the task of the researcher was to let the world of the describer, or the situation as it existed for the subject, reveal itself through the description in an unbiased way. The five stages of the qualitative analysis were as follows:

1.  The researcher viewed each of the 12 music therapy session videotapes and transcribed all of the verbal dialogue of each session onto a word processor. She also read through all of the weekly logs and post-group questionnaires of each subject.
2.  The researcher then read through the transcripts of subjects' verbal dialogue and the post-group questionnaires and logs (a second time), looking for individual descriptions of the underlying components of subjects' performance anxiety; subjects' overall experience of group music therapy; and subjects' report of change due to music therapy intervention.
3.  The researcher then organized individual descriptions of each member under the above categories.
4.  The researcher then reflected upon the above categories (with data still in the subjects' original language). Redundancies were eliminated and essential information from each category was then extracted and organized into more specific subcategories.

5. The researcher then attempted to interpret the meaning of the above subcategories in the light of relevant psychological and music therapy theories.

In order to avoid perceptual bias on the part of the researcher, several videotapes, questionnaires and logs were randomly selected to be independently evaluated by another person trained in the phenomenological method. This person was blind to the theoretical expectations of the study and had no interest in any particular outcome. Using the Pearson Correlation Co-efficient, the inter-rater reliability was found to be .87, representing high reliability between the two raters.

## Procedure

Performance tests were conducted with subjects during the second, sixth (mid-point) and twelfth sessions. Stephen Foster's "Slumber Song" was assigned to the subjects at the end of the first session. The piece was chosen for its simplicity, beauty and potential to evoke deep feelings. Subjects were asked to learn the piece and to perform it for the group the following week. The same piece was to be performed by the subjects mid-group as well as during the final group session.

The performance test was used diagnostically by therapists to obtain information from subjects regarding their "lived" experience of music performance. This included subjects' experience of being in a "test" situation; attitudes towards preparation and interpretation of the performance piece; musicianship; body/mind integration while performing; communicative ability; creativity; and coping skills.

## RESULTS

The underlying components of performance anxiety as extracted from the qualitative statements data are described below. The constituents are ranked according to the frequency of qualifying statements made by subjects.

*1. Inner critic*

According to subjects, the inner critic represented negative self-talk which seemed to have originated from harsh judgments of parents, teachers and peers in response to past performance situations. The subjects reported that the inner critic became more active in situations where they felt their expression of self would be evaluated in some way.

The first step in transforming the "inner critic" was for subjects to become aware of the introjected "voices" that had instilled the harsh judgment of their music. This was done while the musicians were actually performing in the group music therapy context. By unearthing these voices, the subjects were consequently able to become aware of the emotions which were associated with the voices. Subjects found that on a deeper level, the self reacted to these voices with feelings of anger, sadness, helplessness, guilt, and fear. It was actually these emotions which blocked the full expression of the music and prevented the musicians from experiencing fulfillment during their performances. As the musicians became aware of the negative inner voices and the feelings underlying them, they were then able to make choices, based on their own realistic assessments of their musical performances, as to which voices were helpful and which voices needed to be relinquished. The musicians received support and encouragement in making these choices from the group members and therapists.

*2. Ambivalent association with primary instrument*

Most subjects felt pressured to play "perfectly" while performing on their primary instruments. They felt they would be personally judged while playing their primary instruments and were fearful of making mistakes. They did not worry so much, however, while improvising on instruments other than their primary ones. In this musical context, they felt they would not be judged. They could relax and enjoy themselves.

From a psychoanalytic perspective, the relationship between the musician and his music often reflects his primary relationship with mother (Benenzon 1982; Racker 1951; Diamond 1981). If the musician did not work through early separation/individuation issues, his instrument often becomes a substitute for the "loved/hated" object (mother) and his ambivalence towards mother is then projected onto his relationship with his instrument. His severe judgmental attitude towards his primary instrument becomes symbolic of the quality of his relationship with his expressive self. Unconsciously he feels that if he plays badly or makes mistakes, he will not receive his mother's love. He is still dependent on her approval and acknowledgment and is frightened that if he is not perfect, he will be rejected. This creates anxiety for the musician every time he is about to perform before an audience, which, according to Gabbard (1979), is also representative of mother.

As could be seen in this study, several subjects actually turned the unexpressed feelings underlying their anxiety (mostly anger and guilt), against themselves and their instruments (symbolic extensions of themselves) during their practice sessions and actual performances. This behavior was experienced by several musicians as a form of self-punishment, both psychologically and physically. It is hypothesized that this "masochistic" approach to playing music may be a contributing factor to the "overuse" syndrome in certain musicians.

The music therapist helped the musicians to move the focus away from their fears of making mistakes and being rejected towards creating new bonds with their instruments in the spirit of compassion and unconditional self-acceptance. Musicians were encouraged to enter into the process of getting to know their instruments as if they were new friends— loving them, accepting them for better or for worse. This helped them to release their ambivalence towards their instruments (and their own expressive selves) and to value their uniqueness and creativity.

*3. Lack of commitment to music performance*

Fear of being judged was a common experience of all subjects. Subjects reported that in order to deal with this fear, a part of themselves became detached from the performance experience, so that the whole self was not put on the line, "subject to attack." Subjects reported anticipating failure as opposed to success in the performance situation. They felt they had to protect themselves in case they made a mistake or did something "inappropriate" while playing music.

The above behavior, in its extreme state, has been defined by Kaplan (1969, 65) as depersonalization,

> A split between a functioning and an observing self, with pronounced spatial disorientation. The observing self perceives the functioning self as off at a distance, operating mechanically before an audience which is also perceived as quite distant.

The subjects' abovementioned behavior may also be representative of Winnicott's (1971) description of the "false self." Because the musicians feared rejection and abandonment by the audience, and at the same time wanted their love and approval, they would split off or dissociate from the fear and its underlying emotions of sadness, anger, frustration, etc., and would pretend through the "false self" that they were secure and willing to please the audience. Because the musicians were not allowing themselves to be totally present in their musical experience, they were unable to communicate the music with the emotional intensity needed to engage the giving and receiving feedback loop with the audience. In the end, this caused even more frustration, as a part of the musician's psyche was "frozen" during the performance, and remained frozen, unable to be melted by the creative fire of the particular piece of music he was performing.

The music therapist encouraged the anxious musicians to become aware of the feelings underlying their anxiety responses. When working with actual performance pieces, the musicians were asked to let the music carry the emotions they may have been suppressing. Frequently these were feelings of sadness, longing and anger. Most group members chose performance pieces which actually embodied the emotions that they had the most difficulty accepting in themselves. The music therapist helped the musicians to use the music itself to draw forth the emotion in conflict or its polarity, in order to resolve past music-related traumas and to facilitate personality integration. The problem with depersonalization was that the musicians were disconnected from the emotional content of the music (and from themselves). They were, in fact, identified with their negative self-image, which in effect was a cover-up for deeper emotional issues.

*4. Inadequate preparation (with regard to performance piece, "Slumber Song")*

Some subjects did not prepare adequately to perform the piece for the group. A few subjects explained that by not preparing well enough, they would then have an excuse in case they made mistakes, or "screwed up" the piece. In this way, the audience would not have such high expectations of them.

This kind of thinking shows a rather negative association with performance, anticipating failure as opposed to success. It also may reflect the musicians' initial resistance to the therapy process. This behavior also shows the musicians' lack of commitment to performing music, a lack of self-esteem and a lack of belief that if one prepared well, one would do well. Musicians often projected their own highly critical expectations onto the audience and felt they would be laughed at or rejected if they were unable to live up to these expectations.

The music therapist helped to inspire a deeper sense of purpose in the performing musicians. She encouraged them to focus on the meaning inherent in the music and to filter out ego-identification and self-involvement. Through active techniques which had the potential to induce "peak" experiences, music therapy helped to reawaken the original sense of joy in sharing music that many musicians had lost due to mixed messages (good/bad judgment) from parents, teachers, and peer pressures.

*5. Underdeveloped will and lack of focus related to music performance*

A common component of performance anxiety as reported by subjects was the feeling of being out of control due to nervousness during a performance. Subjects experienced shaking (in their voices, hands, knees, and ankles), shortness of breath and heart palpitations as symptoms of performance stress. Because these bodily symptoms led to a feeling of being out of control, subjects would try to control them by forcing the mind to suppress the nervous reaction. This in turn would take the focus off the music, as attention was needed to keep the bodily sensations in check. The breath would lock, the body would become rigid and musical expression became stifled. This would create feelings of anger and hopelessness in subjects. They realized that they were conditioned to respond to the negative stress syndrome while performing, rather than to the pull of the music itself.

One of the detrimental ways of dealing with anxiety is attempting to control the feeling state of being out of control. When one is feeling out of control, it is important to come back to center and to become the observer of the different dynamics (both inner and outer) which are occurring. This technique has been called "focusing" (Gendlin 1978). During an actual performance, however, it is quite difficult to do this. The music therapist gave the performers opportunities to allow themselves to feel out of control in "reality rehearsal" performance situations and to study the dynamics of this state. The yogic technique of breath awareness (Rama 1986) was taught to the musicians so that the breath would become the home base to return to when feelings or thoughts began to overwhelm them. Focusing on and learning to control the breath calms the autonomic nervous system and allows the physical symptoms to subside. The musicians could then return their focus to the music, use their will to affirm their purpose, and channel their creative energy (nervousness/excitement) directly into the music.

*6. Discomfort in sharing one's music with the audience.*

Most subjects reported that expressing emotions such as loneliness, anger, joy, and love were difficult for them to do musically. One subject said that connecting intimately with a small audience was more difficult than singing to an anonymous audience, "out there." During the group improvisations subjects found that communicating through singing directly to another group member was more difficult than just playing instruments together. They often reacted nervously when they were mirrored musically by the therapists and by other group members. One subject felt that the audience might get "squeamish" if she got too close to them while performing. All subjects reported having fears of playing solo in front of an audience or being the leader of an ensemble or improvisation group.

Mayman (1974) writes about the shame dynamic, a sense of feeling naked and unable to hide one's shame (underlying repressed memories of the excitement and exhilaration of early childhood nudity) as being part of the stage fright syndrome. According to Mayman, the performer is torn between the desire to expose himself to prove he is a fully equipped sexual being and the fear that the onlooker will find his equipment laughable (p. 386). The shame dynamic not only applies to the child's sexual feelings, but to any intense emotions which he feels may not be acceptable to or acknowledged by significant others.

Gabbard (1979) writes that separation anxiety, a child's fear of asserting himself as a separate individual against the regressive pull of symbiosis (Mahler et al. 1975), is an important dynamic in the stage fright syndrome. Shields (1986) has found in her clinical experience that many musicians have conflicts around mother-child symbiotic formation. From a psychoanalytic perspective it would seem that most musicians in this study were still psychologically bound to their introjected "mother" and were dependent on her for the fulfillment of primitive needs such as nurturing, belongingness, approval, etc. According to Mahler's theory, if they were to release their narcissistic bond with mother, these musicians would probably experience much fear and anxiety, as they would then come face to face with the realization that they were fully responsible for themselves. Also, the anxious musician might fear that, if he attempts to separate from mother, she would withdraw the love and support she had offered in the past and he would be left alone in the world without a safety net.

When dealing with the issue of separation/individuation, the music therapist first helped the musicians to become aware of their underlying dependency on significant others for acknowledgement, approval, and love, and how this affected their performance experiences. She then encouraged them to take some time to reflect on the kind of music which they really enjoyed playing—or music with which they felt they could deeply identify during this particular stage of their lives. Often this was not the music on which they were focusing at the time. Several subjects seemed to have been molded into musical "clones" by teachers and significant others. Because of their dependency on these individuals, they were often too fearful of expressing their own musical opinions and desires.

In searching for their own unique forms of musical expression, the musicians began to experiment with songs from childhood, various kinds of ethnic music, other genres of music, including improvisation. Some musicians were satisfied with their current repertoire. Often they needed only to free themselves from the harsh judgment they placed upon themselves while playing music to enjoy their playing and to be nurtured by the musical experience. In the music therapy context, musicians began to bond with their own music—with their own selves. The music became the transitional object (Tyson 1981) as the musicians gradually began to separate from "mother" and develop their own musical-self identities.

Subjects' musical identities were also developed through the process of vocal improvisation. Khan (1983) describes the voice as the mirror of the soul, or Self. In the music therapy group, the musicians were encouraged to let go of the judgments they placed upon their vocal expression, to go within and allow vocal self-statement to emerge, and to share these with the group. They were asked not to think, but to feel the music emanating from their source—the hara (belly) and to allow it just to be in its own unique sound form and pulse. Through contacting the musical "self," the musicians were connected to their own "inner music" (Nordoff and Robbins 1977; Priestley 1975). It is only from the space of one's inner music that true motivation for creativity and growth can be activated.

In further developing the self, musicians were encouraged during "reality rehearsal" performances to make contact with the "audience," and to become aware of the thoughts, feelings, and bodily sensations which emerged during the performance process which blocked this contact. If painful feelings emerged it was suggested that the energy of these feelings (perhaps stemming from past traumas) be accepted fully by the musicians and then channelled back into their music to enhance the musical expression.

According to object relations theory (Winnicott 1971; Kernberg 1975), individuals who have a weak sense of self often create a "narcissistic shell" around themselves which prevents them from making emotional contact with others. During the group improvisations, as well as in individual work, the music therapist reflected back to the musicians, both musically and verbally, certain self-revealing communications which they had made, to help them see and hear themselves as they exist authentically in the here-and-now. Mirroring helped the musicians to become aware of their self and to own it. In this way, they had also to deal with the fact that someone was really listening to them, really being with them. This was sometimes threatening for several subjects. Mirroring during the music therapy process helped to diminish the sense of unreality that the overly self-involved musicians felt about themselves and strengthened their sense of personal identity.

## 7. Weak sense of self

Many subjects reported that they found it difficult to separate their own thoughts and feelings from the critical judgment of others. Their moods seemed to change based on how others viewed them. One subject reported that she felt like a vacuum that was filled with the opinions, beliefs, and judgment of teachers, peers, and parents. Two subjects had fears of boring people with their music. Some subjects realized their overriding need for approval when playing music. During the group improvisations, subjects became aware of their patterns of conformity within the group structure as well as their inclinations to act out or rebel against the group norms. Some subjects had difficulty playing music for their own enjoyment and experienced music as drudgery, "just a job."

Again, these data reflected the musicians' weak sense of identity and low self-esteem. This particular personality structure might suggest a form of narcissistic personality disorder (Emmons 1987). Because the abovementioned musicians had weak associations with self, they were constantly seeking recognition and approval from others. Also in alignment with the theories of narcissism, it appeared that many of the musicians in this study were fearful of the imagined intensity of their emotions. Because of this fear, their emotions were often repressed. The repression caused a lack of enthusiasm towards performance and weakened self-motivation. During the first few group improvisations, subjects evidenced extreme shifts in mood from conformity to hostility during their musical interactions. There was a lack of true musical relationship among group members. The subjects were self-involved and found it difficult to put their music forward.

Because subjects were often cut off from their emotional selves, the technical aspects of the music became overvalued. There was a striving for perfection and no allowance for making mistakes. These musicians tended to be left-brain dominant (Diamond 1985). This imbalance fostered an assertive, aggressive behavior which apparently did not allow much time for repose, reflection, reverie and emotional expression (right-brain attributes). The musicians' ability to play and their sense of wholeness were forces into the background of consciousness.

Through breath awareness, relaxation exercises and musical improvisation in a supportive, playful atmosphere, subjects were encouraged to unwind their self-judgment and aggressive behavior, to soften their competitive attitudes and to cultivate gentleness and self-acceptance. Being in a group situation with other musicians with similar problems seemed to reduce feelings of aloneness and vulnerability, as the musicians began to allow the hidden parts of themselves to emerge during the group process. Group members began to interact musically and verbally, and deeper levels of sharing unfolded as the therapy progressed. Self-involvement also decreased as a sense of community was experienced among group members.

*8. Ambivalent relationship with audience*

Most subjects had inaccurate perceptions of audience attitudes and needs. They projected inner fears and wishes onto the audience and often worried about what the audience might be thinking of them. Some of the fears experienced by subjects were that the audience would: a) be overly critical, b) fall asleep while they were performing, c) only go to performances because they were obligated.

The musicians' role is one of outward-directed communication (Diamond 1983; Havas 1973). The subjects in this study seemed to be generally more concerned with their own inner needs and projections with regard to musical performance than with the goal of communicating music to the audience. This state of excessive self-involvement seems to be an attribute of most adults with neurotic anxiety (Diamond 1987). It is possible that subjects may have unconsciously perceived the audience as parental object, whose rejection of them at a critical growth period had created ambivalent feelings: the desire to be accepted and loved coupled with feelings of hopelessness, despair, and anger from perceiving themselves as unlovable. It was hypothesized that subjects were repeatedly re-enacting this inner conflict under the guise of musical performance, with the hope of some resolution of the painful feelings that had become a part of their self-systems.

Because of the intensity of the abovementioned submerged feelings, the audience was perceived by several subjects as something to be feared, and if their trauma was great, to be avoided. These musicians seemed to enclose themselves in a "narcissistic shell" which prevented them from really making contact with the audience. Because their fear was so great, the same subjects actually pretended that the audience (mother/father) was not really there, which suggests a form of defensive denial. They may have been trying to prove to the significant others, through the performance experience, that they would not fall apart with them (Kernberg 1975) (even though they had never completely introjected them in the first place—which is the most likely cause of their deep sense of insecurity). Performing then became a test of mastery as opposed to a gift of giving, i.e., "Can I get through this [the performance] without making any mistakes?"

The abovementioned component of performance anxiety was again related to subjects' unresolved dependency issues. The music therapist first helped subjects to bond with their own music and cultivated the soil of the subjects' own musical identities. Once subjects began to establish a positive relationship with their own music, they were then encouraged to share their music with group members during group improvisations and actual performances. In this way, the subjects began to bond musically with others. As the subjects began to strengthen the bond with their own music and their relationships with others, they were then encouraged to use their own music (both vocal and instrumental) creatively in the form in improvisations and compositions, utilizing story-telling techniques, imagery, and the creative will, to resolve emotional polarities and to fill the "holes" in their development. According to Kenny (1985, 9),

> Music is the expressive connective tissue guiding us into wholeness.


## DISCUSSION

In summary, eight key components emerged from the qualitative data which seem to contribute to the performance anxiety syndrome in selected professional musicians:

- an "inner critic;"
- ambivalent association with primary instrument;
- inadequate preparation for performance;
- lack of commitment to performance;
- underdeveloped will and lack of focus related to performance;
- discomfort in sharing one's music with the audience;
- weak sense of self; and
- ambivalent relationship with the audience.

In reviewing the abovementioned data it appeared that therapy subjects were generally overly self-involved due to certain psychological factors and were estranged from a healthy relationship with their own music and with the audience. It is suggested that the group music therapy context gave the musicians an opportunity to become aware of these factors (the thoughts, feelings, and bodily sensations underlying their anxiety reactions) while actually performing for group members and therapists during the course of therapy. Music itself was used as a self-reflecting and transformational tool to assist the musicians in achieving greater self-awareness, developing stronger relationships with their own creative potential and dealing with their anxiety constructively. It is believed that the interpersonal interactions fostered among group members and therapists during the course of therapy were also helpful in resolving conflicts around the musicians' relationship with the audience as well as their relationships with significant others. Although self-report data suggest that the changes experienced by subjects during the course of therapy transferred readily into their real life performance situations, it is yet to be seen whether these changes will continue past the initial therapy period. A follow-up study in planned to collect data which will explore this possibility.

## REFERENCE LIST

Appel, S. 1976. Modifying solo performance anxiety in adult pianists. *Journal of Music Therapy* 13(1):3-15.

Benenzon, R.O. 1982. *Music Therapy in Child Psychosis.* Springfield, IL: Thomas.

Brantigan, T. A. et al. 1979. The effect of beta blockage on stage fright. *Rocky Mountain Medical Journal* 76(5):227-232.

Diamond, J. 1981. *The Life Energy in Music Volume I: Notes on Music and Sound.* Valley Cottage: Archaeus Press.

_____. 1983. *The Life Energy in Music, Volume II: As in Life, So in Music.* Valley Cottage: Archaeus Press.

_____. 1985. *Life Energy.* New York: Dodd, Mead and Company Inc.

_____. 1987. Personal communication.

Emmons, R.A. 1987. Narcissism: Theory and measurement. *Journal of Personality and Social Psychology* 52 (1): 11-17.

Fishbein, M.; Middlestadt, S.E.; Orsatti, V.; et al. 1988 Medical problems among ICSOM musicians. *Med. Probl. Perform. Art.* 3:1-8.

Gabbard, G.O. 1979. Stage fright. *American Journal of Psychoanalysis* 60:383-391.

Gendlin;, E.T. 1978. *Focusing.* New York: Bantam Books.

Giorgi, A. 1975. *Duquesne Studies in Phenomenological Psychology II.* Edited by A. Giorgi, C. Fischer, E. Murray. Pittsburgh: Duquesne University Press.

Havas, K. 1973. *Stage Fright, Its Causes and Cures with Special Reference to Violin Playing.* London: Bosworth and Co.

Hesser, B. 1985. Advanced clinical training in music therapy. *Music Therapy* 5(1):66-73.

Kaplan, D. 1969. On stage fright. *Drama Rev.* 14:60-83.

Kendrick, M. J. et al. 1982. Cognitive and behavioral therapy for musical performance anxiety. *Journal of Counseling and Clinical Psychology* 50(3):353-362.

Kenny, C.B. 1985. Music therapy: A whole systems approach. *Music Therapy* 5(1):3-12.

Kernberg, O. 1975. *Borderline conditions and Pathological Narcissism.* New York: Jason Aronson.

Khan, H.I. 1983. *The Music of Life.* Santa Fe, NM: Omega Press.

Mahler, M.; Pine, F.; and Bergman, A. 1975. *The Psychological Birth of the Human Infant.* New York: Basic Books.

Mayman, M. 1974. The shame experience, the shame dynamic, and shame personalities in psychotherapy. Presented at APA Annual Meeting, September 1974. Unpublished.

Montello, L. 1989. Utilizing music therapy as a mode of treatment for the performance stress of professional musicians. Thesis, New York University, New York.

Nordoff, P., and Robbins, C. 1977. *Creative Music Therapy.* New York: The John Day Co.

Piperek, M. 1981. *Stress and Music.* Vienna: Wilhelm Braumueller.

Priestley, M. 1975. *Music Therapy in Action.* London: Constable.

Racker, H. 1951. Contribution to psychoanalysis of music. *American Imago* 8:129-263.

Raeburn, S. 1987 Occupational stress and coping in a sample of rock musicians. *Med. Probl. Perform. Art.* 2:41-48.

Rama, S. 1986. *The Path of Fire and Light.* Honesdale: Himalayan Publishers.

Shields, A. 1986. *Expressive Therapy,* Edited by A. Robbins. New York: Human Science Press.

Sweeney, G.A., and Horan, J.J. 1982. Separate and combined effects of cue-controlled relaxation and cognitive restructuring in the treatment of music performance anxiety. *Journal of Counseling Psychology* 29(5):486-497.

Tyson, F. 1981. *Psychiatric Music Therapy.* New York: Fred Widner and Sons, Inc.

Winnicott, D.W. 1971. *Playing and Reality.* London: Tavistock.

# MUSCLE PAIN SYNDROMES IN PERFORMING ARTISTS: MEDICAL EVALUATION OF THE PERFORMER WITH PAIN

Richard J. Lederman

Occupational pain syndromes are a heterogeneous, and in some cases, poorly defined group of disorders which have been recognized for almost 300 years (Ramazzini 1940). The term itself implies some connection with the patient's occupation although the relationship is not always clear and unequivocal. At one end of the spectrum would be a very well localized and unifocal pain associated with a readily recognized source of trauma and clear signs of tissue injury. At the other end of this spectrum are the diffuse or multifocal and sometimes poorly localized pain syndromes, generally "musculoskeletal" in character, waxing and waning in severity but associated with and attributed to activity in the work place, and often of uncertain etiology. Over the years a number of terms have been used to describe these ailments, including cumulative trauma disorders, occupational cervicobrachial syndrome, overuse syndrome, regional pain syndrome, repetition strain injury, and tendinitis. Currently, overuse syndrome seems to be preferred in Performing Arts Medicine. This may be defined as the symptoms and signs associated with apparent injury to tissues which have been stressed beyond their biological limits. Any body tissue may be excessively stressed, but the majority of overuse disorders appear to involve the muscle-tendon unit or the joints and associated ligaments (Lederman and Calabrese 1986).

Pain appears to be the most common symptom among performers who seek medical care (Hochberg et al. 1983; Knishkowy and Lederman 1986). The prevalence of pain syndromes among performers, particularly instrumentalists, has been the subject of a number of recent investigations. Fry (1986) interviewed members of eight orchestras and found that 64% (312/485) had playing-related pain. Caldron et al. (1986) surveyed instrumental musicians in music schools and professional ensembles in the Northeast Ohio area. Among 250 string and keyboard instrumentalists, 59% were identified as having musculoskeletal symptoms. The International Conference of Symphony and Opera Musicians (ICSOM) surveyed its 48 member orchestras by questionnaire. Of 2,122 respondents, 76% had what was described as a severe medical problem affecting performance (Fishbein et al. 1988) and 58% had a severe musculoskeletal complaint or ailment (Middlestadt and Fishbein 1989). Surveys have also been carried out on groups of student musicians at both secondary and conservatory levels, with prevalence rates of playing-related pain ranging from about 10% to as high as 56% (Fry 1987; Lockwood 1986; Fry et al. 1988). Despite what appears to be a large number of instrumental musicians reporting playing-related pain, a substantial percentage of these may not consult medical practitioners. In our survey only 63% of symptomatic respondents had sought medical help (Caldron et al. 1986). There is some evidence that this may be changing, at least in part because of the growth and increasing recognition of Performing Arts Medicine as a specialty (Lockwood 1989).

A few generalizations can be gleaned from the various surveys mentioned above and from reports from various centers describing their experience with instrumentalists. Playing-related symptoms, including particularly those characterized as musculoskeletal, are more common in women than men. Keyboard and string instrumentalists are more likely to have musculoskeletal playing-related symptoms than woodwind or brass players. Characteristic patterns of involvement have also been seen. For example, string instrumentalists, particularly violinists and violists, are more likely to have problems with the left hand and arm, whereas keyboard players tend to have more problems with the right upper limb.

The approach to medical evaluation of the instrumental musician or other performer is in many ways no different from that of any patient. The first step involves a determination of the major problem or symptoms which have led the performer to seek medical consultation. The performer may, like other patients of today, be remarkably sophisticated medically, as the result of self-education or numerous prior contacts with health care professionals. Others may be surprisingly naive and unsophisticated. In either case, the performer may attempt to describe the problem by using terminology peculiar to music or the specific instrument. Just as the health care practitioner dealing with dancers must be conversant with such terms as *en pointe, grand plié*, and *turnout*, so must the physician or other health care practitioner seeing instrumental musicians develop some familiarity with the language of musicians. If the medical history is punctuated by such words as *embouchure, arpeggio, vibrato, tremolo, spiccato*, or *frog*, this should not represent a major impediment in the attempt to elucidate the nature of the musician's complaint.

While pain is most frequently mentioned by the instrumental musician, other complaints may also be reported, including stiffness, cramping, fatigability, tightness, swelling, numbness, tingling, burning, weakness, lack of control, impaired dexterity, or some sort of involuntary movement. These may be present alone or in various combinations. The history of these symptoms must be pursued further, eliciting information regarding the onset, development, character, intensity, time course, frequency or regularity of occurrence, relationship to playing or other activities, and factors which appear to aggravate or ameliorate the symptom or symptoms.

A detailed risk factor analysis should also be undertaken with special emphasis on the circumstances surrounding the onset of each symptom. Specific questions must be asked regarding recent changes in playing or practice schedule, particularly the time spent playing and the intensity of that activity. Both time and intensity are likely to increase as an audition, recital, or jury approaches. Recent changes in techniques or playing may precipitate new symptoms, often triggered by exposure to a new teacher or even by an attempt to reproduce something observed in another performer. A new instrument can also precipitate new symptoms as the instrumentalist may have to modify technique to achieve the desired result. At times, the performer may describe a recent alteration in technique that may actually represent a compensation for a playing-related symptom rather than the cause of that symptom without actually realizing that this change has been made. This can be misleading. Careful inquiry into the practice habits and circumstances of practicing and playing is also important. Total playing time and duration of practice sessions should be detailed. The time of day when playing or practicing is done may be important as well. It is further important to inquire about the repertoire and to get some idea of the technical difficulty and degree of comfort that the performer has with the particular pieces being studied or played. For ensemble players, position in the orchestra or other group, crowding and sight lines, problems with height of stands and with chairs, and other mechanical factors may be relevant. Information regarding nonmusical activities may be important in elucidating the mechanism of symptom production. A detailed inquiry into economic and psychosocial factors is also necessary and these aspects may not be spontaneously offered as is so often the case with many patients.

One must also elicit information regarding the general medical background including previous or chronic illness, medications, recreational drug usage including alcohol, and family history. At times, supplementary information may have to be obtained from family, friends, colleagues, teachers, and orchestra management, always of course with the full understanding and knowledge of the musician/patient. Confidentiality is often a major concern of the performer and a violation of this trust is unacceptable.

The scope and focus of the physical examination of the instrumental musician must be guided, as it is in any medical evaluation, by the history and by the major complaint. The emphasis in the instrumental performer with pain is generally on careful musculoskeletal and neurological assessment. General observations would include overall body habitus and configuration. Craniofacial structure, neck length and thickness, shoulder and upper trunk posture, spinal configuration, general assessment of muscle development, soft tissue swelling, and skin changes may all be noted on simple inspection. Range-of-motion, both passive and active, of neck, thoracolumbar spine, and proximal as well as distal limb joints are assessed. Restricted mobility, hyperlaxity, and asymmetry are particularly looked for.

On palpation one searches for areas of tenderness over joints, tendons, muscles, points of nerve entrapment, or subcutaneous tissues. Tightness, spasm, and trigger points with or without palpable bands or nodules in muscle may be important diagnostically. Crepitation, swelling, and nodular thickening of joints or tendon sheath is noted. Provocative maneuvers looking for nerve entrapment or subluxation are carried out and one looks for thickened or atrophic nerves where they are accessible.

The neurological examination is traditionally divided into systems, although it may be performed in many different ways. Mental status is continuously assessed from the moment of introduction to the patient but formal testing may be required in some circumstances. The cranial nerve examination particularly includes sensory testing on the face and jaw and facial muscle assessment as well as palate and tongue function in the wind instrumentalist. Motor examination includes evaluation of muscle tone, bulk, and strength as well as fine motor control. The sensory examination is usually focused on identifying radicular or peripheral nerve syndromes. Special techniques of sensory testing are rarely required but two point discrimination on the fingertips or lip may be particularly useful in some situations. Testing of tendon reflexes in the upper limbs may include not only the biceps, triceps, and brachioradialis but also finger flexor and pectoral tendons as well.

It is always desirable and often critical to be able to examine the instrumentalist in the act of playing. This requires only some advance warning and instruction to the musician playing a readily portable instrument but may require something more for the harpist, pianist, or church organist. The physician cannot of course be expected to be an expert musician or even to have working knowledge of any, let alone all, instruments. Music teachers may justifiably express concerns that the physician may be overstepping his or her area of competence with this portion of the examination. Nonetheless, even a musically naive physician may be able to make important if not critical observations based upon an understanding of posture, muscle function, and ergonomics. Recognition of mechanically inefficient or unnecessary movements, contorted postures, and excessive tension in playing may be extremely important in the assessment of the playing-related symptoms. Obviously, the physician with some knowledge of the instrument or technique of playing will have a distinct advantage and some of this may be learned in the office as well as in the concert hall. In some cases it is desirable to enlist the help of another instrumentalist or a teacher to provide a different perspective and technical advice. Again, one must be very cautious to respect the sensitivity of patient and not to jeopardize a student-teacher relationship by bringing in another teacher without careful consideration of the implications of this action.

Examination of the instrumentalist while playing is not only important but absolutely essential for identification of occupational cramp or focal dystonia. Many of these curious disorders occur only in the act of playing and simply cannot be recognized in any other setting. It may be particularly important to record a portion of the examination with instrument on video tape for subsequent review as well as for baseline comparison.

Following the history and examination, there may still be a need for further testing. This may run the gamut of procedures available but some general guidelines can be suggested. A variety of blood analyses may be useful, including screening for collagen-vascular disease, endocrine dysfunction, inflammatory disorders, and metabolic abnormalities. X-rays of the neck, lower spine, shoulders, elbows, wrists, or hands may be useful, looking for degenerative disc or joint disease, bone spurs, congenital anomalies, and primary bone disorders. Radionucleide scanning may be helpful in identifying areas of inflammation or infection. Computed tomographic (CT) scanning and magnetic resonance imaging (MRI) may be utilized to study the head, neck, brachial plexus, or upper limb structures. Electrodiagnostic procedures including nerve conduction study, needle electromyography, and, on occasion, somatosensory evoked potentials may all be helpful when nerve entrapment or some other peripheral nerve disorder is being considered. A number of other less well-established and in some cases, less well-validated procedures for studying trunk and limb function, including kinesiologic EMG, thermography, motion analysis, and MRI spectroscopy are utilized in some laboratories and may prove helpful.

Ultimately, evaluation as well as management of the various playing-related problems of performing artists, including the pain syndromes, may involve a multidisciplinary approach, utilizing the resources available in many of the multispecialty clinics which have evolved for this purpose. It is not unusual for a disabled performer consulting our group or a similar clinic to be seen by a neurologist, rheumatologist, ortheopedist, hand surgeon, physiatrist, psychiatrist or psychologist, physical therapist, and occupational therapist for a complex and chronic upper extremity disorder. As has been mentioned above, this may be supplemented by consultation with an instrumental teacher or performer, preferably one who feels comfortable with and has considerable experience in the analysis of performance problems.

The therapeutic approach to management of these problems may be complicated and require a similar multidisciplinary effort. Some aspects of this are dealt with by others in this symposium. The ultimate goal, of course, is to ensure that the disabled performer is once again capable of returning to his or her art, to brighten and enrich our lives.

## REFERENCE LIST

Caldron, P.H.; Calabrese, L.H.; Clough, J.D.; Lederman, R.J.; Williams, G.; and Leatherman, J. 1986. A survey of musculoskeletal problems encountered in high-level musicians. *Med. Probl. Perform. Art.* 1:136-139.

Fishbein, M.; Middlestadt S.E.; Ottati, V.; Straus, S.; and Ellis, A. 1988. Medical problems among ICSOM musicians. Overview of a national survey. *Med. Probl. Perform. Art.* 3:1-8.

Fry, H.J.H. 1986. Incidence of overuse syndrome in the symphony orchestra. *Med. Probl. Perform. Art.* 1:51-55.

_____. 1987. Prevalence of overuse (injury) syndrome in Australian music schools. *Br. J. Ind. Med.* 44:35-40.

Fry, H.J.H.; Ross, P.; and Rutherford, M. 1988. Music-related overuse in secondary schools. Med. Probl. Perform. Art. 3:133-134.

Hochberg, F.H.; Leffert, R.D.; Heller, M.D.; and Merriman, L. 1983. Hand difficulties among musicians. *JAMA* 249:1869-1872.

Knishkowy, B. and Lederman R.J. 1986. Instrumental musicians with upper extremity disorders: A follow-up study. *Med. Probl. Perform. Art.* 1:85-59.

Lederman, R.J. and Calabrese, L.H. 1986. Overuse syndromes in instrumentalists. *Med. Probl. Perform. Art.* 1:85-89.

Lockwood A.H. 1986. Medical problems in secondary school-aged musicians. *Med. Probl. Perform Art.* 3:129-132.

_____. 1989. Medical problems of musicians. *N. Engl. J. Med.* 320:221-227.

Middlestadt, S.E.; and Fishbein, M. 1989. The prevalence of severe musculoskeletal problems among male and female symphony orchestra string players. *Med. Probl. Perform. Art.* 4:41-48.

Ramazzini, B. 1940. *Diseases of Workers* (1713). Revised and translated by W.C. Wright. Chicago: University of Chicago.

# APPLICATIONS OF MIDI TECHNOLOGY IN ASSESSMENTS OF PERFORMANCE SKILLS

Paul Salmon
Jonathan Newmark

We have adapted MIDI technology for use as a clinical and pedagogic tool. MIDI, or Musical Instrument Digital Interface, is a generic term for a category of computer software originally designed by the music industry for the rapid scoring of up to eight tracks of music which are entered into any ordinary synthesizer keyboard. Originally the specifications for commercial MIDI packages, contained in a central package called a sequencer, were trade secrets, and researchers had no access to them. In the last three years, however, at least one manufacturer of MIDI software has published its specifications in hopes of establishing an industry standard. We have used this information to extract data from the MIDI package which allows us to characterize quite precisely parameters of performance both of exercises designed to bring out disordered function and of actual keyboard works. This paper summarizes our initial studies demonstrating the use of MIDI technology in assessing both disordered function and individual performances of musical works.

## DESCRIPTION OF THE SYSTEM

We use commercial software created by the OPCODE Corporation, in a Macintosh Plus personal computer connected to a YAMAHA pf80 model keyboard. We have described our initial method previously (Salmon and Newmark 1989). The data obtained consist of numerical measures of the time of key press and release, which is measured in small and precise timing units, and of key velocity, which is proportional to loudness, measured in units of comparable precision. In our initial modification of the software these data were provided in tabular form, with each line of the table corresponding to a "MIDI event" defined as a key press or release. In the more recently improved version of the program, called VISION by the OPCODE Corporation, we are able immediately to create a graphical picture of this information, of which examples are shown. The program can also generate, within about five seconds, a bar-graph picture of duration or key velocity as a function of time. We create hard copies of these graphs by reproducing them on a printer.

## ASSESSMENTS OF PATIENTS WITH UPPER LIMB DYSFUNCTION

The assessment of movement disorders has long been handicapped by a lack of objective measures to quantify the degree of dysfunction. This may be exemplified by the recent tendency of movement disorders journals to include videotapes as part of the patient description. Other than such "living pictures" or classical terms such as "chorieform" or "athetotic," there is no quantifiable way to specify degrees of dysfunction. Musician patients, who depend occupationally upon fine motor control in small distal muscles, are particularly prone to unusual movement disorders, the nature of which evokes much controversy (Newmark and Hochberg 1987).

In an early study (performed before we had the later OPCODE VISION program), we measured the degree of dysfunction seen in repetitive finger tapping in a 26-year-old rock guitarist with a stable motor control dysfunction of the right third finger (Salmon and Newmark 1989). Even in this cumbersome early form of the program we easily demonstrated laterality and finger specificity of his dyscoordination.

More recently we have used the improved version of the program to document the degree of dysfunction and response to treatment of a 41-year-old nonmusician with a predominantly right-sided cerebellar tremor as a result of traumatic cerebellar hemorrhage from a motor vehicle accident. This patient responds quite well clinically to small doses of benzodiazepines. The patient has a great inability to hold down four fingers while playing the fifth. Two hours after an oral dose of 10 mg diazepam, his ability to hold these fingers down has improved. We quantify the degree of improvement by counting the discontinuities (what we have termed "intrusions"). On the patient's largely asymptomatic left side, there was also improvement which was not easily picked up clinically.

This patient demonstrates that MIDI technology can quantify degrees of dysfunction even in a nonmusician unfamiliar with the keyboard, and indicates that this technology may eventually prove to be useful in rehabilitation settings for patients with movement difficulties due to a variety of problems, including brachial plexus injuries, stroke-induced mono- or hemiplegia, and Parkinsonism.

## ASSESSMENT OF PERFORMANCE IN MUSICIANS

Our modification of MIDI technology allows a bird's eye view of a performance in quantitative terms. With practice the observer can make valid statements about the performance. This program is considerably easier to use than either our earlier version or the only comparable program in the published literature (Shaffer 1980).

The first example,[*] a MIDI-based recording of a measure from Jehain Alain's *Litanies,* well known to organists, illustrates the sensitivity of the MIDI system to variations in touch and timing between right and left hands. The right hand, playing block chords, is accompanied by the left, playing a series of staccato chords in a rapid-fire fashion. This measure is technically quite difficult to play. Performers who have used this system in

---

[*] Please contact authors for a copy of this cassette with these examples.

our initial trials comment that visual, in addition to auditory, feedback of their performances makes it easier to adjust and correct problematic finger movements, because they have access to a permanent, visual record against which to compare subsequent performances.

The next example shows how this feature allows documentation of differences in the performance of a player in different circumstances or on different days. Two performances recorded several days apart by the same organists of an excerpt from an organ prelude by Buxtehude are shown. Between these two recordings the player had practiced the work carefully. The MIDI program quantifies the "smoothing out the rough edges." In particular, the note duration is down, meaning that his dexterity has improved and/or that the tempo is slightly faster, and the variation in loudness or velocity also is reduced.

A performance of the Minuet from Johann Sebastian Bach's *Partita No. 1* in Bb for harpsichord is shown. This work has the fortunate characteristics of having a left-hand part almost entirely composed of eighth notes and a right-hand part almost entirely composed of sixteenth notes. Since is was originally written to be performed on the harpsichord, an instrument without the capacity for individual note volume gradation, most musicians would agree that a modern performance on the piano should attempt to keep the note volume and duration fairly consistent throughout the work. In particular, the natural tendency, at least in beginners, to play louder with the thumb should be curbed. In this performance, the player played the first strain of the minuet in a more legato, almost 19th-century style, and then changed for the second strain to a drier, more staccato style which more closely approximates the sound of the harpsichord.

One may reasonably object that the aim of practicing a musical work is not to play it with mathematical rhythmic or volume precision. Of course, a "good" performance will contain rhythmic and volume variations, and we certainly intend no criticism of these. We do feel, however, that the MIDI program will find its use in the study of the acquisition of motor programs and behaviors, including the rhythmic and volume variations characteristic of idiomatic playing, and in the quantification of phenomena related to the keyboard which heretofore have only been documentable by acoustic recording.

## REFERENCE LIST

Newmark, J., and Hochberg, F.H. 1987. Isolated painless manual incoordination in 57 musicians. *J. Neurol. Neurosurg. Psychiat.* 50:291-295.

Salmon, P. and Newmark, J. 1989. Clinical applications of MIDI technology. *Med. Prob. Perf. Art.* 4:25-31.

Shaffer, L.H. 1980. Analysing piano performance: A study of concert pianists. In *Tutorials in Motor Behavior* edited by G.E. Stalmach & J. Requin. North-Holland: Amsterdam.

# TREATMENT APPROACHES IN THE PERFORMER WITH CERVICO-BRACHIAL PAIN

John T. Myers

The occupational therapist and physical therapist who treat instrumentalists must work together to avoid overlap and to complement each other's treatment. The following discussion combines both treatment approaches.

The goals of treating muscle pain syndromes include: identifying problems through the evaluation, correcting these problems, decreasing or abolishing symptoms, and reestablishing the desired functional level in playing, performing, and everyday living.

The evaluation is in two parts—the history and the physical. Each can be further subdivided as follows.

## HISTORY EVALUATION

The symptom history investigates the type of symptoms, duration, location(s), frequency, and relationship of symptoms to various activities.

The treatment history includes any attempt the musician has made to alleviate these symptoms including previous physician visits, medications, modalities, exercises, therapies, chiropractic care, Feldenkrais or Alexander treatments, massotherapy, or others.

We ask for a description of the playing schedule including the number, frequency and length of breaks. We ask about the use of warm-up or cool-down activities, sudden or gradual changes in playing time, and changes from the normal routine (such as a different style of music, or a change in technique). If a number of different instruments are played, each may affect symptoms differently.

Sources of tension are discussed including work, home life, school or others that may be mentioned. Students may be adversely affected by a number of these stressors, and are well represented in our particular patient population. We ask about any activities that may aggravate symptoms including other jobs, driving, writing, typing or housework. (These may commonly increase postural or upper extremity symptoms.)

Finally, the general activity and fitness level of the patient is evaluated including the type/frequency/duration of any regular exercise they may do and any effect on symptoms. We might inquire into how much rest they get, and what they do to reduce stress.

## PHYSICAL EVALUATION

This always includes a postural evaluation, looking at alignment and noting any abnormalities in sitting, standing, and with the instrument. Of particular interest is the head and neck positioning, low back region, and scapular positioning. We also look at the way the instrument is positioned or held, height of rests, or any other adaptation that the patients may make to interface with the instrument. Often in patients we will see a forward head, and rounded shoulders. Abnormal positioning or posture can set up biomechanical abnormalities that cause problems or pain.

Range of motion in the spine and extremities is compared to "normal." We look for any significant limitations, excesses, pain or joint instability. These findings may be abnormal, but may not necessarily cause a problem. In many cases we may find abnormalities, but if these are not directly or even indirectly part of the problem, we use the philosophy "if it ain't broke, don't fix it." Empirically we find a large number of patients with distal upper extremity ligamentous laxity ("double jointedness") which usually does not appear to be a part of their problem. It seems prevalent in violinists, especially those with a greater level of talent. (This can be a "chicken or egg" dilemma: does playing cause the laxity, or does laxity somehow predispose to better skills?)

Strength testing is usually done on patients with many variations depending on need. Gross testing gives us a "feel" for the strength around a particular joint, while specific isolated single muscle testing gives us very detailed information about the condition of a particular muscle. At times, testing of endurance may also be necessary, especially in an overuse situation. Other special strength tests are often used including pinch strength and grip strength. When testing strength we may have to purposely stress the muscle to test it in a "real-life" situation (such as in playing the instrument), by putting it in awkward positions, putting the muscle on a stretch before contracting it, or holding the instrument. The muscles can be palpated for tenderness in the belly or bulky portion of the muscle, as well as along the origin of the muscle and its tendon. Signs of weakness, pain or irritation are noted.

Flexibility testing examines the amount of muscle tightness present. The ability of the muscle to lengthen passively is tested, looking for pain with stretching. Any areas of tightness or tension during activity or rest are noted. Trigger points (thickened, tender areas in muscles) may indicate chronic muscle imbalances or tension.

Other special tests of a variety of types may be used, depending on the need or indication. In cases of neurological complaints, sensation is usually tested. We might do testing of the cervical spine to close down the foramen (the opening in the bones of the cervical spine where the nerves exit) to see if the problem originates in the neck. Other common tests that we might use include those for carpal tunnel syndrome and thoracic outlet syndrome. The shoulder complex is a common area for problems and often needs a thorough evaluation and special testing. This might include testing for impingement or problems with the rotator cuff mechanism. The wrist and hand are also cited as areas of frequent problems, and tests for tendonitis, and instability are frequently used. The special testing that is done varies, and depends on the patient's complaints and symptoms.

## TREATMENT PLAN

After collecting the history and physical evaluation information, the therapists follow a problem solving model to formulate a comprehensive treatment plan. Because we see patients from all over the country and frequently they cannot come back to see us very often (if at all), they must be instructed in a home program and progression.

There are many options for treatment. Often patients will need assistance in their program from start to finish, and much of what we do is education.

Patients need to know how to warm up the muscles before activity (to lengthen tissues, increase circulation, prepare for the physical demands placed on the tissues, and prevent injury), as well as cool-down techniques for after activity. We will often encourage them to use normal instrument warm-ups by starting slowly and playing scales. (Teachers/instructors may be more helpful in providing specific warm-ups, as long as the patient understands the principles.) We talk to the patients about a gradually progressive playing program to increase their pain-free time on the instrument. We talk to them about the use of breaks, to give the body a chance to recuperate. We may have to ask the patient to rest in some form. (There are difference types of rest ranging from relative rest, to complete rest, to immobilization with a splint.) We often ask the musician to consult with an instructor regarding their technique on their instrument. Changing their technique is very difficult for most musicians and may affect their amount of playing time and playing quality initially. We are not experts in technique, but we can see things which are physically stressful and refer to the expert instructors to help find an acceptable and less stressful alternative method for the patient. Patients are instructed in proper posture, especially relating to their instrument. This is one of the hardest things for them to change, as it requires constant, conscious attention at first. People can consciously change it, but will quickly shift back to old habits . We may have to teach the patient stretching or strengthening exercises to help attain and maintain their new posture. We may teach the patient body mechanics (how to use the body and posture efficiently in activities) if they are having problems or pain with activities. With any aggravating activity we will try and show them how to do the activity more efficiently and comfortably.

We may also have to work with adapting equipment for the patient. For example we might suggest changing the height of a music stand to decrease neck strain, or increase the height of a shoulder rest for a violinist to avoid hiking the shoulder and protracting the head forward. Often, simple discussions about the choice of the chair, or use of a lumbar roll can make practice time much easier.

We find that most patients have some muscle imbalances during their evaluation (i.e., muscle tightness, weakness, opposing muscle groups with wrong strength ratios.) These may or may not be causing pain and need to be corrected. For example, many patients may have mild weakness in their deltoid muscles, but this is rarely a clinical cause of a problem and we usually ignore it. A major imbalance frequently seen is an increased tightness in the pectoral muscles and shoulder protractors, with weaknesses in the retractor muscles attaching the scapulae to the thoracic spine. The end result is a posture with the shoulders rolled forward and the shoulder blades abducted from the center of the spine. This appears to cause weakness of the adductors of the scapula and we suspect that it can lead to overuse syndromes in the forearms. (This may be related to the NDT theory and "fixing.")

We try to increase endurance in the muscles through exercises, which may include using repetitions to allow for longer activity tolerance. The goal is to maintain strength and coordination for the activity over time. In addition, the progressive playing schedule, which allows for greater lengths of time practicing on the instrument, will also increase endurance.

We encourage aerobic fitness because the life of a musician is often fairly sedentary and stressful. General aerobic fitness programming helps many physiological functions, including decreasing stress and improving mood.
While many of our patients come to use because of pain, we do not always see pain as a major problem. Pain is usually a symptom of some other problem. We do try to help the patient decrease their pain by correcting the underlying problems, using stretching techniques, rest, use of modalities such as heat/ice, and relaxation techniques.

Because patients are so busy professionally and often come from far away, they have to understand the concepts of the problem and the principles of self-treatment. They must know what to expect when they start their program, what symptoms to pay attention to and which can be ignored. Patients have to be able to build up the exercise programs (for example, adding weight or increasing their playing time). Once pain-free, patients may need some preventative stretches, postural techniques or strengthening exercises.

Due to the nature of the patient population and the complexity of their problems, their activity level, symptoms, and lifestyle must be evaluated and treated as a whole. While generalizing is usually frowned upon, I feel that this patient population is a joy to treat because of their level of dedication, enthusiasm, desire to learn, and active participation in their care. One word of warning that goes along with this level of enthusiasm is that the patient may overdo the therapeutic exercise program, and this can also cause problems for them.

# THE MUSICIAN'S HAND IN THE SURGEON'S HAND: DEFINED SYMPTOMS—UNUSUAL DEFICITS

Nikolaus Ell
Peter Haussmann

## 1. INTRODUCTION

The hand—we need and use it all day long. It is our tool for eating, care of the body, and work. It is a physical bridge between loving persons and the psychological bridge between people by means of gesticulation. It also enables the musician to produce and modulate tones for creation of the wonderful world of sound and music.

The aim of this paper is to present some basic information about the hand and some of its more frequent diseases with regard to their special effects on musicians. The surgeon's problems concerning uncommon deficits will be explained by means of some examples.

The complexity of the hand is because of its unusual dual function as an organ of sense and performance at the same time. There are several functional systems: the systems of bones and joints, the motor system, the system of lymphatic vessels and blood supply, and that of feeling. Because of the interconnection of the different systems, even slight disorders in one system can effect serious disturbances of the function of the complete hand.

## ANATOMY AND PHYSIOLOGY

First, here are some basic anatomical and physiological facts.

### The Bone and Joint System

The bone and joint system of the hand consists of the distal radius and ulna, the 8 carpal bones, the 5 metacarpal bones, 2 phalanges of the thumb, 3 phalanges of the fingers, connected by joints of very different shapes and functions.

Some joints show a preference for mobility, like the joint between carpus and the thumb's metacarpal bone, some others a preference for stability, like the joints between distal carpal bones and the metacarpal bones 2 to 5. However, for most joints of the hand, mobility in one or two directions and stability in the others is important.

Abnormalities may occur either with pathological instability of bones and joints or in painful and reduced mobility of joints as well as in malposition and shortening of bones.

## The Motor System

The motor system is composed of the extrinsic and the intrinsic muscle systems and their innervation. The muscles of the *extrinsic system* are mainly located in the forearm, connected to the wrist and several joints of fingers by long tendons, which stretch inside a synovial sheath within certain regions of the hand. The extensor tendons extend the proximal joints of the fingers, partly the middle ones. Additional extensor tendons for the thumb exist. The flexor tendons flex the middle and distal joints of fingers, independently of the position of the proximal finger joint.

The *intrinsic system* muscles are located inside the hand, separated into several anatomical and functional groups. Essentially, they are responsible for substantial parts of the thumb's movement, for the flexion of the proximal finger joints and for the extension of the middle and distal joints, and for the spreading and adduction of the fingers.

All are involved in the *innervation* of the extrinsic system's three basic nerves of the hand, the median, ulnar, and radial nerves, while the intrinsic system is only served by the median and ulnar nerves.

There is a clearly differentiated balance between the functional muscle groups in the two systems themselves as well as between the intrinsic and extrinsic muscles, controlled by the nervous system based on will, use, and training, on the data of the sensory system and on the rules of agonist and antagonist.

Failures of the motor system may occur in many points beginning at common, degenerative or rheumatic inflammation of the tendon's vagina, the tendon's rupture, even a minimal change of the tendon's length and direction, the contracture of muscles and partial or complete loss of motor innervation connected with nerve-compression syndromes or traumatic dissection.

## The Blood and Lymphatic System

The blood and lymphatic system consists of two main arteries, the ulnar and radial artery, and some smaller ones, forming two arterial arcades inside the palm of the hand. Each finger has two larger palmar arteries and two smaller dorsal ones.

There are two systems of veins, a deep and a superficial one, flowing into the lower and upper arm main veins. Also, two systems of lymphatic vessels exist, the first stations of lymph nodes are the elbow and the axilla.

Fortunately, problems occur very seldom in this system. They may occur because of thrombosis of either ulnar or radial artery, because of high-grade arteriosclerosis, because of injury or because of lymphatic edema.

## The Sensory System

The task of the hand as sensory organ is mainly given to the ulnar and median nerves, less to the radial nerve.

First, there is the sensitivity to the tension of muscle and tendon and the sensitivity of the joints, which inform the brain about the position of arm, hand and fingers, and about velocity.

Secondly, there is sensitivity for touch, pain, temperature, pressure, 2-point-discrimination, vibration. This is located in the skin, mainly in the fingertips. To achieve this, each finger and the thumb has two dorsal and, more importantly, two palmar sensory nerves.

Problems can occur either in general neurological diseases like diabetic or alcoholic polyneuropathia or in local defects of the nerves, like nerve-compression syndrome of the upper extremity or injuries to the nerves.

## DEFINED SYMPTOMS AND DISEASES

We divide the diseases of the hand into one group of defined symptoms and diseases, in which we can correlate physical problems with known methods of treatment quite well, and into another group of unusual deficits, in which standard procedure is not possible.

In the *defined diseases* group the problems appear at an earlier stage in musicians than in the average population. The reason may be, that a weakening of the hand's function is perceived earlier by a person who needs a very distinct capability in his hand, or that by intensive daily use the complaints proceed rapidly.

The most frequent disorders are presented below. In these diseases the surgeon can specify the reason, kind of treatment, prognosis, and time of recovery fairly accurately. These are some of the most important defined diseases.

## Nerve-Compression Syndromes

All three main nerves of the arm can be stricken with this disease, and in several levels of the arm. It is caused by external compression or internal anatomical alteration (Kaeser

1984). The result of compression over a long period is always anatomical and functional damage of the nerve, which can be reversible partially or totally by early surgical treatment. The damage may affect either the motor (Haussmann 1984) or the sensory portion of the nerve, but often both are involved. The symptoms are usually pains in the arms at night, loss of muscle power, and reduction of feeling in the early stages, muscle atrophy, loss of feeling altogether, and trophic ulcera in late stages.

Surgical treatment is indicated if there is no spontaneous remission within 2 to 3 months from the beginning of the compression. Generally the operation includes freeing the nerve from all compressing anatomical structures by various ways, dividing the epineurium and sometimes displacing the nerve. The earlier the surgical treatment takes place, the more successful the operation.

The most frequent compression syndrome are the carpal tunnel syndrome and the ulnar nerve entrapment of the elbow.

*The Carpal Tunnel Syndrome*

This is produced by compression of the median nerve in the palmar side of the wrist. In its early stages in the average population it causes mainly pain in the arms and a slight reduction of feeling in the fingers 1 to 4. Musicians however very soon feel a reduction of sensitivity for judgement of vibration, pressure, and 2-point discrimination and a reduction of power in thumb opposition and key pinching as well as a loss of endurance. In cases of extended practice or concertizing, the pianist often complains of increasing paraesthetic, even painful sensations in the fingers.

In late stages with their subtotal or total loss of sensation and atrophy of thenar muscles, patients are considerably impaired. Most musicians will no longer be able to play their instruments up to a professional standard.

*Ulnar Nerve Entrapment Syndrome*

The ulnar nerve entrapment syndrome is produced by compression of the ulnar nerve in the sulcus ulnaris of the elbow, or by habitual luxation of the nerve around the epicondylus ulnaris (Figure 1). In the average patient the complaints are slight in early stages, the reduction of sensation affects the 4th and 5th fingers.

The musician however is more seriously impaired, not only by the lessening of sensation, but much more by the reduction of the ability to spread the fingers, specially of the abduction of the 5th finger, and the lack of ability to extend completely the middle and distal joints of the 4th and 5th fingers (Figure 2).

In late stages, spreading of fingers is completely impossible caused by atrophy of the ulnar-innervated intrinsic muscles. Contractures of the abovementioned joints of 4th and 5th fingers are often found beside loss of sensation of these fingers, and ulcera. Depending of instrument, the musician may have to change profession.

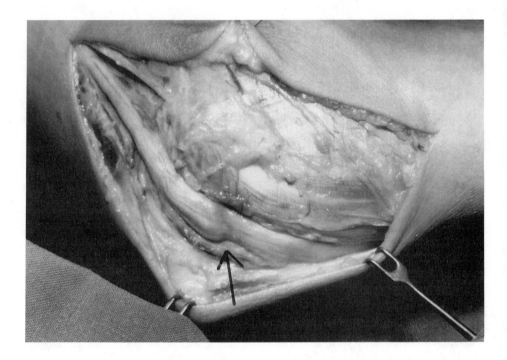

*Figure 1.*
*Intraoperative finding of a high-degree compression of ulnar nerve at the elbow (sulcus ulnaris). The reduced diameter of ulnar nerve after resection of compression structures is marked (arrow).*

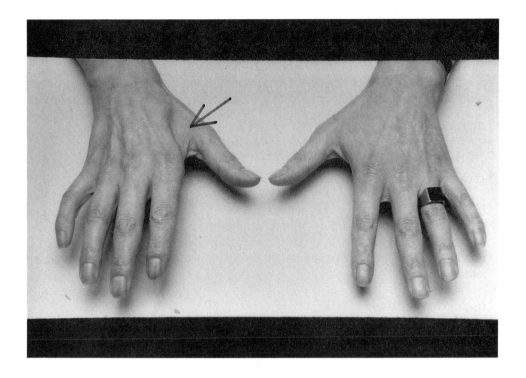

*Figure 2.*
*Clinical findings of ulnar nerve entrapment at elbow: Atrophy of some intrinsic muscles (for example, M. Interosseus I, marked by arrow) or the right hand, reduction of spreading of fingers, loss of complete extension of 4th and 5th fingers.*

## Tenosynovitis

This condition is an inflammatory, but nonrheumatic disorder of the tendon sheaths, and is one of the most frequent disorders of the musician's hand (Hochberg et al. 1983). We see mostly tenosynovitis of the flexor tendons, with or without "snapping fingers" and the tenosynovitis of the thumb's extensor tendons. The condition is usually of a degenerative type and the complaint may be worsened by intensive practice.

The common tenosynovitis of flexor tendons produces only minor complaints from the average patient, namely swelling of palm and fingers and stiffness of joints in the morning. Musicians however will additionally complain about diminished speed and endurance. Nonsurgical treatment by antiphlogistic methods and temporary reduction of practice is necessary.

*Tenosynovitis Stenosans*

This condition of the flexor tendons is marked by the snapping of one or several fingers and thumb with various degrees of impairment in the average patient, but usually considerably impaired performance in the instrumentalist because of pains and loss of free finger mobility, and uncontrolled moving of fingers. In this case, surgical treatment improved the situation immediately.

*Tenosynovitis of the Thumb Extensor Tendons*

In this condition there are also various degrees of complaints in the usual patient. If the condition is acute the musician will not be able to play his instrument if he needs a frequent adductive movement of his thumb, abduction of the thumb or extension or maximal flexion of the proximal joint of the thumb. Surgical treatment brings prompt relief.

## Dupuytren's Disease

This is the fibromatosis of the palmar fascia, a simultaneous growing and shrinking of the aponeurotic tissue in the palm of hand between the skin and the flexor tendons. Mainly men over 40 are afflicted with this disease. Predispositions are diabetes, hepatic disorders, and heredity. Beside the palm of the hand, thumb and fingers may be also affected, usually the 4th or 5th fingers.

In the early stages, there will be found either only hard nodes in the palm of the hand, sometimes sensitive to pressure, or additionally slight flexion contracture of the proximal finger joints. Complaints in the average population are rare. In the musician on the other hand, troubles can arise if a constant pressure on the palm of the hand or the need for full finger extension and abduction is inherent in the practice of the instrument (Figure 3).

In the late stages, flexion contracture of one or several fingers or adduction and flexion contracture of the thumb are to be found. Daily life and craftsmen's work is very impaired. Depending on the instrument, most musicians are completely unable to practice because of loss of extension, spreading and abduction of fingers and thumb (Figure 4).

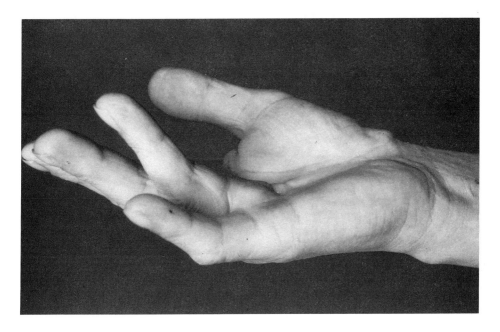

*Figure 3.*
*Dupuytren's disease: early stage. Slight flexion contracture of mainly the 4th*
*finger; nodes in the palm.*

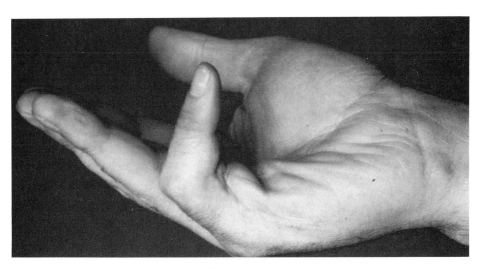

*Figure 4.*
*Dupuytren's disease: late stage. 70-degree flexion contracture of 5th finger middle*
*joint, slight flexion contracture of proximal joint of all fingers.*

Nonsurgical treatment like radiation or enzymatic therapy has never proved to be very successful. If the patient complains about disability, surgical treatment is indicated even in early stages.

Surgery is unavoidable in late stages, if professional ability is to be restored and daily life to be improved. Various kinds of operation exist. In our clinic, we excise very accurately all pathological tissue, always with the use of a head-on-microscope. The aim is free finger movement and avoidance of recurrent disease. Depending on the seriousness of the condition, this operation can be one of the most difficult in hand surgery, taking sometimes many hours of surgical work.

## Malposition of Bones and Joints and Nonunion of Bones

Problems arise in the average patient mainly in cases of extreme malposition, considerable instability of joints and bones and in cases of special needs for profession or hobby.

Much slighter disorders, on the other hand, often induce the musician to ask for medical aid with the frequently found reduction of power and mobility of concerned or neighboring joints, and early posttraumatic arthrosis with its pain following extended performance.

The preoperative situations and the types of treatment are too variable to be explained here in detail. Generally, the aim of the surgeon is to reconstruct precisely the former anatomy and function to avoid further worsening at least.

## Arthrosis

Arthrosis means destruction and frequently malposition of joints. The main causes of this disease are former injury, infection, or gout, but above all there is idiopathic arthrosis, which is believed to be hereditary. One or several joints may be affected by arthrosis.

In the average population there is a high incidence of arthrosis, but only about 50% report problems to their doctors (Stellbrink, G. 1981). The extent of problems with musicians depends greatly on their instrument. Arthrotic joints, which are inflamed by pressure or frequent movement, cause pain and therefore loss of endurance and the instability of the joints reduces the quality of performance.

All nonsurgical treatment should be tried before operation, because there are disadvantages with any of the various types of operation. The type of operation used, generally arthrodesis, autoartroplastic, prosthesis or simple denervation, depends on the level of pain complaints and on the need for stability or mobility in the concerned joint.

In addition in musicians, the general decision of which surgical treatment, like the details of a planned operation, need careful deliberation, much experience and a demonstration of performance by the patient on his instrument before operation. For example, the angle of the distal joint arthrodesis in a guitarist must be about double that of a pianist.

## Rheumatic Arthritis

Here we include all diseases of the rheumatic group, which affect the joints and tendons of the hand. These are autoallergic diseases causing severe inflammation and having a destructive character for tendons, joints, and blood vessels. For any patient this diagnosis means a drastic diminishing of his quality of life with a prognosis of lifelong medical treatment and many operations.

For a musician with active, multifocal rheumatic disease which involves his hands, we have to advise him/her to look for a new profession in the longer term.

Even in the early stages, when average patients are not greatly impaired, musicians will be troubled by pains when practicing and by loss of endurance, reduction of speed and loss of mobility.

Our example shows a professional guitarist with a buttonhole deformity of the 5th finger in the early stages of arthritis (figure 5). This deformity is caused by a lesion of the extensor system of the middle joint of the finger. It is characterized by the loss of free extension of the middle joint and simultaneous loss of flexion of the distal finger joint in cases of only slight flexion of the middle joint. Therefore the guitarist is able to control exact pressure on the upper strings, for which middle and distal finger joints have to be inflected considerably, but not onto the lower strings, where the middle joint needs only a slight flexion position (Figures 6 and 7).

*Figure 5.*
*Buttonhole deformity of 5th finger: loss of free middle joint extension*
*disturbance of distal joint flexion.*

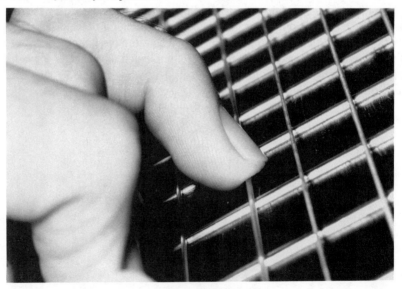

*Figure 6.*
*Buttonhole deformity: exact finger-tip pressure onto upper strings.*

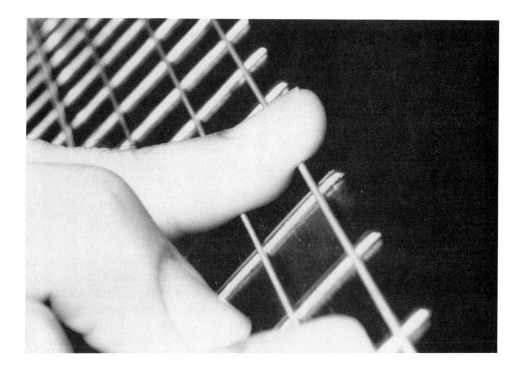

*Figure 7.*
*Buttonhole deformity: inexact pressure on lower string (E), the A string is visibly touched, too.*

Later stages will produce destruction of several joints, rupture of tendons, malposition of joints and worse. Surgical treatment in combination with medicine can effectively slow down this process, but the ability to perform professionally will generally not return for a musician.

### Injuries of the Hand

Treatment here requires all the theoretical knowledge, the experience and the practical skill of the hand surgeon, including microsurgery. Injuries of the hand are often related to reduction of mobility and reduction of muscle power for a long time, depending on the extent of the injury.

In the average patient, problems are usually reported after serious, combined injuries. In musicians, even slight reduction of the function in one system of the hand can handicap professional performance.

In acute injuries with wounds, we try to reconstruct all the systems of the hand, as in these emergency cases we do not know very much about the patient's expectations and needs. In the surgical treatment of earlier injuries, we can plan the operation better and can take into consideration the special needs of a musician. In these cases too we encourage the patient to play his instrument.

At this point it should be mentioned that for surgical treatment to be successful a perfect operation must be provided with specialized high quality physiotherapy afterwards.


## UNUSUAL DEFICITS

In this category, problems occur in the function of the hand only in people who use their hands in an unusual way for their professions or hobbies.

In these cases repeated and thorough medical examinations are necessary. It is necessary first to ascertain whether the cause of the disturbance of the hands lies inside the hand or outside. Cervical syndromes, thoracic outlet syndrome, focal systonic movements, problems of shoulder, elbow, and of lower arm rotation have to be excluded. Special attention has to be paid to the results of Wagner (1979, 1981, 1987). Also general neurological and psychiatric problems have to be seen.

Some unusual deficits in musicians are reported, for example, disturbed movement of the index (McGregor and Glover, 1988), acro-osteolysis in guitarists (Destouet and Murphy 1981), or osteoarthropathy in pianists (Bard et al. 1984) induced by the extensor tendons.

If the cause of disorder is definitely inside the hand, an operation may be indicated. The safety of the planned surgical treatment, the prognosis and success rate is still not very good. Thus the surgeon's experience will be needed and also his specialized understanding of the difficult interactions of the hand's different systems.

Each case of this group is very different. A systematic presentation is impossible. Therefore, just a few examples of this group, treated in our clinic, are presented.

### Patient L.D. - Cello

This patient suffered from a steep proximal-phalanx fracture of the left index finger. To avoid further dislocation and for speedy remobilization an osteosynthesis was performed. The result was a shifting of the middle and distal phalanx 2mm in the direction of the third finger and a slight deviation and rotation of 5 degrees in the same direction. This is usually tolerable for an average patient.

Some weeks after resuming practice on his cello, the patient complained of having difficulty, especially in the playing of octaves. Because of the minimal deviation and shift, combined with the physiological tendency of the index to the ulnar side of the thenar during grip, the radial abduction of the index was reduced and the index crossed over the third finger in fist grip.

After a careful analysis of the problem, we corrected by osteotomy, performing a needed radial deviation of 5 degrees and radial rotation of 10 degrees. Two months after this osteotomy the patient can now play his instrument up to a professional standard again.

## Patient G.J. - Oboe

He came to our office because of a very small node on the palmar side of the index middle joint. Whenever he bent this joint it was very painful and professional performance was impossible.

During surgery, we found a neurofibroma of the radial digital nerve of the index. This tumor was excised by use of a microscope. Some weeks later the musician was able to perform perfectly with no pain.

## Patient J.W. - Organ

This man suffered a distal radius fracture 3 years ago, including a fracture of the processus styloideus of the ulna. He complains of a painful and reduced ulnar abduction of the wrist. The X rays show a pseudoarthrosis of the processus styloideus ulnae combined with dislocation. Clinical finding, X rays, and the patient's symptoms all agree. So we will perform surgery to reposition and refix the processus styloideus ulnae.

## Patient M.F. - Clarinet

In this case the disease is not unusual, but the treatment had to be adapted for a professional need. After intensive practice on his clarinet, a spontaneous rupture of the long extensor tendon of thumb took place. This deficit called "drummer's thumb" in German, causes considerable reduction of extension and abduction of the thumb. The usual surgical treatment is a transfer of one of the two index fingers extensor tendons to the thumb, but it is combined with a reduction of the index finger and thumb's extension power and speed.

Therefore we chose the much more complicated surgical procedure and postoperative physical therapy and interposed a free tendon graft aiming to conserve full extension power and speed of both thumb and index finger. Our preoperative deliberations were confirmed. Three months after surgery the patient can play his instrument again without any impairment.

### Patient M.H. - Keyboard

This musicians complained of a reduction of speed in trills using the index finger or the right hand. Although we made several medical examinations including observing the patient playing the piano, we could find no clear cause. Neurological and psychiatric consultations showed no result. Also an examination by Prof. Wagner in Hannover, Germany failed to find the answer. So a surgical treatment was not possible. But from this case we learned that we still do not know enough about hand problems of musicians and we must set to work on these problems.

## CONCLUSION

The higher the expectation of healthy function of the hand and the more difficult and unusual the disease, the more the changes in all the systems of the hand and their balance as the result of surgical treatment have to be considered. Thus it is even more crucial to consult a highly specialized hand surgeon, with his theoretical and practical knowledge, including skill in microsurgery.

It can be very helpful if the surgeon himself is trained in playing an instrument to improve insight into the musician's problems. Additionally, preoperative demonstration by the patient on his instrument is very helpful for better analysis of problems and for optimal results.

## REFERENCE LIST

Bard, C.C.; Sylvestre, J.J.; and Dussault, R.G. 1984. Hand osteoarthropathia in pianists. *J. Can. Assoc. Radiol.* 35(2):154-158.

Destouet, J.M., and Murphy, W.A. 1981. Guitar player acro-osteolysis. *Skeletal Radiol.* 6(4):275-277.

Haussmann, P. 1984. Microsurgical treatment of isolated lesions of the motor branches in the hand and forearm. In *Handbook of Microsurgery* Vol. 1, edited by W.L. Olszewski, 173-200. Boca Raton, FL: CRC Press, Inc.

Hochberg, F.H.; Leffert, R.D.; Heller, M.D. and Merriman, L. 1983. Hand difficulties among musicians. *JAMA* 249(14):1869-1872.

Kaeser, H.E. 1984. Allgemeines zu den Kompressionsneuropathien (Compression syndromes of peripheral nerves — general ideas). *Basler Handchirurgische*

*Arbeitstagung* 30 June 1984, edited by H. Nigst. Stuttgart: Hippokrates (published 1986).

McGregor, I.A., and Glover, L. 1988. The E-flat hand. *J. Hand. Surg. (Am).* 13(5):692-693.

Stellbrink, G. 1981. Erkrankung der Gelenke (Diseases of the joints). In *Handchirurgie* Vol. 1, edited by J. Nigst, D. Buck-Gramcko, and H. Millesi, 20.1-20.8. Stuttgart, New York: Thieme.

Wagner, C. 1979. Der Fall Werner M (The patient Werner M.). *Orchester* 27:728-735.

_____. 1981. Die Natur der Hand als Ursache spieltechnischer Probleme am Klavier (The nature of the hand as a handicap in piano playing). In *Dokumentation 1982 EPTA* (European Piano Teachers' Association). Germany: further bibliographical information not available.

_____. 1987. Welche Anforderung stellt das Instrumentalspiel an die menschliche Hand? (What demands does playing an instrument make on the hand?) *Handchir. Mikrochir. Plast. Chir.* 19(1):23-32.

# PULMONARY AND CARDIOVASCULAR ASPECTS OF MUSIC MAKING

Fawzi P. Habboushe

In a short dissertation such as this, either a partial list of salient problems or a rather more thorough introduction to a particular problem or fundamental issue could be undertaken. This paper will attempt to discuss several pressing issues. Both disabilities resulting from music making and the understanding of some of the biological fundamentals for better music making will be considered.

Because of the sparse amount written on this subject as it applies to musicians specifically, and in the interest of exploring relevant material, the author being a surgeon, has taken the liberty of identifying a few areas pertinent to this subject from the surgical, medical, and basic science literature, and also whenever possible, from the musical literature and his own professional experience.

The cardiopulmonary system obviously forms an integral part of the body function in any task. In most activities, it provides various amounts of raw biological support to the functioning organism. The amount of gaseous exchange and oxygen delivery, as well as fluid and metabolite distribution, is dependent upon the immediate energy requirements dictated by the task. On the other hand, some of the musical requirements will not only demand the basic cardiopulmonary energy needed for the activity but will also necessitate delivery of finely regulated and precisely controlled aliquots appropriate to the circumstance (Bouhuys 1974). These well controlled circulatory and ventilatory surges are manifested in bursts or smooth transitions, as needed, for example in a wind player's execution of a musical passage with its *pianos* and *fortes*, *staccatos* and *legatos* (Cugell 1986). During such a passage the cardiopulmonary system satisfies:

1. The BASIC common needs for sustaining the body, exclusive of the actual playing of the instrument;
2. The INCREASED demand for the amount of activity the actual playing represents over and above the basic needs;
3. The FLUCTUATING needs as dictated by the nuances of the musical passage. These activities indicated above are sustained together in one coordinated and inseparable whole (Bouhuys 1974), and;
4. The PERFORMANCE related increased demand for cardiovascular output relative to the stress of the performance or rehearsal.

Clearly, the cardiopulmonary system must be trained in conjunction with the musical training of the individual. For the best performance, the musicians' psychological, neurological, musculoskeletal functions as well as gross and fine movements, coordination, sense of rhythm and pitch and a number of other functions, are all executed simultaneously and intertwined with the precise cardiac and pulmonary activity demanded, as one productive whole. Any flaw in any of the systems or functions requires immediate adjustments of the other systems and functions, with a possible effect on the musical.

There are several categories of cardiorespiratory needs according to instrument. These are broadly divided into :

1. Instruments not dependent on breathing in sound production, such as stringed instruments, the harp, piano, percussion, and conducting. The coordination of cardiorespiratory needs may be critical, but is not directly linked to the production of sounds.
2. Wind instruments need precise and well coordinated cardiorespiratory excursion tailored perfectly to and integrated with the conditions of the playing. Recordings of airway pressure and respiration reflect these transient changes (Cugell 1968; Bouhuys 1974). Furthermore, the instrument has to be applied to the embouchure and supported by the arms in a very precise and well programmed manner to secure proper intonation and dynamics for each individual note played (Farkas 1986).
3. Singing is produced by an integral part of the body and is therefore different from other instruments as it requires no support from the arms. No additional effort is expended to retain the instrument against the embouchure. Nonetheless as with wind instruments, precise cardiorespiratory requirements have to be met.

## THE ROLE OF THE PEDAGOGUE

It is important to us as physicians, surgeons and therapists to understand how the musician can be better served in ailments relative to musical performance. Of equal interest is an understanding of normal performance and how the mechanisms involved can be more efficiently improved by this understanding. This necessitates a full dialogue with musical pedagogues. As a surgeon and conductor, the author feels that although a pedagogical function is served by the activities of the conductor, the unique input of the pedagogue is essential to the musical as well as the medical well-being of the musician. Needless to say, the conductor may serve a special role in directing the musician to the proper resource, medical or musical for appropriate resolution of the problem.

Dysfunction varies depending upon the instrument played. Likewise, modalities of rehabilitation and cure also vary. We must obtain the appropriate perspective and insight, both from our medical and musical experience, and from experienced performers and teachers. Of significance to this perspective is the place, experience, and active participation of the pedagogue. Unlike Dr. Arnold Jacobs, the world renowned brass pedagogue of the Chicago Symphony Orchestra (Stewart 1987), few teachers have actually been involved in the scientific laboratory side of the discipline, so it is important to provide the opportunity and proper medical terminology for these pedagogues to allow them to be able to converse fluently both scientifically and artistically. Conversely, the scientist and clinician must thoroughly understand the musical aspects of playing.

## DYSFUNCTION

For purposes of this article, dysfunction has been classified according to its origin and involved body system in the following manner: general fitness and pathology.

### General Fitness

Problems in fitness are potentially ubiquitous and may result in generalized deconditioning. This is analogous to the unfit athlete who requires a certain degree of baseline fitness to be able to practice for the special athletic endeavor intended. Similarly, the musician requires a minimum degree of strength and endurance in certain body parts or musculoskeletal regions that are involved in playing. To be able to remain at a peak level of performance, a good musician should engage in certain calisthenics, weight lifting and physical exercises as appropriate to the instrument played.This has been suggested by internationally known brass pedagogues (Farkas 1986). Strength and endurance each serves a specific function in playing. They concern not only the total body, but also specific arm and weight bearing muscles, and, for the wind player and vocalist, respiratory muscles.

### Respiratory Muscle Strength and Endurance

The concept of respiratory muscle training originated from the more common, sports-related, skeletal muscle training. Leith and Bradley (1976) first reported the application of these principles to the respiratory muscles of normal humans. They clearly demonstrated that respiratory muscle strength increased in response to specific strength training programs. Similarly, respiratory muscle endurance increased in response to specific endurance training programs. In strength training, muscle hypertrophy results. This occurs with low repetition of high intensity stimuli similar to the predominantly isometric exercises of weight lifters. On the other hand, endurance exercises result in increased oxidative capacity without change in muscle fiber size. This results from high repetitions of low intensity stimuli, as in the predominantly isometric exercises of the marathon runner.

To achieve positive results, there are certain fundamentals which must be observed for skeletal muscle training, including respiratory muscles. These include the phenomena of overload, specificity, and reversibility.

*Overload*

For a muscle fiber to increase its structural capability, functional capability or both, its capacity must be taxed beyond some critical level (overloaded). To generalize this principle to music teaching, it is important to consider the contradiction of the old adage "no pain no gain" (a form of overload) and the more recent discovery of the many overuse and abuse syndromes in the performing musician. In considering this apparent dilemma it must be noted, that the amount and intensity of the exercise involved may be important variables. On the other hand, the word "overuse" has become so widely used, that it may mean different things to different people. Furthermore, overuse applies to the muscles involved. However, other structures such as other muscles, nerves, blood supply, and their associated ligamentous structures may also be involved. No scientific study has yet assessed the sequencing of exercises in musical practice either to prevent or to induce the so called "overuse" condition. Thus, to utilize properly the principle of *overload*, the knowledge of its relationship to the concepts of overuse must be considered.

*Specificity*

The second requirement for training is specificity. This involves the direction of a specific exercise to a particular muscle or muscle group. This specific stimulus must be applied in an overload fashion. Thus, for adaptation to occur, the loading must be beyond the critical threshold.

*Reversibility*

Finally reversibility implies that conditioning is in fact transient, requiring some maintenance activities to retain the conditioned state. This principle reinforces the common observation that continued or regular practice is needed to remain at the optimum level of performance.

While keeping in mind the so-called overuse and abuse syndromes, these principles may be applied, adapted and scientifically tested, and ultimately may enhance and clarify the pedagogical aspects of music making.

*Drugs and Medications.*

Given the current availability of drugs, therapeutic or recreational, legal or illicit, and overindulgence of many (alcohol, caffeine, theophylline, theobromine and nicotine), it is important to consider the effects of these substances on any activity. This is particularly true in the area of musical performance with its intricate and exacting psychological, mental and physical requirements. Of consequence also are the many mood alterations and cognitive dysfunctions caused by many drugs, especially illicit ones. The author believes that as musicians downplay their medical problems, the silence and pervasiveness of substance abuse could be easily one of their most serious problems.

On a happier note, it has been found convincingly that methylxanthines, including caffeine, have an augmentative effect on the contractility and muscle force of the diaphragmatic muscle (Whittmann and Kelsen 1982; Supinski et al. 1984). This is probably not specific to that muscle but rather generalized. On the other hand, the ubiquitous benzodiazapines, with their reducing effect on the tetanic tension of skeletal muscles may have the opposite effect. Furthermore, calcium channel blockers, with their differential dose-related effects on various muscle types and sites, introduce new and very interesting possibilities.


## PATHOLOGY

Pathological derangements may occur in one or more organ systems. These derangements are divided into three different categories based upon the relationship of the problem to the actual playing of the instrument :

## 1. Problems caused by playing that in turn affect performance

These may result from faulty or overzealous use of the instrument, and are exemplified by the various frequently reported so-called overuse syndromes. Because of their close relationship to technique and intensity of playing, these problems may be called pedagogical. While a pedagogue may not be directly at fault, his or her involvement may be required in supervising practice in subjects with this problem. For example, the overuse pain and weakness of the hand in a pianist may be managed by a program of rest and exercise. In addition to other specific treatments, partial and/or total return to playing may be supervised by the pedagogue involved. The author has seen for instance a case of subcutaneous emphysema in a twenty-year-old man who developed this condition as a result of overzealous playing of the highest register of the trumpet at high dynamic levels. Subsequent work up and management were prescribed, and the emphysema subsided spontaneously with rest and abstinence from playing. Furthermore, a strong recommendation was made to work with a teacher and this resulted in a positive outcome for the patient.

## 2. Conditions not resulting from playing, but affecting musical performance

Most conditions that seriously affect musicians fall into this category, for instance, problems of the cardiorespiratory system. A common example is the case of a severe common cold. More seriously, an acute asthmatic attack may be severe enough to totally disable the patient for a period of time. In this instance, the patient does not necessarily acquire the attack a direct result of playing. However, bronchospasm may itself compromise playing. Asthma of course is an interesting and special example, as it may interact with the playing in certain cases.

*Bronchospastic conditions* may classically present as asthma, but may be both allergic or non-allergic types. Regardless of the type, they have interesting, complex and not fully understood etiologies. In addition, there are incomplete as well as sometimes totally satisfying therapeutic strategies. Some of these conditions undoubtedly may be caused by frequent aspirations or so called microaspirations(Mays et al. 1976; DeMeester et al. 1980; Pellegrini et al. 1979). In the case of gastro-esophagal reflux as etiology, a confirmation is usually fairly easy to attain with 24 hour pH monitoring. Management in this case is relatively easy when full compliance is obtained. Only rarely does the need for surgical intervention involving antireflux procedures arise. Of significance is the fact that the incidence of this problem in the general population is not fully known, nor is its specific incidence documented in the musician, particularly the wind player or singer. It appears that the Valsalva maneuver, inherent in the act of singing or playing of wind instruments, may augment the frequency or extent of the aspiration when it occurs. Not to be underestimated is the potential contribution of alcohol usage, smoking, and caffeine with their influence on gastric secretion and the lower esophageal sphincter. A variety of therapeutic means may improve this condition and include the use of antacids and H2 blockers. These latter reduce acid although they have no apparent effect on the lower esophageal sphincter. Metoclopramide on the other hand is a dopamine agonist which has dual effects in that it increases lower esophageal sphincter pressure while improving gastric emptying (McCallum et al. 1977).

*Asthma*, as a clinical entity, is heterogeneous with its etiologies and presentations. It is traditionally attributed to allergic causes in atopic individuals with IGE mediation. There appears to be another type of asthma in which atopic history is not a feature. In both, however, there appears to be an early reaction phase in which bronchospasm is the main feature. A late inflammatory phase can occur in both also. Its primary manifestation is a heightened increase in tracheobronchial reactivity. Offending agents are not only allergens, such as pollen but also chemical, psychological and physical precipitating causes. In the latter situation cold air can trigger a bronchospastic attack. Furthermore, exercise or excessive activity causes a type of asthma known as exercise asthma. The latter can be completely averted with pretreatment with bronchodilators. Furthermore, there is evidence that in the variety which is triggered by cold air, the alpha-adrenergic blocker Phentolamine, partially alleviated bronchospasm (Walden et al. 1984).

In asthma, the common offending agent is a mediator of bronchospasm such as histamine, certain leukotrienes and prostoglandins. These are liberated usually, but not exclusively, from the mast cell. This cell may release these mediators by actions of allergens, parasympathetic overflow of afferent impulses, or by many other factors. The cell membrane is destabilized by these agents thereby causing this release. Cromolyn sodium is an agent that is known to stabilize mast cell membrane and prevent mediator release. Therefore this agent can help to prevent this release if pretreatment is instituted.

While histamine is not the only offending mediator, the mast cell contains the entire amount of histamine in the body. Mast cells undergo selective hyperplasia in allergic and nonallergic asthma by about ten fold compared to normals. A 20 milligram dose of Cromolyn or a 200 microgram of Albuterol given 15 minutes prior to an allergic challenge attenuates not only the airway response but also the circulating levels of the mediators of the immediate asthmatic reaction, histamine and neutrophil chemotactic factor (Howarth and Holgate 1984). With regard to prevention, specially for the allergic types, H1 antagonists have been favoured. In the more recent past chlorpheniramine with its undesirable and frequent side effects on the central nervous system has become replaced by Astemizole and Terfenadine. In addition to the absence of a central side effect, these drugs have an advantage in that they are more potent. Their effect on asthma is in attenuating the bronchospasm, rather than relieving it (Holgate et al 1985). It is likely that the bronchoconstriction which is resistant to Terfenadine may be a result of newly found mediators such as LTC4 and PGD2 which are potent airway contractile agents.

It should be noted that as an attack progresses from its immediate to delayed phase, there develops an increase in mucous secretion, which further increases resistance to air exchange due to its critical effect on reduction of the radius of the bronchi. In addition, mucosal edema may further aggravate the problem. This inflammatory reaction is a complex one and is responsible for prolonging the attack. It requires considerably more time to resolve than the bronchospasm itself. It has been well documented that after the symptomatic resolution of an asthmatic, attack fully 30% of functional loss remains. This might require up to a week to resolve completely.

Medications to relieve an attack and to prevent it are available with varying but fairly uniform success. Bronchodilators in the form of beta-agonists act on the smooth muscle cell to release the spasm. These agents are available with variable side effects such as the tendency to arrhythmia and tremor. Through a different biochemical route, theophylline produces the same benefit with its specific side effects. The use of both agents can be additive in response and in side effects, and the literature, in the more recent past, seems to support elimination of theophylline from the treatment regimen. Steroids, when used, have to be attended to carefully. In their long term use in the musician, it should be recognized that they may cause negative nitrogen balance with associated weakness, loss of protein framework, and a host of other problems.

The influence of wind instrument playing on the state of the respiratory tract in the patient with chronic obstructive lung disease, including asthma, is not clear (Farkas 1986). It would appear to be a double-edged sword. When playing produces negative consequences, then prophylactic and therapeutic management should be an area of our concentration. When playing yields positive results then it falls into the domain of music therapy where a great deal of interdisciplinary interphasing is needed. Wind instrument playing may have the effect of PEEP (positive end expiratory pressure), thereby encouraging uniform ventilation and tending to decrease arteriovenous shunt.

The asthmatic musician needs to be restudied from the standpoint of the medical field. To illustrate, consider an issue that normally does not appear significant in the average patient, who is not using his respiratory bellows with the same endurance requirements and precision as the musician. Bronchospasm is aggravated or precipitated in the asthmatic patient by taking a deep inspiration (Gayrard et al. 1975). In the wind player, who depends on frequent deep breaths to execute his task, this means a decrease of his vital capacity, a correlate of timed vital capacity (FEV1) in the asthmatic (Dulfano et al. 1953). This clearly is doubly negative with compounding loss. Not only does the patient lose air flow but also the length the breath may be held. Many patients with moderate decrease of FEV1 and FVC are in no distress, and therefore the issue may not be as apparent (McFadden et al. 1973). Furthermore end expiratory pressure increase coincident with the blowing will decrease airway resistance. The whole issue of the work of breathing must, and can be assessed in the wind player and singer.

*Surgical Considerations*

*Surgical operations* play a major role in causing a degree of temporary or permanent disability. Thus, common procedures will interfere with the performance of musicians to various degrees, from temporarily to permanently. Especially significant are operations on the chest or abdomen that may result in a serious hindrance to performance.

It is commonly but erroneously believed that the respiratory muscle involved in singing and playing wind instruments is the diaphragm. This of course is partly true. In addition, abdominal muscles, thoracic muscles, both intercostals, as well as extrathoracic muscles, are intimately involved with proper playing (Wang and Josenhans 1971). It is a common experience for the surgeon that subcostal incisions such as for biliary, pancreatic, and splenic surgery are associated with greater ventilatory disability than midline non-muscle cutting operations. A patient with a Kocher incision (subcostal muscle cutting incision) suffers from serious compromise of ventilatory functions as opposed to a similar patient with a midline incision. This is not only more severe but also usually of longer duration. A choice of incisions that is compatible with intact muscle function is the better choice whenever possible. More recently laparascopic and laser performed cholecyssectomy and other surgery have resulted in very transient and minimal disability.

More importantly when the operative intervention is that of the chest cavity, more dysfunction will result unless certain precautions are taken. *First*, the cavity violated is that of the more critical cardiovascular and respiratory organs. *Secondly*, the incisions made are usually fairly large. *Thirdly*, and most importantly, these incisions are usually done with extensive *muscle cutting* of layers that are intimately used in the act of breathing as well as in singing and blowing of a wind instrument. The exception is midline sternotomy in which there is minimal muscle interference. Furthermore many other instrumentalists, for whom the chest is not involved in performance, will suffer disability resulting from limited respiratory reserve and from limitation of the use of the arm in full range in certain instances. The muscles are of course approximated at the end of the procedure, but again healing occurs not by muscle but by fibrous tissue, and maturation may take many months or years.

Thoracotomy causes many derangements including the decrease of thoracic compliance. This latter implies that the ease of expansion of the chest is diminished, thereby making breathing harder and requiring greater energy. This is a restrictive type of respiratory dysfunction and occurs as a result of postoperative pain, pleural effusion, the presence of chest tubes, and incision of the intercostal and chest wall muscles. The decrease in vital capacity to 60-70% of baseline on the first postoperative day takes about seven days to return to the preoperative value. If on the other hand significant pain persists, then this restrictive ventilatory pattern may take up to several months to resolve.

The use of muscle *splitting* incisions located high up on the chest are preferable and very effective. This higher location avoids to a great extent the lower more compliant portion of the chest. Appropriate transection of the intercostal muscle fibers at the rib and proper approximation at the conclusion of the operation may help. Delicate and atraumatic handling of the tissues, with good hemostasis further reduce these chest compliance problems. Finally the use of intercostal nerve block or cryotreatment to reduce postoperative intercostal pain along with the other modalities may result in the reduction of both temporary and permanent disability. It is advisable to avoid incisions in the diaphragm as much as possible and to making nerve-sparing incisions with attention to avoiding interference with the vasculature of the diaphragm when such surgery is absolutely necessary.

Muscle splitting as opposed to muscle cutting operations of the chest, published first in France (Noirclerc et al. 1973; Mitchell et al. 1976) are thought to produce much less disability. These appear to avoid most of the essential drawbacks of the usual muscle cutting method. The problem is that these methods are not generally used in the United States. Furthermore, surgeons who use these methods may not be comfortable with them because of the perceived lack of surgical exposure. In fact exposure is just as good providing the right kind of attention is paid to pertinent details. Experience tells us that these incisions are superior and result in much less morbidity than their muscle cutting counterparts.

In breast surgery for carcinoma, amputation of the breast with reconstruction may cause more potential deficits than lumpectomy, lymph node dissection and radiation.

## 3. Conditions that neither affect playing nor are the direct result of playing

In this category for example, a broken leg does not usually affect a hornist, while certainly a broken arm resulting from a fall might seriously disable that musician.

To fully understand cardiopulmonary function and derangement in wind instrument playing, we must address a physiological phenomenon called the Valsalva maneuver.

### The Valsalva Maneuver

A common physiological condition that is an integral part of the playing of any wind instrument or singing is a modification of the so called Valsalva maneuver which is well known and fairly well studied in the human. It is important to clarify that the studies done in this area of music performance are limited. In fact, any similarities to the Valsalva are in fact speculative and by inference only until hard data are collected directly from the musicians with proper research.

The Valsalva maneuver is a procedure in which the subject is asked to exhale against a closed glottis after taking a breath. This is analogous to the common condition of lifting weights, or bearing down as in child birth or on defecation. While the true physiological procedure used in playing wind instruments is not fully tested, it is speculated to be much like the Valsalva maneuver with the following exceptions present in wind playing:
1. The glottis is not completely closed.
2. The air column within the respiratory system is in a state of vibration.
3. The vibrating air column includes the resonance area above the larynx in the singer or the wind instrument, as the case may be.
4. There is a delicate and dynamic coordination of the respiratory, abdominal, and diaphragmatic muscles and the throat muscles that regulate the generation and amount of pressure, and control as well the flow of air through the glottis and upper airway.
5. The magnitude of the intra-airway pressures and and the amount of time they are sustained are different. These vary in different instruments at different volumes and different pitches.

In general, the higher the pitch the higher the pressure is in the air system; similarly, the higher the decibels, the higher the pressure produced. This is in contradistinction to the usual definition of the Valsalva maneuver as a test. It is usually measured as an intra-airway pressure of 40mm Hg. for 10 to 20 seconds. Tucker et al. (1971) measured intraoral pressures in young musicians (Figure 1).

| INSTRUMENT | MMHG | |
|---|---|---|
| French Horn | 55.3 | +/-6.9 |
| Trumpet | 103.3 | +/-10.3 |
| Trombone | 67.9 | +/-9.9 |

*Figure 1. Intraoral Pressures in Young Subjects*

Intraoral pressures are a function of pitch and of loudness. Similarly Stone (1874) reported oral pressures for various instruments. These were measured at a loudness considered to be *mezzoforte* and reported in inches of water. They are here approximated to the nearest mm Hg. (Figure 2).

| | LOW FREQUENCY | HIGH FREQUENCY |
|---|---|---|
| Oboe | 29 | 55 |
| Clarinet | 49 | 26 |
| Bassoon | 39 | 78 |
| Horn | 16 | 88 |
| Cornet | 32 | 110 |
| Trumpet | 39 | 107 |
| Euphonium | 10 | 130 |
| Bombardon | 10 | 117 |

*Figure 2. Intraoral Pressures in mm Hg in Subjects at mezzoforte*

It is evident that of all the musical instruments, some of the highest pressures come from trumpets and cornets. Similarly, Berger has found that in ten trumpet players, the intraoral pressures varied with frequency and loudness sounds (Figure 3). Because of these variables, it is obvious that the true answer must come from direct and valid measurements on subjects under specific musical conditions. Short of this, we can only make inferences from the physiological findings from current studies of the Valsalva maneuver and analogize to the musical condition.

| FREQUENCY (CPS.) | SOFT | LOUD |
|---|---|---|
| 175 | 3 | 13 |
| 932 | 25 | 65 |

*Figure 3. Ten Trumpets. Intraoral Pressure (Mm Hg.).*

In the Valsalva maneuver there are four phases in a set of two groups, i.e. two phases in each group. In the first group, the subject is straining and covers the first two phases. In the second group, the subject releases the strain for the third and fourth phases. With the "onset of straining" (phase I) there is transient increase in blood pressure presumably due to the direct increase of intrathoracic pressure. In the "late strain phase" (phase II), decreased venous return causes a gradual decrease in pulse pressure and stroke volume. This is referred to as the "active phase" of the maneuver. The decrease in pulse pressure causes a reflex increase in heart rate. With the "onset of release" (phase III) there is a transient decrease in blood pressure resulting from decreased thoracic pressure, and an increase in thoracic volume resulting in pooling of blood in the chest. The last part (phase IV) occurs rapidly and is called the "overshoot" phase. This arterial pressure overshoot is subject to conflicting explanations. The most accepted explanation involves the sympathetic drive resulting from the preceding relative hypotension with or without reflex baroceptor bradycardia. Figure 4 below illustrates these four phases more clearly.

| GROUP 1 (Strain) |
|---|
| PHASE I ONSET OF STRAINING |
| transient increase of B.P. *(intrathoracic pressure increase and volume decrease)* |
| PHASE II {ACTIVE} LATE STRAIN |
| gradual decrease of P.P. with reflex increase of H.R., decrease of S.V. *(decrease of venous return)* |
| GROUP 2 (Release) |
| PHASE III ONSET OF RELEASE |
| transient decrease of B.P. *(intrathoracic pressure decrease and volume increase with pooling)* |
| PHASE IV OVERSHOOT |
| increase of of B.P. and bradycardia *(? sympathetic drive from relative preceding hypotension OR baroceptor bradycardia* |

*Figure 4. The Valsalva Maneuver (40mm Hg for 15 seconds) see text*

In clinical medicine, it is known that the Valsalva maneuver has the theoretical possibility of precipitating arrhythmias or angina. It is known to cause syncope especially in the elderly whose reflex compensatory mechanisms to decrease venous return are impaired. Whether this has anything to do with the reported frequent arrhythmias in brass players (Tucker et al. 1971; Nizet et al. 1976) has not been clearly tested.

It is however encouraging to point out that the maneuver is well known for its ability to terminate paroxysmal supraventricular tachycardia. This results from the increased parasympathetic drive attendant with phase IV (late release phase). In addition, the termination of some ventricular tachycardias has been reported (Waxman et al. 1980). This seems to be related to a decrease in the size of the heart during the maneuver, through a decrease in the automaticity of the Purkinje fibers.

In the syndrome called long QT interval, named for the electrocardiographic finding of the long QT interval in which there is a tendency for ventricular fibrillation, this phenomenon does not occur until a condition similar to the late phase III of the Valsalva is experienced. This apparently causes reflex sympathetic stimulation with attendant possible T-wave alternans and ventricular tachycardia. In some patients this can be suppressed with beta blockers.

With a view to considering the effect of the maneuver on coronary artery disease, one must entertain the possibility of arrhythmias. More importantly the effect of the Valsalva on myocardial oxygen demand and supply is the issue. Hemodynamic studies during the maneuver in patients with angina pectoris have demonstrated that lowering of the left ventricular end diastolic pressure accompanies disappearance of the angina. This suggests a decrease in oxygen demand. Support for this observation comes from a study (Labovitz et al. 1985) in which both normal subjects as well as patients with proven coronary artery disease had statistically significant improvement in the ejection fraction and the left ventricular end systolic and end diastolic pressures. Some authors have also reported a decrease in coronary blood flow (Bechimol et al. 1972). Others have demonstrated potentially dangerous cardiac arrhythmias induced by the maneuver in patients with angina (Lamb et al. 1958 ).

Whether the Valsalva maneuver is friend or foe to the musician, especially the musician with coronary artery disease remains to be seen. The maneuver can suggest abnormalities by the response obtained and the way that response differs from normal. This latter subject is beyond the scope of this paper.

Whereas this article does not pretend to be all inclusive or exhaustive in any way, it may be appropriate to mention that there are many conditions that have either been defined as cardiothoracic medicine music problems or have been alluded to in the literature as possible problems. They range from the thoracic outlet syndromes to the interesting reports of metaplasia of the respiratory mucosa in wind players, and coccidia in bagpipes.

## REFERENCE LIST

Bechimol, A.; Wang, T.F.; Desser, K.B.; and Gartlan, J.L., Jr. 1972. The Valsalva maneuver and coronary arterial blood flow velocity: Studies in man. *Ann. Intern. Med.* 77:357-360.

Berger, K.W. Respiratory and articulatory factors in wind instrument performance. *J. Appl. Physiol.* 20 (6): 12117-1221.

Bouhuys, A. 1974. Voluntary breathing acts: Speech, singing and wind-instrument playing. In *Breathing: Physiology, Environment, and Lung Disease*, edited by A. Bouhuys, 253-256. New York: Grune and Stratton.

Cugell, D.W. 1986. Interaction of chest wall and abdominal muscles in wind instrument players: A preliminary report. *Cleve. Clin. Q.* 53(1):15-20.

DeMeester, T.R.; Wang, C.I.; Wernly, J.A.; Pelligrini, C.A.; Little, A.G.; Klementschitch, P.; Bermudez, G.; Johnson, L.F.; and Skinner, D.B. 1980. Technique, implications and clinical use of 24 hour esophageal pH monitoring. *J. Thorac, Cardiocasc. Surg.* 79:656-70.

Dulfano, M.J.; Herschfus, J.A.; and Segal, M.S. (1953). Timed vital capacity in bronchial asthma. *J. Allergy* 24:309-315.

Farkas, P. 1986. Medical problems of wind players: A musician's perspective. *Cleve. Quin. Q.* 53(1):33-37.

Gayrard, P.; Orehek, J.; Grimaud, C.; and Charpin, J. 1975. Bronchoconstrictor effects of a deep inspiration in patients with asthma. *Am. Rev. Respir. Dis.* 111:433-439.

Holgate, S.T.; Emanuel, M.B.; and Howarth, P.H. 1985. Astemizole and H1-antihistamines in asthma. *J. Allergy Clin. Immunol* 76:375-82.

Howarth, P.H., and Holgate, S.T. 1984. Comparative trial of two non sedative H1-antihistamines, Terfanadine and Astemizole, for hay fever. *Thorax* 39:668-672.

Labovitz, A.J.; Dincer, B.; Mudd, G.; Aker, U.T.; and Kennedy, H.L. 1985. The effects of Valsalva maneuver on global and segmental left ventricular function in the presence and absence of coronary artery disease. *Am. Heart J.* 109:259-264.

Lamb, L.E.; Dermksian, G.; and Sarnoff, C.A. 1958. Significant cardiac arrhythmias induced by common respiratory maneuvers. *Am. J. Cardiol.* 2:463-571.

Leith, D.E., and Bradley, M. 1976. Ventilatory muscle strength and endurance training. *J. Appl. Physiol.* 41:508-516.

Mays, E.E., Dubois, J.J.; and Hamilton, G.B. 1976. Pulmonary fibrosis associated with tracheobronchial aspiration. *Chest* 69(4):512-5.

McCallum R.W.; Ippoliti, A.F.; Cooney, C., et al. 1977. A controlled trial of metoclopramide in symptomatic gastroesophageal reflux. *N. Engl. J. Med.* 296:354-7.

McFadden, E.R, Jr.; Kiser, R.; and DeGroot, W.J. 1973. Acute bronchial asthma. *N. Engl. J. Med.* 288:221-5.

Mitchell, R.; Angell, W.; and Wuerflein, R. 1976. Simplified lateral chest incision for most thoracotomies other than sternotomy. *Ann. Thrac. Surg.* 22:284-6.

Nizet, P.M.; Borgia, J.F.; and Horvath, S.M. 1976. Wandering atrial pacemaker (prevalence in French hornists). *J. Electrocardiology* 9(1):51-52.

Noirclerc, M.; Dor, V.; and Chauvin, G. 1973. Extensive lateral thoracotomy without muscle section. *Ann. Chir. Thorac. Cardiovasc.* 12:181-184.

Pellegrini, C.A.; DeMeester, T.R.; Johnson, L.F.; and Skinner, D.B. 1979. Gastroesophageal reflux and pulmonary aspiration: Incidence, functional abnormality, and results of surgical therapy. *Surgery* 86:110-9.

Stewart, M.D. 1987. *Arnold Jacobs: The Legacy of a Master.* Northfield, IL: The Instrumentalist Publishing Company.

Stone, W.H. 1874. On wind-pressure in the human lungs during performance on wind instruments. *Phil. Mag.* 48(316):113-114.

Supinski, G.S.; Deal, E.S. jr.; Kelsen, S.G. 1984. The effects of caffeine and theophylline on diaphragm contractility. *Amer. Rev. Resp. Dis.* Sept.: 130 (3): 429-33.

Tucker, A.; Faulkner, M.E.; and Horvath, S.M. 1971. Electrocardiography and lung function in brass instrument players. *Arch Environ. Health* 23:327-334.

Walden, S.M.; Bleeker, E.R.; Chahal, K.; Britt, E.J.; Masing, P.; and Permutt, S. 1984. Effect of alpha-adrenergic blockade on exercise-induced asthma and conditioned cold air. *Am. Rev. Respir.* 130:357-362.

Wang, C.S., and Josenhans, W.T. 1971. Contribution of diaphragmatic/abdominal displacement to ventilation in supine man. *J. Appl. Physiol.* 31(4):576-580.

Waxman, M.B.; Wald, R.W.; Finley, J.P.; Bonet, J.F.; Downar, E.; and Sharma, A.D. 1980. Valsalva termination of ventricular tachycardia. *Circulation* 62:843-851.

Whittmann, T.A., and Kelsen, S. 1982. The effect of caffeine on diaphragmatic muscle force in normal hamsters. *Am. Rev. Respir. Dis.* 126:499-504.

# VI

## TOWARDS STANDARDS OF RESEARCH IN MUSICMEDICINE AND MUSIC THERAPY

# TOWARD A RESEARCH STANDARD IN MUSICMEDICINE/MUSIC THERAPY: A PROPOSAL FOR A MULTIMODAL APPROACH

Ralph Spintge
Roland Droh

**M**usic seems to be the most intense emotional and aesthetic means of communication in human culture. Emotion in this sense is taken as the central program for human behavior control (Spintge 1990a).

In this paper we address methods of emotion research and their application in Music Therapy and MusicMedicine. Looking into emotional behavior one has to consider the different modalities or components of emotion, namely: the cognitive-verbal; the vegetative-physiological; the nonverbal-psycho-motoric behavior; and the situational subjective feelings. Figure 1 shows our model of emotion as it relates to the human brain and its functional position in human life.

An emotion is the central control or program for observable behavior and subjective experience and feelings. We believe that there is no behavior without emotion. Neurophysiological research demonstrates that music influences all modalities of emotion effectively and therapeutically where appropriate (Spintge 1987, 1988, 1990b).

A multimodal monitoring system is applied to monitor the emotional and therapeutical effects of music:

1. The cognitive-verbal behavioral component is described by using psychological tests (Thematic Apperception Test [TAT], State-Trait-Anxiety-Inventory [STAI], Zerssen's Scale of Subjective Feeling). Verbal behavior, verbal expressions and their content are also analyzed.

2. Vegetative-physiological behavior is quantified by monitoring peripheral parameters and central nervous parameters. Peripheral parameters include pulse rate, blood pressure beat-to-beat, EKG, heart rate variability, respiratory rate and rhythmicity, skin temperature, finger-plethysmography, oxygen consumption, $CO_2$ production, etc. Central nervous parameters include blood levels of neurohormones like beta-endorphine, ACTH, etc. In addition, a new method of noninvasive monitoring of the central neurovegetative state concerning cardio-respiratory functions and central nervous control processes is used (Koepchen et al. 1989; Abel et al. 1989; Koepchen et al. page 40 in this volume).

3.  Nonverbal, psychomotoric behavior is described by analyzing facial expression (Scherer 1984; Ekman 1982), by observing conversion phenomena like biting one's nails, fiddling with something, etc. Also external or internal fight-flight reactions are tabulated.

4.  Situational subjective feelings are evaluated through pre-, intra- and post treatment questionnaires and interviews.

The multimodal monitoring system described above is used perioperatively. This is a situation which creates a standardized emotional state of "anxiety." Thus we are measuring in a "real" situation, where we also want to work with our therapeutic musical interventions later. At the same time data acquisition is integrated into the everyday routine of the respective medical treatments without disturbing the patient, the doctor or any part of the situation. This holds true not only for receptive application of music, but also for active music therapy, where we can use modern techniques of telemetric monitoring.

All measurements and observations are made by one observer in order to obtain consistent, comparable, and replicable information as far as possible. All therapeutic interventions are standardized regarding sequence, method, verbal contact between staff and patient and, general behavior of the staff. Standardized procedural checklists are used. More details of the procedures used have been described in Spintge (1981, 1988) and Spintge and Droh (1987). The multimodal method has been developed and substantiated in a series of controlled, randomized clinical studies in dental treatment (Oyama, Hatano et al. 1983), during surgery (Oyama, Sato et al. 1983), and during labor and delivery (Halpaap et al. 1987; Halpaap 1988).

Concerning the cognitive-verbal component of emotion, the frequency of perioperative anxiety in the music group dropped from 70% preoperatively to 20% perioperatively. The control group showed a drop from 70% to about 40% respectively. Of the 75,000 patients, 95% welcomed our selection of anxiolytic music and confirmed its beneficial effects.

Concerning the nonverbal, psycho-motoric behavior, fight-flight reactions were not seen at all in the music groups in any studies, whereas in the control groups, about 1% of 5,000 patients per year showed these kinds of behavioral reactions.

Concerning the subjective feelings of the patients, 95% of 75,000 patients evaluated in the postoperative questionnaires confirmed that music had a marked and anxiolytic effect, calming them and alleviating anxiety and distress.

Concerning the vegetative-physiological modality of emotion, all monitored parameters (peripheral and central) showed that music groups did significantly better than the control groups (Spintge 1981; Oyama et al. 1983a, 1983b; Halpaap et al 1987). This held true not only for relatively short treatment as in dentistry and surgery, but also for long lasting distress situations as in obstetrics (for a day or more). Last but not least this also led to a reduction in drugs like sedatives, analgesics and anesthetics down to 50% of the usual dosage. Using our multimodal method meant that we were assured consistent and replicable information from all these studies. However, the decisive precondition needed to gain such results is to control strictly all possible interference from emotional and cognitive stimuli in the research setting. To achieve this it is always necessary to work in an interdisciplinary team, comprising expertise in medicine, music therapy, musicology, psychology, and statistics.

I believe that music, like any other medical drug, should be used only in cooperation with a physician and taking into consideration the following criteria:
1. Ingredients (title, instrumentation, interpretation, arrangement, size of orchestra, live/recorded, active/receptive, etc.);
2. Dosage (duration of application, intensity, loudness/volume, etc.);
3. Indications (patient's choice, applications to the situation, i.e., waiting/treatment, etc);
4. Effects (sleep-inducing, relaxing, cheering-up, motivating, exciting, pain relief);
5. Side effects/risk (epileptic seizure, "drug dependency");
6. Contraindications (exciting music in cardiac rehabilitation; drug addiction; sedative music in physical rehabilitation);
7. Ways of application (active/receptive, single/group, loudspeaker/earphones, stereo/mono, wire/wireless, analog/digital, etc.).

A multimodal method of emotion research and its application to music therapy means that we can now analyze and describe quantitatively and qualitatively some important parts of music therapy processes, thus achieving reasonable and responsible control of this kind of therapeutic intervention. Music therapy, dance therapy, and art therapy in general are medical therapies, so they have to fulfill the same standards of excellence as any other medical therapy and must be subject to the same controls of effectiveness and quality. Of course we always have to consider that art itself cannot be quantified, so that there is often the need for a pure qualitative description of the therapeutic means used. But in general the reputation of music therapy/music medicine and its acknowledgement by the medical community depends on how it meets the scientific and therapeutic standards of state-of-the-art healthcare and science.

The scientific instruments and methods are at our disposal. They should be used by interdisciplinary research teams which will benefit from the expertise of music therapists, music psychologists, psychologists, educators, physicians, and scientists.

## REFERENCE LIST

Abel, H.H.; Klüssendorf, D.; and Koepchen, H.P. 1989. New approach to analyzing the neurovegetative in man. In *Innovations in Physiological Anaesthesia and Monitoring*, edited by R. Droh and R. Spintge, 21-34. Berlin, Heidelberg, New York: Springer.

Ekman, P. 1982. *Emotion in the Human Face*, 2nd Ed. Cambridge, Cambridge University Press.

Halpaap, B.B. 1988. Musik als Anxiolytikum in der Geburtshilfe (Music as an anxiolytic in obstetrics). Medical Dissertation, Free University of Berlin.

Halpaap, B.B.; Spintge, R.; Droh, R.; Kummert, W.; and Kögel, W. 1987. Angstlösende Musik in der Geburtshilfe (Anxiolytic music in obstetrics). In *Musik in der Medizin* (Music in Medicine), edited by R. Spintge and R. Droh, 232-242. Berlin, Heidelberg, New York: Springer.

Koepchen, H.P.; Abel, H.H.; and Klüssendorf, D. 1989. Physiological concepts of cardiovascular and respiratory control: Theoretical basis and applicability in man. In *Innovations in Physiological Anaesthesia and Monitoring*, edited by R. Droh and R. Spintge, 3-21. Berlin, Heidelberg, New York: Springer.

Oyama, T.; Hatano, K.; Sato, Y.; Kudo, M.; Spintge, R.; and Droh, R. 1983. Endocrine effects of anxiolytic music in dental patients. In *Angst, Schmerz, Musik in der Anästhesie* (Anxiety, Pain and Music in Anesthesia), edited by R. Spintge and R. Droh, 143-146. Grenzach: Editiones Roche.

Oyama, T.; Sato, Y.; Kudo, M.; Spintge, R.; and Droh, R. 1983. Effects of anxiolytic music on endocrine function in surgical patients. In *Angst, Schmerz, Musik in der Anästhesie* (Anxiety, Pain and Music in Anesthesia), edited by R. Spintge and R. Droh, 147-152. Grenzach: Editiones Roche.

Scherer, K.R., and Ekman, P. (Eds.) 1984. *Approaches to Emotion*. New York: Hillsdale.

Spintge, R. 1981. Psychologische und psycho-therapeutische Methoden der Verminderung präoperativer Angst. (Psychological and psychotherapeutic methods to reduce preoperative anxiety.) Medical dissertation, University of Bonn.

Spintge, R. 1988. Music as a physiotherapeutic and emotional means in medicine. *Int. J. Music-, Dance-, and Art Therapy* 2(3) (Münster):75-80.

Spintge, R. 1990a. The neurophysiology of emotions and its therapeutic application in music therapy and music medicine. *Journal of Music Therapy* - Special issue on Music and Medicine. Washington, NAMT.

Spintge, R. 1990b. *Musik-Medizin. Physiologische Grundlagen.* (MusicMedicine. Physiological basics). Stuttgart: Fischer.

Spintge, R. and Droh, R. 1987. *Musik in der Medizin.* Music in Medicine. Berlin, Heidelberg, New York: Springer.

# A MODEL OF EMOTION —
## central behavioral program with
## intelligent cortico-thalamic filter [ 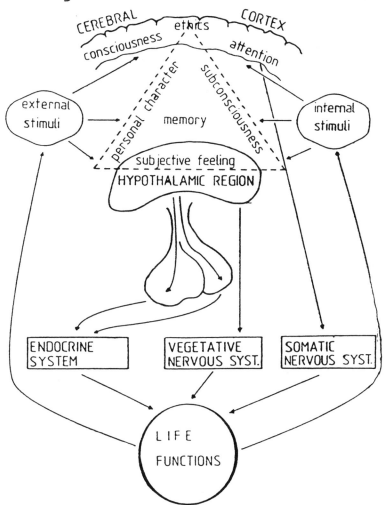 ]

*Figure 1. Model of Emotion*

*This paper is dedicated to Prof. A. Schmölz, Vienna.*

# THE MUSICAL DIALOGUE IN MUSIC THERAPY PROCESS RESEARCH

T. Timmermann
S. Bauer
N. Scheytt-Hölzer
S. Schmidt
H. Kächele
H. Baitsch

## MUSIC THERAPY AS A TARGET OF PSYCHOTHERAPY RESEARCH

The field of psychotherapy research as portrayed by the voluminous *Handbook of Psychotherapy and Behavior Change* (Garfield and Bergin 1986) has not yet discovered the so-called nonverbal psychotherapies. Right or wrong it is a fact that these have developed outside of academia and have not found the acknowledgement they deserve. However, in psychosomatic and psychiatric institutions there is a well developed field of nonverbal therapies with therapists who as a rule have semi-academic training, acquiring their skills in specialist schools, such as the Vienna School of Music Therapy which is a part of the Academy of Music and which requires a high standard of musical skills and formal training as a prerequisite and delivers a three year course in close liaison with the departments of psychosomatic medicine and psychiatry. Therapists trained there provide an opportunity for their patients to experience the affective aspects of a nonverbal interaction style which is highly welcomed as an additional form of therapy by the verbally oriented psychotherapists. At the same time the value of this work is reduced when the effects of nonverbal therapy have to be continued in a more conventional verbal psychotherapy setting. Even if these activities were only additional ingredients for fruitful work with patients who need an intensification of their capacities to experience emotions, it would be worthwhile and long overdue to evaluate their effectiveness by means of a sound methodology of psychotherapy research.

### Definition

Strotzka (1975) suggests that music therapy can be considered as a form of psychotherapy as it is a conscious and planned interactional process to influence behavioral disturbances and states of suffering. A consensus of patients, therapists, and society as a whole considers these problems worthy of psychological treatment (by verbal and nonverbal communication) with a defined goal (diminution of symptoms and or structural change of the personality) using teachable techniques with a basis of a theory of normal and abnormal behavior.

## Indication

The question of differential indication for music therapy is the subject of many clinical discussions. Like all therapists, music therapists often think they know best whom to treat and when to begin treatment. Systematic studies on this question and on outcome are still rare (Strobel and Huppmann 1978). The clinical literature is full of specific claims especially for so-called psychosomatic patients. A growing number of music therapists have made these kinds of claims for borderline pathology, schizophrenia (Oswald 1965), eating disorders (Loos 1986, 1989; Tarr-Königer 1990) and so on. Specific clinical fields have a certain amount of consistency and first monographs on topics like autism (Alvin 1988) are available. Drawing a conclusion from the clinical literature there is no doubt that such interventions can be as helpful as any other psychotherapeutic techniques. The question of differential effects however has not yet been addressed nor do we know very much about which preconditions respond most favorably to such treatment. In this fairly young field we may characterize our work by a high spirit of discovery.

What methods are used? Are they psychological or musicological in nature or are they a mixture of both dating back to centuries of the application of music to induce affective change?

### Specific and Nonspecific Factors

As there are many aspects involving relationships that we know from other forms of therapy (Orlinsky & Howard 1986, 311-385) it is probable that many of the mechanisms that have been dealt with under the notion of nonspecific factors are part and parcel of music therapy work. The nature of the specific factors is less clear; therefore it should be the aim of systematic research to focus on them. Calling for controlled outcome studies to demonstrate the effectiveness of music therapy (Vocke 1985, 468-474) before embarking on process research is likely to produce a host of results that will not be very impressive in terms of differential outcome. Therefore we should initiate studies to understand better the processes that are operating in musical dialogues. The relationship of the music elements of the process to the other aspects if it—and these are not only verbal but also other communicative channels that even in verbal psychotherapy are of considerable importance—seems to us one of the prime goals to focus upon first. Is it possible to specify the communicational processes in various channels? Are there different tasks for the different aspects of the communication process or are there, what Stern (1984) aptly called "amodal transformations?" For the development of research into the process of music therapy we are confronted with the task of starting a descriptory and classificatory research program.

Our study is geared toward such a descriptive task. Taking up Grawe's (1988) challenge for intensive single case analysis we have begun to develop a strategy for investigating processes in music therapy. We will describe the main feature of our approach which by its heuristic nature is stimulating hypothesis formation and will add to our experience on how to fund music therapy research with small grants[1] (Orlinsky 1987).

We began by videotaping ten sessions of a patient who was in psychoanalytic treatment. This was also taperecorded. The video recording allows us to study different aspects of the complex interaction where verbal exchange, the movements of both participants in the room, gestural components, and the looked-for musical exchange provide a host of observational data.

The leading question of our first study took its departure from the clinical conviction that in the musical dialogue between patient and therapist the therapist is able to detect characteristic repetitive patterns. So we set out to ask if there is an expertise among music therapists in identifying characteristics of music interaction that are related to a patient's psychopathology.

## SAMPLING OF SIGNIFICANT MUSICAL DIALOGUES

Musical dialogue means free improvised expression and interaction with instruments and voice. The therapist's "playful" interaction with the patient, sometimes even considered as "acting in or out" (Abs 1989) or as a kind of "holding" (Priestley 1983), supporting or complementary reactions according to the specific moment in the process afford the patient the opportunity to study his usual patterns of affect and behavior in a relationship and to risk new ways of playing and experimentations in the safe setting of a therapeutic situation. The therapist's attitude is imbued with an intuitive empathy: simultaneously he/she is abstinently reflecting the interaction, controlling his/her counter-transference. A shared reflection of the musical experiences is important and meaningful with patients who are able to do this, to help to integrate what has happened.

### Hypothesis

*Music therapists work under the assumption that the musical (in the widest sense of the word) expression and interaction with the therapist represent the core structures of the patient's personality and behavior.*

*Research to support this assumption is still rare.*

---

[1]   This study was supported by the Klöckner Foundation (Essen) and by the Breuninger Foundation (Stuttgart).

Our study group's first question was if and in what way the typical features of interaction between patient and therapist in the setting of a free musical improvisation can be identified and described verbally and by representation in a specific code. Then we asked: can these typical features be recognized by a group of experienced music therapists?

## Patient

The patient in our study agreed to participate in a ten session experimental intervention of music therapy, simultaneous to his ongoing psychoanalytic treatment. He was diagnosed as having a schizoid relationship personality disorder. The regulation and control of intimate relationship is the main theme of the treatment. He perceives the therapist as extremely powerful and tries to control him. He checks out the limits handling the rules of the therapy setting like a child (Thomä and Kächele 1991, 142).

His specific symptomatology consists of perverse actions. In situations when he feels overpowered by others he withdraws. Alone in his room he ties himself up with chains, which he locks up and through which he sends an electric current. To free himself becomes more and more dangerous. This arouses him sexually. He has never had intimate relationships with women. Intellectually he can control nearness and distance because he is very adroit on the verbal level. The personality can be described as inhibited specially in terms of aggression, insecure, passive, and extremely easy to hurt.

## Setting

The music therapy intervention took place in a music therapy room with carpet floor and a wide range of instruments. Drums and other rhythm instruments, flutes, a harp, a bass, etc., easily available to the patient. The therapist and the patient agreed upon:

- Meeting once a week for one hour for a total of ten sessions;
- Freely choosing instruments (or voice);
- Playing freely on the instruments;
- Talking about experiences.

## Pattern

During the intervention the patient often interrupted the musical dialogues, accusing the therapist of being too loud, too quick, too skilled, etc. The therapist felt more and more imprisoned. It seemed to him that whatever he did was wrong. This stereotyped, unconscious role induction aroused specific countertransference feelings in the therapist: he understood that the patient did to him what he had suffered from in his early childhood.

## Documentation

The experimental intervention was recorded by a fixed video camera. Before and after each session mood questionnaires (Janke and Debus 1971) and therapy session reports were filled out by the patient and the therapist. Immediately after the session the therapist produced a spontaneous affective protocol. Later he formulated a detailed report on the basis of the videotape. The weekly supervision with another music therapist was also recorded as well as the psychoanalytic sessions that paralleled the experimental intervention.

## Significant Episodes

In the clinical "macro" process the therapist gets information on the patient's psychopathologic structures by repetitions. Affective and cognitive processes direct the attention to specific patterns of behavior. To demonstrate these to an outside person one would have to choose sequences in which the patient interacts with the therapist in some typical manner.

The therapists (TT) and two colleagues (SB and NS) with similar training independently chose short sequences which they felt most convincingly demonstrated the specific pattern of interaction. The criteria were fairly intuitive. They used two perspectives for the selection of significant episodes:

1. Repetitive patters: rhythmic, melodic and/or communicative, e.g. the patient interrupts the dialogue; for this patient this was a very typical pattern of interaction and therefore a clinically meaningful choice.

2. Patterns of change (Rice and Greenberg 1984): moments where the patient's musical expression and interacting behavior differ from the usual patterns.

For each significant episode the music therapist composed a verbal description of his own sequences. In a joint meeting they discussed the material and agreed on eight scenes with a mean length of two minutes. In order to control the clinical validity of our selection we invited different rater groups: music therapists, psychotherapists and lay people.

## RATING OF SIGNIFICANT MUSICAL DIALOGUES

As consensual validation of our selection of the significant episodes constitutes a further step in developing our research program we were interested in the expertise of other music therapists in recognizing such patterns.

1.  Do they classify these musical interactions in ways that are pertinent to an understanding of the personality of patients?
2.  Are these patterns recognizable only when present in the therapeutic sessions or are they also identifiable when music therapists are mere observers listening to audio recordings of sessions or even watching videotapes?
3.  Do they share the therapist's view of the interactional patterns?
4.  Is it also possible for other psychotherapists or even lay people to identify these patterns?

In order to answer these questions, we developed a questionnaire, which was administered to three groups of raters: twenty music therapists, ten psychotherapists, twenty lay people. The criterion for selection of music therapists and psychotherapists was simply considerable clinical experience.

Ratings of the music—as is known from music-psychology—usually reflect the subjective experience of the listener and are in general related to the piece of music as a whole. Our study had to disentangle the part played by the patient and the part played by the therapist, which eventually leads to far reaching consequences for the recording. Since we were especially interested in the interaction of players, we included items covering relationship aspects developed in psychotherapy research.

The questionnaire consisted of two parts. Raters were told to answer the ten questions of Part 1 immediately after having seen and listened to one significant episode. At the end of the rating session they were asked to answer three additional questions, relating to their general impressions which made up Part 2.

The questions of Part 1 referred to the way both patient and therapist played their instruments, how they may have felt during their play and how the interaction looked. We elicited different information:

a)  The adjective checklist (shortened version of Janke and Debus 1971), was composed of twenty-six words expressing moods and feeling states and emotional behavior. Each item was rated on a line of 10 cm.

The Janke-Debus questionnaire has been analyzed for its factorial structure which has led to nine well established categories. As we were interested in a clinically relevant description of this particular patient we preferred to construct a category system tailor-made for this patient (see below).

b)  Brief free descriptions of the patient's and therapist's musical behavior. This material will enhance our inventory of qualifying expressions about the hard-to-grasp nonverbal experiences.

c) We used Luborsky's "Core Conflictual Relationship Theme" standard categories (Luborsky and Kächele 1988, 95) to formulate typical relationship patterns, e.g.:
  • "The patient tries to attract the therapist's attention" or
  • "The patient wants to dominate the therapist."
The raters had to decide whether statements similar to these were right or wrong with respect to a certain episode.

For each of the eight significant episodes these three ratings were performed separately for patient and therapist. In addition one question referred to the role relationships of the interaction directly as conceptualized by Racker (1968)—"Was the relationship more concordant or complementary or even discordant?"

A further question in Part 1 should catch ideas of the raters as to what they themselves would have done "being in the shoes of the therapist" in this episode, quoting Strupp's idea when he analyzed "psychotherapists in action" (1960).
To summarize their impressions of the whole material the raters had to answer the three following questions in Part 2 of the questionnaire.

a) Please characterize the personality of the patient.
b) What is the main problem of the patient in your opinion?
c) What are the technical difficulties of the therapist?

The free answers of the raters were analyzed by categorizing them into the same six categories as used for the adjective-checklist:

1) Symptomatology;
2) Refusal of relationship;
3) Inner tension, aggressiveness;
4) "Healthy behavior;"
5) Depression, resignation;
6) Feeling threatened, being afraid of loss of control.

As the therapist's free comments on the sessions will be coded in the same way, a comparison is feasible.

Quantitive analysis is still under way; statistical results are not yet available. We are working on a group-statistic approach as well as on finding out which single significant event most concerned the various raters. However, these questions are not yet the focus of our present work.

**REPRESENTING MUSIC DIALOGUES: PROBLEMS OF TRANSCRIPTION IN MUSIC THERAPY**

Research into the process of Music Therapy using video tapes can be approached by rating procedures as discussed above. A more direct investigation needs representation of the musical interaction. The history of representing psychotherapy dialogues is linked with the introduction of tape recording in the fifties and the development of tape recording systems to standardize the subtleties of spoken language in linguistic form (Gottschalk and Auerbach 1966).

Our intention was to find our how the music, which patient and therapist improvise during their music therapy session, could be graphically represented in such a way that the music can be repeated by a trained music therapist. This way the single therapeutic event becomes an identifiable object of investigation. But how can one write down improvised music? Traditional music notation is inadequate for putting on paper music which only in part leans towards traditional music and which is very different from conventional music. Even so, music therapists should use our conventional notation system whenever possible to facilitate the reproduction of a particular piece of "therapy music." On the other hand when "therapy music" goes beyond the boundaries of traditional music it makes sense to use some of the signs and symbols which are used by contemporary composers (Karkoschka 1966). since there is no uniform musical notation system in the field of New Music, it seems more than justifiable to choose any kind of sign language which appears suitable for one's own work. Here, it is very important to give very clear instructions concerning how the signs are to be interpreted by the player.

Our aim was to devise a language which enables the researcher to reproduce the musical interaction with a sufficient degree of similarity. The first example illustrates this.

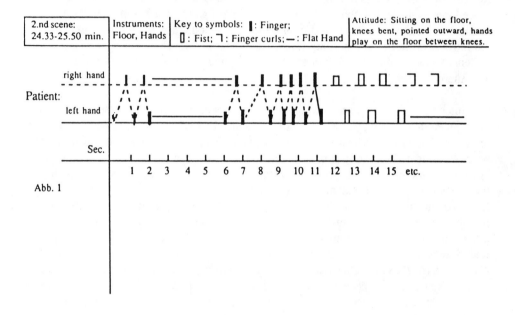

| 2.nd scene: 24.33-25.50 min. | Instruments: Floor, Hands | Key to symbols: ▌: Finger; ▯ : Fist; ⌐ : Finger curls; — : Flat Hand | Attitude: Sitting on the floor, knees bent, pointed outward, hands play on the floor between knees. |

Abb. 1

*Figure 1.*

*This figure represents a time axis plus two other horizontal lines—the left-hand-line and right-hand-line—where on each of the two one can see specific signs. The meaning of the signs is given at the top of the sheet, along with the description of the patient's physical position while playing, and the name of the instrument being used in this particular episode.*

Three types of scores were developed which we consider indispensable for our research program.

*Score 1* (called "Nachspielpartitur in German) from which we took the above example is a literal transcription or "sound for sound" transcription of the so-called "significant episodes." As the duration of one "significant episode" in our sample is no more than three minutes, the time scale one uses should be rather fine grained. We decided to use the scale of one second equalling one centimeter. In the case of many sounds occurring in a smaller space of time, the scale used could be of one second equalling two centimeters, and so on (Figure 2).

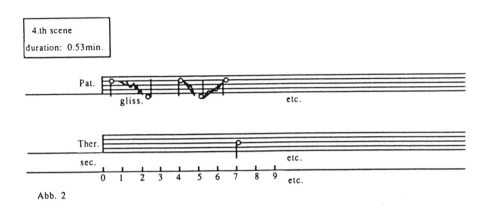

*Figure 2.*

The musical event, the "dialogue" or "interaction" can now be analyzed. Having identified sounds, phrases and dynamics the structure of interaction can be examined. The literal transcription is clearly a very complicated and time-consuming procedure. We realized, that in this particular part of research a second person is helpful to perform the task, where one person plays the data-analysis part, the other person the transcription part.

*Score 2* ("Balkenpartitur"), aims to catch the whole session, representing in a very simple way the point at which each of the participants starts and stops playing. The On-Off pattern analysis which has proved fruitful in psychotherapy research (Marsden 1971, 345-408) may be successful in music therapy research. The time scale used here is two centimeters for each minute. The graphics for both therapist and patient are put one below the other so that the external observer having no information about the musical contents of the session can quickly discern who played how much and when; also: did therapist and patient play together? always? never? how much? who started? who interrupted? and so forth. The so-called "Balkanpartitur" could also be helpful in determining the significant episodes: why not choose, before knowing what music was played, the episodes where the structure of interaction is in some way unusual (see Figure 3)? And why should one not think that patterns of interaction which are very similar to each other will have musical similarities as well? We think this may be an interesting point of research: What kind of relationship exists between structure and material?

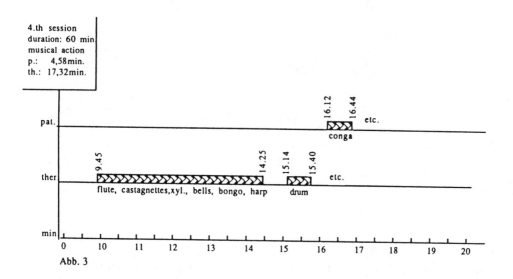

*Figure 3.*

*Score 3* is the graphic representation of all the musical repetitive patterns of the patient. Here we discern the familiar topic of pattern analysis in psychotherapy research. We can expect and do indeed find repetitive structures not only in verbal conversation but also in musical dialogue. In this case we discovered rhythmic and melodic patterns as well as "the-way-of-playing" patterns. The so-called "Spielmuster" are easy to detect once one gets to know the patient better. Of course, we are not only looking for repetition but we also assume that there will be change. With growing professional experience the music therapist will discover the patterns of change immediately. The following example of our study displays a number of patterns which have been extracted from the material (Figures 4a and 4b).

rhythmic patterns:

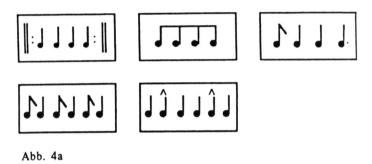

Abb. 4a

*Figure 4a.*

melodic patterns:

Abb. 4b

*Figure 4b.*

The patient used very regular, monotonous rhythmic patterns. We discovered five main patterns almost all of them in 4/4 modality. The last pattern was different as the patient was playing very regularly on one side, but putting his accents very irregularly on the other. The melodic patterns are characterized by very small intervals, such as seconds, by unfinished scales and by the frequent use of glissandi.

The last pattern seems to be different as the patient used a new interval: the third. It is interesting to know that he never repeated this little melody, whereas he used all the other melodic patterns at least five or six times.

Our personal experience with the three types of notation has helped our clinical work. We think that the evaluation of the implementation of this descriptive system may increase diagnostic approaches and the evaluation of therapeutic techniques.

## REFERENCE LIST

Abs, B. 1989. Agieren und Mitagieren in der musiktherapeutischen Behandlung (Acting and co-acting in music therapy treatment). *Musiktherapeutische Umschau* 10(1): 33-49.

Alvin, J. 1988. *Musik und Musiktherapie für behinderte und autistische Kinder (Music and Music Therapy for Retarded and Autistic Children)*. Stuttgart: Fischer.

Gottschalk, L.A., and Auerbach, A. 1966. *Methods of Research in Psychotherapy*. New York: Meredith Publishing Company.

Garfield, S., and Bergin, A.E. (Eds.) 1986. *Handbook of Psychotherapy and Behavior Change*. 3rd ed. New York: Wiley.

Grawe, K. 1988. Zurück zur psychotherapeutischen Einzelfallforschung (Back to single case research in psychotherapy). *Z. Klin. Psychol.* 17:1-7.

Janke, W., and Debus, G. 1971. *Die Eigenschafts-Wörterliste (The List of Adjectives)*. Göttingen: Hogrefe.

Karkoschka, E. 1966. *Das Schriftbild der Neuen Musik (The Look of New Music Notation)*. Celle: Herman Moeck Verlag.

Loos, G.K. 1986. *Spiel-Räume. Musiktherapie mit einer Magersüchtigen und anderen frühgestörten Patienten*. (Places to play in: Music therapy with an anorexic female and other early disturbed patients) Frankfurt: S. Fischer.

_____. 1989. Anorexie—eine Frauenkrankheit—eine Zeiterscheinung. Musiktherapie als Behandlungsform bei Eßstörungen (Anorexia — a women's disease — a modern phenomenon. Music therapy as treatment for eating disorders). *Musiktherapie Umschau* 10:105-131.

Luborsky, L., and Kächele, H. (Hrg). 1988. *Der zentrale Beziehungskonflikt (The Core Conflictual Relationship)*. Ulm: PSZ-Verlag.

Marsden, K. 1971. Content-analytic studies in psychotherapy. In *Handbook of Psychotherapy and Behavior Change*, edited by A.E. Bergin and S. Garfield. New York: Wiley.

Orlinsky, D. 1987. *How to do Psychotherapy Research Without a Grant*. Ulm: PSZ Verlag.

Orlinsky, D., and Howard, K. 1986. Process and outcome in psychotherapy. In *Handbook of Psychotherapy and Behavior Change*, edited by A.E. Bergin and S. Garfield. New York: Wiley.

Oswald, J. 1965. Musiktherapeutische Erfahrungen bei chronischer Schizophrenie (Music therapy experiences with chronic schizophrenia). *Wiener Zschr. Nervenheilkunde* 22:260-270.

Priestley, M. 1983. *Analytische Musiktherapie (Analytical Music Therapy)*. Stuttgart: Fischer.

Racker, H. 1968. *Transference and Countertransference*. New York: International University Press.

Rice, L., and Greenberg, L. 1984. *Patterns of Change. Intensive Analysis of Psychotherapy Process*. New York: Guilford.

Stern, D. 1984. *The Interpersonal World of the Infant. A View from Psychoanalysis and Developmental Psychology*. New York: Basic Books.

Strobel, W., and Huppmann, G. 1978. *Musiktherapie (Music Therapy)*. Göttingen: Hogrefe.

Strotzka, H. (Hrg). 1975. *Psychotherapie: Grundlagen, Verfahren, Indikationen (Psychotherapy: Basics, Procedures, Indications)*. Munich, Vienna, Baltimore: Urban and Schwarzenberg.

Strupp, H.H. 1960. *Psychotherapists in Action: Explorations of the Therapists' Contribution to the Treatment Process*. New York: Grune.

Thomä, H., and Kächele, H. 1991. *Psychoanalytic Practice*. Vol. II: Dialogues. Berlin, Heidelberg, New York: Springer.

Tarr-Königer, I. 1990. *Bulime und Widerstand. Ein musiktherapeutisch orientierter Ansatz (Bulimia and Resistance. A Music Therapy Oriented Procedure)*. Heidelberg: Roland Asanger.

Vocke, J. 1985. Empirische Forschung. In *Musikpsychologie. Ein Handbuch in Schlüsselbegriffen* (Empirical Research. In *Music Psychology. A Handbook in Keywords)*, edited by H. Bruhn, R. Oerter, and H. Rösing. Munich, Vienna, Baltimore: Urban and Schwarzenberg.

# META-ANALYSIS OF RESEARCH IN MUSIC AND MEDICAL TREATMENT: EFFECT SIZE AS A BASIS FOR COMPARISON ACROSS MULTIPLE DEPENDENT AND INDEPENDENT VARIABLES

Jayne Standley

## INTRODUCTION

The volume of empirical studies on the effects of music in medical treatment continues to grow and has achieved a quantity which can provide important information with implications for the course of future research and for clinical applications. A comprehensive review of the literature on music in medicine conducted in 1983 revealed over 90 entries (Slesnick 1983).

In 1986 Standley obtained and reviewed over 98 references on this topic and identified 30 empirical studies which were amenable to a comprehensive meta-analysis of characteristics and results (Standley 1986). The effect size of music by each dependent variable was then statistically calculated and results compared and contrasted across multiple variables. Further, results were transferred to clinical applications and implications for techniques of music therapy treatment were identified and described.

Since that comprehensive analysis a large number of studies have been added to the research literature, many representing unique applications of music in medicine and many resulting in the replication of prior findings. A recent search by this author revealed 54 references which have accrued on this topic in addition to those considered in 1986.

The purpose of the current study is to expand and update the existing meta-analysis database on the topic of music in medicine in order to integrate results of the two groups of studies, summarize findings of as complete a body of empirical results as possible, and delineate the most current implications for uses of music in medical treatment.

## META-ANALYSIS PROCEDURES AND RESULTS

Meta-analysis is differentiated from primary analysis (original analysis of data in a research study) and secondary analysis (the reanalysis of data for the purpose of answering the original research question with better statistical techniques or for answering new questions with the original data) of research results. Meta-analysis is the application of a variety of techniques of measurement and statistical analysis to identify effect sizes (quantitative summaries of the properties and findings of individual studies) which can then be compared and contrasted across multiple variables (Glass et al. 1984).

TABLE 1

| Author | Year | Source | Type of Patient | Research Location | No. | Age | % Female | No. of Groups | Design Type | Independ. Variable | Dependent Variable | Type Meas. | Pain Present | Type Music | Music Function |
|---|---|---|---|---|---|---|---|---|---|---|---|---|---|---|---|
| 1. Roter | 1957 | Thesis | Medical | Univ.Med Arts Center | 451 | Adults | 73 | 3 | Posttest only | Music | Pleasure | SR | No | Taped listening | Mood Stimulus |
| 2. Ammon | 1968 | Journal | Respiratory distress | Gen/Children Hospital | 20 | Infants | 65 | 2 | Exp/Con | Music | Respirations | SR / PO | Yes | Taped listening | Sedative |
| 3. Budzynski, et al. | 1970 | Journal | Chronic headache | Biofeedback Clinic | 5 | Adults | 80 | 1 | AB | Tones | EMG Headache intensity | PO / SR | Yes | Contingent tones | Audioanalgesic |
| 4. Epstein, et al. | 1974 | Journal | Headache | Univ. Med. Center | 1 | Adult | 0 | 1 | ABAB | Music | EMG Headache | PO | Yes | Taped listening | Audioanalgesic |
| 5. Crago | 1980 | Dissertation | Open heart surgery | Univ. Med. Center | 40 | Adults | 0 | 2 | Exp/Con | Music/ relax | Pain Sleep Anxiety Analgesic Anxiety Hos. Days Lis. Time Relax | SR SR PO PO SR SR BO BO | Yes | Taped listening | Audioanalgesic |
| 6. Hoffman | 1980 | Thesis | Hyper-tensive | Univ. Med. Center | 19 | Adults | 74 | 1 | Pre/Post Test | Relax/ Imagry/ Ocean & Music | BP Relax | PO SR | No | Taped listening | Sedative |
| 7. Corah, et al. | 1981 | Journal | Dental | Dental School | 80 | Adults | 50 | 4 | Exp/Con | Music & vol. control / Relax. Music / Music | Anxiety Autonomic sensation | SR SR | Yes | Taped listening | Audioanalgesic |
| 8. Kamin, et al. | 1982 | Book of Proceed. | Surgical | Sports Clinic | 50 | Adults | 0 | 2 | Exp/Con | Music | Stress hormone | PO | Yes | Taped listening | Anxiolytic/ anesthetic |
| 9. Schneider | 1982 | Dissert-ation | Burn | Burn Hospital | 5 | Children | 40 | 1 | ABAB | Music/ suggest./relax. | Pain | BO | Yes | Taped listening | Audioanalgesic |
| 10. Spintge | 1982 | Book of Proceed. | Surgical | Sports Clinic | 400 | Adults | 29 | 4 | Exp/Con | Music | Amt. of anesthet. | SR | Yes | Taped listening | Anxiolytic/ anesthetic |
| 11. Spintge & Droh | 1982 | Book of Proceed. | Surgical | Sports Clinic | 1910 | Adults | 27 | 1 | Posttest only | Music | Choice of anesthet. | SR | Yes | Taped listening | Anxiolytic/ anesthetic |
| 12. Brook | 1984 | Thesis | Obstetric | General Hospital | 40 | Adults | 100 | 2 | Exp/Con | Music | Pulse Time | PO BO | Yes | Taped listening | Audioanalgesic |
| 13. Sammons | 1984 | Journal | Obstetric | Hospital Birth Cent. HMO/Milit. Hosp. | 54 | Adults | 100 | 2 | Exp/Con | Music | Apgar Choice of music | PO BO SR | Yes | Taped listening | Audioanalgesic |

SR = Self Report   PO = Physiologically Observed   BO = Behaviorally Observed

**TABLE 1 Continued**

| Author | Year | Source | Type of Patient | Research Location | No. | Age | % Female | No. of Groups | Design Type | Independ. Variable | Dependent Variable | Type Meas. | Pain Present | Type Music | Music Function |
|---|---|---|---|---|---|---|---|---|---|---|---|---|---|---|---|
| 14. Tanioka et al. | 1984 | Book of Proceed. | Surgical | National Hospital | 30 | Adults | 63 | 2 | Exp/Con | Music | Hormones | PO | Yes | Taped listening | Audioanalgesic |
| 15. Cofrancesco | 1985 | Journal | Stroke | Rehab. Facilities | 3 | Adults | ? | 1 | AB | Music/Exercise | Grasp | PO | No | Taped Participation Exercise | Structure for Exercise |
| 16. Frank | 1985 | Journal | Cancer | University Hospital | 15 | Adults | 87 | 1 | AB | Music/Imagery | Emesis, Nausea, Anxiety | SR, SR, SR | Yes | Taped listening | Antiemetic |
| 17. Rider | 1985 | Journal | Spinal cord injury | Spinal Pain Clinic | 23 | ? | ? | 1 | Repeat. measures | Relax/music, Relax/imagery | Pain, EMG | SR/PO, SR/PO | Yes | Taped listening | Audioanalgesic |
| 18. Roberts | 1986 | Thesis | Brain-injured | General Hospital | 10 | Adults | 67 | 2 | Pre/Post | Pref. music imagery | ICP | PO/PO | ? | Taped listening | Decrease ICP |
| 19. Sanderson | 1986 | Thesis | Surgical | General Hospital | 60 | Adults | 47 | 2 | Exp/Con | Music | Ver. pain, Obs. pain, Medication, BP, Anxiety, BP | BO, BO, BO, PO, SR/PO, SR/PO | Yes | Taped listening | Audioanalgesic |
| 20. Lininger | 1987 | Thesis | Neonates | Hospital | 36 | Infants | 56 | 3 | Exp/Con | Music (Inst/Voc) | Crying | BO | No | Taped listening | Sedative |
| 21. Martin | 1987 | Thesis | Chronic Headache | Biofeedback Clinic | 60 | Adults | 65 | 3 | Exp/Con | Music, Relax., Biofeed. | EMG | BO | Yes | Taped listening | Audioanalgesic |
| 22. Metzler & Berman | 1987 | Unpub. | Bronchoscopy | General Hospital | 31 | Adults | ? | 2 | Exp/Con | Music | Pulse | PO | Yes | Taped listening | Anxiolitic |
| 23. Ward | 1987 | Thesis | Burn | Burn Center | 5 | Adults | 80 | 1 | AB | Music/relax. | Pulse, Pain | PO, BO | Yes | Taped listening | Audioanalgesic |
| 24. Schieffelin | 1988 | Unpub. | Stevens-Johnson Syndrome | Children's Hospital | 1 | Child | 0 | 1 | AB | Music | Crying | BO | Yes | Taped Participation | Audioanalgesic |
| 25. Gfeller et al. | 1989 | Unpub. | Dental | Dental Clinic | 40 | Adolesc./Adults | 50 | 4 | Exp/Exp | Music/sugges. | Helplessness | SR | Yes | Taped listening | Audioanalgesic |
| 26. Caine | 1989 | Thesis | Neonates | General Hospital | 52 | Infants | 58 | 4 | Exp/Con | Music | Wt. gain, Length of Hosp., Nonstress behav., Caloric Intake | PO, BO, PO, BO | Yes | Taped listening | Audioanalgesic |

## TABLE 2

| Author | Variable Analyzed | Data Provided | Effect Size |
|---|---|---|---|
| 1. Roter | Perceived benefit: Patients | % | .28 |
|  | Visitors | % | .26 |
| 2. Ammon | Reduction in respiration rate: | means, s.d. | 3.15 |
| 3. Budzynski, et al. | EMG reduction | means, p, n | 1.76 |
|  | Headache intensity | means, p, n | 1.76 |
| 4. Epstein, et al. | EMG reduction | F, means | 1.00 |
| 5. Crago | Headache intensity | % | .59 |
|  | Music/relax. vs. music alone: |  |  |
|  | Pain | t, n | .87 |
|  | Sleep satisfaction | t, n | .42 |
|  | Amount of analgesics | t, n | .30 |
|  | Anxiety | t, n | .41 |
|  | Days in hospital | t, n | -.51 |
|  | Time listening | t, n | .45 |
|  | Relaxation | t, n | .88 |
| 6. Hoffman | BP reduction | means, p, n | .83 |
| 7. Corah, et al. | Music alone: Anxiety | F, means | -.39 |
|  | Autonomic sensation | F, means | .47 |
| 8. Kamin, et al. | % Cortisol below upper normal limit: |  |  |
|  | 10 min. before anesthesia | % | .42 |
|  | just prior to anesthesia | % | .67 |
|  | 15 min. after incision | % | .44 |
|  | 20 min. after extubation | % | .80 |
| 9. Schneider | Observed pain | p, n | .70 |
| 10. Spintge | Effect of epidural anesthesia: | % | .42 |
| 11. Spintge & Droh | Choice to reuse epidural anesthesia: | % | 1.12 |
| 12. Brook | Pulse | means, p | .73 |
|  | Cm dilation/second | means, p | .52 |
|  | Infant Apgar of multipara mothers | means, p | .73 |
| 13. Sammons | Music used in labor | % | .44 |
| 14. Tanioka et al. | Cortisol-1hr. of operation | % | .75 |
| 15. Cofrancesco | Grasp strength | means, s.d. | 1.94 |
| 16. Frank | Emesis intensity | means, s.d. | .47 |
|  | Emesis length | means, s.d. | .33 |
|  | Nausea intensity | means, s.d. | 0.00 |
|  | Nausea length | means, s.d. | .36 |
|  | Anxiety | means, s.d. | .63 |
| 17. Rider | Pain & EMG by music selection: |  | Pain / EMG |
|  | Reich | t, n | 1.55 / .50 |
|  | Metheny | t, n | 1.16 / 1.90 |
|  | Entrainment | t, n | 1.51 / 2.03 |
|  | Crystal | t, n | .96 / 1.56 |
|  | Debussy | t, n | 2.11 / .33 |
|  | No music | t, n | .96 / 1.52 |
|  | Preferred music | t, n | .59 / .91 |
| 18. Roberts | Decreased ICP, BP: |  | ICP / BP |
|  | Preferred music/silence | t, n | .67 / .49 |
|  | Preferred/sedative music | t, n | 1.21 / .03 |
| 19. Sanderson | Preoperative anxiety | means, s.d. | 1.02 |
|  | BP stabilization | % | .55 |
|  | Verbalized pain | means, s.d. | .58 |
|  | Time observed without pain | means, s.d. | .89 |
|  | Amount of medication | means, s.d. | .50 |
| 20. Lininger | Crying time: |  |  |
|  | Instrumental/no music | means, s.d. | .26 |
|  | Vocal/instrumental music | means, s.d. | .15 |
|  | Vocal/no music | means, s.d. | .72 |
| 21. Martin | EMG reduction (all 3 conditions): |  |  |
|  | 35 minutes | t, n | 2.38 |
|  | 26-30 minutes | t, n | 2.10 |
|  | 18-25 minutes | t, n | 1.22 |
| 22. Metzler & Berman | Pulse | % | .39 |
| 23. Ward | Pulse | means, s.d. | .50 |
|  | Observed pain | means, s.d. | 1.52 |
|  | SR pain | means, s.d. | .48 |
| 24. Schieffelin | Crying frequency | means, s.d. | 1.23 |
| 25. Gfeller | Helplessness | t, n | .94 |
|  | Weight gain | t, n | .71 |
| 26. Caine | Length hospital stay | t, n | .56 |
|  | Formula intake-ICU | t, n | -.59 |
|  | Nonstress behaviors | t, n | .05 |

The procedure of this study was identical to that of the original study and followed the three basic steps of a meta-analysis as outlined by Getsie et al. (1985):

1. A complete literature search was conducted to find all possible members of the defined population of studies whether published or unpublished sources;
2. The characteristics and findings of the collected studies were identified, described, and categorized;
3. The composite findings were statistically analyzed and results converted to computed Effect Size.

The population for analysis was defined as all empirical studies on the effects of music in actual (not simulated) medical/dental treatment which were additional to those analyzed in 1986. Sources searched included the computerized indexes PsycLIT, Dissertation Abstracts Ondisc from 1980 to the present, and MEDLINE. Printed sources searched included *Master's Theses in Music Therapy* (Maranto and Bruscia, 1988), the journals in music therapy since 1985 (*Journal of Music Therapy, Music Therapy*, and *Music Therapy Perspectives*), and the proceedings of the International Society of Music and Medicine (1982 and 1984).

A total of 54 references on this topic were identified and copies obtained through interlibrary loan. Of these, 26 qualified for inclusion in the meta-analysis by containing empirical data; utilizing actual, not simulated, pain stimuli; utilizing music as an independent variable; utilizing subjects who were actual patients with medical/dental diagnoses; and reporting results in a format amenable to replicated data analysis.

Table 1 shows the complete analysis of the characteristics of each of these 26 studies in chronological order and includes the following: authors, year, source, patient type, clinical location of research, total sample size, subjects' age range, percentage of female subjects, number of groups in the experimental design, type of experimental design, independent variables tested, dependent variables measured, coding by type of dependent measure (whether psychological and based on staff or self-report, physiological, or behaviorally observed), presence of pain, and stated function of the music.

Table 2 shows the format of reported data and the calculated Effect Size for each of 74 dependent variables organized by author. All effect sizes were estimated according to procedures outlined by Glass et al. (1984).

Once each dependent variable had a value on a linear scale of effect, then the multiple studies could be compared according to the characteristics identified and categorized in Table 1. Results of this current meta-analysis were combined with those in the original study yielding a total of 56 empirical studies and 129 dependent measures included in the following comparisons of effect size. Estimated effect sizes ranged from 3.28 (meaning the music condition was more than 3 standard deviations greater in desired effect than the control condition) to - .59. Only 4 of the 129 variables had a negative sign, meaning that for those dependent measures the music condition was less beneficial than the nonmusic condition. Several of these negative results were from studies where other dependent measures showed a positive reaction to music. The overall mean effect size for all 129 dependent measures was .88. Tables 3 through 12 provide other comparisons of these data.

Design characteristics are included in Tables 3 through 5. Sources of studies included in these analyses are primarily published (N=77) vs. unpublished (N=52). Published sources which are not refereed yield a similar effect size (1.0) as those which are refereed, (1.00) while unpublished theses and dissertations yield a smaller effect size (.69) after undergoing academic review (Table 3). Studies which utilize a research design with experimental and control groups also yield a much more conservative effect (.70) than do those using subjects as their own control (1.14) or with posttest only (1.14) (Table 4). Sample size affects the data with very small (.96) and very large groups (1.03) yielding the largest effect sizes, while studies with 31-60 subjects (.71) and 61-100 subjects (.85) yield the smallest (Table 5).

TABLE 3
Mean Effect Size by Type of Source

|  | Published | | Unpublished | |
|  | Refereed | Non-refereed | Thesis-Dis. | Non-Refereed |
|---|---|---|---|---|
| $\overline{ES}$ | 1.00 | 1.00 | .69 | .70 |
| N | 61 | 16 | 48 | 4 |

N=129

TABLE 4
Mean Effect Size by Type of Research Design

|     | Experimental/ Control Groups | Subject as Own Control | Posttest Only |
|-----|------------------------------|------------------------|---------------|
| $\overline{ES}$ | .70 | 1.14 | 1.14 |
| N   | 76 | 43 | 10 |

N=129

TABLE 5
Mean Effect Size by Sample Size

|     | ≤10 | 11-30 | 31-60 | 61-100 | >100 |
|-----|------|-------|-------|--------|------|
| $\overline{ES}$ | .96 | .96 | .71 | .85 | 1.03 |
| N   | 22 | 42 | 45 | 5 | 15 |

N=129

Tables 6 through 9 compare effect sizes by subject demographics. Table 6 shows mean effect size by sex of subjects and reveals that women react more favorably to music than do men. The studies with 100% women are almost exclusively obstetrical, studies with dependent measures that yield relatively low effects to music (See Table 9). Yet, women in these studies achieved an average effect size of .70 vs. that for studies with all males of .57.

TABLE 6
Mean Effect Size by Sex of Subjects

|  | Females | | Males | |
|  | 51-99% | 100% | 51-99% | 100% |
|---|---|---|---|---|
| $\overline{ES}$ | .87 | .70 | .82 | .57 |
| N | 42 | 22 | 16 | 14 |

N=94

The subjects' ages seem greatly to affect reported effects of music (Table 7). Infants (.47) react very differently than do adults (.86) while children and adolescents show the greatest response (1.12). It may be that the children and adolescents in these studies are reflecting the differential attraction to music that is apparent in commercial sales data, i.e., that the great majority of records and tapes are purchased by teenagers and pre-teens. Infants have the shortest history of relating to music in the environment and, therefore, may not yet have learned to "respond" as do other ages of subjects.

TABLE 7
Mean Effect Size by Age of Subjects

|  | Infants | Children/ Adolescents | Adults |
|---|---|---|---|
| $\overline{ES}$ | .47 | 1.12 | .86 |
| N | 13 | 9 | 93 |

N=115

The mean effect sizes yielded by patient diagnosis are shown in Table 8. Dental and chronic migraine headache studies have the highest effect sizes (1.54) while studies of neonates, again, yield the lowest effects (.24).

Across the diagnoses, it appears that the effects of music are differentiated by severity: level of pain, anxiety, and prognosis. It is interesting to note that when pain is the only diagnostic characteristic considered (Table 9) the effect size is greater (.95) than when pain is not a usual symptom of the diagnosis (.70). Combining the results of Tables 8 and 9 would seem to clarify the extent to which music specifically alleviates pain. When the pain is temporary (dental and headaches) and not the "deep" pain of ischemic muscle tissue (childbirth, surgery, or cancer) then music is more effective.

TABLE 8
Mean Effect Size by Patient Diagnosis

| Diagnosis | $\overline{ES}$ | N |
|---|---|---|
| Dental | 1.54 | 8 |
| Chronic Migraine Headache | 1.54 | 7 |
| Respiratory Problems | 1.46 | 3 |
| Chronic Pain | 1.26 | 14 |
| Physically Impaired | 1.17 | 4 |
| Cardiac Intensive Care | 1.14 | 4 |
| Kidney Dialysis | 1.09 | 2 |
| Burn | .89 | 5 |
| Abortion | .84 | 2 |
| Surgical | .78 | 30 |
| Obstetrical | .64 | 17 |
| Coma | .60 | 4 |
| Families of patients | .44 | 4 |
| Cancer | .43 | 8 |
| Neonates | .24 | 12 |

N=124

TABLE 9
Mean Effect Size by Pain vs. No Pain Diagnoses

|  | No Pain | Pain | Unknown |
|---|---|---|---|
| $\overline{ES}$ | .95 | .70 | .60 |
| N | 102 | 11 | 16 |

N=129

TABLE 10
Mean Effect Size by Type of Dependent Measure

|  | Physiological Data | Behaviorally Observed Data | Self-Report Data |
|---|---|---|---|
| ES | .94 | 1.00 | .76 |
| N | 51 | 34 | 44 |

N=129

Tables 10 and 11 provide comparisons of effect size according to characteristics of dependent measures. Table 10 shows that patient self-report is the most conservative measure of the effect of music (.76) while measurement of physiological data (.94) and behavioral observation of patient responses (1.00) yield greater effect sizes which are relatively comparable.

Specific dependent measures included in more than one study are listed in Table 11 in order of effect. Respiration rate is strongest (1.58), followed by EMG (1.39) and amount of analgesic medication used by patients (1.31). Low effects are achieved when infant behaviors are monitored (movement ES=.17); crying ES=.30; and weight gain ES=.46). Low effects are also achieved when days of hospitalization (.23) and degree of nausea/emesis (.29) are quantified.

TABLE 11
Mean Effect Size by Dependent Measure

| | $\overline{ES}$ | N |
|---|---|---|
| Respiratory Rate | 1.58 | 2 |
| EMG | 1.39 | 13 |
| Amount of Analgesics | 1.31 | 7 |
| Pain (Self-Report) | 1.16 | 16 |
| Pulse | 1.10 | 7 |
| Relaxation | 1.10 | 2 |
| Pain (Observed) | 1.01 | 10 |
| Intracranial Pressure | .94 | 2 |
| Attitudes | .87 | 7 |
| Stress Hormones | .76 | 8 |
| Anxiety | .72 | 12 |
| Blood Pressure | .69 | 8 |
| Length of Labor | .57 | 2 |
| Infant Weight Gain | .46 | 3 |
| Amount of Anesthesia | .36 | 2 |
| Infant Crying | .30 | 4 |
| Emesis/Nausea | .29 | 4 |
| Days in Hospital | .23 | 3 |
| Infant Movement | .17 | 2 |

N=114

The final table (12) shows the difference in effect size when recorded music is used (.86) versus live music performance or participation with the music therapist (1.10). Even though the number of empirical studies using live music is small (N=12), these data do seem to confirm the medical impact that the music therapist has when adapting the musical event to meet the specific needs of the patient.

TABLE 12
Mean Effect Size by Live vs. Recorded Music

|        | Live | Recorded |
|--------|------|----------|
| $\overline{ES}$ | 1.10 | .86 |
| N      | 12   | 117      |

N=129

## DISCUSSION

The comparisons afforded by meta-analysis have implication for improvement of applied music techniques in the medical setting and for future research on this topic. In order for music to be a viable medical component, its therapeutic methodology must fulfill the expectations of the medical model, i.e., an a priori determination of treatment protocol dictated by a specific diagnosis and proven options. Further, treatment options must provide specific, calculated outcomes by frequency and duration of applications systematically documented to readily identify positive or negative consequences. Meta-analysis data can provide a valuable research methodology for identifying such parameters for the use of music with specific medical problems and for establishing effective music therapy techniques.

Additionally, meta-analysis data may provide a basis for differentiation of professional resources. For instance, if music is most effective with pain symptoms without serious consequences and live music is the most effective form of music treatment, then perhaps the resources of the professional music therapist might focus on personal interactions with those with serious illnesses or trauma while other professions focus on the use of taped music as a background for another primary medical treatment.

An interdisciplinary approach to treatment combing the medical expertise of physicians and nurses with the counseling and music expertise of music therapists would obviously enhance health benefits to many patients. The continued cooperation of all medical professions to promote the most effective, documented techniques amongst the myriad uses of music is critical.

Progressive applications of music to other diagnostic categories might be predicted by generalization of the evidence of conditions under which music appears to be effective.

While transfer of knowledge gained and interdisciplinary applications may lead to further discovery of the medical benefits of music, it is of course crucial that the existing database continues to grow. Comprehensive review and analysis of the literature can prove helpful in suggesting where research is needed or indicated, but it is the role of the investigator to provide the future documentation that will lead to advancement in clinical applications. This meta-analysis not only demonstrates that the data base on music and medical treatment is strong and burgeoning due to the avid interest and productivity of researchers from many professions, but also reconfirms that more research is warranted and needed from all.

## REFERENCE LIST

Ammon, K. 1968. The effects of music on children in respiratory distress. *American Nurses' Association Clinical Sessions*, 127-133.

Brook, E. 1984. Soothing music during the active phase of labor: Physiologic effect of mother and infant. Unpublished Master's Thesis, University of Florida.

Budzynski, T.; Stoyva, J.; and Adler, C. 1970. Feedback-induced muscle relaxation: Application to tension headache. *Journal of Behavior Therapy and Experimental Psychiatry* 1:205-211.

Caine, J. 1989. The effects of music on the selected stress behaviors, weight, caloric and formula intake, and length of hospital stay of premature and low birth weight neonates in a newborn intensive care unit. Unpublished master's thesis, The Florida State University.

Cofrancesco, E. 1985. The effect of music therapy on hand grasp strength and functional task performance in stroke patients. *Journal of Music Therapy* 22(3):125-149.

Corah, N.; Gale, E.; Pace, L.; and Seyrek, S. 1981. Relaxation and musical programming as means of reducing psychological stress during dental procedures. *Journal of the American Dental Association* 103:232-234.

Crago, B. 1980. Reducing the stress of hospitalization for open heart surgery. Unpublished dissertation, University of Massachusetts.

Epstein, L; Hersen, M; and Hemphill, D. 1974. Music feedback in the treatment of tension headache: An experimental case study. *Journal of Behavior Therapy and Experimental Psychiatry* 5:59-63.

Frank, J. 1985. The effects of music therapy and guided visual imagery on chemotherapy induced nausea and vomiting. *Oncology Nursing Forum* 12(5):47-52.

Getsie, R.; Langer, P.; and Glass, G. 1985. Meta-analysis of the effects of type and combination of feedback on children's discrimination learning. *Review of Educational Research* 55(1):9-22.

Gfeller, K.; Logan, H.; and Walker, J. 1990. The effect of auditory distraction and suggestion on tolerance for dental restorations in adolescents and young adults. *Journal of Music Therapy* 27 (1): 13-23.

Glass, G.; McGaw, M.; and Smith, M. 1984. *Meta-analysis in Social Research*. Beverly Hills, CA: Sage Publications.

Hoffman, J. 1974. Management of essential hypertension through relaxation training with sound. Unpublished master's thesis, University of Kansas.

Kamin, A.; Kamin, H.; Spintge, R.; and Droh, R. 1982. Endocrine effect of anxiolytic music and psychological counseling before surgery. In *Angst, Schmerz, Musik in der Anasthesie*, edited by R. Droh and R. Spintge, 163-166. Basel: Editiones Roche.

Lininger, L. 1987. The effects of instrumental and vocal lullabies on the crying behavior of newborn infants. Unpublished master's thesis, Southern Methodist University.

Maranto, C. and Bruscia, K. (Eds.) 1988. *Master's Theses in Music Therapy: Index and Abstracts*. Philadelphia: Temple University, Esther Boyer College of Music.

Martin, M. 1987. The influence of combining preferred music with progressive relaxation and biofeedback techniques on frontalis muscle. Unpublished master's thesis, Southern Methodist University.

Metzler, R. and Berman, T. 1987. The effect of sedative music on the anxiety of bronchoscopy patients. Paper presented at the Annual Conference, International Society of Music in Medicine, Lüdenscheid.

Roberts, C. 1986. Music: A nursing intervention for increased intracranial pressure. Unpublished master's thesis, Grand Valley State College.

Roter, M. 1957. The use of music in medical reception rooms. Unpublished master's thesis, University of Kansas.

Rider, M. 1985. Entrainment mechanisms are involved in pain reduction, muscle relaxation, and music-mediated imagery. *Journal of Music Therapy* 22(4):183-192.

Sammons, L. 1984. The use of music by women in childbirth. *Journal of Nurse-Midwifery* 29(4):266-270.

Sanderson, S. 1986. The effect of music on reducing preoperative anxiety and postoperative anxiety and pain in the recovery room. Unpublished master's thesis, The Florida State University.

Scheiffelin, C. 1988. A case study: Stevens-Johnson Syndrome. Paper presented at the Annual Conference, Southeastern Conference of the National Association for Music Therapy, Inc., April, Tallahassee.

Schneider, F. 1982. Assessment and evaluation of audio-analgesic effects on the pain experience of acutely burned children during dressing changes. Unpublished dissertation, University of Cincinnati.

Slesnick, J. 1983. Music in medicine: A critical review. Unpublished master's thesis, Hahnemann University.

Spintge, R. 1982. Psychophysiological surgery preparation with and without anxiolytic music. In *Angst, Schmerz, Musik in der Anasthesie*, edited by R. Droh and R. Spintge, 77-88. Basel: Editiones Roche.

Spintge, R., and Droh, R. 1982. The pre-operative condition of 1910 patients exposed to anxiolytic music and Rohypnol (Flurazepam) before receiving an epidural anesthetic.

In *Angst, Schmerz, Musik in der Anasthesie*, edited by R. Droh and R. Spintge, 193-196. Basel: Editiones Roche.

Standley, J. 1986. Music research in medical/dental treatment: Meta-analysis and clinical applications. *Journal of Music Therapy* 23(2):56-122.

Tanioka, F.; Takazawa, T.; Kamata, S.; Kudo, M.; Matsuki, A.; and Oyama, T. 1985. Hormonal effect of anxiolytic music in patients during surgical operations under epidural anesthesia. In *Music in Medicine,* edited by R. Droh and R. Spintge, 285-290. Basel: Editiones Roche.

Ward, L. 1987. The use of music and relaxation techniques to reduce pain of burn patients during daily debridement. Unpublished master's thesis, The Florida State University.

# A MODEL FOR INTERNATIONAL INFORMATION MANAGEMENT IN ARTS-MEDICINE

Richard A. Lippin
Judith E. Schaeffer
Thomas Sherman
Karen L. Barton

## INTRODUCTION AND HISTORY OF ARTS-MEDICINE

The value of the relationship between the healing arts and the creative arts has been discussed since antiquity. The ancient Greeks recognized this connection with the temples of medicine. These temples were built in places of great natural beauty. A combination of diet, massage, various baths, and incubation sleeps was used for diagnosis and treatment. The head of Aesculapius, the founder of the cult which practiced this early form of medicine, was immortalized on Greek coins as early as 150 B.C. Examples of this coin are today a part of the medical prints collections at the Philadelphia Museum of Art (Douglas 1986).

Medical illustration developed in the Middle Ages with the work of Erhard Reuwich. During that period medicinal plants were used extensively in medical treatment. Since it was important that medical practitioners be able to identify these plants, a handbook which combined medical and botanical knowledge was published in 1485. Reuwich provided the illustrations for this early text.

During the Renaissance, artists such as Leonardo da Vinci spent much time studying anatomy to improve their artistic representations. Scholars today can visualize the medical history of the period through such works as Bellini's "Visit to a Plaque Patient." This artistic visualization of medical history continues through the post-Renaissance, most notably in the works of Rembrandt and Eakins.

Dr. Robert Root-Bernstein (1987) of Michigan State University has documented the relationship between achievement in science or medicine and involvement in the arts throughout the 19th and 20th centuries. The special relationship between medicine and music is reflected in the number of accomplished physician musicians and the large number of physician orchestras that have existed for over a century in many countries.

The arts therapy movement began during World War II. There are now over 140 graduate programs in the field and a large number of professional associations, journals, and activities.

The Center for Safety in the Arts, founded in New York City in 1977, has dedicated over 10 years of work toward understanding safety issues in the arts. They place a particular emphasis on toxicity in the visual arts.

In 1977 Johns Hopkins University and Hospital established the Committee on Cultural and Social Affairs and Dr. George B. Udvarhelyi was appointed its Chairman. Since that time Dr. Udvarhelyi has established a model cultural program for medical university campuses utilizing innovative methods for incorporating international quality arts within the campus intellectual milieu. Dr. Udvarhelyi has contributed to the rehumanizing of health education and health institutions.

The medical problems of world class pianists like Leon Fleischer and Gary Graffman in the late 1970s led to the founding in this country of some early clinics which specialized in the treatment of musicians. The evolution of the arts-medicine movement followed in the early 1980s.

The formation of the International Arts-Medicine Association [IAMA] in 1985 recognized that there were a large number of activities occurring on a global basis that dealt with one or more aspects of the relationship between the arts and medicine. Much information was being generated, but no umbrella organization was facilitating networking, coordinating activities, or collecting, storing, and managing information in this growing, important field. Therefore, the first of IAMA's goals was to provide a forum for communication between professionals in the arts and health.

In 1989 physicians Alice G. Brandfonbrener and Richard J. Lederman founded the Performing Arts Medicine Association (PAMA). Membership in the nonprofit organization is limited to physicians. PAMA is dedicated to providing leadership in the field of performing arts-medicine, including treatment, education, and research.

It is our belief that we are now entering a cycle in world culture in which a reexploration of the comprehensive relationship between the arts and medicine seems warranted. Such a focus would recognize the value in interdisciplinary approaches to problem solving in this time of enormous societal crisis.

This new Renaissance, unlike others in the past, has the advantage of being driven by high technology, rapid and advanced communications technologies, and significant advances in neuroscience. Today's Renaissance man or woman combines a traditional intellectual curiosity with a 20th century sense of the diversity of information sources available to feed that curiosity.

## THE NEED FOR INFORMATION

Recognizing that there is a diversity of information sources available and accessing these sources are two entirely different exercises.

One of IAMA's basic premises is to provide a forum for communication between the arts and medical sectors. IAMA has recently decided as an organization to focus on global information management in arts-medicine. Multi-lingual international information exchange in the arts and medicine is achievable with current computer and telecommunications technology and organizational and cross-cultural cooperation. There is a need for accessing a central data base which combines the relevant materials from existing arts and medical data bases and incorporates the new arts-medicine journals and newsletters as well as proceedings from arts-medicine conferences.

## EFFORTS IN INFORMATION MANAGEMENT TO DATE

The vast resources of the United States National Library of Medicine, a branch of the National Institutes of Health located in Bethesda, MD, provide enormous opportunities for collaboration on arts-medicine information management. The Medical Literature Analysis and Retrieval System [MEDLARS], is a leading online bibliographical data base of medical information. It covers over 25 years and over 3,000 journals. It can be accessed through a nationwide network of more than 5,8000 universities, medical school, hospitals, government agencies, and commercial organizations. The MEDLARS system contains some 8 million references to journal articles and books in the health sciences. Most of these references were published after 1965.

Former IAMA Board Member Dr. James Ferguson serves as a liaison between IAMA and the National Library of Medicine [NLM]. Dr. Ferguson has supplied IAMA with sample printouts utilizing the NLM's vast computer capabilities. He is exploring potential uses of NLM data bases as they relate to arts-medicine topics.

In April of 1986, the NLM published a specialized bibliography known as "Medicine and the Arts." The bibliography was prepared in conjunction with the colloquium "Medicine and the Arts: Two Faces of Humanity" held at the NLM in April of 1986. The subjects covered in this specialized bibliography include both medical themes in art and literature and the physician as artist. This medicine and arts specialized bibliography include journal articles, periodical, and monographs, including bibliographies.

IAMA has been actively petitioning the NLM to index journals which address the emerging field of arts-medicine so that those journals can become part of this huge computerized medical data base.

Dr. Michael McCann, founder and current president of the Center for Safety in the Arts [CSA], had dedicated over a decade of his professional career to providing information both to professionals and consumers on safety issues in the arts, with a strong emphasis on toxic hazards in the visual arts. CSA's newsletter *Art Hazard News*, has been placed on the computer bulletin board of the Western States' Federation, known as ARTSNET, which is online 24 hours a day, 7 days a week.

The CSA also publishes "data sheets," many of which will become part of the ARTSNET online network. In addition, CSA publishes an annual Special Resources Issue which is a compilation of resource organizations for arts-medicine. It includes government agencies, occupational health organizations and clinics, poison control centers, arts-medicine services, and other relevant listing. Dr. McCann, under CSA, has also developed the Art Hazard Information Center, which was designed to provide written and telephone answers to inquiries about high risks in the arts for the disabled.

In September of 1988, the Library of Medical and Chirurgical Faculty (Maryland State Medical Society) designated itself as the International Clearinghouse for Resources and Publications on the Medical Problems of Musicians. The Clearinghouse is a concept built around the work of Susan E. Harman, Associate Librarian at the Library who has been accumulating articles on medical problems of musicians for 9 years. The Clearinghouse with a nucleus of approximately 600 reprints and several bibliographies, has a long term goal of acquiring an original copy of everything published on this subject. The current emphasis is on English-language journal articles pertaining to instrumental musicians. However, the staff is expanding the collection to include other musicians, more books and foreign languages. The collection also includes ephemeral material such as lists of clinics, information from the National Flute Association Dysfunction Committee, summaries of conference presentations and newsletters from several organizations including IAMA. Clearinghouse information will be organized so that it is available and useful to physicians, other health care professionals, musicians, educators and researchers. Plans are under way to combine the bibliographies and create subject data of entry access. A music medicine section has been set up on the faculty's computer bulletin board system, MED-SIG, so that information on the field can be shared. At the same time, historical and rare materials are also being sought. Contributions of any type of material on the subject from authors, publishers, and organizations are most welcome. The Clearinghouse may be accessed by phone, letter, fax or in person.

Dr. Richard Ratzan, an emergency room physician from the University of Connecticut and a recognized scholar in medicine and literature, has independently developed several extensive, interdisciplinary bibliographies which are computerized in conjunction with arts-medicine conferences that Dr. Ratzan has organized. Among these bibliographies are, "Arts and Medicine—Diagnosing the Canvas," and "The Sound of Healing: Music and

Medicine" (both available from IAMA). Dr. Ratzan's bibliographies and conferences reflect his comprehensive grasp of arts-medicine which includes arts therapy as well as clinical arts-medicine topics. Dr. Ratzan serves as a Board Member of the IAMA. His ability to generate bibliographies is an asset to IAMA's information management focus.

Perhaps the most exciting development from IAMA's perspective to date in information management is the work of Dr. Charles Eagle, Professor of Music Therapy, Head, Department of Music Therapy, Medicine and Health at Southern Methodist University, Dallas, TX. Dr. Eagle has dedicated a significant portion of his professional life to developing and publishing music therapy and music psychology indexes and, more recently, has been developing a music medicine information management system known as The Computer-Assisted Information Retrieval Service System for Music Medicine [CAIRSS]. His goals for the the project are to provide a data base of information relevant to:

1. The function of music in medical specialties; and
2. The treatment of performing musicians.

As of August 1989, over 1,000 reference had been entered. The material is divided into a variety of categories including medical specialties and medical settings. There are over 1,500 key words in all. Dr. Eagle began by carefully selecting related bibliographical citations from a variety of medical journals and then medically related citations from music therapy and music psychology journals. Next, duplicate copies of the articles were ordered. Then the articles were organized by years and by medical specialties. Computerization began with material published in 1988 and Dr. Eagle is now working backwards through the 1980s and 1970s. Dr. Eagle has identified the music type that is referenced in each article. Abstracts are included if present. Otherwise, an abstract is composed in Dr. Eagle's offices. Dr. Eagle's goal has been the conceptual formulation of music medicine. Combining words from music and from medicine into a coherent assembly for the understanding of both musicians and physicians continues to be his challenge. Perhaps Dr. Eagle has provided a model in his music medicine data base which could be applied to other arts-medicine disciplines such as voice, dance and the visual arts.

In the Spring of 1988, IAMA entered into an agreement with the Institute for Scientific Information [ISI], a Philadelphia-based world leader in scientific and humanities information management. Specifically, each week since May, 1988, ISI has provided IAMA with a report of the latest arts-medicine related citations added to their extensive data base. These reports are marketed by ISI as part of its weekly subscription service *Research Alerts*.

ISI's former *Research Alert* Specialist, Judith Schaeffer, Chairman of IAMA's Information Management committee, has constructed a detailed and personal profile of arts-medicine interests. Each week this profile is searched against the latest science, social science, arts, and humanities journals. One benefit of *Research Alert* is that it is more comprehensive and thorough than competing services because it gives multi-disciplinary journal coverage. Furthermore, each topic search profile consists of source author names, words and word stems, as well as the names of cited authors and publications. *Research Alert* and ISI's document delivery service "The Genuine Article" are available through a world-wide network of company offices and agents.

It is IAMA's hope that this formal affiliation with ISI will permit IAMA to develop a plan to distribute critical and timely information on arts-medicine topics to its growing international membership.

The data bases just reviewed are a few of the many sources of arts-medicine information currently available to the diligent researcher. A recent survey of online data bases identified over 150 commercial data bases which could contain material of interest to arts-medicine in the broadest use of the term (Hall and Brown 1983; Online Data Bases 1987).

A sample search for articles relating to performance anxiety or stage fright was conducted in five of these data bases. SCISearch, SSCISearch, MEDLINE, PSYCHOINFO, and EMBASE, the online version of Excerpta Medica. To simplify the results, only articles published in 1988 were retrieved. Nine articles were identified. Six of these appeared in only one of the five data bases. None of the articles appeared in all five. Only one article appeared in four of the five. SSCISearch, MEDLINE, PSYCHOINFO, and EMBASE each contained articles unique to that data base.

Among the existing articles which provide a forum for communication and would pride a significant contribution to a comprehensive data base are *Medical Problems of Performing Artists*, *The Journal of Voice*, *The Arts in Psychotherapy*, and *The Japanese Bulletin of Part-Psychotherapy*. None of the data bases used for the test reference question includes all of these journals.

Several newsletters exist which could be added to our data base. These include the *IAMA Newsletter*, *The International Newsletter of Music Therapy*, and *Hospital Art News*, among many which address some aspect of arts-medicine.

We must learn more about the existence of relevant arts and performing arts journals and newsletters which address arts-medicine topics. We need our members and readers to help in identifying other journals and other newsletters which could contribute to an improved information management system in arts-medicine. We also need to lobby to get these publications included in the standard online data bases that are currently our chief means of identifying arts-medicine related materials.

## AMI, A PROPOSED COMPREHENSIVE, INTERDISCIPLINARY, INTERNATIONAL MODEL FOR INFORMATION MANAGEMENT

The goal of AMI is to collect, organize and distribute arts-medicine information internationally to artists, health professionals and the general public. AMI will become the primary source of arts-medicine information in the world.

Audiences for AMI services will include but not be limited to:

1. Arts-medicine information managers;
2. Arts-medicine organizations;
3. Arts organizations;
4. Medical organizations;
5. Individual professionals, artists, and consumers.

Decisions on which audiences to address first will be based on such considerations as whose need is the greatest and which audience has the funds necessary to pay for the service or is most likely to attract foundation, corporation or government funding.

Kinds of information included in the AMI data base will include but not be limited to:

1. Events such as conferences, symposia, and workshops;
2. News of new clinics, publications, and discoveries;
3. Names of organizations, artists, health professionals, and clinics in the field;
4. Information regarding publications such as articles, books, bibliographies, and abstracts;
5. Funding sources for arts-medicine projects and research.

Collection will occur continuously. AMI will obtain information from such sources as publications in the field, clipping services and submissions from interested organizations and individuals. Periodically, AMI will publish bibliographies and reviews of the literature on certain arts-medicine topics. These reports will be made available to members at no cost and sold to nonmembers. Among potential sources of information for the reviews are more than forty electronically searchable data bases. AMI will respond to written, telephoned, or faxed requests for information. Responses will include referral to members of the AMI network as well as or in lieu of written reports.

A great deal of medical information has already been assimilated into electronically accessible data bases; much arts information, such as that addressing the field of arts therapy, has not been.

In order to permit the sorting of information on parameters such as date or location of events for practitioners and clinics, and to facilitate communication among members, AMI will require the development of customized software for its data base management system. All collaborating organizations and individuals will use the customized software.

Information obtained and maintained by AMI will be distributed through such means as the *IAMA Newsletter,* occasional literature reviews, bibliographies and other articles, press releases and media events, conference presentations, a computer bulletin board system, and a national/international information service. Through its computer bulletin board system, AMI members and the general public will have access to some or all of AMI's collected information and will be able to communicate electronically on arts-medicine related subjects. AMI information will be available publicly or privately through various national and international electronic information services such as CompuServe and GEnie.

AMI specialist staff or contractors under staff supervision will collect, organize, and distribute ongoing information. AMI members will be entitled to a certain number of hours of search services free and will be billed at an hourly fee if they wish the search to continue. Nonmembers will be billed at an hourly fee.

AMI will develop collaborative relationships with the small number of other organizations and individuals currently managing arts-medicine information. Network Members will be remunerated for collecting and organizing information distributed by AMI and may be asked to cover part of the costs of developing the customized software.

The Information Management Committee of the IAMA Board, along with selected additional representatives from the AMI Information Network will oversee AMI operations and establish policies for approval by the IAMA Board.


## CONCLUSIONS AND RECOMMENDATIONS

Arts-medicine, comprehensively defined, has established itself as a new, worldwide, scientific, and social movement which encompasses performing arts-medicine, visual arts-medicine, creative arts therapy, and the increasing use of the arts in the rehumanizing of health education and health institutions.

Perhaps the most difficult challenge of an arts-medicine information strategy is to teach ourselves the interdisciplinary language of medicine and the arts. Those of us in health professions must learn the "language" of the arts and vice versa. Also, our definition of IAMA as an international arts-medicine organization presents challenges related to the complexities, sensitivities, and subtleties of foreign language translations.

We are convinced that modern health care will increasingly emphasize the application of currently known information regarding basic health care issues. It is a given that much of the basis for primary preventive medicine is education through information exchange. Consumerism is motivating patients, including artists and performing artists, to enhance their knowledge and, hence, their involvement in their own health care management. In addition, there is a major movement to provide medical consumers with information pertaining to the skills, capacities, and experiences of the vast provider network so that intelligent and informed choices can be made.

Clearly, easy access to timely, accurate and affordable information is one of the keys to improving health care in the future, and this is certainly applicable to arts-medicine as well. Since information in this field is currently decentralized, with arts and medical information existing in many distinctly different data bases, the need exists to develop a centralized, interdisciplinary data base which is accessible to a worldwide arts-medicine constituency. Rapid advances in information technology, including satellite technology, printing technology, personal computer technology, and other major breakthroughs in communication permit data to be managed, stored, and exchanged in ways we only dreamed of in the past.

On of the observations which led to the founding of IAMA in the mid-1980s was that arts-medicine activities were occurring all over the world and growing in number and quality. This was the stimulus for proposing an umbrella, "coordinating" organization. Through a centralized international arts-medicine information clearinghouse which we are calling AMI [Arts-Medicine Information], IAMA can serve as the "central nervous system" or brain which can "think globally" for arts-medicine by collecting, organizing, and appropriately disseminating information on arts-medicine around the world.

Independent organizations in the arts and medicine will continue to carry out successful local, national, and, in some cases, international activities that are less dependent on central clearinghouse functions.

The clearinghouse data base should be easily accessible, multi-lingual and affordable. The IAMA, with its extensive worldwide network of health and arts professionals and its strong information-management committee comprised of individuals and institutions which have already developed one or more components of an arts-medicine information network, has proposed AMI. AMI, as envisioned by its proponents, would fulfill the criteria of accessibility, multi-linguality and affordability.

Given appropriate funding, acceptance, and cooperation from all components of the arts-medicine community, AMI should be available for use within a two to three year time frame. Anticipated benefits to the arts community and those health care providers involved with this community are predicted to be considerable. Response to a mailing designed to ascertain scope of interest has been encouraging. To cite one example, Rosalie Rebollo Pratt, Executive Director of the International Association of Music for the Handicapped, has sent a compilation of research papers from eight separate interdisciplinary and international symposia for inclusion in AMI's growing data base.

It is time to recognize the international importance of the arts-medicine movement. It is time to apply more information management and communications technologies to strengthen interdisciplinary and cross-cultural bridges where they exist in the arts and medicine and to build them where they do not.

## REFERENCE  LIST

Douglas, W.G.T. 1986. Art and medicine. In *The Oxford Companion to Medicine*, edited by J. Walton, P.B. Beeson, and R.B. Scott, 1:90. New York: Oxford University Press.

Hall, J.L. and Brown, M.J. *Online Bibliographic Data Bases: A Directory and Sourcebook*, 3rd Ed. London: Aslib.

Online Data Bases in the Medical and Life Sciences. 1987. New York: Cuadra/Elsevier.

Root-Bernstein, R.S. 1987. Harmony and beauty in medical research. *Journal of Molecular and Cellular Cardiology* 19: 1043-1051.

# AMI NETWORK ORGANIZATIONS
## as of August, 1989

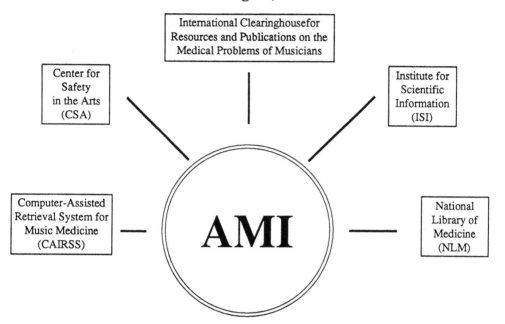

International Clearinghousefor Resources and Publications on the Medical Problems of Musicians

Center for Safety in the Arts (CSA)

Institute for Scientific Information (ISI)

Computer-Assisted Retrieval System for Music Medicine (CAIRSS)

**AMI**

National Library of Medicine (NLM)

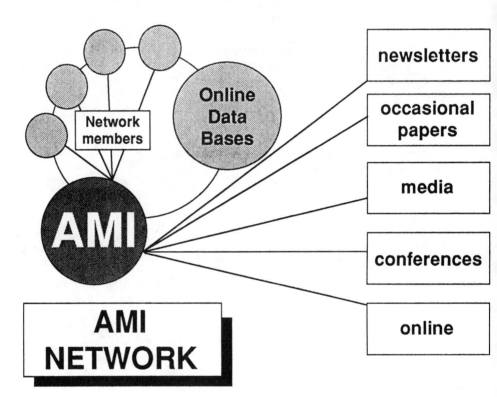

# RETRIEVING THE LITERATURE OF MUSICMEDICINE

Charles T. Eagle

## INTRODUCTION

A number of years ago, my friend and mentor—E. Thayer Gaston—wrote that "without practice and research, theory is impotent and unproven; without theory and research, practice is blind; and without theory and practice, research is inapplicable" (Gaston 1968, 408). (See Figure 1).

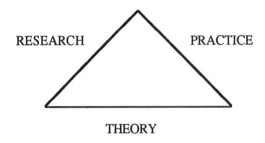

RESEARCH       PRACTICE

THEORY

Therefore:

— Without practice and research, theory is impotent and unproven

— Without theory and research, practice is blind

— Without theory and practice, research is inapplicable

*Figure 1.   Formula for Success in a Discipline*

Assuming that theory, practice, and research are the three essential interfacing rubrics in any discipline, in this case MusicMedicine, the following question arises: *Who's* doing *what*, and *where in the world* is it being done—this theorizing about, this practicing and this researching of the use and function of music in medical therapy?

The purpose of this paper is to attempt at least a partial answer to this question. In so doing, I will provide you with a personal odyssey of my twenty-year search of the literature relevant to MusicMedicine. My story, therefore, will be in an historical context. In this context, I hope to provide you with information regarding my attempt to find the literature in MusicMedicine, to collate it and to find the proper tools to do the collating, and to disseminate the results of the search and collation.


## BACKGROUND

So that you will have some idea of the philosophy underpinning this paper, I want to write briefly of my professional background. My full-time teaching began in 1953. I taught for the ensuing five years at the elementary and secondary school levels, as well as at the university. I conducted bands and orchestras, and taught instrumental music, both privately and in class. Then, in 1958, I switched professions by accepting a position in pharmaceutical research and sales. For over six years, I studied anatomy and physiology, and detailed physicians, nurses, and pharmacists about the actions of certain pharmaceuticals in persons suffering from such conditions as pain, allergy, smooth and skeletal muscle spasm. In 1964, I enrolled at the University of Kansas to pursue a doctor of philosophy degree. Eventually, my doctoral major became music education with an equivalency in music therapy, with minors in research design and statistics, and special education.

While at the University, I came under the influence of Dr. E. Thayer Gaston who has been called "the father of music therapy." A brilliant trumpet performer, exquisite psychologist, and Socratic teacher, Dr. Gaston obtained his first university degree in pre-medicine. He did not go to medical school, but later obtained a doctorate in educational psychology. His primary and pervading interest during all his professional life was something he called "the influence of music on behavior." It is quite obvious that music does affect behavior, he said, so how and when does music affect such human attributes as heart beat, stomatological functioning, and skin conductance? Then, he said, how can this knowledge be used to reduce human suffering?

For a period of three years beginning in 1966, I worked as a music therapist in Topeka, Kansas. During the same time, Dr. Gaston and I were also conducting research on the function of music in therapy with alcoholic patients, utilizing the hallucinogenic drug LSD, or lysergic acid diethylamide (Gaston and Eagle 1970). In doing so, we worked very closely with the psychiatrists and psychologists of the Menninger School of Psychiatry. I remember asking Dr. Gaston why there was no bona fide, full-fledged doctoral degree in music therapy? He said: "Because we don't know enough; there is not a body of research literature to support a doctorate in music therapy."

I have never forgotten Dr. Gaston's remark. And in fact, I began then and continue now to challenge his assumption, for in 1969 I began a concerted search for published, medically-related literature. Over the next eight years, I applied for and received nine grants to help me in my bibliographical search, six of which were funded by the National Association for Music Therapy of the USA.


## RESULTING INDEXES

It became abundantly clear to me that there existed a clear "need for a single, comprehensive index of pertinent periodical literature pertaining to the influence of music on behavior" (Eagle 1976). This need was especially acute for music therapy practitioners. In compiling the reference work,

> The initial task was to locate the sources of relevant bibliography. Thus, related periodicals and indexes were reviewed. Then the format and arrangement of the bibliographical entries for the [eventually published] *Music Therapy Index* were determined by consulting with librarians...It was agreed that logical presentation and completeness of coverage were of high priority in maximizing the usefulness of the *Index*. It was further agreed that manual indexing would be impractical and that, therefore, the *Index* would have to be computer-generated and based on keywords taken from the titles from the [published] journal articles. (p. vii)


### Music Therapy Index, Volume 1

To resolve the purpose of bringing together the literature of music therapy, a philosophy was needed—literally, a study of the wisdom of the current thinking of music therapy. As can be seen in Figure 2, the philosophy which guided my initial efforts in literature search in the late 1960s and early 1970s was interdisciplinary-centered. Therefore, music therapy—as then defined and practiced—was at the center of my search universe.

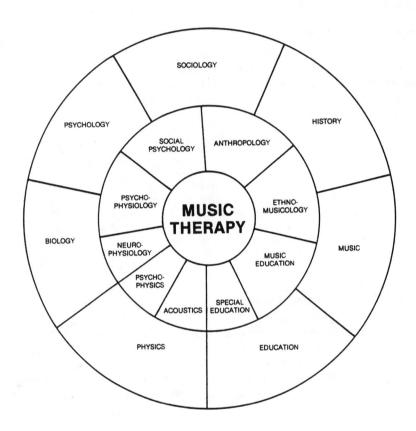

*Figure 2.    Bibliographical Universe for Music Therapy Index, Volume 1.*

Out of this universe, five leading questions guided my resolve to bring together the music therapy literature:

1. *What* are "relevant" references?
2. *Where* are such references to be found?
3. *How* are the references to be formatted?  That is, what is the most effective way of presenting the bibliographical entries?

4. *How* do I make use of a computer to facilitate the project? That is, what kind of computer software and hardware is needed to get the job done?
5. *How* are the results of the project to be disseminated? That is, how do I get my accumulated information to those who need and want it?

Using the wholistic notion illustrated in Figure 2 and these five questions, I was able to answer these questions in the initial bibliographical retrieval process. "Relevant" references were those published between 1960 and 1975, and taken directly from the publications in music therapy, music psychology, and music education. In addition, I obtained medical and psychological references from printed editions of *Hospital Literature Index, Index Medicus,* and *Psychological Abstracts.* In these indexes, I looked for relevant citations under the headings of "acoustics" and "sound," as well as "music" and "music therapy." The result was the publication of the word-and-author prepared *Music Therapy Index, Volume 1* (Eagle) in 1976, published under the auspices of the National Association for Music Therapy.

## Music Psychology Index, Volume 2

After the publication of *Music Therapy Index* and as I continued the information retrieval project, my philosophy underlying it was modified. I defined "music as organized, organizing sounds and silences in a flow of time" (Eagle 1978). This definition was influenced greatly by my reading of concepts stemming from quantum physics, and my continuing reflection on Dr. Gaston's phrase, "the influence of music on behavior." Therefore, I concluded that, because vibration—hence physical frequency—is the essence of all being and because music is organized vibrational frequency, an additional, more inclusive guiding question should be asked:

> Can we get a better perspective of the essence [of the use and function] of music if we [also] study unorganized sound defined as noise? . . . In what ways do these [vibrational] musical and nonmusical sounds influence behavior? What are the biological effects? Physiological? Neurological? Psychological? Sociological? Anthropological? Acoustical? Educational? [As well as] therapeutic?

An attempt to illustrate this emerging and expanding philosophy, as well as the complexity inherent in the networking system, can be seen in Figure 3. Thus, as I continued my search, I considered bibliographical citations found in other data bases under the following rubrics: acoustics, vibration, and sound, as well as music, music therapy, nursing, and medicine. Eventually, I changed the title of the next publication to the *Music Psychology Index, Volume 2* (Eagle 1978), which I thought would illustrate better the expanded data base. The subtitle reflects even better the expanding of my outlook, that is: *The International Interdisciplinary Index of the Influence of Music on Behavior: References to the Literature from the Natural and Behavioral Sciences and the Fine and*

*Therapeutic Arts for the Years 1976-77. Volume 2* was published in 1978 under the
auspices of the Institute for Therapeutics Research.

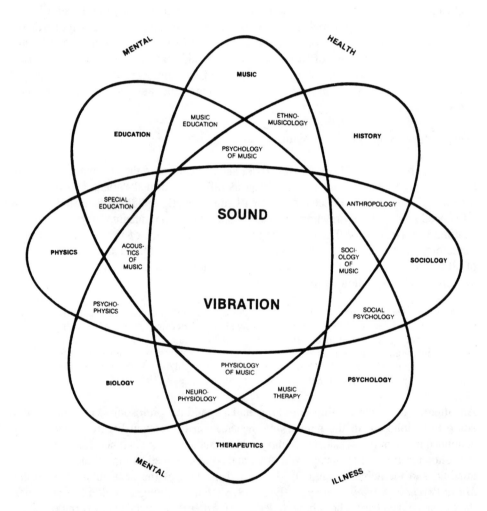

*Figure 3.    Bibliographical Universe for Music Psychology Index, Volume 2.*

## Music Psychology Index, Volume 3

I continued to collect bibliographical citations, in much the same manner. The culmination came with the publication of the *Music Psychology Index, Volume 3* (Eagle and Miniter 1984), the citations of which were published in 1978, 1979, and 1980.

The summary data from the three published index volumes are impressive. Their content reflects an analysis of over 100,000 citations. In the three, you will find over 6,000 bibliographical entries, published between 1960 to 1980, cited under more than 16,000 keywords and names of authors. The citations appeared in over 800 different journals published in 36 different countries.

But all good things must come to an end and with the publication of *Volume 3*, I stopped the project. The enormity of it was simply overwhelming. First, my wholistic, undergirding philosophy and the several guiding questions had led me literally to thousands of pieces of relevant literature. Secondly, the so-called revolution in computer hardware and software was in full swing by the early 1980s, and I realized that a change in my computer technology was needed. Thirdly, I also realized that an index built on a thesaurus of words from titles of articles and their authors, but not from the article itself, was inadequate. The convergence of these major factors led me to the conclusion that a complete overhaul of the project was needed. But I had not the time, the energy, nor the financial resources to continue.

## RETRIEVAL RESURRECTED

The years since 1980 have been my professional "Decade of Discovery." I have discovered, or have had reinforced, concepts from such seemingly diverse disciplines as biology, chemistry, family therapy, neuroscience, music, quantum physics, and systems theory. More specifically, I recall attending a medical meeting in Phoenix, Arizona in 1980. While there, I discovered the work of Swiss physician Dr. Hans Jenny (1974a, 1974b). When I saw photographs of the results of his having projected frequencies and amplitudes—that is, musical pitches and loudnesses—through various physical media, I was astounded. Pictures that looked like sand dollars and backsides of turtles, human eyes and vertebra left me in a deep silent state of spiritual contemplation.

In 1982, I discovered physician Larry Dossey's then-new book, *Space, Time and Medicine*, in which Dr. Dossey beautifully explains the relationship between the concepts from quantum physics to the world of medicine—indeed, the world of healing. This led me to the writings of such physicists as Fritjof Capra, Paul Davies, David Peat, Fred Alan Wolf, among others. Concepts, such as Einstein's special and general theories of relativity, Heisenberg's uncertainty principle, and Bohm's implicate order, have led me to formulate what I call a "theory of quantum musichanics."

In 1984, I attempted to bring together my thoughts about these networking topics through a presentation of a paper entitled, "A Quantum Interfacing System for Music and Medicine," at the Second International Symposium of the International Society for Music in Medicine (Eagle 1987). (The First Symposium was held in 1982, nurtured and directed by Dr. Roland Droh and Dr. Ralph Spintge.) In 1985, the International Arts-Medicine Association began publishing its newsletter under the direction of the founding president, Dr. Richard Lippin. In 1986, the first issue of *Medical Problems of Performing Artists* appeared under the editorship of Dr. Alice Brandfonbrenner, and in October of 1986, the Third Symposium of the Society was held. An increasing number of national and international conferences ensued, concerning the function of music in medical specialties and the remedying of medically-related problems of performing musicians.

But not only were physicians becoming increasingly aware of the healing phenomenon of music; music therapists and educators were becoming aware of the increasing interest of physicians in the function of music in their practices. For example, Dr. Arthur Harvey sponsored conferences at Western Kentucky University in 1986 and again in 1987. Dr. Rosalie Pratt has been responsible for several relevant international conferences during the 1980s. I have also noticed an increasing number of more medically-related presentations at the annual conferences of the National Association for Music Therapy, primarily under the leadership of Dr. Cheryl Maranto.

Sensitive to this activity, in 1988 I began once again to review the related literature. But this time, in contrast to the approach taken in preparation of my previous data base and consequent three index publications, I did computer-assisted searches of the *medical* literature relevant only to the keywords "music" and "music therapy," as well as searching by hand other relevant publications in music therapy. In other words, I focused on the use and function of music in medical specialties and medical settings.

As a starting point, I started the search for references published in 1988 and worked backwards in time. Having found the pertinent bibliographical citations, I ordered copies of the articles. Using a commercial software program called "Bookends" (Ashwell 1985), I input the pertinent information obtained from each article to an inexpensive Apple IIe. Figure 4 displays an example of the fields of information used in inputting a bibliographical entry.

| | |
|---|---|
| AUTHOR(S): | Godec, C.J. |
| TITLE: | Clinical application of Pavlov conditioning reflexes in treatment of urinary incontinence |
| JOURNAL/BOOK: | Urology*Urology |
| VOLUME/EDITOR: | (USA) 22:4(1983) |
| PAGE(S): | 397-400, ISSN 0900-4295 |
| LEGEND: | Case study; 32-year-old woman with a history of stress incontinence; 5 references. |
| MUSIC TYPE(S): | N/A |
| ABSTRACT: | A new method of treatment of urinary incontinence is described. A tape recorder with two outlets generates musical stimuli. One outlet brings direct unconverted musical stimuli to the patient's ear, the other outlet conveys the musical stimuli to a converter where the musical pulses are converted into electrical stimuli which are then applied to the patient's anus. At first simultaneous application of stimuli into the ear and anus is performed and anal pressure response recorded. After conditioning takes place, music is applied to the patient's ear, stimulation to the anus is disconnected, and only anal pressure response is recorded. The patients are conditioned enough to generate good anal response to aural stimulation only. (By author) |
| ABSTRACT, CONT: | |
| KEYWORD(S): | Godec, C.J./urology/Pavlov/incontinence/music therapy/anus/ biofeedback/psychotherapy/conditioned reflex/bladder |
| SUBFILE/PUB: | Dialog:Medline |
| CLASSIFICATION: | j |

*Figure 4.    Fields of Information in a Computerized Entry*

After the initial input of this information for 1,000 articles, editing was begun—and it is still going on. Then, a listing of keywords from each article was printed. From the output, I have been attempting to build a thesaurus of compatible terminology from the medical, music, and music therapy professions. Many are the nights I have sat at my desk with copies of *Harrison's Principles of Internal Medicine* (Wintrobe et al. 1974), *Taber's Cyclopedic Medical Dictionary* (Thomas 1981), *The Merck Manual* (Holvey 1972), and the *Physicians Desk Reference* (1987),—laying side by side with *The Norton/Grove Concise Encyclopedia of Music* (Sadie 1988) and *Harvard Dictionary of Music* (Apel

1969). In short, I am in the process of building not only a data base for MusicMedicine, but also a language base.

Now comes the time for searching my MusicMedicine data base using the keyword listing. Using any word or combination of words, I do a computerized search. The fruit of my keyword search results in finding entries in the data base and then the final output takes the format as shown in Figure 5

---

Godec, C.J. Clinical application of Pavlov conditioning reflexes in treatment of urinary incontinence. *Urology* (USA), 22:4(1983) 397-400, ISSN 0990-4295.
  *Legend*: Case study; 32-year-old woman with a history of stress incontinence; 5 references.
  *Music Type(s)*: N/A

A new method of treatment of urinary incontinence is described. A tape recorder with two outlets generates musical stimuli. One outlet brings direct unconverted musical stimuli
to the patient's ear, the other outlet conveys the musical stimuli to a converter where the musical pulses are converted into electrical stimuli which are then applied to the patient's anus. At first simultaneous application of stimuli into the ear and anus is performed and anal pressure response recorded. After conditioning takes place, music is applied to the patient's ear, stimulation to the anus is disconnected, and only anal pressure response is recorded. The patients are conditioned enough to generate good anal response to aural stimulation only. (By author)

---

*Figure 5.   Format of Entry Output*

I have spent only the last year designing and formulating the data base for MusicMedicine, although 20 years of experience in information retrieval in MusicMedicine, therapy, and psychology preceded it. In June 1989, I stopped inputting entries. I have spent the intervening time in analyzing what has been done thus far and rethinking the process. Here are my conclusions to date:

1.  Of the 1,000 relevant-to-music-medicine bibliographical entries computerized thus far, I have over 4,000 articles in my file cabinets that have not been entered. And more articles are arriving at my office every week.
2.  As seen in Figure 6, professionals in 34 medical specialties have published articles in which "music" or "music therapy" is a keyword. The specialty and

general medical journals in which they appear number 347. In addition, I have inputted relevant entries from 20 music and 5 music therapy journals, for a grand total of 372 journals.

| SPECIALITY | NUMBER OF JOURNALS |
|---|---|
| ADOLESCENT MEDICINE | 2 |
| ALLERGY 1 | |
| ANESTHESIOLOGY | 6 |
| BEHAVIOR MEDICINE | 6 |
| DENTISTRY | 21 |
| DERMATOLOGY | 2 |
| FAMILY PRACTICE | 1 |
| FORENSIC MEDICINE | 1 |
| GENETICS, MEDICINE | 2 |
| GERIATRICS | 5 |
| INTERNAL MEDICINE: | 3 |
|     CARDIOLOGY | 5 |
|     GASTROENTEROLOGY | 3 |
|     HEMATOLOGY | 2 |
|     ONCOLOGY | 1 |
|     RHEUMATOLOGY | 2 |
| NEUROLOGY | 14 |
| NEUROSURGERY | 2 |
| NURSING 29 | |
| OBSTETRICS & GYNECOLOGY | 2 |
| OPTHALMOLOGY | 3 |
| OTOLARYNGOLOGY | 27 |
| PATHOLOGY | 1 |
| PEDIATRICS | 18 |
| PHYSICAL MEDICINE | 2 |
| PREVENTIVE MEDICINE: | 2 |
|     AEROSPACE MEDICINE | 1 |
|     OCCUPATIONAL MEDICINE | 2 |
|     PUBLIC HEALTH | 5 |
| PSYCHIATRY | 27 |
| PSYCHIATRY (CHILD) | 3 |
| PSYCHOLOGY, MEDICINE | 29 |
| RADIOLOGY | 2 |
| SURGERY 11 | |
| UROLOGY | 1 |
| Thus, 34 medical specialties, publishing | 244 speciality journals |
| Plus, | |
|     + J. Am. Med. Assoc.; N. Eng. J. Med; etc. | 103 general med. jnls. |
|     + J. Music. Ther.; Med. Probs. Perf. Art.; etc. | 5 music therapy jnls. |
|     + Piano Q.; Senza Sordino; etc. | 20 music jnls. |
| Grand total | 372 journals |

*Figure 6. Medical Specialities and Journals (N = 1,000 articles)*

3. As seen in Figure 7, the relevant journals have been published in 36 different countries.

---

**JOURNAL COUNTRY OF ORIGIN**

| | |
|---|---|
| ARGENTINA | ISRAEL |
| AUSTRALIA | ITALY |
| AUSTRIA | |
| | JAPAN |
| BELGIUM | |
| BRAZIL | MEXICO |
| BULGARIA | |
| | NETHERLANDS |
| CANADA | NEW ZEALAND |
| CHINA | NORWAY |
| CZECHOSLOVAKIA | |
| | PAKISTAN |
| DENMARK | POLAND |
| | PUERTO RICO |
| ENGLAND | |
| | ROMANIA |
| FINLAND | |
| FRANCE | SOUTH AFRICA |
| | SPAIN |
| GERMANY, WEST | SWEDEN |
| GERMANY, EAST | SWITZERLAND |
| | |
| HUNGARY | USA |
| | USSR |
| INDIA | |
| IRELAND | YUGOSLAVIA |

36 = total country of origin journals

---

*Figure 7. Journal Country of Origin*

4. Of the 46 computer files, the keywords of only 3 have been edited. The keywords in these 3 number over 1,400.

## CONCLUSION

In this paper, I have attempted to assure you that there is a large body of literature relevant to MusicMedicine. In a professionally historical manner, I have presented you with clues which provide data showing us, in broad conclusive terms, who is doing what in MusicMedicine, and where in the world it is being done. In doing so, I have shown you more of what I have not done, rather than what I have. What I have created is in a most primitive state of existence.

The preliminary work I have done thus far in building a computerized data base in MusicMedicine, however, does show the need for worldwide collaboration in the endeavor. No one person can do the work alone. For example, I could work full-time beginning now and still not be able to keep up with the "information explosion" in MusicMedicine. We need a networking system which would allow for immediate interfacing between and among researchers, clinicians, and theorizers of MusicMedicine. This interfacing includes electronic mail, bulletin board, and information retrieval. With specific regard to the latter, we need a team of editors throughout the world, who can gather the information from their professional sources. Then, we need to decide upon the computer software and hardware to facilitate the dissemination of the information. In short, we need the people to be involved who will work at the realization of this project, and of course, the money to get the job done.

I am ready to devote the remaining portion of my lifetime to seeing that the job of MusicMedicine is done. Because as surely as creativity arises out of discipline, good theory, practice, and research arises out of good bibliography. As we prepare the way for the emergence of the art-science of music-medicine in the 21st century, we must provide the means for our successors to build that future.

## REFERENCE LIST

Apel, W. 1969. *Harvard Dictionary of Music.* Cambridge, MA: Harvard University Press.

Ashwell, J.D. 1985. *Bookends Extended: A Reference Management System.* Birmingham, MI: Sensible Software.

Dossey, L. 1982. *Space, Time and Medicine.* Boulder, CO: Shambhala.

Eagle, C.T. (Ed.) 1976. *Music Therapy Index Volume 1.* Lawrence, KS: National Association for Music Therapy.

_____. 1978. *Music Psychology Index Volume 2.* Denton, TX: Institute for Therapeutics Research.

_____. 1987 A quantum interfacing system for music and medicine. In *Music and Medicine*, edited by R. Spintge and R. Droh, 389-411. New York: Springer-Verlag.

Eagle, C.T., and J.J. Miniter (Eds.) 1984. *Music Psychology Index Volume 3*. Denton, TX: Institute for Therapeutics Research and Phoenix, AZ: Oryx Press.

Gaston, E.T. 1968. Planning and understanding research. In *Music in Therapy*, edited by E.T. Gaston. New York: Macmillan.

Gaston E.T., and Eagle, C.T. 1970. The function of music in LSD therapy for alcoholic patients *Journal of Music Therapy* 7(1):3-19.

Holvey, D.N. (Ed.) 1972. *The Merck Manual*. Rahway, NJ: Merck.

Jenny, H. 1974a. *Cymatics (Vol. 1)*. Basel: Basilius Presse.

_____. 1974b. *Cymatics (Vol. 2)*. Basel: Basilius Presse.

*Physicians' Desk Reference* (41st ed). Oradell, NJ: Medical Economic.

Sadie, S. (Ed.) 1988. *The Norton/Grove Concise Encyclopedia of Music*. New York: Norton.

Thomas, C.L. (Ed.) 1981. *Taber's Cyclopedic Medical Dictionary* (14th ed.). Philadelphia: F.A. Davis.

Wintrobe, M.W.; Thorn, G.W.; Adams, R.D.; Braunwald, E.; Isselbacker, K.J.; and Persdorf, R.G. (Eds.) 1974. *Harrison's Principles of Internal Medicine* (7th ed). New York: McGraw-Hill.

# MUSIC THERAPY AS AN ADDITIONAL COURSE AT THE UNIVERSITY OF WESTPHALIA (WESTFÄLISCHE WILHELMS-UNIVERSITÄT MÜNSTER)

Ekkehard Kreft

## THE SITUATION IN WESTERN COUNTRIES APART FROM THE FRG

Training centers for music therapy in the USA and in Europe are usually part of music schools. Since 1950, 75 such centers have been established within music schools in the USA. Music therapy as course of study was introduced to London's Guildhall School of Music and Drama in 1958 and to the "Hochschule für Musik und Darstellende Kunst" in Vienna in 1959. Since 1971, there have been German congresses of music therapy and in 1973, the German Society for Music Therapy was founded in Heidelberg.

## THE SITUATION IN THE FEDERAL REPUBLIC OF GERMANY

Apart from the Vienna Hochschule, where the music therapy course is completed with a state-recognized diploma, there are now seven music therapy courses in the Federal Republic of Germany. These are linked to music schools (Hamburg, Berlin), to universities (Witten-Herdecke, Münster, Giessen), and to specialized institutions of higher education (Heidelberg, Frankfurt), and they comprise courses which last between four and six semesters.

## DEVELOPMENT OF MUSIC THERAPY AS AN ADDITIONAL COURSE OF STUDY AT THE UNIVERSITY OF WESTPHALIA

Efforts to establish music therapy as a additional course of study at the University of Westphalia date back to 1983.

Some dates:

- 8 October 1987: Authorization of the Music Therapy Syllabus as an additional course of study.
- 18 March 1988: Authorization of the Music Therapy Syllabus with a diploma as final examination.

- Music Therapy was first offered in the winter semester of 1987/1988, with possible matriculation. 14 students signed up.
- On 19 May, 1988, I was made managing director of the Music Therapy course.
- On 29 May 1989, the examining board for diploma examinations was installed, and I was elected director of this board.
- In the winter semester of 1989/90 we intend to obtain a professorship for this course, which has so far been conducted by assigned teachers.
- As of the Fall 1989, 47 students were enrolled for the Music Therapy course. Six students passed the diploma examinations successfully in the winter semester of 1989-1990.

## THE COURSE

The qualifications for access to the additional course of Music Therapy are both the general certificate for matriculation requirements and the First State Exam for teaching at primary or secondary level with music as a subject.

These qualifications are relevant for the University of Westphalia only. The aim of the course is to provide the students with additional scientific, musical, and professional qualifications in training for the work of a music therapist. They can increase their theoretical knowledge and the practical abilities gathered in previous courses. The course trains students to become music therapists by way of applied, educational, and research-oriented fields of study. It is the goal of the course to supply students of music therapy with professional competence based on scientific, artistic, and practical abilities so that they can later pursue their work in an independent and responsible way. In consequence, they should be able to give adequate support to people needing music therapy treatment. Music therapy as an additional course should also provide future music therapists with the medical knowledge necessary for successful cooperation in a general therapeutic program.

### Duration of the Course

The additional course of Music Therapy generally takes four semesters. The course has a total of at least 65 units.[1] These consist of 24 units in Music Therapy, 14 units in Medicine, and 27 units spent on practical training in therapeutic institutions.

---

1   In the German university system, the students have a choice of optional courses each semester. The weekly lessons of the individual semesters are added up at the end of their studies; these lessons are referred to as obligatory "units" here.

## Contents of the Course

The course comprises medical studies as well as the improvement of practical (i.e. musical) knowledge and abilities. In a second stage, these new insights are evaluated and practically applied.

*Teaching Arrangements and Lectures*
The teaching arrangements are generally the following:

- Lectures
- Seminars
- Tutorials
- Practical Training

**Lectures** give an integral insight into medical and psychological knowledge both basic and specialist, and they deal with methodology in a larger context.

**Seminars** deal with complex questions and concepts of music therapy by way of talks and discussions.

**Tutorials** are devoted to the planning, execution, evaluation, and theory of methods of music therapy. They refer to active and passive, single and group therapy.

**Practical Training** provides the opportunity to get acquainted with the range of professional activities of the music therapist. Students will visit various therapeutic institutions and work there under the supervision of the doctors and other music therapists. They will thus gather experience about the situations of therapists and clients, which usually proves very helpful for their further theoretical studies.

Music therapy as an additional course of study is subdivided into the following disciplines:

- Music Therapy
- Medicine
- Practical Training in Music Therapy

1. **Music Therapy** (24 units)

   *Musical Psychology* (lectures, tutorials: 6 units)
   These lessons deal with aspects of research into perception and reception, with musical socialization, with applied music psychology, and with

discussions about the relevance of these subjects to the work of the music therapist.

*Theoretical Music Therapy* (seminars: 6 units)
These lessons deal with the history and methodology of music therapy, fundamental research, and practical abilities concerning observation, planning, performance, evaluation and reflection of both, active and receptive, single and group therapies.

*Practical Music Therapy*
  a. Methods of Music Therapy (tutorials: 6 units)
     Students are trained to employ different methods of music therapy. They work on their own and under supervision, and learn to consider the individual needs of each particular group of clients.
  b. Rhythmics (tutorials: 6 units)
     These tutorials are designed to develop facility with strict and free improvisation of music and movement, using the student's main instrument, his or her voice, percussion instruments, and therapeutic music in groups.

2. **Medicine** (14 units)
   The Faculty of Medicine offers tuition in subjects relevant to the the practical work of music therapy and for the positioning of music therapy within a general concept of therapy as follows:

   *Fundamentals* (lectures: 5 units)
   Neurophysiology and physiology of the senses with special reference to the central and vegetative nervous systems.

   *Medical Psychology and Psychosomatic Medicine* (lectures: 2 units)

   *Psychiatry* (lectures: 6 units)
   These give insights into various diseases, including their symptoms, genesis, progress, and treatment.

   *Psychosomatics and Psychiatry of Infancy and Adolescence* (lectures: 2 units)

   *Selected Cases of Neurological Pathography* (lectures: 2 units)

   *Disturbances of Hearing, Voice, and Speech* (lectures: 2 units)

3. **Practical Courses in Music Therapy** (27 units)

The practical courses are an integral part of music therapy as an additional course of study. They give an insight into therapeutic institutions and thus offer vital experience both for the study course and the student's future profession. They take two different forms:

*Block Practical Courses* (practical: 18 units)

These are block practicals with a duration of 6 weeks. The students can attend these practical courses individually or in groups.

*"Semester Practical" Courses - stretching over 3 semesters* (practical: 9 units)

Students work in hospitals for three semesters and spend at least 9 units there in addition to the course during semester time.

## Diploma Examinations

The examinations for the diploma consist of three elements:

- the thesis,
- the written test,
- the vivas.

The first of these is the thesis with a time limit of four months. The thesis is to show that the candidate is capable of handling a problem in an independent and scholarly way and within a limited span of time.

For the written test the candidate has the choice of three subjects from different areas of music therapy (time: 4 hours).

The vivas are to be taken in medicine and music therapy (45 minutes for music therapy, 30 minutes for medicine).

The candidate passes the examinations if the individual grades and the grade of the thesis are at least "sufficient" (i.e., 4.0 in a system of grades ranging from 1 to 6 with 1 as the best grade). The final grade is made up as follows:

- 40% from the thesis
- 20% from the written test
- 20% from the viva in medicine
- 20% from the viva in music therapy.

## OVERVIEW

In order to give an accurate description of the aims of music therapy as an additional course of study with reference to the teaching of it, one has to take a wide range of occupational activities into consideration, which include both clinical and nonclinical occupations. Since the clinical sector is sufficiently recognized at the moment and clinical components are largely realized (psychiatry, orthopedics, anesthesia), I will concentrate on the nonclinical range.

### Socially Disturbed Children

In discussions, school teachers always stress the fact that a quota of their pupils have to be regarded as socially disturbed. Many teachers think therefore that music therapy ought to be incorporated into the methods of nonspecialized schools. This could be seen as a precautionary measure with children so threatened by various social factors.

The "Realschule" (school leading to the General Certificate of Education Ordinary Level) of Herten/Westphalia may serve as an example of work in music, sports, and theater. In a talk in the autumn of 1988 the headmaster of this Catholic-run school said that a considerable number of his students from the 5th to the 7th grade had started to behave in a more motivated and independent way after taking part in the abovementioned projects. Those pupils had previously been socially unstable because of their deprived backgrounds. According to him, the performance of the boys and girls in question had improved considerably, so that these potential problem pupils had become successful ones.

### Delinquent Young People

A second area of therapeutic activities is concerned with the resocialization of threatened or delinquent young people outside school. Drug problems increasingly lead to criminal offences, such as prostitution of both girls and boys, and petty crimes which can lead to stigmatization of these young people. This applies to youngsters who generally live in unstable surroundings. Instead of sending them to institutions, social workers care for them in socio-pedagogic shelters. The "Caritas-Verband" (a charitable organization) of Münster is a good example of this. They have no-cost projects where they look after threatened youths and can motivate them to get acquainted with music and to use music for independent creativity.

### The Elderly

Nowadays, attention is usually directed to the younger generation whereas the elderly, who do not work any more, are hardly considered. I am not referring to the simple physical care in old-age homes. It is well known that elderly people often suffer from fear of isolation or from the idea that they are not needed. The factor of loneliness in old age presents an increasing threat. Consequently it will be necessary in the future to develop the therapeutic, and especially the musically therapeutic, aspect of dealing with elderly people. This will help them not only to occupy themselves satisfactorily in their free time, but also to maintain and reactivate social relations. First steps in this direction can be observed, although they are scarce—homes or sanatoriums for the elderly rarely have their own therapist.

p. 117- 140

p. 201- 224